More Than Screen Deep

Toward Every-Citizen Interfaces to the Nation's Information Infrastructure

Toward an Every-Citizen Interface to the Nation's Information
Infrastructure Steering Committee

Computer Science and Telecommunications Board

Commission on Physical Sciences, Mathematics, and Applications

National Research Council

NATIONAL ACADEMY PRESS
Washington, D.C. 1997

...eport was approved by the Governing Board ...mbers are drawn from the councils of the ...cademy of Engineering, and the Institute of ...ponsible for the report were chosen for their special competences and with regard for appropriate balance.

This report has been reviewed by a group other than the authors according to procedures approved by a Report Review Committee consisting of members of the National Academy of Sciences, the National Academy of Engineering, and the Institute of Medicine.

Support for this project was provided by the National Science Foundation under Grant No. IRI-9529473. Any opinions, findings, conclusions, or recommendations expressed in this material are those of the authors and do not necessarily reflect the views of the National Science Foundation.

Library of Congress Cataloging-in-Publication Data

More than screen deep : toward every-citizen interfaces to the
    nation's information infrastructure / Toward an Every-Citizen
    Interface to the Nation's Information Infrastructure Steering
    Committee, Computer Science and Telecommunications Board, Commission
    on Physical Sciences, Mathematics, and Applications, National
    Research Council.
        p. cm.
    Summary report from a workshop held in August 1996.
    Includes bibliographical references.
    ISBN 0-309-06357-4 (pbk. : acid-free paper)
    1. User interfaces (Computer systems)—Congresses. 2. Human-
computer interaction—Congresses. 3. Information superhighway—
United States—Congresses. I. National Research Council (U.S.).
Toward an Every-Citizen Interface to the Nation's Information
Infrastructure Steering Committee.
QA76.9.U83M67 1997
303.48′3—dc21   97-21211

Additional copies of this report are available from National Academy Press, 2101 Constitution Avenue, N.W., Lockbox 285, Washington, D.C. 20055; (800)624-6242 or (202)334-3313 (in the Washington metropolitan area); Internet, http://www.nap.edu

TOWARD AN EVERY-CITIZEN INTERFACE TO THE NATION'S INFORMATION INFRASTRUCTURE STEERING COMMITTEE

The National Academy of Sciences is a private, nonprofit, self-perpetuating society of distinguished scholars engaged in scientific and engineering research, dedicated to the furtherance of science and technology and to their use for the general welfare. Upon the authority of the charter granted to it by the Congress in 1863, the Academy has a mandate that requires it to advise the federal government on scientific and technical matters. Dr. Bruce Alberts is president of the National Academy of Sciences.

The National Academy of Engineering was established in 1964, under the charter of the National Academy of Sciences, as a parallel organization of outstanding engineers. It is autonomous in its administration and in the selection of its members, sharing with the National Academy of Sciences the responsibility for advising the federal government. The National Academy of Engineering also sponsors engineering programs aimed at meeting national needs, encourages education and research, and recognizes the superior achievements of engineers. Dr. William A. Wulf is president of the National Academy of Engineering.

The Institute of Medicine was established in 1970 by the National Academy of Sciences to secure the services of eminent members of appropriate professions in the examination of policy matters pertaining to the health of the public. The Institute acts under the responsibility given to the National Academy of Sciences by its congressional charter to be an adviser to the federal government and, upon its own initiative, to identify issues of medical care, research, and education. Dr. Kenneth I. Shine is president of the Institute of Medicine.

The National Research Council was organized by the National Academy of Sciences in 1916 to associate the broad community of science and technology with the Academy's purposes of furthering knowledge and advising the federal government. Functioning in accordance with general policies determined by the Academy, the Council has become the principal operating agency of both the National Academy of Sciences and the National Academy of Engineering in providing services to the government, the public, and the scientific and engineering communities. The Council is administered jointly by both Academies and the Institute of Medicine. Dr. Bruce Alberts and Dr. William A. Wulf are chairman and vice chairman, respectively, of the National Research Council.

PREFACE

The spread of information systems and, in particular, information infrastructure throughout the economy and social fabric raises questions about the technology's ease of use by different people, from those with limited technical know-how to those with various disabilities to the so-called power users who push for higher performance on many dimensions. In response to a request from the National Science Foundation, the Computer Science and Telecommunications Board (CSTB) of the National Research Council convened a steering committee to evaluate and suggest fruitful directions for progress in user interfaces to computing and communications systems. The charge to the steering committee is best presented by quoting from the project prospectus, which called for a workshop to "determine the state-of-the-art of research in CS [computer science] and other disciplines, identify the questions most important to investigate next . . . , identify what is known from research on the longer-term problems that will aid in near-term human-computer communications design, and identify important long-term research issues." The steering committee met in March 1996 to plan a two-day workshop that was held in August 1996 (the agenda and participants are listed in Appendix A) and then met again in September 1996 to plan the structure and format of this summary report. It relied primarily on electronic mail for its subsequent interactions, including electronic mail with the larger set of workshop participants.

The workshop participants, like the steering committee, included experts from multiple disciplines—computing and communications software and hardware, psychology, sociology, human factors, design, and economics—and experts experienced with applications in specific domains (e.g., health and education) and with the needs and experiences of a wide range of subpopulations (e.g., people with physical disabilities; those with low-income and/or limited education). Whether from a computer science, social science, or application-domain perspective, all had experience working with a variety of computing and communications system users, and all were asked to draw on their practical experience. It was anticipated that viewing earlier, more technically focused treatments of user interfaces through the lens of a familiar life domain would reveal neglected issues, unidentified challenges, unexpected convergences, or new directions for research or action. The participants pooled their skills to make suggestions concerning how to build interfaces that will enable the broadest-possible spectrum of citizenry to interact easily and effectively with the nation's information infrastructure to obtain as many services as is reasonable.

The workshop demonstrated the value of assembling a very diverse group of experts embodying many complementary perspectives; it also demonstrated how differently people in different disciplines—or people with different subspecialties within a given discipline—perceive, analyze, and discuss the experiences and needs of users of computing and communications systems. That recognition implies that the workshop should be seen as part of a process of interdisciplinary convening and exchange that should continue. That process may require special effort and encouragement through activities like the one responsible for this report.

The role of the steering committee was not only to organize the workshop but also to sift through the many inputs to distill key themes, ideas, and recommendations. The results compose Part I of the present report, which is a synthesis and distillation primarily of workshop-related inputs and which focuses on research opportunities. Its contribution lies in its integration of a very diverse set of perspectives to illuminate directions for research, with emphasis on directions that blend multiple disciplines. Part I does not purport to be a comprehensive treatise on either user interfaces or the entire set of problems inherent in the challenge of broadening public access to the national information infrastructure (NII), nor does it focus on the important subset of problems associated with NII applications in support of the rights and responsibilities of citizenship. For those seeking more detail and a mapping of ideas to sources, position papers contributed by workshop participants (several containing bibliographies) are included in Part II. Additional position papers can be found on the World Wide Web at http://www2.nas.edu/CSTBWEB).

The steering committee is grateful to the many people who contributed to its deliberations and to this report. The workshop participants generated a lively set of discussions and commented on early drafts derived from panel discussions. The steering committee is particularly grateful to those who also contributed position statements (see Part II), brief outlines of the state of the art in specific areas (distributed with the workshop program to participants), and comments on a draft of this report. H. Rex Hartson (Virginia Polytechnic Institute), who was unable to attend the workshop, generously supplied a special overview of the user interface landscape, which is the lead segment of Part II. Terry Winograd (Stanford University), Ben Shneiderman (University of Maryland), and Nathan Shedroff (vivid studios), who were also unable to attend, provided position papers.

Several workshop participants and a few individuals with no formal participation in the project provided extraordinary inputs to this report. Austin Henderson (Apple Computer) made significant contributions to the committee's thinking about collaboration and information dimensions. Johanna Moore (University of Pittsburgh) assisted in the revision of the discussion on agent technology by collecting input from other participants and integrating it with her own suggestions. Candace Sidner (Lotus Development Corporation) and C. Raymond Perrault (SRI International) contributed additional insights, references, and text describing natural language understanding and processing. Blake Hannaford (University of Washington) contributed text describing commercial and research trends relating to haptic and tactile interfaces, and David Warner (Syracuse University) provided input on medical applications for such technology. Julia Hirschberg (AT&T Research Laboratories) and Pierre Isabelle (Center for Information Technology Innovation) provided state-of-the-art reviews for text-to-speech synthesis and machine translation, respectively. Jason Leigh (University of Illinois at Chicago) supplied a substantial part of the graphics and virtual reality reference list. CommerceNet (http://www.commerce.net) and Nielsen Media Research (http://www. nielsenmedia.com/commercenet) generously provided results of their Internet Demographics Survey. Michael North (North Communications) and Marc Regberg (Venture Development Corporation) supplied reference materials on kiosks and their uses. David Crocker (Brandenburg Consulting) created an electronic mail discussion list that supported post-workshop exchanges by the workshop participants and the steering committee.

The anonymous reviewers of this report provided an invaluable, if sometimes confounding, sanity check on the steering committee's early efforts to synthesize its impressions and conclusions. The range of comments, criticisms, and suggestions was as broad as the other inputs to the project, but collectively they guided the steering committee in tightening and reinforcing its presentation.

John Godfrey, a CSTB research associate until February 1997, put considerable effort into organizing the workshop and working with the steering committee as it developed this report. Rob Cheng, a graduate student at the Massachussetts Institute of Technology, prepared background research and other materials for the workshop as a summer intern with CSTB. Finally, the committee thanks Gary Strong, of the National Science Foundation, for both making this project possible and providing ongoing encouragement.

Alan W. Biermann, *Chair*
Toward an Every-Citizen Interface to the
Nation's Information Infrastructure
Steering Committee

CONTENTS

On Application Areas

On Selected Population Groups

On Key Processes

APPENDIXES

EXECUTIVE SUMMARY

INTERFACES FOR EVERYONE

Computing, communications technologies, and associated enterprises advanced enough in the early 1990s for the national information infrastructure (NII) to be accepted as public infrastructure. As a result, concern is growing about what will be required to enable most if not all of the public to use NII resources. The opportunity for broad public access and use reflects many factors, among them the technologies used directly by people as part of their interactions with the information and communications systems that make up the NII. This report outlines issues and directions for progress in developing interface technologies that will enable increasing numbers of people to use the NII effectively. Drawing from a late 1996 workshop hosted by the Computer Science and Telecommunications Board, the steering committee responsible for this project derived ideas for research in computing, communications, and social science to advance the underlying sciences and enable development of innovative, implementable concepts for interfaces that are more usable and capable than today's technologies and are accessible by as many people as possible.

The NII is dominated by computing and communications systems, and the human-machine or user interface represents the means by which people communicate with a particular system and the machines and people connected to it. In this report such technologies are referred to as every-citizen interfaces (ECIs), reflecting the project's mission to examine what might be required for every citizen to be able to use the resources available through the NII. ECIs are defined broadly as including input and output hardware and software as well as design and performance characteristics of applications—such as ease and speed of communication—that influence the overall experience of a person or group of people working in a system. The concern of the study is that, even though the usability of systems has improved substantially over many years, current interfaces still exclude many people from effective NII access. Most obvious are individuals with physical and other disabilities, but as articles in even the national and business press attest, people without such distinguishing characteristics, even expert users of NII systems, experience difficulties that constrain or even preclude their full use of NII resources.

The steering committee emphasizes that effective technological research on and development of ECIs must be grounded in a well-considered understanding of the needs and behavior of people. Achieving ECIs is thus an interdisciplinary endeavor involving computing-related science and engineering disciplines as well as social science disciplines. Progress toward developing improved ECIs will require basic research in theory, modeling, and conceptualization; experimental research involving building, evaluating, and testing of artifacts; and empirical social science research assessing segments of the population and how people actually work with different systems. In all cases, data, methodology, and tools are themselves targets for research or research support.

Certainly, however, the needed ECI-related research discussed in this report accounts for only part of the challenge of making NII resources broadly accessible. Policies aimed at promoting universal access to the NII must be developed that address economic factors, such as a person's ability to pay for communication and information services and access devices, as well as social and psychological factors, such as organizational, family, and peer group support, and personal preferences. Although the importance of such factors is clear, examination of them is beyond the scope of this report, which focuses primarily on issues related to computing, information, and communications technologies.

TECHNOLOGIES FOR HUMAN-MACHINE COMMUNICATION BY EVERY CITIZEN

At this time and for the foreseeable future, enlarging the set of options for human-machine communication, not replacing older technologies with new per se, is a broad goal for ECI research. Making a full range of options available involves continued improvements in mainstream interface technologies, such as graphical direct manipulation interfaces and typed and menu-selected command line interfaces, as well as research on modes that are currently not widely available. Recent advances in the performance and the commercial deployment of speech recognition and natural language processing technologies, for example, indicate their promise for future interfaces. In the last several years, progress in research and in the development of commercial products points to credible prospects for software agents as aids to ordinary citizens. Major progress in virtual reality technologies and three-dimensional user interfaces generally suggests their near-term availability. A variety of ideas are being generated for collaboration and communications technologies. Other options such as gesture recognition, pointing devices, and haptic devices are being proposed and in some cases developed and installed. Together, these technologies provide a rich set of opportunities to create new human-machine interface paradigms for the coming years.

Just as the NII is more than a single entity, so also will ECIs be diverse and varied. No single interface can be used by absolutely everyone, because people differ in ways relevant to the design of the technologies they use and because for a given person the activities and conditions of use for technologies vary: graphical user interfaces are problematic for blind people and also for people driving cars, for example. Experts who have concentrated on meeting the needs of users with specific limitations have discovered not only that it is possible to achieve adaptations of conventional interfaces to suit those users (giving rise to prototypes and commercial systems), but also that such adaptations often prove attractive and useful to many others. Such experiences underscore the value of medium and modality independence for future ECIs. Research and experience with real systems show that cross-disability access is compatible with diversity in the look and feel of an interface and that providing for it does not imply compromising capabilities that are useful to people without disabilities. In the language of this project, aiming for use by every citizen can enhance use by ordinary citizens. Even the seemingly ordinary are heterogeneous: the general population varies greatly in computer skills (e.g., from novice to expert); in the ability to speak, read, and write English; in personal cognitive styles (e.g., from linguistic/verbal to spatial/visual); and in personal propensity for using complex technological gadgets.

Other motivations for ensuring the versatility and adaptability of user interface technologies in the NII context include the desirability of achieving nomadicity, the ability of people to use the NII effectively regardless of their location, and the quality of available computing or communications equipment and services, which may vary depending on whether users are on the road, in the office, or en route between locations. Another more commercial motivation for emphasizing versatile and adaptable interfacing is the drive by relevant businesses to produce mass-market technologies. Although in the early 1990s popular discussions of the NII focused

on the use of personal computers (PCs) and the Internet as an NII component, more recent experiences with commercialization and public acceptance are leading to a broader view in the late 1990s of an NII accessed by
PCs, telephones, televisions, and a myriad of consumer electronics and
other devices. Some of these devices have primary purposes other than
computing and communications but incorporate embedded systems that
allow for connection with networked infrastructure and therefore integration with other computing and communications systems. This diversifica-
tion further broadens the range of people, activities, and environments that
can be supported by the NII and thus represents one of the requirements
for effective ECIs; it underscores the value of certain kinds of research, such
as research and development to lower costs or foster compatibility. Taken
together, the evolving set of motivations for facilitating human-machine
communication gives rise to a range of ECI desiderata: flexibility, adaptability, ease of learning, compatibility, affordability, and so on.

SYNTHESIZING A RESEARCH AGENDA

An important starting point in building a research agenda is to ask
what people's computing, communication, and information needs are
with respect to the NII and how these needs can be met. This approach
involves studying people doing ordinary tasks with and without technological aids and asking how new technologies might improve the process.
It can also include gathering data from existing applications as input to
guide new designs. Proposed systems can then be simulated or built in
prototype for testing, refinement, and evaluation. Work of this kind can
in turn guide decisions in technical areas concerning specific perceived
needs and new research goals. A complementary approach is to study
technical areas to discover fundamental mechanisms that can serve in
providing support when they are needed. The pursuit of the two paths
together can lead to an eventual synthesis of truly usable and important
new aids for future communities.

Generally with this view in mind, the steering committee crystallized
three recommendations that are summarized here and are presented in
detail in Chapter 7. The first is that a major new effort be launched to seek
new paradigms for human-machine interaction. The research community recognizes the success achieved by technologies developed two or
more decades ago but also sees many indications that better alternatives
are needed and are possible. Among the drawbacks of or problems with
current technologies are that they are too finely tuned to the peculiarities
of the technologically elite, too inflexible for the variety of applications
and environments that the NII will offer, and too inaccessible to ordinary
users or to individuals with disabilities. New, better interfaces are needed

that utilize a variety of technologies that are now becoming available, that are usable by a broader cross section of people, that take advantage of the opportunities afforded by the NII, and that emphasize the new role of technology in society as a mediator among individuals, groups of individuals, and networked machines. Elaborating on this recommendation, the steering committee in Chapter 7 specifies a series of properties and characteristics that it thinks new and improved interfaces should have, including learnability, modality and medium independence, and a strong capability for supporting group activities.

The steering committee's second recommendation encourages investment in research on the component subsystems needed for ECIs and emphasizes the importance of studies of human and organizational behaviors and ways that technology can support them. It encourages research on a variety of potentially useful technologies, including input technologies (such as speech recognition, natural language processing, computer vision, gesture sensing, and multimodal input languages) and output technologies (such as flexible, portable, and compact displays, high-resolution displays, virtual reality, haptic devices, mechanical actuators, voice and artificial sound, and multimodal generation of output) that can help to maximize human-machine communication by more closely matching machine audio, visual, and mechanical capabilities to those of humans. This second recommendation also emphasizes the importance of developing modality and medium independence so that individual systems can be used by a variety of people in a variety of situations, and it recognizes the importance of agent technologies that can aid in interpreting and responding appropriately to users' needs.

The steering committee's third recommendation encourages research at the systems level that assembles the many subsystem components referred to in its second recommendation. It encourages the development of theories and architectures for collaboration and problem solving; emphasizes continued studies in human-centered design methodologies and social science research into how well the public is being served by new and proposed technologies; and underscores the importance of building experimental human-machine systems to test, refine, and measure the effectiveness of various proposed systems.

Because they have not been emphasized in other research or may have unusual payoffs in achieving improved ECIs, the steering committee chose to designate some areas for highest-priority consideration and accordingly emphasizes the following:

1. Undertake psychological, sociological, and historical studies to determine the needs of every citizen in the context of the NII and thus to

provide guidance to technologists concerning what needs to be created and what will not work for real users.

2. Encourage additional research on speech recognition and the associated natural language processing so that speech can become a viable option for input in a variety of NII-related applications. Speech recognition and natural language processing are each important; speech as an output option calls for research related to speech synthesis. The steering committee was impressed regarding both the broad need for such capabilities and the recent progress in the field supporting the hypothesis that speech will soon become usable for at least some interface applications.

3. Develop technologies that enable modality and medium independence for as many applications as possible, in order to support the goals of nomadicity, compatibility of interfaces with a variety of hardware types, and usability by people with disabilities.

4. Develop theories and architectures that support collaboration among networked people. The new opportunities offered by the NII will come to fruition only if technologies are developed that enable collaboration.

5. Build experimental human-machine systems, for individual users and groups, using proposed technologies or simulations of them. Test them, refine them, install them in applications environments, and measure their effectiveness.

The steering committee emphasizes the importance of there being a strong experimental component in upcoming studies.

PART I

1

INTRODUCTION

Information infrastructure—local, national, and global—holds the promise of connecting people of all ages and descriptions to other people; to business, government, and other organizations; and more generally to sources of information, art, entertainment, and more. We can only begin to imagine the transformations that might unfold. Obvious trends are illustrated by activities on the World Wide Web and innovations in telephony and cable television networks, with improvements in network and device support for finding, viewing, or exchanging text and growth in audio and video exchange over alternative media. Although the most common examples relate to white-collar activities, the same technologies are beginning to reshape service and goods production jobs as well. More speculative are the possibilities arising from greater and more explicit networking of computing and communications systems embedded in all manner of consumer and producer devices—including systems in automobiles and home appliances as well as systems associated with manufacturing and service process automation.

Within this context, the question arises as to whether the many proposed benefits of the new technologies will be available to ordinary citizens. Specifically, will these technologies have interfaces that are usable by the broad spectrum of people who may wish to use national information infrastructure (NII) resources? In cases where they will not, what new research is needed to make such interfaces available? This report examines these questions and their solutions as analyzed by the authoring steering committee.[1]

As a start for the study, the steering committee notes that good interface design can help the spread of technologies. For example, one can point to the movement of personal computers from offices to homes and the growth of electronic game systems (e.g., Nintendo and Sega) that run on special or general-purpose computers. In the last several years, we have also witnessed the explosive growth of the World Wide Web and its use by individuals, schools and universities, companies, governmental units, and nonprofit organizations. Another area of growth involves the 800- and 900-number telephone services and experiments in electronic banking, meter reading, and other specialized data services to the home, as well as the rise of "freenets" and other local public network services.

Yet problems with many interfaces have also been observed. Interfaces often frustrate or are of limited use to many users, restricting access and use.[2] Problems begin with those who do use these technologies despite some apparent difficulties. They suffer from repetitive stress syndrome and from the effects of low input/output bandwidths, overly restrictive computational formats, information overload, and many other problems. Market research also shows that today's costs of owning a personal computer, in the home or office, are very high once the various support costs are factored in.[3] Other problems relate to those who do not or cannot use the information infrastructure. Current interfaces are among a variety of factors that limit use today by those who have physical, sensory, cognitive, language, and learning difficulties and by those whose activities or environments impose constraints on what they can do and how. Despite an enormous number of smart people working to improve interfaces, this is an area characterized by tough problems, many of which are getting tougher as the user population and its demands grow. As Bruce Tognazzini observed at the August 1996 workshop, "While critical roadwork needs to be done in building the nation's information superhighway, we cannot afford any longer to ignore the cars. Our 1960s rattletrap hardware and 1970s rattletrap interfaces and software are not up to the task of every-citizen access to this nation's information infrastructure."

Based on its study of such problems, the steering committee recommends an aggressive research program, funded by government and private sources, that examines both the human performance side of interfaces and the interface technologies, current and potential. Certainly such funding has played a major role historically in breaking new ground in interface design, and even greater reasons exist now for its continuance. One need only look at the roots of current graphical interfaces, notably the Apple Computer Macintosh operating system, which built on the earlier Xerox PARC SmallTalk and Alto systems and yet earlier work at SRI and RAND.[4] Another example is the Internet, which can be traced to

BOX 1.1
Constraints Imposed by Commercial Conditions

Serving every citizen implies not just technical feasibility, but also that there are products available on the market and, in particular, that many information infrastructure products take on the character of mass-market goods and services, which is not the case today for most computer-based products. If they prove relatively expensive, are virtual reality and many other of the newest technologies likely to find their way into everyday life? Economists and people in industry note that high prices are common early in technology markets; consumer advocates caution against the inherent exclusion implied by high prices.

The observed rate of progress is a function of the marketplace: vendors offer technology that sells, using their best guess about what people will buy in sufficient volumes and rushing to fill narrow market windows. Market pressures affect what kinds of interfaces are available in several ways. Rapid product life cycles, for example, militate against long-term evaluation and testing (implicitly relying on market response testing) and emphasize incremental changes that allow vendors to continue to sell what sells, in part to facilitate transfer of skills among successful products. An example is the evolution and growth in market dominance over more than a decade of graphical user interfaces that involve windows, icons, menus, and pointers. Even in a marketplace characterized by rapid change, facilitating the adoption of new technology by the existing base of users is as important to industry as assimilating uninitiated or previously unserved users. In computing, as in telephony and television, the existing base represents a known market that vendors do not want to abandon or alienate; this base provides vendors the incentive to moderate the pace of change.[1] Market pacing also reflects perceptions about what people will buy, other things being equal. Early videotext and recent cable television and on-line service market trials foundered because they failed to appeal to consumers.

---

[1] Controlled rate of change is reinforced by regulation in television contexts, and some speculate that the growing user base of the Internet will also prove to be a conservative force.

federally funded network research and deployment (CSTB, 1994a, 1995). These developments show that major progress can be made in spreading the use of technologies. They also illustrate a fruitful combination of public and private investment in research and development. Box 1.1 outlines the influence of commercial conditions on interface availability.

A significant research opportunity (and challenge!) is presented by the need to narrow the gap between the capabilities provided in today's interface products and the capabilities that computer science and interface design researchers believe are possible.[5] Research that can contribute to advancing innovative concepts and that can promote better understanding of what technology works well to make interfaces more usable, useful, and accessible is the focus of this report.

DEFINITIONS, KEY CONCEPTS, AND PARAMETERS

The steering committee established definitions for the major terms that appear in the subtitle of this report: *Toward Every-Citizen Interfaces to the Nation's Information Infrastructure.* The term "every citizen" represents the steering committee's desire to consider the needs of people of all ages and physical abilities, races and ethnicities, education and ability levels, economic backgrounds, cognitive styles, and personal inclinations. It overcomes the homogenization suggested by a term used early in the project, "ordinary citizen," but also includes people who are ordinary in the sense that they are not distinguished by special needs, such as accommodation of disabilities. The term opens up consideration not only of conventional office and household equipment and services but also of systems in production manufacturing and service environments, systems embedded in equipment designed for purposes other than computing and communications, and public access systems such as public kiosks.

Associated with this definition are several principles:[6]

• Promoting broader (every-citizen) access does not necessarily imply making all systems accessible to literally all users; rather, the goal can be expressed quite usefully in terms of enabling many more people to use the information infrastructure well than do at present. (See Chapter 2 for data concerning the current demographic patterns of NII use and the distribution in the U.S. population of special characteristics such as sensory disabilities and illiteracy.)

• Ease of use does not necessarily imply no personal effort in learning or mastery.

• Improvements aimed at meeting special needs, for example, those of partially disabled persons, may benefit other (even all) users.

The steering committee defines the "interface" to a system as encompassing the various means by which people communicate and interact with the system to engage and guide what it does, the nature of the dialogue, and the means by which the system communicates its responses. The interface includes input/output hardware and software—the actuators, keyboard, speech recognition, and so forth—that people may employ for input and the visual, audio, and other representations that the system returns as its output. It also includes application characteristics such as information management and presentation, collaborative and other group interaction dimensions, and sharing of labor and responsibility between people and systems (e.g., by means of autonomous agents). The technical facilities (e.g., communications, computation) supporting people's interaction with systems are also part of the interface because their performance directly influences the experiences people have using a system—the interface in its broadest sense. For example, an important dimension of an interface is the amount of time delay encountered when using a particular system; this depends on the available communications bandwidth, processor speed, and memory capacity as well as the design and function of the input/output components. An interface may connect a person to a machine, an application program of some kind, other people, or a combination of such entities. The definition used in this report is more comprehensive than may be traditional; the steering committee's goal is to avoid the slippage that comes when the interface and application are narrowly defined and important issues are lost in an unfortunate gap that falls between them.

Because the NII and the population are inherently diverse and heterogeneous, it is unreasonable to expect to have a single every-citizen interface to the NII. The variety of users, applications, and vendors mandates a corresponding variety of interfaces. These will include present-day telephones and computers (including both portable and full-featured desktop or room systems), inexpensive network computers and various portable computing and communications systems, a variety of devices that can be worn on one's body or installed in a vehicle, and systems embedded in equipment and services with other primary purposes.[7]

The term "national information infrastructure" as used here means the collection of communications systems in the United States and the set of computers and information stores and services that may be accessible through them. It includes the telephone system, the radio and television networks, all of the libraries and computers in the country, and a long list of other communications and storage facilities and services (CSTB, 1996). Of course, elements of the information infrastructure have always existed, but the term "NII" was coined recently because of the possibility of tying together a great many (if not all) of these elements into an integrated network complex that will be accessible (with some limitations) to essentially everyone. The Internet is a significant part of the NII, but it is important not to equate it with the much richer and more complex NII as a whole. The NII concept implies that the paradigm for the coming century is one of networked machines, collaborative computing, ubiquitous and possibly continuous access, and group interactions over networks of all kinds.[8]

Of course, interface improvement is not sufficient for maximizing the utility of the information infrastructure. Other factors outside the scope of this report include the appeal of the content and activities made available (do people want to use the information infrastructure more, or are advocates projecting their own tastes?), regulatory and legal conditions that affect the nature and pricing of communications products that compose and depend on the infrastructure, free speech protections and intellectual property controls that shape what information is available through different components of the infrastructure, and political processes based on value judgments about how technology can be leveraged to meet societal objectives (themselves subjective) and decisions about the allocation of public resources to technology relative to other uses. All of these factors combine to shape who uses the information infrastructure and how, when, where, why, and how well. They indicate why public policy is an important element of context. In this context, the Americans with Disabilities Act and the Telecommunications Reform Act are recent examples of public policy interventions to promote more and easier use of the information infrastructure (and other facilities) by every citizen; the Telecommunications Reform Act, for example, contains language requiring that product design incorporate features enabling access by people with disabilities.[9]

ADDITIONAL COMMENTS

There is a vital interaction between the shape of the technology and the public and private objectives for its use, drawing implicitly on ideas associated with universal service in telecommunications or equitable access more broadly viewed. For example, the expression "every-citizen interface" led some contributors to this report to suggest framing research relative to objectives concerning how much of the population can undertake certain activities associated with exercising the rights and responsibilities of citizenship (e.g., sending and receiving e-mail, querying a government agency, or participating via the network in a multiweek organized educational experience). Others pointed to problems in framing such objectives—how much of the population constitutes critical mass or social equity? What activities are most essential to enable? How can their achievement be paid for if they are not likely to emerge from the marketplace?[10] Contributors to this project noted, therefore, that given what people can and do do with today's information infrastructure (including activities that substitute for use of other technologies), prematurely promoting broader access and use might result in either underused resources or a diversion of personal and institutional resources from less to more expensive technologies currently used in somewhat similar ways. Overall, the difficulty of getting many things right, at the same time, suggests that serving every citizen will take time—and that research can help accelerate the progress.

Questions of timing and the incidence of costs and benefits are familiar ones in the evolution and diffusion of new technologies. What stands out in the context of the information infrastructure, however, is the strong belief by many that the associated technologies, including their interfaces, have public-interest ramifications that should be considered in decision making about associated computer and social science research agendas.[11] The steering committee shares that belief but reports that this project provides evidence of divergent views about specific opportunities and needs: consensus on social objectives and how trade-offs should be made is difficult to attain or define. Discussions and disagreements among workshop participants point to the value of developing applications and access technologies, including interfaces, concurrently. They also explain why some issues are identifiable only through actual use of an interface.

SYNTHESIZING A RESEARCH AGENDA

The starting point for user interface improvement comes in multiple forms—there is no single approach to recommend. The visual approach is epitomized in commercial graphical user interfaces. Commercial speech synthesis and recognition systems exist, but they are restricted in applicability and bandwidth compared to visual interfaces. Menus are common in many kinds of systems, yet today's systems point to limitations in how they are implemented. But their success suggests that, for the near, medium, and even longer terms, progress will come through introducing more options that meet more needs rather than in eliminating the incumbents.

The next milestone depends on one's vision of the future. From almost any angle—technical, social, business, or policy—disagreements exist. Overall, the future may be reached incrementally, by extrapolating from and building directly on earlier successes. A large variety of new technologies are being pioneered that could potentially address people's needs. They include speech recognition and generation, virtual reality and advanced graphics systems, haptic devices, advanced database query mechanisms, and intelligent agents, all aided by much faster processing and greater memory than were available before. In most cases, substantial research is needed before the functionality, reliability, and appropriateness of new technologies for use by different people will be understood to the point that such technologies can be widely used.

Incremental improvements will take place; they should be considered part of the (moving) baseline. For example, more conservative members of the community point to the successes of direct manipulation interfaces and suggest that development efforts should build on them. The future may also be radically different as a result of technical breakthroughs or transformations arising from cumulative incremental developments. Some of the more visionary objectives come out of the (sub)discipline of artificial intelligence and involve credible and useful realization of natural language and intelligent systems. But to experts from other subdisciplines, those visions will not work or may be undesirable because of what they imply for complexity, control, and time investment to develop. Other tensions relate to emphasis on support for real-world communities and interactions versus support for artificial worlds and virtual environments. These are not inconsistent, but reflect different preferences and assumptions regarding people, activities, and allocation of resources. Some of the difference in perspective reflects differing views of the desirability of automating different functions or of different approaches to simplifying technology (e.g., whether functions should be hidden). What is simple, easy to use or learn, or even helpful is a matter of opinion. Some reflect attention to different segments of society: attention to information components of work and other activity tends to emphasize white-collar activities, raising questions about support for other kinds of activities, including those that may have little connection to information finding and manipulation (such as the purely recreational). Yet other differences arise in contemplating the larger architecture of the evolving information infrastructure: What is likely or preferable as the locus of intelligence, processing, various input/output functions, and so on? What capabilities belong in what kind of user device, and what capabilities belong in the network? Will one approach dominate, or will multiple solutions be sustainable technically and economically? How these issues are sorted out bears on end-user device and service options (technical features and costs), the cost structure of information and communications service providers, and the features and qualities desired in interfaces. The range of issues and their interactions underscore the value of joining social and computer science perspectives because technical capability is only a piece of the puzzle.

This project has shown that experts differ strongly in their views about what visions should shape the agenda for future user interface research. Those differences reflect the inherent biases of personal concentration and investment in a given subdiscipline, as well as differential understanding and evaluation of what has and has not worked in the past, varying orientations to medium- and long-term time horizons, relative openness to new or synthetic ideas/approaches, diverging values and frameworks, and myriad other factors. The increasing scale and diversity of the research effort make it harder for people to know about and understand progress outside their own niche; uneven understanding can be constraining in an inherently multifaceted arena. This report tries to be catholic in its approach, accepting the value of incremental and radical, as well as foreseeable and speculative, approaches and embracing the promise offered by multiple technologies and the interaction of technical and social science perspectives.

Interface research must proceed along many dimensions to accommodate every citizen and to sustain the marketplace of ideas and experimentation that composes a healthy research enterprise. It is already proceeding along multiple paths because of the fragmentation and multidisciplinary nature of the research community. Many different and often disagreeing communities exist: those oriented toward speech and those toward visual systems, those oriented toward artificial intelligence and those toward direct manipulation, those oriented toward meeting the needs of people who have disabilities or are disadvantaged, and those oriented toward the high-end, fully enabled, resource-rich users (these are characteristics often found among the early adopters of any new technology). These and other differences characterize the technical community; they are complemented by differing approaches among a variety of social sciences—psychology (e.g., cognitive, perception, social, industrial), sociology, anthropology, and economics—that offer valuable insights into how and why people use the information infrastructure and how those uses can be better in one or more ways. Diversity in research does not imply that all ideas are equivalent in merit or priority, but rather that there are risks in focusing too soon and too narrowly and that there is value in reassessing the prospects of certain technologies as conditions change. The diversity in research outlooks evidenced in this project underscores both the value of fostering interdisciplinary research and the challenge of undertaking such collaborations.

Progress toward achieving ECIs will involve basic research in theory, modeling, and conceptualization; experimental research involving evaluating, testing, and implementing artifacts; and empirical social science research assessing segments of the population and how people actually work with different systems. In all cases, data, methodology, and tools are themselves targets for research or research support.

ORGANIZATION OF THIS REPORT

Part I of this report represents the steering committee's synthesis of the factors shaping goals for ECI design (Chapter 2) and issues and directions for research in relevant and promising areas (Chapters 3 through 6). The cross-cutting issue of design and evaluation is covered in Chapter 4. Chapter 7 presents overarching conclusions and recommendations developed by the steering committee. Part II includes selected position papers prepared for the project's August 1996 workshop. These papers contain additional details on overall and specific ECI issues and the authors' personal recommendations for further research. Additional position papers are posted on the World Wide Web at http://www2.nas.edu/CSTBWEB.

NOTES

1. Use of the NII is, of course, a matter of individual choice. Although many factors affect who chooses to use what technology, when, where, how, and how well, contemporary experience shows that many people seem to want to use infrastructure technologies. Further, economists have shown that individuals benefit from widespread use of network technologies, suggesting that enabling use by more of the population will benefit more than just those newly accommodated. Broader deployment, if not ubiquity, and broader use allow for the economic and social benefits of what economists call network externalities—individuals gain value and appreciate networked systems more as more people become connected users. Even if advocacy based on the social or societal value of enhanced information infrastructures is premature, as some skeptics argue, the evidence for the promise of the technologies is great enough to make continued efforts to improve interfaces a wise national investment.

2. Some of the difficulty reflects the explosion in numbers of features and capabilities in the software and information infrastructure, a result of which is to make the older WIMP (windows, icons, menus, and pointers) interfaces more clumsy to use. Whereas an early-1980s desktop-style interface might be used with perhaps 50 documents, orders-of-magnitude more documents might be used in late-1990s applications.

3. Many of these support costs reflect limitations of today's interfaces, inasmuch as they involve ongoing training, consultation, and third-party adaptation of how a system is configured to meet the user's needs; these costs can be compounded by significant operating costs for telephone and cable television service. Note that even mouse pointing devices confound people initially, as recognized by Microsoft's inclusion of a solitaire game with Windows software packages.

4. Others building on that research legacy include Motif, the evolution of the Microsoft Windows line through Windows 95, and Mosaic and other Web browsers.

5. Context and motivation are provided by changing needs, an example of which is the contrast between searching a single document and searching vast repositories of documents (with the Library of Congress providing the canonical example). Research can enable a competitive marketplace to produce a wider variety of interfaces and applications, supporting citizen choice based on individual perceptions of needs and wants.

6. Other principles or goals can be framed as a function of value judgments about what people should be able to do and under what circumstances. Goals related to specific applications such as health care, education, or other domains can be very helpful in suggesting attributes for interfaces, and these are the focus of separate literatures, references to which are scattered throughout this report. For example, as Sproull and Faraj (1995) point out, policy discussions of the Internet and other electronic networks tend to assume that these media are mainly informational in nature and that users chiefly want better ways to browse and find the information they desire or to send information to others. Empirical social science studies suggest a contrasting view of users as complex social beings whose information needs are inextricably bound up with a collection of other ends that are communicative, participatory, and social in nature.

7. The expectation that computer and communications systems will take many forms and be used in many contexts underscores a caution voiced by some project contributors against "personal computer centrism": many devices and systems present many interface needs. The proliferation of technology promises ubiquity—eventually—and calls attention to the context of use: there is an evolution of what Mark Weiser, a workshop participant from Xerox PARC, has called "personal information infrastructures," and systems can be differentiated or used in common among personal, household, organizational, and public facility or public space environments.

8. Taking advantage of improvements in the cost, performance, and capabilities of the underlying hardware technologies, as well as the basic and applied interface research that has made possible today's successful commercial implementations, today's successful infrastructure products (epitomized by Internet services now extending to audio and video delivery) are often creatures of software. User interfaces are also driven increasingly by software, which can increase (or decrease) the accessibility of computer-based products to meet varying needs. Hardware improvements have enabled faster computing speed, one of the key sources of advances found in commercial graphical and, to a lesser degree, speech recognition and synthesis user interfaces.

As Gregg Vanderheiden (1996) explained in testimony to the Federal Communications Commission:

> Software determines the user interface more than hardware: In today's computers and most telecommunication and enhanced telecommunication devices, the user interface is almost entirely defined by the software rather than the hardware. Although the hardware provides some limits on what the software can do, the bulk of the user interface is determined by the software. Work with Apple Computer, IBM, Microsoft, and others in computer operating systems has shown how much disability access can be achieved without making any hardware changes. Software can be used to make mouse functions operable from the keyboard for those who cannot operate a mouse. Software can allow screen displays to be made accessible to individuals with low vision or blindness, and information emitted by speakers to be displayed visually for individuals who are blind—all without any changes in the hardware. In fact, the accessibility of almost any product can be tremendously enhanced by modifying nothing more than the instructions (the software) which govern its behavior. On the other hand, relatively little can be done to make a product more cross-disability accessibility without addressing the software issue.

9. Section 255: Access by Individuals with Disabilities.

    (a) DEFINITIONS—As used in this section—
        1. DISABILITY—The term "disability" has the meaning given to it by section 3(2)(A) of the Americans with Disabilities Act of 1990 (42 U.S.C. 12102(2)(A)).
        2. READILY ACHIEVABLE—The term "readily achievable" has the meaning given to it by section 301 (9) of that Act (42 U.S.C. 12181(9)).

    (b) MANUFACTURING—A manufacturer of telecommunications equipment or customer premises equipment shall ensure that the equipment is designed, developed, and fabricated to be accessible to and usable by individuals with disabilities, if readily achievable.

    (c) TELECOMMUNICATIONS SERVICES—A provider of telecommunications services shall ensure that the service is accessible to and usable by individuals with disabilities, if readily achievable.

    (d) COMPATIBILITY—Whenever the requirements of subsections (b) and (c) are not readily achievable, such a manufacturer or provider shall ensure that the equipment or service is compatible with existing peripheral devices or specialized customer premises equipment commonly used by individuals with disabilities to achieve access, if readily achievable.

(e)   GUIDELINES—Within 18 months after the date of enactment of the Telecommunications Act of 1996, the Architectural and Transportation Barriers Compliance Board shall develop guidelines for accessibility of telecommunications equipment and customer premises equipment in conjunction with the Commission. The Board shall review and update the guidelines periodically.

10.   Lee Sproull, Boston University, personal communication.
11.   This is central to the linkage with universal telecommunications service, a concept many seek to expand from telephony, and to the discussion of public access points, from network access computers in libraries to kiosks in shopping malls.

2

REQUIREMENTS FOR EFFECTIVE
EVERY-CITIZEN INTERFACES

In addition to giving us new tools or techniques for carrying out the activities we are already doing, communications and information technologies will provide new opportunities for doing things we cannot currently do: viewing the invisible; hearing the unhearable; shrinking the world or ourselves in real time in order to better explore, learn, or interact with the real or virtual worlds; enhancing our sensory, physical, or cognitive skills; and tackling tasks we would otherwise never attempt because of the physical demands. Not only will what we do and how we do it affect the way interfaces should be designed, but the way we design the interfaces will also have profound effects on the way we do things. At the same time, substantial growth in information quantity and diversity is affecting both activities and the nature of the information infrastructure from the inside out, suggesting alternative perspectives for interface designers to consider. The steering committee expected that viewing existing interfaces through the lens of a familiar life domain would reveal neglected issues, unidentified challenges, unexpected convergences, or new directions for research or action. Accordingly, the workshop convened by the steering committee generated examples of trends, needs, and anticipated developments in education and lifelong learning, selected work environments, and home life, civic life, and social life.

This chapter begins with a high-level overview of the almost kaleidoscopic interplay of task, environment, information, and user attributes to which effective ECIs must be responsive. The overview of tasks, environments, and users provides the basis for an enumeration in the rest of the chapter of the qualities desired from every-citizen interfaces (ECIs). The steering committee emphasizes that this overview, synthesized from workshop discussions and supporting materials, is impressionistic rather than complete. More completeness is both beyond the scope of this report and problematic: the ease of extrapolating from what we see and do today may be misleading about the future, although contemporary experiences do illuminate what does and does not work well.[1] In particular, contemporary examples emphasize the characteristics of contemporary personal computers and, to a lesser extent, telephones and televisions; tomorrow's information infrastructure will draw more on embedded systems and different kinds of devices, too (Verity and Judge, 1996).

DIVERSITY OF DEMANDS TO BE MET BY EVERY-CITIZEN INTERFACES

The interdisciplinary nature of the workshop discussions provided evidence for the contributions to technical development of better interfaces from better understanding of the social context and "domestication" of system use. For example, how does the new technology change or become integrated into household and community routines? How is the definition of home computing evolving? As explained by social scientists, that understanding should be informed by a history of social change associated with computing and communications systems, leveraging descriptive data and analysis to anticipate the amount and style of use. For example, what are the roles of service features, early experiences, and social influences in the adoption and use of networked infrastructure by mainstream users? Longitudinal, multimethodological field research may be especially important for systems intended for public access (e.g., library resident and kiosk systems[2]). It may also help in understanding how public knowledge, understanding, and educational needs about security and trustworthiness should be factored into technical decision making. For example, how far can one go in providing anonymity and/or privacy protection to citizens without huge increases in cost or effort associated with use of the national information infrastructure (NII)? Is technology that is aimed mainly at protecting institutional (government or corporate/proprietary) information generalizable, or do individuals present specific additional requirements?

Today's Diverse Uses of Information and Communications Technologies

Reliable, comprehensive, and up-to-date data about everyday uses to which people currently put information technology are in short supply,

TABLE 2.1   Computer Use at Home

Application	Percentage of Users by Age Group[a]				
	0-14 Years	15-39 Years	40-59 Years	60+ Years	Adults Age 15+ Years
E-mail	1	25	35	38	29
Bulletin boards	2	8	8	8	8
Communications	NA	18	24	24	20
Databases	NA	18	25	21	21
Spreadsheets	1	18	24	20	20
Word processing	26	58	64	57	60
Games	85	20	19	19	19
Graphics	15	14	14	10	14
Household records and finance	NA	15	20	17	17
Work at home	NA	22	33	21	26
Connect to work from home	NA	8	9	4	8
Home-based business	NA	4	6	6	5
School assignments	40	33	14	2	24
Educational programs	39	13	18	14	15
Learning computer use	25	21	20	15	20
Programming	3	8	9	7	9

NA, not applicable.

[a] Percentages are the proportion of people who had a computer at home (not the percentage of total U.S. population) and used it for the indicated purpose.

SOURCES: U.S. Bureau of the Census, Current Population Survey, October 1993; RAND (1995, p. 185).

but what is available provides important insights. Table 2.1 summarizes data from the U.S. Bureau of the Census about computer use by adults and children who have access to a computer at home (22.8 percent of U.S. households at the time of the survey). The Census Bureau data were collected in 1993 in the Current Population Survey, which uses a statistically valid sample of the U.S. population (unlike on-line surveys and most market research reports). The 1993 data are the most recent available from the Census Bureau concerning the country's home computer use; unfortunately, the 1993 survey predated the widespread growth in popularity of the World Wide Web and did not ask about Web use. More recent private surveys (e.g., Hoffman et al., 1996) provide only snapshots, since the combination of broadening use of personal computers and frequent introductions of new software and services leads to relatively frequent changes in who is doing what.

Table 2.1 suggests that work, learning, entertainment, household chores (e.g., bookkeeping), and social/collegial contact (e.g., bulletin boards) have all become part of everyday household computer use. For example, learning—including formal education—is not restricted to household members in the kindergarten through high school age range. Rather, a sizable proportion of adults who have home computers have been doing school assignments on them (24 percent), using educational programs (15 percent), and investing time in learning about computer use (21 percent). Word processing seems to have been the dominant application for adults (60 percent reported its use), probably because it figures into so many other activities (e.g., bulletin boards, e-mail, home-based business, remote work, school assignments).

Excluding word processing, e-mail has the highest incidence of home use among adults (29 percent) in the Census Bureau data. More recent data add support to the conclusion that communication is a dominant reason for computers (Sandberg, 1996). A representative example is provided by Forrester Research, which estimated that about 15 percent of all Americans (not just those with home computers and thus a different measure than the Census Bureau data cited above) communicate by e-mail at work and/or at home, up from 2 percent in 1992 (*Investor's Business Daily*, 1997). Typical of market research optimism, Forrester predicts that growth in the use of personal computers in homes and corporate Internet access will drive e-mail use up to 50 percent of the U.S. population within 5 years.

Use of home computers for work-related purposes appears to be increasing. According to an International Data Corporation (IDC) study, the number of households with full- or part-time self-employed home workers reached 20 million in 1996. IDC found that these households lead U.S. households overall in their rates of personal computer (PC) ownership (56.5 percent compared to 35 percent), on-line service use (27.5 percent compared to 21.1 percent), and Internet use (23.1 percent compared to 15.9 percent), and they are more likely to use on-line and Internet services than households with home computers but no home workers. IDC segments home offices according to whether they are used by self-employed home workers or by people with "corporate home offices" (i.e., those who work elsewhere and telecommute or bring work home after hours). Perhaps because of financial and training support from their employers, the latter group have even higher rates of PC ownership and network use than self-employed home workers. Although these data cannot be compared directly to the Census Bureau data in Table 2.1,[3] IDC's finding of 10 percent growth in home offices in 1995-1996, combined with the high rates of computer and network use observed among such offices, suggests that doing paid work at home is a more common use of computers and networks now than in 1993.

TABLE 2.2   Internet Use in the Past Three Months (all data represent percentages of the U.S. population)

Category	People in Computer Households (%)	People Using Networks (%)
Income quartile		
1	15	2
2	34	8
3	43	10
4	68	21
Education level		
< HS	26	5
HS or more	32	6
B.A. or more	59	23
Gender		
Male	41	12
Female	52	6
Age		
< 20	50	14
20-39	41	12
40-59	43	9
> 59	15	2

NOTE: Getting an accurate picture of the distribution of computer and network use among U.S. citizens is not straightforward. Numerous samples are used to generate publicized survey data, but close examination shows that despite care in the planning of sample design, the actual data must be adjusted statistically (through the use of weights) to achieve meaningful and accurate inferences about the U.S. population. In addition, what is being measured is often neither clear nor consistent. Survey researchers have observed, for example, that people often do not understand enough about their equipment or services to answer questions reliably; questions about activities and uses tend to yield more accurate and consistent results. Another factor inspiring caution about reported data is that there is significant "churn" in the PC application and services markets: people start and stop activity relatively often, but it is too soon to describe either long-term attrition rates or consistent patterns in how use varies over time and among different categories of people.

SOURCE: "CommerceNet/Nielsen Media Research Internet Demographics Study for Fall 1995 and Spring 1996 Recontact," Nielsen Interactive Services, Dunedin, FL, August 1996.

Recent research on Internet use in the United States draws on the 1995 CommerceNet/Nielsen Internet Demographic Survey (CNIDS), a telephone survey conducted in August 1995 (see Table 2.2).[4] Unlike the 1993 Census Bureau survey, this survey examined Web use, which is a subset of Internet use since one must use the Internet to reach the Web, but not vice versa. Researchers for Project 2000 at Vanderbilt University found

TABLE 2.3   Internet and Web Use by Frequent Internet Users

	High Web Use[a]		Low Web Use[a]		No Web Use[a]	
	Male	Female	Male	Female	Male	Female
Gender (%)	78	22	72	28	56	44
Activities performed on Internet (%)[b]						
Communication	37	41	30	28	22	42
Interactive discussion (chat)	9	6	12	12	2	9
Noninteractive discussion	19	24	9	7	15	10
Download software	15	10	8	6	1	4
Use another computer	16	5	7	6	4	7
Activities performed on Web (%)[b]						
Search for product/service information	72	56	49	33		
Search for company/organization information	72	67	56	45		
Search for other information	86	83	66	66		
Browse/explore	95	91	87	82		
Make purchase based on Web information	29	18	17	8		
Ever used Web for business	57	46	44	30		
Total in segment	4.9 million		4.6 million		3.4 million	

[a]All three segments are frequent Internet users (once per week or more often). Frequency of Web use is defined on a 4-point scale.

[b]Percentage of segment that named the activity as frequently performed.

SOURCE: Project 2000 (Hoffman et al., 1996).

that 28.8 million people in the United States who are 16 or older had access to the Internet at home, work, and/or school; 16.4 million actually used the Internet at some time in the previous 3 months; 11.5 million had used the Web; and 1.5 million had used the Web to buy something. Table 2.3 presents detailed findings about a subset of the population—the 12.9 million people identified as frequent Internet users (once per week or more), segmented by gender and amount of Web use. Among the interesting findings from this table are that women are much more likely than men to use the Internet for communication (e.g., e-mail, noninteractive discussions on news groups and bulletin boards, and interactive chat discussions) and that men are more likely than women to download software, use a computer remotely over the Internet, make purchases based on information gathered on the Web, or use the Web for business.

Project 2000's (Hoffman et al., 1996) finding of 11.5 million Web users in 1995 suggests rapid growth in the use of this relatively new application in the NII. Information-gathering activity predominates on the Web, with a much smaller share of people using it to plan or make purchases. Web use is constantly evolving, however, and this August 1995 snapshot took place before tools for publishing one's own Web page became widely available.[5]

Because access to the Internet from work and school as well as from home is included, the Project 2000/CNIDS data are not directly comparable to the 1993 Census Bureau data in Table 2.1. Nevertheless, it is significant that both surveys found communication to be the most common use of the Internet. This finding squares with detailed field observations gathered in Carnegie Mellon University's HomeNet project (Kraut et al., 1996), described at the workshop by Sara Kiesler and Robert Kraut. The HomeNet project gave 48 families of varied demographic backgrounds computers, Internet connections, and technical support for a year. In pretrial questionnaires, participants did not expect that computers would be useful for interpersonal communications. However, communicating with friends and family via e-mail proved to be the dominant reason for use of the Internet, especially among teenagers, and e-mail use turned out to be a strong predictor of Web use—but not vice versa. Teenagers also were likely to become the household experts and most frequent users of networked information and communications media.

Similarly, civic networks report that communication is the incentive that draws most of their participants on-line (Anderson et al., 1995), and other anecdotal and case study evidence also points to growth in networked activity among children, especially at home rather than at school. While large income- and education-based differences exist in the access of primary and secondary school students to these media, a 1994 *Times Mirror* survey of technology in American households found "virtually no socioeconomic differences in how often and for what purposes children use computers if present in the home."

Public, civic, and social activities are hardest to represent with robust data (Kraut et al., 1996). Every study of civic networks has reported that access increases community attachment and political involvement (e.g., Anderson et al., 1995). Yet such findings reflect selection bias—respondents are those who have opted for civic network membership. More objective data are available in the nationally representative 1994 *Times Mirror* household technology survey. The survey established that individuals with network access from home were significantly more likely to know the answers to questions about their current political environment than their computer-owning peers without network access. These results are mirrored in enterprise-level research: those who use an organization's network have more knowledge about it and feel more positive about it than those who do not (Huff et al., 1989; Kraut et al., 1992).

Lifelong Learning

Evolution of the nation's information infrastructure makes clear that it presents opportunities and challenges to people of all ages, who must learn how to assimilate it into their lives. Continuous changes in technology (and in the mix of activities that make up our lives) imply that people will confront the need to learn new systems or activities at multiple points during their lives, notwithstanding people's changing willingness and ability to learn over time. Today's teenagers, for example, emerge from various studies as leading-edge users and innovators, but those qualities will not necessarily endure over time since a number of circumstances differentiate teenagers from other age groups. Making learning a part of life and the implications this has on how, under the influence of new media, human beings will think, create, work, learn, and collaborate in the future constitute a major consideration for the design of every-citizen interfaces to the NII; recognition of these concerns contributes to the rise of programmatic support for lifelong learning in a variety of contexts. The lifelong learning challenge illustrates the need for interfaces and other elements of technology that transcend today's "gift-wrapping" approach to education, training, and learning in which the tradition of rote learning is "wrapped" in the mantle of new technologies such as multimedia or the World Wide Web (Rubin, 1996; Wasser, 1996).[6] See Gerhard Fischer's and Wallace Feurzeig's position papers in this volume for a fuller discussion.

Lifelong learning is grounded in a variety of descriptive and prescriptive goals, such as the following:

• Learning should take place in the context of authentic, complex problems (because learning is more effective when people understand its impact).

• Learning should be embedded in the pursuit of intrinsically rewarding activities. Motivation is an enduring concern.

• Learning on demand needs to be supported because change is inevitable, complete coverage of relevant information and knowledge is impossible, and obsolescence of acquired skills and knowledge is unavoidable.[7]

• Organizational and collaborative learning must be supported to leverage limited individual human minds and to meet collective organizational needs.

• Skills and processes that support learning as a lifetime habit, that reflect a realistic view of what should be considered basic skills in a society that assumes broader use of information technology, and that transcend the school-to-work transition must be developed.[8]

Research is needed to enable successful pursuit of all of these goals.

The organizational emphasis that is emerging in a variety of work environments is as a growing and recurrent theme, in part because the NII concept emphasizes the interconnection of groups of people (see Chapter 5). At the workshop, John Thomas, of NYNEX, explained that more frequent and less regular changes in work environments imply that "assimilative learning," which is incremental and oriented to information acquisition, will be supplemented increasingly by "accommodative learning," which relates to more substantial change in perspective and activities. In a variety of contexts, communities of practice exist that may provide vehicles and contexts for learning that may generate requirements for new interfaces (see the position paper by Charles Cleary in this volume).

Growing Use in Home, Civic, and Social Activities

The growing penetration of computing and communications into home settings and social activities is increasing their commonality with white-collar work. It is possible, as Mark Weiser, of Xerox, mused at the workshop, to begin to talk about personal information infrastructures— which are elements of or complements to the larger NII. The personal and social impacts are changing with the technologies and their uses. For example, as a tool for social interaction, the typewriting-telegraphy nature of today's applications seem to trade off isolation in the immediate environment for dispersed community on the net.[9] With progress in networking technology and access, evolving interfaces are expected to enable tomorrow's electronic communities to see, hear, and touch each other, meeting face to face, safely and anonymously, in cyberspace (see Box 2.1). Already, people are using even typed text interfaces in multiuser domains (MUDs) and multiuser domains/object-oriented (MOOs) to experiment with alternative identities and other behaviors that relate to self-image; two- and three-dimensional avatars are also providing vehicles for play, expression, and experimentation that underscore the potential for social impact that is only beginning to be recognized.

The challenge of making interfaces appealing and easy to learn is greater in home and social contexts, inasmuch as people at work have no choice but to learn and make the best of systems available to them, whereas the success of home applications depends more on individual discretion and desire, which are in large part a response to the interface along with the associated content and specifics of the application. These lessons are repeated regularly in market trials of new services and consumer electronics. Home settings also reflect the dynamics of families, which are different from other kinds of groups or institutions. At the

BOX 2.1
Evolution of Social Interaction

America is staying home. In the 1980s, futurist Faith Popcorn labeled the phenomenon "cocooning." Now she is suggesting that we have entered into an even more isolated phase—"burrowing"—as we go beyond physical withdrawal into emotional withdrawal as well: "Some of us are too overwhelmed or exhausted by the stress of life to bother to return . . . even the phone calls of friends we really want to talk to." The next stage she predicts is "clanning," where we will cluster like birds of a feather into clans of 20 to 20,000 members. That trend is upon us today, and cyberspace is facilitating its growth. In the early part of this century, on a warm summer evening, you could find people sitting on their front porches, calling out to friends and neighbors passing in the street. People lived in communities, knowing who their neighbors were and what they were up to. Radio brought little alteration, except that people might leave their front door open, so that the sounds of "One Man's Family" or "The Shadow" might brighten their evening. Then television came and everything changed. Today, you can walk down those same streets and never see a soul. The only signs of life are the telltale bluish glow of the TV sets within.

The resulting social isolation has brought about a new form of instant intimacy. Television shows have devolved from formal stage presentations and movies down to a peek into that interesting neighbor's window down the street (an augmentation of the same peek we used to take in person). You can now watch people just like yourselves losing their pants at a wedding, revealing graphic details of their marital infidelities, or being shot or arrested, all in living color right on your TV.

Today, we are engaging in the myth of a set-top box that will connect to the family TV set, around which everyone will cluster, watching in rapture as Dad traverses a labyrinth of baseball statistics or Mom pays the bills. Interactive services do not invite partnership. In the coming decade the single blue glow of the living room TV will be replaced with a separate glow for every member of the family. This has already happened at my house, where we have moved our computers into the living room, so that we can be together while we work and play on our own. With the advent of continuous speech recognition and vocal conversation on the Internet, we may finally be driven into separate rooms, spending time with each other through our viewports and offering greetings as we pass through the hall.

SOURCE: Adapted from a background paper prepared for the August 1996 workshop by Bruce Tognazzini, Healtheon Corporation.

workshop, Patricia Brennan, for example, noted that apparently shared tasks are often defined very differently by different people. This condition suggests added value for tools that allow different people to assign different interpretations to tasks and arrive at a common endpoint.

Another clear difference between home and institutional settings (work, school, and public access points such as libraries) is that equipment and networks at home are paid for by individual users. The relatively greater cost burden of network use by self-owned and very small businesses is reflected in the finding of the 1996 IDC and 1993 Census Bureau surveys that self-employed individuals lagged the general population in access to network services (including access from home, work, or school), despite leading the general population in personal computer ownership. In work settings, the institution provides both equipment and support (training, help, and other resources), which are important for the assimilation of information technology. In contrast, home users presumably must invest discretionary income in acquiring computing and communications systems and associated help, consulting, and training. Less demanding designs for which less help is needed and systems with better built-in help support than is typical at present could reduce these burdens. This premium on usability in home settings is one reason the term appliance has been used with greater frequency to describe an ease-of-use objective for future access devices. The problem of meeting user support needs is compounded, of course, in the case of people with inferior devices or systems (e.g., for reasons of affordability), except inasmuch as their designs require less support. Also, systems that are more self-contained or sealed as a process of being more appliance like may imply a need for disability access features to be built in, on the assumption that modifications will become more difficult. Building in such access may also become a requirement for the shared systems that may be more typical of institutional (e.g., employers or schools) or public contexts (e.g., kiosks) than homes (Government Information Technology Systems (GITS), 1995).

Civic activities may involve use of the NII from home or other settings, including public facilities, such as libraries. Examples of civic uses include motor vehicle registrations and renewals of driver licenses; finding and filing income tax forms, getting refunds or paying owed amounts; commenting on a proposed rezoning or a national forest land management plan during a public comment period; and monitoring the agendas and actions of government units at all levels (GITS, 1995). As a class, government-supported efforts (e.g., under the Digital Library Initiative and various NII access initiatives) should be of particular interest to interface researchers because they are inherently more amenable to data gathering and analysis that can be discussed publicly than proprietary efforts, yet this potential is not exploited for the most part. Many experiments are under way at local, state, and federal levels of government and social service organizations, and many workshop participants urged the use of these nascent efforts for study about what works, what does not, what is missing, and so on. Where possible, comparisons to corresponding research in other countries is desirable.

Information as a Common Currency

Contemporary experimentation with the World Wide Web, the Internet, and even telephony and television provide what are expected to be only hints of future information exchange. In the work world alone, it feeds expectations that employees will need to connect to the open world of cyberspace to access their colleagues around the world, vast on-line libraries, and video, audio, and data feeds from news services offering everything from this minute's news to archived video and print history. Along with technical access, people must have the skills and tools to find, comprehend, and work with information; current technologies show both progress and limitations in all three areas. These skills and tools present an alternative, cross-cutting perspective to interface contexts from that presented by applications, tasks, or activities.

Today's technology, built to meet obsolete constraints of the 1960s and 1970s, focuses users' attention and work patterns on the tool instead of the information: they must first decide what tool set they wish to use and then open a document inside that tool set before they can proceed with their work. If people want to gather information, they must use their browser. If they want to include that information in their own work, they must transport it from the browser into their productivity tool. When they want to write a memo, they do so in their word processor, where spell checking is only a click away (but typically absent from e-mail editors).

There are interactions between the nature of information and its presentation that are sensitive to interface design. Recent experiments with hypermedia and multimedia show the potential for new forms of presenting and representing information, both of which involve technical challenges; they may also enable new forms of information, per se, illustrated today by emerging uses in the creative arts and attempts by authors to write specifically for the electronic medium. At the workshop, Louis Hecht, of the Open Geographic Information Systems Consortium, for example, referred to the power of nontextual electronic representations, such as digital maps and virtual reality, for moving "our individual minds and collective culture away from text-induced linear, sequential thinking toward nonlinear thinking. . . . Virtual reality applications will employ spatial representations of real spatial phenomena, but they will also employ spatial representations of nonspatial phenomena, simply because our brains are hardwired for solving problems in three-dimensional space."

Drawing from her experiences working with humanities scholars, Susan Hockey (then with the Center for Electronic Texts in the Humanities) described, at the workshop, how documents can be viewed as complex data structures; digital annotations and hypertext representations of textual documents can include nonlinear links and can show layers of value and meaning that paper cannot. Box 2.2 provides examples from humanities scholarship of how the Standard Generalized Markup Language can be used to encode logical structure, change over time, and other aspects, enabling powerful new ways of understanding and analyzing information.[10] Hockey's illustrations emphasize that interfaces should be seen as part of a system that not only presents or represents but also can influence interpretation of and options for working with information.

Interfaces inherently constrain the user's view because their designers must make compromises between burgeoning choices of information and limitations on display space and bandwidth for communication or reception. Those choices might be made for many reasons and in many ways; technology is not neutral. It is important to recognize that there are choices and that, by shaping the presentation of information, interface design may affect use. Most obviously, for example, for those with sensory disabilities, information that is presented in only one modality may not be accessible. The overtly political debate of the mid-1990s about whether and how to control obscenity in networked infrastructure is a harbinger of other debates; technical tools (e.g., information filters, labels, blocking systems) developed in that context and the associated public policy frameworks will influence demand for interface features and may be transferable to other contexts.[11] Public and private decision making about whether and how to label and block information will, of course, reflect a combination of perceptions of technological options and a variety of nontechnical factors.

Reflecting on the workshop and a draft of this report, workshop participant Susan Brummel, of the General Services Administration, characterized the challenge of providing support for multiple views:

> In order for citizens to construct personal, community, and action-oriented views, they need multiple technology "viewers" to see their views relative to others, to conduct the discourse that keeps views "eased"— pliant and flexible relative to achieving the overall agreed-upon purpose—and "easeled"—angled and standing in the best possible light to capture the current and proposed view as it emerges. They also need to be able to be accountable to themselves and others for what they have agreed to do. We haven't graduated to the availability of devices that accommodate greater relativity beyond viewpoint, to reflect for example "view-plane" (multiple views with their respective coherence/interference patterns), "view-sphere" (multiple views over a complete cycle or course of action), "view-torus" (multiple long views as dynamic cultural influences as a whole, swell, crest, crash/transform, reform, and so on). How do we see the flow patterns that enable us to be eased up above the noise—and hold a balanced, steady course?

BOX 2.2
Representing Humanities Texts

Information in the arts and humanities can take many forms, and it can be studied for many different purposes. Humanities primary source texts may take the form of literary works, historical documents, manuscripts, papyri, inscriptions, coins, transcriptions of spoken texts, or dictionaries, and they can be written in any natural language. This information is characterized more than anything by its complexity. It may include variant readings, variant spellings, marginal notes, annotations of various kinds, cancellations, and interlineations, as well as nonstandard characters. Literary texts rarely conform to the simple document structure required by most current text retrieval systems. Plays consist of acts, scenes, speeches, stage directions, cast lists, and so forth. There are very many different types of verse. Systems for processing literary texts must also be able to handle different languages and alphabets, both in terms of analyzing the structure of words and displaying the text in the correct script.

Most textual information in electronic form is intended to be used in a document retrieval system where a typical user wants to find all the documents about a certain topic. For primary source material in textual form, this is less likely to be the major application. A user may want to locate a quotation, compare the vocabulary of the characters in a novel, examine the rhyme and sound patterns in verse, or even find out whether a particular word is used at all. These types of searches require an accurate text and one that is encoded to make certain features explicit.

Ever since Father Busa began to create the first humanities electronic text in 1949, effort has concentrated on finding ways to represent the characteristics of texts such that they can be manipulated easily. Most early projects attempted to transcribe electronic texts by maintaining as accurate reproduction of the original as possible. Typographic features were faithfully encoded, and many texts were prepared before it was fully realized how ambiguous typography can be. For example, italic can be used to represent titles, foreign words, or emphasized words, making it impossible to retrieve only foreign words.

In late 1987 the humanities computing community became one of the earliest groups to adopt the Standard Generalized Markup Language (SGML) when it began a major project called the Text Encoding Initiative (TEI). The TEI has developed an SGML application that can handle many different types of humanities electronic texts. It includes tags not only for the structural features of the text, but also for analysis and interpretation. The TEI includes SGML tag sets for prose, verse, drama, transcriptions of speech, dictionaries, and terminological data, as well as analytical features, transcription of manuscripts, names and dates, language corpora, and a sophisticated method for hypertext linking both within and outside the current document. The TEI consists of about 400 possible tags, but very few are mandatory. The philosophy is that one person can encode a text for the features he or she is interested in. Another person can then take that text and add encoding for other features. The TEI makes it possible to encode multiple and possibly conflicting views in the same document, thus allowing for differences of opinion in interpretations of the material.

SOURCE: Excerpted from position paper by Susan Hockey available on-line at http://www2.nas.edu/CSTBWEB.

Constraints on views will reflect the differing incentives and possibilities in both private and public quarters of cyberspace. Emerging debates about privacy of personal data illustrate that even private uses (e.g., health data, which may be used by patients, physicians, health care organizations, health insurers, employers, government benefits providers, medical researchers) are not without policy constraints. In private domains, various restrictions may be both legal and either sought after or a concomitant of use (e.g., restrictions on use of company-owned resources by employers). In public access systems, other constraints may be embodied in system design. In general, nonpersonal systems and interfaces may limit what every citizen can do with them, at least in the near to medium terms.

Range of Environments in Which Access Is Needed—Requirement for Nomadicity

In a period of rapid technical and social change, not much can or should be taken for granted. Two things, however, seem evident from the course of development of the NII, to date:

• A person's physical location at any time during the day will make less and less difference to his or her ability to carry out most any activity associated with information processing, communication, and electronic transactions.

• Since electronic interaction is likely to become integral to education, employment, and daily living, not having access to these emerging technologies will have increasingly negative ramifications for individuals who are unable to access them for various reasons—not being able to understand them, not being able physically to use them, not being able to afford devices and other end systems (or the communications, capacity and service to use them to access the NII).

The range of environments where people can access networked infrastructures is growing. With miniaturization and advances in wireless communications, and architectures for distributed computing that may place fewer demands on at least some classes of devices, people will no longer need to be tied to a workstation or carry a large device for access to computing, communications, and information services and functions. At the same time, growth in the variety of network-attachable devices in homes (not only computers, but also televisions, stereos, systems for managing energy consumption, and many others) implies networking within the home and additional hardware or software that supports both interconnections and management of home-based devices and systems. The quality of communications capacity to homes and other remote locations depends on the evolution of associated services (people differ as to their optimism about what will be deployed to homes and when; see the section titled "The Communications Infrastructure" in Chapter 3); the prospect of greater networking within homes raises questions about household economics that compound those presented by PC ownership. Nevertheless, interface research should contemplate possible changes in networking capacity and services and alternative architectures, which embody alternative expectations for what functionality will be in terminating devices, hosts or servers, and the network itself.

A number of conceptual frameworks—untethered computing and communications or nomadicity,[12] ubiquity, and universality—have in common the vision of systems and, therefore, interfaces that can be used anywhere, anytime: while a person is sitting at a desk, driving a car, sitting in an easy chair, participating in a meeting, sitting in a library, walking down the street, sitting on the beach, walking through a noisy shopping mall, taking a shower, or relaxing in a bathtub. The challenge of operability across environments is being pursued in the context of specific kinds of jobs, such as maintenance work, which involves problem solving, distributed corporate knowledge, and people who move among locations and need to communicate both in transit and from afar (see, for example, the position paper by Daniel Siewiorek in this volume). At least some systems and interfaces will also need to be operable in hostile environments—when camping or hiking, in factories, or on a battlefield.

Ubiquitous computing and communications implies that many people will need to access their device (or devices) in very different environments even on the same day. Different environments will put constraints on what type of physical and sensory input techniques will work under what circumstances and conditions (e.g., it is difficult to use a keyboard when walking, difficult and dangerous to use an input method that requires vision when driving a car; keyboard use is fine when sitting at a desk, but speech input may not be acceptable in a shared environment), as well as the types of display or other output techniques that will be accessible and usable or not (in a noisy mall, in the midst of a meeting, while at the library, while driving a car).

Some devices and systems will be personally purchased and owned, while others will be public in nature. For personal systems an individual can do a certain amount of selecting among systems to meet personal needs or preferences and can even make modifications if necessary. Public systems, on the other hand, must be operable without modification by all individuals who may come upon them, implying suitability for people who have any of a wide range or combination of disabilities and also systems that are very easily learned. Institutional systems (e.g., provided by employers or schools) may provide an intermediate level of customization. The contexts of public use may imply greater needs for durability (e.g., because of higher-volume or more intensive use) and ruggedization (e.g., because of public space or outdoor installations). These elements, of course, affect cost. For example, touchscreens are the most common kiosk input device; thinner liquid-crystal display panels with touch membrane overlays are increasingly used to allow shallower kiosk enclosures. Assessments of public kiosks already recognize that there are tradeoffs in a variety of cost elements (including deploying more kiosks to raise proximity to more of the population versus raising the amount of use per kiosk with fewer of them; see GITS, 1995). Expectations for greater use of public access systems, evidenced by experimentation with a variety of kiosk applications, suggests a need to assess their performance and technical requirements more systematically; insights might be gained from contemporary phone booths, automated teller machines, and kiosk systems (GITS, 1995; Venture Development Corporation, 1996a-c).[13]

Range of Users

People who have disabilities or who are older represent a particularly important target community for ECIs, because for people who lack such abilities as walking, seeing, speaking, or hearing, the NII is a medium of communication that allows participation in the nation's civic, social, and economic life on an even footing with fully abled people (see Box 2.3). The goal of developing ECIs does not mean accommodating literally all people in all situations and applications. Some tasks are incompatible with particular disabilities; for example, blind people are not likely to be film editors, even if an interface could be built that somehow enabled them to operate a film editing system.

It should not, however, be too readily assumed that any given task is inherently inaccessible to some people, since trying to figure out how to make the inaccessible accessible can lead to insights that make the task more accessible to and usable by all people. For example, modifications to enlarge fonts on screen to make them more usable by people with visual impairments have been found to be very useful for individuals without visual impairments when using high-resolution screens on laptops. Strategies developed on kiosks to allow them to be used by individuals with low vision or blindness have facilitated use by individuals with literacy problems. Closed captioning on televisions, which was implemented for people who are deaf, is now being used by an even larger number of children and adults who are learning English as a sec-

---

BOX 2.3
Importance of Access to Information Technology for the
Blind and Visually Impaired

Access to information technology is particularly important and valuable for blind and low-vision citizens. The ability to use computers and network services boosts the employment prospects of such people and enables them to participate in on-line communications. The following comments were recently submitted by the American Foundation for the Blind to the Federal Communications Commission:

According to research conducted by the American Foundation for the Blind for the Department of Education, blind and visually impaired people are as likely as the general population to have consumer electronics in their homes, to use personal computers, and to use Internet and on-line services. This, despite the fact that blind persons tend to be poorer, on average, than the general population, and tend to be employed much less often. . . . Since studies have shown that computer users and Internet users tend to have higher income than the general population and that people tend to use computers and the Internet at work, it is particularly noteworthy, given these differences in income and employment, that usage rates for blind and visually impaired persons are similar to the general population, suggesting the increased importance of this access to them. . . . A study completed just before the passage of the Americans with Disabilities Act (ADA) estimates that 43 percent of employed persons who are blind or visually impaired use computers to write (Kirchner, Corinne, and Harkins, Don, Issues and Strategies Toward Improving Employment of Blind or Visually Impaired Persons in Illinois, American Foundation for the Blind, 1991, Table VI-5 (a)).

---

ond language. Nevertheless, efforts to extend accessibility to the NII to as many people as possible must account for the fact that a large number of people have some condition that constrains their ability to use some forms of interfaces.

Altogether, people with physical, sensory, and cognitive disabilities account for 15 to 20 percent of the U.S. population. The Census Bureau regularly measures the number and characteristics of people with specific disabilities.[14] Some 49 million Americans (about 1 in 5) have a disability, defined as a limitation on performing one or more of a range of functional and social activities, such as seeing words in newsprint, engaging in spoken conversation, climbing stairs, shopping, or performing light housework. Of these, 24 million have a severe disability—an inability to perform one or more of these activities.

Although the data do not directly address the use of information technologies, they support some conclusions about interface usability. Among persons 15 and older, 5 percent (9.7 million) report difficulty seeing words and letters in ordinary newsprint, including 1.6 million who are blind; 5.6 percent (10.9 million) have trouble hearing what is said in a conversation with another person (including 0.9 million who are deaf); and 8.3 percent (16.2 million) have difficulty lifting and carrying a full bag of groceries. Difficulty with these tasks implies that certain interfaces could be difficult or impossible to use, such as those requiring reading print on a screen, hearing synthesized speech output, or manipulating a touch screen or mouse.

According to the Census Bureau, the chances of having a disability increase with age, and more than half of persons aged 65 or older have a disability (U.S. Bureau of the Census, 1995). Some degradation of senses and abilities is normal with age. People over 65 account for 12 percent of the U.S. population, but they make up 34 percent of persons with disabilities and 43 percent of persons with severe disabilities (U.S. Bureau of the Census, 1994). As Sara Czaja notes in her position paper (available online at http://www2.nas.edu/CSTBWEB), research on older persons—an increasing share of the population—has found that advanced age is associated with decreased performance working with computers. The precise cause of the decline is not known. Physical disabilities such as decreased vision, decreased hearing, and arthritis probably are involved. Czaja notes that factors other than physical disability may also impair performance for some older people, such as declines in cognitive skills and (for today's older cohorts) less familiarity with information technologies than younger people have. Further research will be required to identify the most significant factors and to find accommodations for the interface limitations of older persons.

Illiteracy is another impediment to effective use of information technology. The *1992 National Adult Literacy Survey* by the U.S. Department of Education estimated that about 21 percent of Americans over age 16 (more than 40 million people) lack more than rudimentary reading and writing skills, including about 4 percent (8 million) who are unable to perform even the simplest literacy tasks.[15] For many of these people, spoken language may be a more accessible form of interaction with information technology than reading output and writing or typing input.[16] The distinction between speaking ability and literacy also applies to younger children, who are expected to be a growing segment of novice NII users. It is also relevant to people whose primary language is not English. For example, at the workshop, Adam Porter drew on his experiences with Latino groups to note the importance of simple predictable interfaces with audio support and culturally appropriate presentations (which may include the ability to shift among languages). It will be important that systems (particularly public systems) allow for cross-cultural flexibility in order to better match people's language, conventions, culture, and so forth.

People also vary in their level of computer expertise and style of interaction with computer systems. Research that quantifies these variations and their implications for interface design, however, is sparse. Overcoming an apparent emphasis in the design of today's information technologies on advanced users at the expense of ordinary people was identified at the workshop as a central part of the every-citizen interface challenge. Bruce Tognazzini (this volume) describes a pervasive tendency in the information technology industry to design "toys for boys"—systems that, by virtue of their complexity, superabundance of features and options, and interaction styles that stress unusual logical and spatial cognitive skills, are much more appealing to and usable by power users than ordinary people.

It is vital to understand that the recognition that people have a range of abilities and styles does not mean that system capabilities valued by advanced users should be eliminated. It would be undesirable to do so; advanced users hold special interest for interface designers because, as in other aspects of information technology, these are the people who push the technology and promote innovation, a good part of which later enters mainstream use. However, even advanced users as a group exhibit a range of abilities that should be accommodated; many individuals who have disabilities (such as blindness) turn out to be some of the best power users, as long as the interfaces stay within their sensory capabilities. Moreover, the economic factors that militate against developing unique interfaces for target groups of people with limited interface abilities—economies of scale, transferability of training and skills, and economies of interoperability with mainstream users)—also constrain or inhibit the development of unique interfaces for the most skilled users.

With multiple input/output modes and graceful progression from novice to expert use, interfaces can be made operable by and efficient for experienced and power users along with everyone else. What was characterized at the workshop as universal design aims to produce interfaces that accommodate a range of user skills and abilities and do not exclude people unnecessarily. For example, a text menu that can be read aloud by a speech synthesizer can be used by blind and low-vision people as an alternative to icons and other graphical displays. Conversely, the graphical alternative, if it uses symbols that are comprehensible without words, can be used better than text by people with poor literacy skills. People who are illiterate in English but can read another language could gain access to English text if machine translation between human languages is available; as Chapter 3 notes, this capability is not out of reach for simple systems with limited vocabularies. In addition, any of these can incorporate shortcuts for advanced users.

The nature of the devices and software applications used for NII access influences how readily they might be made universally accessible. Some devices will be general in nature, such as today's PCs, and used for a wide variety of activities. As Larry Goldberg observes in his position paper in this volume, PCs can run specialized text-to-speech synthesizers and thus make applications accessible to blind or illiterate users. Goldberg expressed concern that low-cost "information appliances" with less general-purpose capability than PCs could preclude add-ons such as speech synthesis and large-print displays. Nevertheless, it is apparent that both general and special-purpose devices will be components of the evolving mix of devices and systems that people carry around with them or that reside in specific environments. That mix presents a software challenge for systems integration. The interaction among multiple technical choices and constraints will provide part of the context for interface development, for example, by increasing the potential for customization.

User ability independence and environment independence are synergistic. Providing better access across the range of environments discussed above (many of which have impacts tantamount to transitory situational disabilities) will end up addressing most of the issues faced by people with disabilities. For example:

• When interfaces are created that will work well in noisy environments, such as small airplanes, construction sites, busy shopping malls, or for people who must be listening to something else while using their device, we will have created interfaces that work well for people who cannot hear well or at all.

• When interfaces are created that will work well for people driving a car or doing something else where it is not safe to look at the device they are operating, we will have created interfaces that can be used by people who cannot see.

• When very small pocket and wearable devices for which it is hard to use a full-sized keyboard or even a large number of keys are developed, we will have developed techniques that can be used by individuals with certain types of physical disabilities.

• When interfaces are created that can be used by people who are doing something that occupies their hands, we will have systems that can be used by people who cannot use their hands.

• When interfaces are created for individuals who are very tired, under a lot of stress, under the influence of drugs (legal or illegal), or simply in the midst of a traumatic event or emergency (and who may have little ability to concentrate or deal with complexity), we will have developed interfaces that can be used by people who naturally have reduced abilities to concentrate or deal with complexity.

REQUIRED ELEMENTS FOR EFFECTIVE
ECI INPUT/OUTPUT SYSTEMS

Effectively addressing the diversity of activities, environments for use, and users requires an entirely new look at interface design. Almost exhausted is the approach that expects the user to come to the interface and adapt to it, an approach that leaves a large portion of society unable to learn or use existing systems effectively or at all. Even those who are using systems today often interact with the interface using what would best be termed superstitious behaviors, and they often use only a small portion of the functionality of their systems.

Input Options

Even though input techniques may be quite different in different environments, they should share operating principles. An improvement over today's techniques would be for users not to have to master three or four completely different interface paradigms in order to be able to operate their devices in different environments. This implies continuity in the metaphor and interface "look and feel" even though operating entirely visually at one point (e.g., in a meeting) or entirely aurally at another (e.g., while driving a car). Users should also be able to transition from one environment to another and from one device to another (e.g., workstation to handheld), and from one mode to another (e.g., visual to voice) in the midst of a task. The challenge relates not only to conventional communications and information devices, such as personal computers and various kinds of telephones, but also other systems, some embedded in very different kinds of equipment, to which the conventional devices may be interconnected or which may supplant those devices for at least some purposes. New types of input, including passive input, gestures, and increased use of speech and natural language, will not replace existing input techniques but rather complement them, providing the user with a wealth of alternate input strategies to select from depending on the task, environment, and personal abilities or preferences. What is natural, interactive, and supportive is subjective, suggesting the expectation for multiple interfaces.

There is a wide range of input options an interface device can offer. These may be built in, or a device may provide a connection point (such as an infrared port) that would allow an individual to easily use alternative input systems with the device. Some of the input options include:

- Typing on a keyboard (still a viable and important interface)—standard, chordic, Braille;
- Alternative keyboards—operable with eyegaze, sip and puff, single switch, etc.;
- Codes (Morse, abbreviation-expansion);
- Handwriting;
- Keypads;
- Speech;
- Gesture;
- Video input—passive, gesture recognition, image interpretation;
- Optical character recognition (OCR)—including recognition of math script;
- Numerous pointing devices;
- Touchscreens;
- Virtual reality—including direct manipulation; and
- Via data link—infrared, radio frequency, cable.

Control Strategies

The strategies used to control a system are similar to the input techniques. These include:

- Verbal techniques (keyboard, speech recognition, alternate keyboards, sign language recognition),
- Gesture,
- Pointing devices,
- Direct manipulation (of the object itself or of virtual objects), and
- Direct thought control.

The specific approaches and technologies chosen for control will vary depending on the size, format, and function of the device. Ideally, of course, the system would incorporate a sufficiently flexible combination of interface techniques to allow it to be used in different environments by individuals with a variety of (dis)abilities to carry out the different tasks specific to the device. As noted above (particularly with portable devices), by the time interfaces are designed to function in the different environments and situations most of the variations for different users will already be accounted for.

Output Options

Similarly, there is a wide range of display options that a device may offer, including:

- Alphanumeric displays;
- Graphic displays (high and low resolution, large and small);
- Auditory output (monophonic, stereophonic, three-dimensional)— speech and sound, including both artificial and natural sounds;
- Tactile (two- and three-dimensional representations as well as Braille presentation of text);
- Olfactory (very low bandwidth);
- Immersive and virtual reality environments (visual, auditory, tactile); and
- Visualization—usually video (two- or three-dimensional) but could also be done verbally.

In looking at the ability to display information in alternative formats, it is useful to differentiate between information that is medium independent and information that is medium specific (and where parallel presentation would be required to provide user choice). Examples of medium-independent information would be information that could be represented purely by ASCII text. Such information can be presented very easily using any number of different modalities, including visually (as printed or displayed text), aurally (as spoken text), or tactilely (as raised letters or Braille). Medium-specific information might be such things as Picasso's *Guernica* or a symphony. With very medium-specific information (such as *Guernica*), it is difficult to convey very much of the information in any other medium. Between these extremes lie a number of other types of information, such as the floor plan of a house, a weather map, a company's logo, or even a movie, which may be primarily or optimally presented in one medium (in this case, visual), but which could also be presented (with varying degrees of success) in a second medium (in this case, auditory through description). Making medium-specific information accessible generally involves creating an information package that includes both the original format (picture, movie, etc.) and alternate presentations that are either in complementary modalities or in medium-independent form. In the case of the photograph or diagram, this might take the form of an audio description (complementary medium) or an ASCII text description (medium-independent). For a movie it might include verbal descriptions of the visual information and visual presentation of the auditory information (e.g., captions).

Again, it is important to note that the same techniques that make medium-specific information accessible to people with different disabilities also makes the information accessible to computers and software agents (which tend to be both deaf and blind). For example, putting captions in movies allows text search engines to find the movies based on dialogue in the movie. It also allows users to jump directly to any point in the movie, speech, documentary, etc., that contains a particular word or phrase. If a photograph or movie is also described and the description is stored in electronic text form, search engines can also locate graphic information based on its description. At the same time, consideration of communication-related disabilities is helpful in understanding how, when, where, and why people's needs differ: speech synthesis can help the visually impaired people, whereas visualization can help hearing-impaired people, and so on.

Characteristics Desired for Effective Interfaces

In exploring possible directions for developing more effective interfaces, workshop participants identified the following characteristics, each of which is discussed in more detail below along with approaches for achieving these goals. It was thought that ECIs would need to be:

- Easy to understand;
- Easy to learn;
- Error tolerant;
- Flexible and adaptable;
- Appropriate and effective for the task;
- Powerful and efficient;
- Inexpensive;
- Portable;
- Compatible;
- Intelligent;
- Supportive of social and group interactions;
- Trustworthy—secure, private, safe, and reliable;
- Information centered; and
- Pleasant to use.

Easy to Understand

Making the interfaces on next-generation devices easier to understand is often equated with making them simpler, but that is not always possible for a given level of reduction in functionality. One place where things can be made simpler is in the removal of unnecessary complexity that does not have anything to do with the task at hand. An analogy can be found in the standard television. When TVs first came out, it was usually necessary for people to understand how to both tune and fine-tune the stations. They also needed to master the vertical and horizontal holds. With advancing electronics, it was possible to eliminate all of these controls and leave the user with only those controls that were really needed in order to accomplish any given task: channel selector, volume control, and perhaps a closed-caption button. The analogy for computers would be to remove all of the work necessary to set up, connect, or make devices work together. The "plug and play" capability commercialized in the Macintosh, which is the trend today, is an example. There are also computers and printers that need only be brought into proximity with each other, at which time they automatically find each other and connect via infrared beam, configuring themselves and requiring only that the user issue a print command in order to print documents. Having systems that are always on and do not need to be started or configured can eliminate a control and leave the system always up and able to provide assistance.

A second strategy that can be used is to create interfaces that provide a better match with the user's abilities, knowledge base, and expectations. Creating interfaces that are more natural and more intuitive can allow individuals to deal with much greater levels of complexity; doing so presupposes an ability to define and measure naturalness and intuitiveness consistently. Rather than "dumbing down" the interface, it can be made to present the situation to the user in a context with which they are already familiar. The ability to communicate with the computer using natural language (either spoken or typed) is a powerful technique here. The use of natural metaphors and virtual environments (either two- or three-dimensional) can also be helpful here, particularly for some types of tasks. Better ability to handle natural gestures, such as pointing, also could play a role here.

Cueing is another technique for making systems easier to understand, particularly where sequences of input are required that would otherwise need to be remembered. With cueing, a user's progress through a sequence is tracked, and the user is given verbal and/or visual prompts leading through the process or offering help.

Layering can be used to create interfaces that are easier to understand yet still allow for the full functionality that may be desired by power users. Layering basically involves the covering up of more advanced features to present a less complex initial interface to the individual. With mastery of a system, an individual can peel back the layers to expose additional functionality. A simple example of layering can be found on some video cassette recorders (VCRs), which present only a basic set of controls on their face and hide additional controls behind a door. Layering is important in order to provide a mechanism for users to slide grace-fully from novice to intermediate to power users. It can also be used to allow advanced systems to function as both an appliance and a tool, depending on the needs and skills of the user.

One goal is to create systems that can function like appliances (i.e., we get good results even if we are not particularly adept) when a person is first learning to use them, but that provide the freedom to use them in more powerful and individual ways as the user's skills increase (i.e., they can become more tool-like). As frequent complaints about VCRs and microwave ovens illustrate, some appliances can be both big sellers and a source of frustration to buyers —presumably because virtually everyone can learn how to do at least the basic functions with them. Designers of other appliances, including more general-purpose computing and com-munications systems, might learn from the problems and attempted solu-tions for such products even if it is reasonable to assume some minimum commitment to learning on the part of users (and that assumption is subject to considerable disagreement).

The ability to slide seamlessly from passive to active/interactive mode can also be used to make systems more accessible and engaging to novice users. For example, systems might be designed to be more like television or videotape in nature, where information or activity sequences occur without much input at all from the user. The systems would be designed, however, such that at any point in time that a user took an interest in a particular portion of the information, he or she would be able to begin interacting with the system. One can think of this in terms of watching television but being able to explore topics as they are presented. How-ever, the basic premise can be taken much further than this analogy and be applied to most any type of education or learning, as well as to activi-ties such as communication, information searches, and even creative ac-tivities where the system starts creating something that the user either can make minor modifications to (as it is happening) or step in and take full control of. Multiuser domains (MUDs) are another example of environ-ments where an individual can take the role of passive observer until such time as he or she feels more confident and wants to step forward and participate more actively.

Easy to Learn

Hand in hand with easy to understand is the need to make systems easy to learn, but there are differences of opinion as to what that should mean, illustrated in comments made at the workshop. Many designers of computer systems observe that success in areas of life involving depth and complexity comes from problem-solving skill (which helps people to overcome minor technical problems on their own) and a willingness to try complex tasks repeatedly until successful. The alternative may involve making the space of possible activities so trivial that there are no potential problems (e.g., pre-set-top box changing of television channels). Some expectation for skill and learning may be realistic, although it should not be an excuse for avoiding improvement.

Some strategies discussed above, such as cueing and the passive/ active strategy, can help an individual learn about the capabilities of a system on the fly as it is being used. Especially with layered systems, such cueing and built-in assistance can allow individuals to naturally evolve an understanding of the additional functions of a device in a more natural manner as they are using the more basic functions of the device.

In addition, overt training functions could be built directly into the devices that would introduce the user to the various functions. Instead of being "tutorial" in nature (like an electronic videotape), these training functions might take the form of mentoring systems, as well as the "follow-then-lead" approaches suggested by the passive-to-active strategy above. (See also discussion under "Supportive of Social and Group Interactions" below and Chapter 5.)

Mechanisms to allow users to learn new techniques and strategies will be important for a couple of reasons. First, there simply may not be any good metaphors or experience base from daily life that matches with all of the functions of a device. Individuals will need to learn new concepts when this happens. Second, the model or real-life metaphor may not be a particularly efficient or effective way of carrying out a task. It may be useful in the beginning, enabling initial use—to write letters, make phone calls, write checks. But over time the same metaphor that worked so well to introduce users to a system may hamper their ability either to understand or to use advanced features. In this case, either specific training modules or on-the-fly training techniques might be used to slide users gracefully forward into higher levels of understanding and additional capabilities.

Social scientists at the workshop noted the appeal of interfaces designed to provide simple but conceptual models (e.g., electronic diagrams) of how things work, what is going on in the application, so that "help" can be better understood or so that people will be able to understand on their own where they are in an interaction. Doing this implies understanding what makes a good model as well as how such models can be designed to convey complex information accurately to nontechnical users at an appropriately general but still useful level of abstraction.

Flexible and Adaptable

One thing that is clear from the above discussion of environments, people, and tasks is that no single interface approach will be sufficient for a device (e.g., only speech or only keyboard). This is true even if one is only trying to address the different environments in which it may be used. For example, speech is one very powerful technique. However, as discussed above, speech is not usable in a noisy environment (e.g., a shopping mall at Christmas), or in a quiet environment (a meeting or library). Similarly, the keyboard, another powerful technique, is not usable when walking or driving a car.

Ideally, therefore systems should exhibit:

• Environment/situation independence—that is, systems should be portable and usable wherever the user happens to be and whatever happens to be going on around the user.

• Equipment independence—that is, systems should work when only low bandwidth is available, when the user switches to a device with a poor display size or resolution (because a high-bandwidth, high-resolution device is unaffordable or because the user is simply in a low-bandwidth access location or is using a very small device).

• User (ability) independence—that is, systems should be usable by all individuals regardless of their visual, hearing, cognitive, or manual abilities.

• Modality independence—that is, systems should not require that users view the information in any particular format or via any particular sense.

• Task appropriateness—that is, systems should allow users to vary the way that information is input or presented to match the particular task a user is engaged in and to match the abilities the user has left given any other tasks being carried out in parallel (not using the particular system).

It is clear that a "least common denominator" strategy will not work (e.g., only using capabilities that everyone has or that could be used in any environment). That approach would require development of an interface with no visual display, no auditory output, no speech input, and no manual controls and that could be used while the individual is distracted or unable to think or concentrate well. This leaves little except direct mind control, which is being explored but seems very speculative at this time.

The alternative is to create flexible modality-independent interfaces: interfaces that allow the user to select the input, control, and display

---

BOX 2.4
Multimedia and Multimodal Interfaces

Mode or modality refers primarily to the human senses used to process incoming information (e.g., vision, audition, taction, olfaction), not mode in the sense of purpose (e.g., word processing mode versus spread sheet mode). Additionally, in its conventional definition, medium refers to both the material object (e.g., paper, video) and the means by which information is conveyed (e.g., a sheet of paper with text on it). These definitions could include the possibility of layering, so that a natural language mode might use written text or speech as media even though those media themselves rely on other modes.

Media and mode are related nontrivially. First, a single medium may support several modalities. For example, a piece of paper may support both language and graphics, just as a visual display may support text, images, and video. Likewise, a single modality may be supported by many media. For example, the language modality can be supported visually (i.e., written language) and aurally (i.e., spoken language). In fact, spoken language can have a visual component (e.g., lip reading). Just as a single medium may support several modalities and a single modality may be supported by many media, many media may support many modalities, and likewise. For example, a multimedia document that includes text, graphics, speech, and video affects several modalities (e.g., visual and auditory perception of natural language, visual perception of images (still and moving), and auditory perception of sounds). Finally, this multimedia and multimodal interaction occurs over time. Therefore, it is necessary to account for the processing of discourse, context shifts, and changes in agent states over time.

SOURCE: Maybury (1994).

---

modalities that best meet the user's current environment, current abilities, and current task. Box 2.4 defines and discusses the relationship between modality and medium; implicit in the distinction is the relationship between input-level (e.g., vision) and higher-level processing (e.g., language or image). This distinction is important in thinking about the appropriate selection of mode and medium for ECIs to use in different circumstances, including strategies that combine multiple modalities and media in a single interaction.

Because an individual will probably need to access information appliances and tools in a wide variety of environments even in a single day, it will be important that modality independence be built into the base product and that it be easy, seamless, and natural to move between modes. As discussed above, it is important that these interfaces accommodate the full range of users, from novice through expert power users. This daily switching among modes also implies the value of a common "look and feel" or underlying metaphor or behavior across the different devices or display formats (e.g., visual versus auditory); see "Supportive of Social and Group Interactions" below for observations on standards. When switching from keyboard and display screen access to the information in a meeting to voice input/output access to information while driving between meetings, the user will want to have the system feel and behave as similarly as possible.

Required Versus Optional Flexibility. Although it is important that users be allowed to tailor their products, they should not be required to do so. Allowing users to adapt the interface to meet their constraints and preferences is important, but setting a system up so that an individual user must tailor it before using it quickly adds complexity to the system. Today, in many cases, to configure a system is much more complex and foreign to users than actually using the product once it is configured.

One powerful concept is a mechanism that would allow the device to recognize the user's needs and adapt to them. This might come either from monitoring the user's behavior or by the user carrying a small card or device (such as a wireless smart card) that contains his or her preferences and that could be automatically read by the device. Issues of privacy arise here, but the card need not identify the person. The card could simply indicate the user's preferred mode for interacting with devices.

It will be important to define and explore the full option space for increasing customizability in access appliances. The ramifications and appropriateness of having an NII identity for every device and system, as some expect to accompany/enable ubiquity, are incompletely understood. Related questions pertain to sustaining greater portability of device identifiers/identities and to enabling grouping of different devices into a new appliance (e.g., via shared object systems).

Appropriate and Effective for the Task

Not all interface techniques are appropriate for all tasks. The flexibility provided needs to allow for the user to select interfaces that best match the particular task. In the attempt to make all services available to all people, it is also important to allow individuals with more advanced skills and full use of all their senses the opportunity to use whatever interface is most effective for them and the task. It will almost always be true that an individual with a reduction in one or more of his or her senses or physical abilities will have a lower bandwidth available for either input or output. This does not necessarily result in lower effectiveness or productivity, but it does imply a narrower-bandwidth input/output channel. A challenge will be to develop interface techniques and flexible information systems that can maximize the efficiency of individuals operating either in constrained environments or with personal constraints with a goal of matching the efficiency of users with high-bandwidth interfaces. This challenge, however, should not be equated with reducing the bandwidth or the interface efficiency for those who do not have physical or sensory disabilities.

Again, it is interesting to note that in looking at collaborative systems, we will be looking at trying to collaborate with a computer—a system that has distinctly impaired vision, hearing, and cognitive abilities. The research aimed at developing interface strategies that work for people with physical and sensory limitations should provide interesting insights for those working on intelligent collaborative machines (and vice versa).

Powerful and Efficient

Expert or "power" users tend to complain about the limitations of contemporary interfaces for meeting some of their needs, although some of those complaints may be shared by novices, too. Upon scrutiny, the complaint may relate at least as much to the application—which may have a limited "understanding" of the user's intentions—as to the interface; judging from the workship, that differentiation confounds much of the discussion of interface needs.

In making an interface easy to understand and flexible, it is important that the system not be "dumbed down" or made less efficient. Through layering, as well as alternate access methods, it is possible to have systems that are both easy to understand and still efficient for individuals who are more experienced or have advanced abilities. Multisensory presentation, short-cuts, and memory-based acceleration techniques are all examples of strategies that can be used to provide higher-bandwidth interfaces for individuals who are able to handle them.

Inexpensive

The vision of interfaces for every citizen implies the availability of systems to much of the population, and that implies affordability. Affordability reflects both the cost to purchase and the cost to own and use a system. The much-hyped rapid change in the information technology marketplace begs questions about the prospects for an access system that does not have to be replaced every 2 years because its functionality has obsolesced—for example, by assuring that when a new interface is needed it can be delivered and installed over a network without a huge user investment in cost and effort or in getting old data to work with new applications. (The same issue applies to hardware.) Tools that facilitate the transfer and implementation of appropriate techniques in commercial products and better testing strategies for evaluating the ability of new devices and interfaces to meet the needs of low-income people (and segments of the mass market) could support affordability and broader access objectives.

Both device and service characteristics will be shaped by the larger context of computer, communications, and consumer electronics trends. CRTs (cathode-ray tubes), for example, have dominated computer displays because the television marketplace drove down the cost of that technology over many years. Communications bandwidth into and out of the home comes at a price, which affects what people choose to do from home and what features they seek or can afford in access devices (today, for example, ISDN service is available at a premium over "plain old telephone service," although emerging data service from cable operators will result in price competition). Meanwhile, debates over the design and commercial viability of so-called network computers raise questions about the architecture of the evolving information infrastructure—what can or must be done in the user's device, what can or must be done in the network, what is centralized and what is distributed, and so on. There are many technical, economic, regulatory, and business factors interacting in the environment within which interface design decisions must be made. Comments at the workshop and on the review draft of this report underscore the wide range of appreciation for the larger environment and for the interactions that shape demand and supply for the technologies for which interfaces are needed.

The needs of lower-income people raise questions about how to lower the historically relatively high cost of access devices (notably PCs), how to gain more functionality from inherently low-cost access devices (such as telephones, televisions, and newer variants of "network computers"), and how to leverage information services at minimal cost. There is no agreement yet on how far one can go with "green screens," how much functionality of the desired/needed type can be achieved without the level of sophistication implied by contemporary graphical user interfaces. Flexibility and options with regard to display can be important. At the workshop, Adam Porter, for example, noted the need in low-income populations for support for presentations on low-bandwidth devices or devices without fixed Internet addresses (e.g., locator systems, services that can be suspended and resumed). Systems that can be used with variable-resolution displays and different bandwidth connections lend themselves to use by individuals with less expensive interface devices. Network services, such as video or auditory communication, which allow the user to degrade the video or audio quality in exchange for lower-cost connections (since fewer packets are being exchanged) can lower usage costs. Also, if information is available in visual, auditory, or ASCII text format, users can select formats that both match their abilities and/or preferences and their pocketbooks. Another important feature might be some advance indication of the resources needed to accomplish a task (and, therefore, the associated costs) prior to its being initiated. This will be particularly important when agent-oriented and other more automated systems are more common.

The expectation for a range of device types raises questions about how to devise criteria for, and enable, applications design that support the required functionality for low-end interfaces at a usable level while providing high-end interfaces the options to exploit their special affordances. This range of support may be especially important for public-interest applications (e.g., delivery of government information and services). For example, are there ways to facilitate support for both information creating/sending and retrieval/reception in even lowend/low-cost access devices? What does it take to achieve flexible data structures/presentations that serve different populations without duplicating content? This kind of exploration of the hows and whys of public-interest applications raises questions about the tradeoffs between multiple interface options and equity attained by efforts to provide the same interface for all users that are outside the scope of this report but that, to the extent they are addressed by political processes, will affect the environment in which interface design decisions are made.

The cost challenge may be particularly great for subpopulations with limitations for which a significant market is not recognized or likely. At the workshop, Candace Sidner, of Lotus Development Corporation, noted the lagging support for blind users associated with recent advances in graphical user interfaces and suggested that similar market dynamics militate against industrial support for research on the use of speech interfaces by users with visual, motor, or linguistic limitations.

Portable

The vision of being able to have a system that will work and be available to the user at any time in any place is dependent on the system being portable. Research on device, network, application, and middleware aspects is proceeding under the nomadic computing aegis; also, with miniaturization continuing at the pace it is, it will be only a matter of time before very powerful systems can be made that are quite small and easily worn. Creating displays and input systems for these very small portable systems, however, will continue to be a challenge. This is especially true if they are to be used in noisy or silent environments where speech cannot be readily used.

Compatible

The new and evolving systems will have to be compatible with legacy systems to at least some extent. This issue is explicit in telephony and television and more de facto in computing; where common, it is associated with slowing the process of change. The convenience of user access to the NII and the impression of high performance in the user interface are greatly enhanced by interoperability (between equipments, networks, applications), consistency (the same or very similar interface is used everywhere), and easy adaptability of a component to an environment ("plug and play," "discovery" of other system entities, quick and easy startup of a new service). All of these requirements suggest the importance of norms and standards.

Much of the "ease of learning" that users will experience with new devices will be a function of the similarity of the new devices to ones they used in the past. Interconnectivity and interoperability are also highly dependent on standards. Thus, standardization can have a profound effect on the familiarity of new devices that individuals may encounter in their environments. That said, experiences such as disagreement over proposed transitions from ON/OFF to 0/1 on power control switches do not promise rapid agreement on interface-related standards. In the marketplace, product differentiation is an important source of profit.

A more important compatibility issue, however, deals with the ability of devices to work with each other. At the present time, interoperability of systems is limited, and even getting a computer to work with printers or other peripherals designed to work with it can be a complicated process.[17] For individuals who require special adaptive interfaces, it is often a nightmare. It should be as easy as bringing a computer and any peripherals near each other or attaching them to get them to work together. However, integration of key features or functions across platforms and services is an issue in the marketplace; it constrains the commercial support for interface commonalities.

"Plug and play" is an urgent necessity for what a user perceives as a hopelessly complex environment of multiple service providers and facilities. The need ranges from carrying a set-top box from one residence to another and having it work when it is plugged in, with minimal human participation through the remote control, to adapting devices to new services and protocols through automatic refreshing of software. It implies system adaptation and convergence, with devices and applications "discovering" one another. Systems research in this area would be very helpful.

Beyond media, universal and secure commercial protocols (for transactions such as credit card and electronic cash purchases) are essential for individual and organizational trust in the NII; they require industry resolution. Advances in encryption technology are becoming widely disseminated, and there are candidate security systems (such as Secure Sockets Layer) for the Internet that use them. Some observers of the evolution of electronic commerce believe that a widely accepted end-to-end paradigm for secure transactions will be in place within 2 years, encouraging expanded commercial use of Web browsers. This suggests the value of further research on user interfaces for commercial transactions, including handshaking palm-top devices, communicating pocketbooks and wallets, and other innovative interfaces.

Although much of the standards-related work is more in the nature of applied research or development than basic research, and although leaders in the academic technical community often disparage standards-related work, the question of whether basic research could facilitate or support standards setting is especially important for systems intended for the broadest possible use. For example, research that could contribute to standards could illuminate options for maintaining a univerally understood paradigm across heterogeneous people, devices, access networks, and locations, using whatever media and media quality are possible in a given situation. In the ECI area, as in others, standards raise concerns about limiting commercial offerings to lowest common denominators, which some maintain is the flip side of highest-possible access.

Intelligent

To achieve much of the friendly, supportive, collaborative, and mentoring characteristics discussed above, it is necessary for the systems to be intelligent. "Intelligence" is an elusive quality, the definition of which differs with the speaker. Although global intelligence would be ideal, even systems that are intelligent only for a limited range of topics or activities could be very useful. Any ability on the part of agents to provide feedback to an individual as to its state or understanding would be helpful, particularly when operating in an anticipatory mode and trying to predict or take semiautonomous action based on its predictions of the user's needs.

There is also much room for progress around elicitation techniques. Often, users are unaware of which questions to ask or what options are available to them. Developing systems that can help users determine what they should do and how they might accomplish their desired goals could be very powerful in helping novices or individuals with less technical skill to master and effectively use the new technologies.

Finally, in considering agent technologies, it is important to realize that agents may be architecturally external to the device or systems we want them to control. This introduces the need for an "external agent" interface to the software system as well: an agent that is probably only going to be able to deal with ASCII text or "medium-independent" interfaces. (For a more extensive discussion of intelligent agents, see Chapter 6.)

Supportive of Social and Group Interactions

Speculation about very large numbers of individuals engaged in various social or interpersonal interactions (e.g., group discussions, visits to public places such as on-line museums or exhibits, doing routine tasks such as checking on the status of a filed Medicare or other insurance claim) raises questions about what can be learned about how to make these kinds of interactions work. (See Chapter 5 for detailed discussions.) For example, what social mechanisms can be evolved or developed or experimentally introduced that will preserve freedom of speech but prevent, reduce, or mitigate destructive individual behaviors so that large-scale network-based interactions can proceed? (This is new territory in social theory.) Will there be a need for significant numbers of human facilitators to give help and support; if so, what tools, interfaces, and other support will they need to enact their roles? What are the critical psychosocial features or dimensions of interactions with people or information that are likely to influence the effectiveness of public-interest activities carried out via networked infrastructure? What differences are introduced by the NII media in these activities? How can NII interface design boost positive effects or damp negative ones? (In discussing some of these questions, workshop participants suggested that clinical communications could provide a test case.) For example, when does a community use setting feel okay? Under what conditions or for what purposes do such settings not feel sufficiently private? (Note that this research question concerns privacy as a psychosocial experience, not as a property of systems per se.) Also, what are electronic analogs of emotional or other reaction that are expressed nonverbally in in-person interactions? Do signs such as :-), sometimes referred to as "emoticons," really work for everyday citizens as nonverbal cues?

More generally, how are the pragmatic dimensions of NII-based interactions to be accommodated? For applications expected to serve large cross-sections of the public, interface design may affect experiences with and perceptions of class-based functionality in interactions between citizens and government agencies or citizens engaged in public-interest activities based on interfaces and hardware platforms. Minimizing class-based distinctions in those interactions can make participation more egalitarian, which may be particularly important in at least some applications, and it should be a consideration in interface and system design. In what ways might the interface representations of participants in a public-interest interchange give status signals or otherwise produce information on socioeconomic status (e.g., because of differences in low-cost or subsidized interfaces and high-end interfaces to public-interest functions)? How can systems for public participation be designed to obliterate status insignia (e.g., based on types of access that indicate very low-end machines, public-access community settings, subsidized users)?

Trustworthy—Secure, Private, Safe, and Reliable

Although information security has often been viewed (and therefore too often dismissed) as specialized, the extension of information infrastructure to more citizens is driving an expansion of security to the broader concept of trustworthiness, linking it to complementary considerations for privacy, safety, and reliability. Protections are needed against both inadvertence and malice in a world of what Mark Weiser has called ubiquitous computing, where personal information infrastructures relate to more general information infrastructure, and where dependence on information infrastructure implies systems to assure trustworthiness of people and systems with which one communicates. Security mechanisms for identification and authentication are likely to become more common elements of interfaces; the question of how much information one should reveal about oneself (and in exchange for what) in that context is open and itself sensitive to technological options as well as broader public policy parameters. For example, a number of technical options for automatically capturing, recording, and even analyzing data about users and their patterns of use (their behavior) are becoming more common but not necessarily apparent to users.

The interface aspects of information security are associated with the challenge of making security solutions more convenient, inexpensive, and more readily accepted and used by people. At the workshop, Stephen Kent, of BBN, noted three research areas, each with long roots: managing confinement (to limit the use of information systems and resources to those authorized), certification (for presumed public key infrastructures as complements to assumed growth in the use of encryption for a variety of protections—of privacy, security, or intellectual property and other rights), and personal tokens for identification and authentication purposes (reflecting the shortcomings of more familiar password-based access control technology). Separation of an identity token from a basic access device may take on growing importance with broader civic use of the NII. For example, identification is required in many dealings with the government; services beyond the simple supply of information require identification and authentication for privacy and security, and so realizing the NII promise involves joint improvement of interfaces and applications to incorporate these functions.[18] Depending on how the interface is designed, it is possible to either enhance or compromise the individual's privacy in carrying out transactions with the systems. This is particularly important around public information systems and systems that can monitor user activity. Overall, enhanced reliability of infrastructure services may be supported by more attention to and integration of studies of physical device reliability, software protocols, and operator errors.

The broadening base of users and applications implies a concern for many dimensions of reliability, which relates to basic system design as well as interfaces. For individuals who are novice or less expert, as well as those with lesser ability (physical, sensory, or cognitive), this includes the ability to help avoid serious and nonreversible errors (although the ECI concept implies this ability is valuable to all). Options relate to strategies to allow more types of actions to be reversed, strategies for requiring confirmation (that do not become so automatic that they are instantly overridden), strategies for identifying and predicting potential mistakes or suspected mistakes, and better cueing techniques for error recovery. For heavier users potentially subject to repetitive strain injuries, the interfaces may be designed in such a way as to help detect potential injury and provide guidance.

Information Centered

The growing pervasiveness of information suggests that interface designers consider a perspective that is information centered, rather than or in addition to one that is application or tool centered. At the workshop, Johanna Moore, of the University of Pittsburgh, described this replacement as a change in the "basic currency" of the NII from applications to information. A fully information-centered approach would allow people to use whatever application they wished and to extract pieces of information from documents—such as lines from a table displayed in a Web page.[19] In a mode-free, information-centered design, people would have one spell checker that could be brought to bear against any text anywhere.

The concept of an information-centered perspective poses hard problems that begin with developing a better understanding of what information is. As the forms of information have diversified and intermixed in the NII, our fundamental concept of information—what we know, how we know it, how we relate to it—has become unstable and must be up-

BOX 2.5
What Is Information?

In addressing the question of how to provide every citizen access to the NII, we inevitably cast our questions, at least in part, in terms of information. We assume that citizens will use the NII to get to information, whether from relatively static information sources such as Web pages, databases, e-mail, newsgroup items, and files, or from more dynamic sources such as people, services, and computations. The interfaces we build for every citizen, and the research supporting their designs, will depend upon and be framed in terms of providing every citizen with access to information.

The centrality of the notion of information to the development of research programs raises the question of whether the concept of information is well understood. If our understanding of this concept rested on foundations held in common and agreed upon by the joint community of researchers, funders, suppliers—of hardware, software, functionality, and content—and the users of interfaces, then one huge area of potential misunderstanding and difficulties could be regarded as safely under control. However, not only is there no such agreement, but many working in the fields that affect interface design and development do not even recognize that there is an issue here. Different communities use the term "information" presuming a certain meaning, without recognition of the alternatives or of the consequences of adopting a particular stance. Different conceptions of information lead to different questions, different approaches, and different ways of evaluating solutions. Given the scale and diversity of the NII, research agendas may have to be reexamined in light of the foundational assumptions they are making about information.

In everyday conversation, "information" refers to facts or knowledge that may be acquired either directly by observation or indirectly by reading or hearing from another. Although there is allowance for error (e.g., "He gave me incorrect information," misinformation), there is usually some presumed authoritative source; the authority might derive from direct observation (and trusted senses) or from the reputation of the source.

There are two predominant formal technical treatments of the concept, one from the mathematical theory of information, the other from philosophical work in semantics. These two treatments differ from the naive conception and from one another.

dated (see Box 2.5). Otherwise, conflicting assumptions will confound people's interactions with information.

An information-centered perspective implies better understanding of the dimensions of information that determine how well people can create, publish, search, browse, retrieve, study, integrate, validate, and use information. How good is the information? Can it be trusted? Is it easily accessible or remote and untouchable? Does it form a part of a larger whole, leading to deep understanding, or does it stand in isolation? Is it useful when found, or does it require an inordinate amount of effort on the part of the finder to comprehend it and concentrate it? Can information from different sources be integrated in meaningful ways? These

1. The mathematical theory of information is concerned with the amount of information and the accuracy with which it is transmitted. It does not consider meaning; neither what the information is "about" nor its truth (or falsity) are factors that play roles in the questions that information theory asks nor the techniques it develops. It is thus clear why the major impact of information theory is on issues of bandwidth, channel, and the like.

2. Philosophical-semantic treatments deal instead with content and meaning; their focus is on how to treat formally the concept that some entity (the sign or message) "carries the information that . . . ."[*] These theories are newer and less well developed than the theory of information. Although they deal explicitly with the "content" aspect of information, which is central to everyday use of the term and the ways in which "every citizen" will conceive of information for the NII, they do not address issues of how information is represented, encoded, or displayed, all of which are also of importance for ECIs. Furthermore, because they are grounded in "truth," they are unable to deal adequately with misinformation or with questions of authoritativeness.

A major issue for the NII, and certainly for ECIs for the NII, is understanding how these three different perspectives—everyday, mathematical, and philosophical-semantic—relate. Integration of these perspectives will be important for economic issues (which view information as a commodity to be paid for), legal issues (e.g., intellectual property rights), and control (e.g., personal view: ownership, conjoint the right to make change). Thus, the NII must ultimately deal with a conception of "information" that encompasses all facets of everyday use of the term. Both the mathematical and semantical theories can contribute to this understanding, but there are facets important to the NII that neither cover.

---

[*]A simple example of the concept, "X carries the information that Y," is "smoke carries the information that fire [is present]." Technically, the issue is that X counterfactually supports Y (i.e., if one has X, then one has Y and, furthermore, if Y weren't around, one wouldn't have X).
SOURCE: Austin Henderson, Apple Computer Corporation.

questions go well beyond requirements for interfaces, but interfaces can support the user seeking to answer such questions. The central concern is dealing with large volumes of information of varying and uncertain quality, recognizing that "quality" can be both subjective and dependent on context.[20]

Research to support better finding and use of information will be complicated by the absence of standard ways to convey the quality of information to people and the dependence of quality on the context of publication or use, suggesting value in a flexible way of representing quality—grounded in a sound sociological understanding of how people use information—so that people can differentiate the quality of information for their own context. Interface approaches should take into account not only the needs of end users but also the larger evolution of the information infrastructure per se: the proliferation of information and changes in its cost structure affect the demand for editing, publishing, and library services as well as the demand for information per se.

Support for searching and retrieving, including catalogs, abstracts, and other tools, are among the challenges. Ben Shneiderman, of the University of Maryland, argues that searching should not be invisible—people should be informed about and have input into choices about the scope, attributes, results, and opportunities for refinement of their queries (Shneiderman et al., 1997). Kept informed, people can learn and grow from novice to expert searchers. In addition, interdisciplinary assessment can illuminate subtle aspects relating to how information and options for tools are presented. For example, according to recent research by Nass and Reeves (1996), interactive media generate fundamental psychosocial cues even where not intended, and other research points to the impact of wording in commands, messages, presentation of images, and so on.

Other challenges relate to the fact that publishing is not a neutral activity, as noted above. Reflecting classical concerns about control over content by those with control over conduits, Apple's Austin Henderson cautioned, at the workshop, that

> failure of the NII [would] be that a small collection of sources broad- or narrowcast their creations to the waiting masses. As the printing press let everybody be a reader, the copier let everybody be a publisher, the personal computer let everybody be a writer, so the real promise of the NII is that it will allow everybody to be an author (create and publish). The NII can give everybody a voice. A deep concern is whether such plurality of voices will be discouraged or encouraged.

Concerns about control over content have shaped past public policy relating to content and equal access in broadcasting (radio and television), antitrust legal inquiries relating to screen displays in computerized reservation systems provided by airlines to travel agents, and recent public statements of information service providers and consumer advocates about screen displays associated with Web browsers and other Internet-related services. Public policy may impose requirements on interface design; technologists should become prepared by recognizing the issue and considering the technical options for representation, display, finding, filtering, and so on. Research on tools for publishing should consider the conflict between the goals of information providers and those of consumers. For example, commercial providers may want to prevent people from mixing and matching parts of services and/or missing the advertising. Already, computer systems vendors have been contending over control and content of the initial displays associated with operating systems and browsers. More generally, Susan Hockey noted, at the workshop, that even apart from explicit digital annotations or hypertext representations, the processes of transcribing a text (including encoding of accented characters) or digitizing an image (including possible enhancements) involves decisions about the intellectual content of the object.

One approach that may affect interface design is to more consistently add metadata to information that could help people—or machines acting on their behalf—to interpret and integrate information. Metadata describe the attributes of information such as format, quality, intended purpose, version, origin, and underlying assumptions. Because everyone views the world differently, integrating information requires a shared description of semantic content. For example, at the workshop, Louis Hecht explained that the Open Geographic Information Systems Consortium Inc. is working on standards for semantic translation because different geodata producers and users give the same geographic feature different names, sets of descriptive parameters, and metadata. Similarly, Kent Wittenburg of Bellcore suggested that research on standardized distributed object-like protocols holds promise for integrating across services, noting that, although commercial services will continue to improve interfaces for searching and browsing, customizing searches across multiple services is a longer-term problem.[21]

According to Craig Knoblock, of the Information Sciences Institute, the most natural way to model the semantic content of information sources is in reference to ontologies—knowledge representations that can be constructed for a given subject area (e.g., stock market data); machine learning technology is needed to automate model generation because the body of information is so large.[22] Because the metadata also will become semantically drifted, Knoblock argued against central standardization: "There is going to have to be some kind of distributed solution, where if you have these information providers that are actually buying this information, they are going to have to change their model and update things. There has to be enough information in the underlying structure that it is easy to make those changes. But there is no way that you can anticipate all those changes."

Moshe Zloof, also at the workshop, cautioned against reinventing lessons from decades of experience with database management. New approaches such as using agents to model the semantics of unstructured data now flooding the Web may be less effective than structuring the data to begin with (e.g., by using a relational database model). As Austin Henderson observed, however, fixed structures—whether embodied in a database or modeled from diverse sources on the Web—inevitably become out of date: "Suddenly my database shifts, not because anything in it shifts, but because the world shifted. This is the well-known problem of semantic drift. . . . [We are] never going to get everyone to agree [on a structure. We are] always going to be in the position of negotiating."

Pleasant to Use

An important factor in attracting new users and helping them overcome their fear of technology is creating interfaces that are naturally attractive and fun to use. A key historic differentiator between home and work, underscored by social scientists at the workshop, is the element of "desirability": home uses of technology have tended to be discretionary, and interfaces or other aspects of technology that do not appeal to consumers are often not used in the home. The HomeNet study, for example, focuses much more on what people want to do than what they need to do, as would be the case at work. At the workshop, Robert Kraut, of Carnegie Mellon University, explained that there is no direct connection among utility, usability, and desirability and that much is not understood about how those qualities do or can relate to each other. Making systems less threatening, less technical looking, more familiar, and more interesting and fun will be important components in creating interfaces that will actually be approachable and used by many individuals. As mentioned above, these systems, however, must gracefully lead to more efficient interface strategies whenever the interesting/fun interfaces are, themselves, not efficient for long-term or general use.

The pleasure, fun, or desirability of use is part of a broader pattern of interaction with behavior that should be considered in designing interfaces. For example, the ability, in a communications context, to see people on screen, especially in real time, can affect how involved an individual is but also tends to result in payment of more attention to physical appearance, associated symbols and cues that can be removed with other communication modes, and increase in cognitive load, which affects attributions to others and persuasiveness. Regardless of context, as Sara Kiesler observed at the workshop, every change in an interface implies changes in social psychology, organizational processes, and other side effects for organizations and individuals—effects that can be studied and anticipated.

Telepresence, in the form of casual video conferencing and collaboration, is the subject of much speculation about how technology can eliminate barriers to intimacy. Although many technologists and business analysts tout video teleconferencing as a possible "killer app" for the NII, Robert Kraut and Sara Kiesler noted that research over 25 years suggests limited payoff to it—conversations accompanied by video are not clearer, information exchange is not better—but some do like it better than simple audioconferencing. Similarly, different attitudes have been recorded for participation in text e-mail versus systems with image transmission. More optimistic technologists hold out the promise that within a year or two some people will be able to glance into the offices—home- or business-based—of perhaps 60 people with whom they normally interact, in contrast to most video conferencing used for remote meetings with many people in attendance. With the advent of wideband digital networks, ease of use, and better quality, the telecommunications center is moving into personal computers or workstations. As the technology becomes more widespread, most meetings could consist of two people collaborating under casual circumstances; as experimentation on the Internet's Mbone multicast system suggests, extremely large (e.g., in the thousands or more participants) or variable-size meetings also will become easier and may become more common. As discussed in Chapters 4 and 5, large group interactions appear to be an area where more understanding of social dynamics is needed.

PULLING IT ALL TOGETHER: ECI INTERFACES IN THE YEAR 20XX

To describe the future is to risk being wrong, but it is a useful technique for showing how it may be possible to integrate the key concepts of an ECI to work seamlessly together to create a whole new paradigm for interaction between information infrastructure and people. A simple scenario, focusing primarily on the input/output aspects, is provided below.

Along with demonstration or prototype projects, scenarios, per se, were suggested by workshop participants as useful elements of an interdisciplinary research program because of their amenability to computer and social science explorations that begin with their design and continue through assessment of the resulting roles/relationships/outcomes under different rules and starting assumptions. As illustrated at the workshop by Michael Traynor's telemedicine scenario, research could develop and explore scenarios that involve multiple stakeholders and diverse interests that converge on cases of NII use. Scenarios might also provide a training/teaching paradigm related to how new media affect extant procedures, expectations, and so on; similarly, simulation games aimed at policy analysis have already shown that scenarios hold promise for providing a framework or vehicle for collaborative policy deliberation among diverse stakeholders and for arriving at negotiated agreements on policy inputs to the NII decision-making process, but the methodology calls for systematic evaluation.

IN THE YEAR 20XX—ONE SCENARIO

It is the year 20XX. Systems with ECIs abound and take a wide variety of forms. Some appear on workstations; others are on accessories carried around as a notepad or cellular phone was carried in the 1990s. These accessories, however, are multifunctional in nature and can be used to access almost any type of information or service available. Many of the ECIs are simply integrated into the environment as part of rooms, vehicles, appliances, and even clothing that people wear. The generalized information systems themselves are integrated so that people can begin a task (e.g., sending a message) in their office on the system built into a desk or wall there and continue the activity seamlessly as they walk out the door to get into their vehicle and leave on a trip.

The systems are modality independent with regard to both input and output. In the office, they may be primarily visual display based (especially if one works in a shared office space). However, as the user gets up and leaves, they are able to seamlessly move from interacting in a visual fashion to interacting in a verbal fashion, completing the "e-mail" as they walk down the hall, get into their vehicle, and head for the airport. While en route, the voice interface can be used to access any of the information transaction or communications systems, in a purely verbal fashion. This might include checking weather "maps," buying a gift for one's spouse, touching base with other colleagues, etc. Since the systems can all work either visually or verbally (words), these same systems work equally well for colleagues who have low vision or blindness or are hard of hearing or deaf. Because the verbal information can be rendered as Braille or speech, the systems could also be used by individuals who are deaf or blind or who are unable to read at all because of specific learning disabilities that prevent them from learning to read or read well visually.

Individuals who have difficulty learning the new systems or new functions on the systems find that there are built-in agents that will help them through whatever task they are interested in and that will interact with them in a friendly, natural language format (or that can interact with the user's own personal agents). They can either speak to the systems aloud, type on the built-in keypad, or use any other technique or device to input information. As users become more expert, they can begin using shorthand phrases, codes, gestures, and other more efficient but less obvious strategies. The user and the systems that the user interacts with develop these strategies naturally over time. These conventions are also passed from one device to another so that users' familiarity with them is interchangeable as they move between physical systems. In addition to using verbal input, many of the systems will have the ability to monitor both the environment around the individual and the individuals themselves for contextual information.

In addition, they can use global positioning systems to determine physically where the individual is and environmental databases to help understand the context or surroundings the individual is in at any point in time. This may include a knowledge of which other people are in the immediate vicinity (inasmuch as they allow this information to be known). With information about the environment, the context, and the individual, the device can much more easily interpret the interactions and requests it receives from the user and may be able to anticipate or facilitate the activities of the user as well.

When an individual does not understand information that is being presented or how to achieve some objective, intelligent agents in the system are available to assist the individual in representing the information in a simpler format or to assist with instructions or with carrying out the activity. Some agents might be autonomous and carry out tasks automatically for the user. Most agents, however, are collaborative and interactive and act more like an intelligent colleague or assistant. They are able to interact with the individual at whatever level and in whatever modality (visual, aural, tactile) is most appropriate and most effective given the environment (noisy, etc.), situation (person's eyes or hands are occupied, or a situation requires silent operation as in a meeting), task, and user abilities or preferences.

Although many situations and environments may require the use of only one or another of the available interface modalities (e.g., visual only, verbal only), there will also be times when the full abilities of the user are available, including simultaneous use of whatever visual, auditory, and tactile manipulative abilities the user may have. In these cases the individual can take advantage of this by using a full immersive environment. For example, the user may use an immersive environment to simulate transport to another virtual environment. Instead of traveling to meet colleagues, the user can sit at a desk and move into a mode where he or she visually, aurally, and manipulatively (and, eventually, tactilely and olfactorially?) joins with other colleagues from around the country in a virtual meeting room where they communicate and exchange virtual documents or exhibits and carry out their meeting. The colleagues around the table who are deaf can have the system invoke a speech recognizer and present its output on the screen. (In the next decade or so, the speech recognition technology will probably still make errors. But for clear speakers and narrow domains of discourse, recognition may be sufficient for understandability.) The text may appear to float in space in front of the speaker, or the user can drag the text displays for different people closer together in the space in front so that it is easier to monitor them simultaneously. People who do not have a hearing impairment also find this feature useful, particularly if they can read faster than they can listen and find it easier to focus attention on a particular verbal stream or to check over what was said when everybody's speech is presented visually. It also allows them to check back over what was said. This is particularly valuable if they are trying to listen to multiple overlapping discourses. Colleagues who are blind or who have difficulty reading any of the printed materials can have the materials presented to them aurally or translated into a form that is easier to understand. Sighted individuals also take advantage of this feature in order to allow them to continue monitoring the situation or demonstration with their eyes while the textual information is being fed to them aurally. Even an individual who is deaf or blind can have the information translated and presented on a special dynamic Braille and tactile display that can be attached to the system.

Immersive environments can be used for a wide range of functions beyond allowing an individual to travel to and visit most any real or simulated spot on earth. They also allow the individual to scale themselves larger or smaller in order to explore or better learn about objects or environments (e.g., the ability to zoom in and out to learn about geography, biology, etc.). They are also used to allow individuals to explore things with their senses that are not available to their senses. This includes seeing the invisible, hearing the inaudible, and translating concepts that have no physical form (such as information) into visual or auditory formats in order to gain new insights. Again, users with all of their senses intact can choose to have the information presented in simultaneous multisensory form. Individuals for whom some senses are weaker or absent have the information presented in forms that best meet their individual abilities and learning styles.

NOTES

1.   In addition, early experiences are often limited indicators of new technology's benefits: the 1980s and early 1990s discussions of the "productivity paradox" suggest that disappointing financial returns from early computing investments reflect relatively simple-minded automation of existing work processes rather than the fundamental restructuring of those processes that has proved necessary to realize the full benefits of computing. See CSTB's *Information Technology in the Service Society* (CSTB, 1994b).

2.   An interagency assessment of issues and opportunities for kiosks in government applications proposed a staged pilot and market test program that would support data gathering and incorporation of feedback into future design and deployment steps (see Government Information Technology Service (GITS), 1995).

3.   The IDC data are at the household level and thus likely to produce higher percentages than the individual-level data from the Census Bureau survey. However even if both data sets were at the individual level, it would still be impossible to draw meaningful comparisons, because they used different sample weightings in order to factor their results to the scale of the whole population. This is one example of the difficulty of identifying trends and making comparisons from survey data in this field.

4.   Project 2000 researchers statistically corrected the CNIDS data to weight the sample in proportion to the U.S. population for gender, age, and education—variables known to affect the likelihood of Internet use. Income was not included because of a high nonresponse relate for income in the CNIDS survey; education, however, is a reasonable proxy for income. The researchers also adjusted the data to omit logically inconsistent responses that the CNIDS had included, such as those from people who initially reported having used the Internet but later in the survey reported the opposite. See Hoffman et al. (1996).

5.   Whether new Web-page publishing tools are readily usable by nonspecialists remains an open question. For an anecdotal account that illustrates the difficulties novices have with such applications (among others), see Rigdon (1996).

6.   Of course, a number of innovative applications of multimedia technology have been introduced for education, but several education experts believe the promise of such technology is only beginning to be tapped.

7.   A further challenge results from the level of exposure to a given environment, situation, or task; for example, there is a difference between a mobile phone one rarely looks at, a phone one never looks at, and a phone one uses frequently.

8.   A related concern is whether there are general skills that people can learn for use in a variety of settings. Does learning in a specific context ever limit the usefulness of the resulting knowledge?

9.   For example, Internet bridge clubs type in bids without idle chit-chat; they sit

locked in their houses, staring at text, punching at keyboards.

10.   By contrast, the encoding features of the Hypertext Markup Language are mainly used to control the appearance of text (e.g., bold type, fonts, blinking text). HTML's descriptive codes are mostly for low-level constructs such as emphasis or indented lists. It has no standard mechanism for indicating common document parts such as author, abstract, keywords, or references. New HTML codes (tags) for such elements could have the side benefit of being interpretable by software agents for automatic indexing and searching. New tags are continually being proposed and implemented; however, the resulting lack of standardization hinders content producers, because a conscientious Web author must test pages to ensure that they appear properly when viewed with a variety of Web browsers that support different overlapping sets of tags (Schulzrinne, 1996).

11.   Note that capabilities for filtering and blocking stand out as features specifically contemplated for children as a subpopulation.

12.   According to the Cross-Industry Working Team (1995), nomadicity refers to the ability of people to easily access a rich set of services, other people, and content while they are on the move, at intermediate stops and at arbitrary destinations; ubiquitous refers to systems that access communications and computing services via the NII and that will be at least as common as today's telephone. Moreover, the NII will facilitate connectivity through a wide range of electronic devices, including portable, mobile, and wireless computing and communications.

13.   U.S. sales of interactive kiosk hardware were $449 million in 1994 and estimated at $610 million for 1995. The retail sector accounts for 84 percent of kiosks installed in 1995, but Venture Development Corporation (VDC, 1996c) expects faster growth in financial, government, and corporate use. Information-dispensing kiosks are about 60 percent of 1995 installations; the remainder are point-of-sale manufacturing kiosks (e.g., greeting card and business card printing) and transactional (e.g., product ordering, driver's license renewal). VDC expects faster growth in transactional kiosks than in information delivery kiosks, partly because return on investment is easier to justify for a kiosk that sells something than for one that gives free information.

14.   The most detailed recent survey of disabilities by the Census Bureau is the 1993 Survey of Income and Program Participation. Although the data are now several years old, it is unlikely that the percentages of people with various disabilities have changed significantly. See http://www.census.gov/hhes/www/disable.html.

15.   The survey involved interviews with over 26,000 adults. It measured skills likely to be required in work, home, and community contexts, such as locating and integrating information in a prose passage; writing new text; interpreting lists, charts, and graphs; and reading and using numerical information (U.S. Department of Education, 1992).

16.   In addition, as Wallace Feurzeig observes in his paper in this volume, spoken-language interfaces allowing literacy training systems to integrate spoken and written communications could enhance training by enabling learners to build on their spoken language abilities.

17.   Interoperability is being advanced through standards such as MPEG for video coding and H.323 for multimedia conferencing. There appears to be a trend for Web-oriented multimedia products (telephony, conferencing) to conform to these standards, which, in the immediate future, will make it much easier to communicate without elaborate prearrangements. Interoperability is also advanced, as described earlier, through the use of transportable software (in a standardized language and virtual machine), which removes the necessity of every party to a session needing to have all of the application software in advance, and distributed object systems, which allow existing applications on diverse computing platforms to interact with one another. Standards are taking on new meaning as a means for facilitating interaction between applications or customizing equipment with

transportable software, rather than being rigid constraints on the equipment. Networks, as well as applications, can be customized with transportable software, and programmable networks are a significant near-future research topic.

18.   How and when these developments take place depends in part on relevant public policy parameters (e.g., the evolution of cryptography policy).

19.   A document-centered approach represents a midpoint, in which people could use various applications, but would still have to access whole documents rather than data from within documents.

20.   At the workshop, Robert Kraut, of Carnegie Mellon University, noted that because information is not a passive, inactive thing, it can have different values for consumers and producers. For example, a babysitter who wants to advertise to parents in the neighborhood probably values that information more than the parent who feels bombarded with advertisements from many sources.

21.   See http://www-db.stanford.edu/~gravano/standards.

22.   Knoblock refers to information in the Web, but the observation applies more generally to all forms of information in the NII.

3

INPUT/OUTPUT TECHNOLOGIES: CURRENT STATUS AND RESEARCH NEEDS

Meeting the every-citizen interface (ECI) criteria described in Chapter 2 will require advances in a number of technology areas. Some involve advances in basic underlying display and interface technologies (higher-resolution visual displays, three-dimensional displays, better voice recognition, better tactile displays, and so on). Others involve advances in our understanding of how to best match these input/output technologies to the sensory, motor, and cognitive capabilties of different users in different and changing environments carrying out a wide variety of tasks. But the new interfaces will need to do more than just physically couple the user to the devices. To meet these visions, the interfaces must have the ability to assist, facilitate, and collaborate with the user in accomplishing tasks.

Subsequent chapters address interface design—the creation of interfaces that make the best-possible use of these human-machine communications technologies—and system attributes that lie beneath the veneer of the interface, such as system intelligence and software support for collaborative activities. This chapter examines the current state and prospective advances in technology areas related directly to communication between a person and a system—hardware and software for input (to the system) and output (to a human). The emphasis is on technical advances that, if implemented in well-designed systems (as stressed in Chapter 4), hold the potential to expand accessibility and usability to many more people than at present. The discussion includes a cluster of speech input/output technologies; natural language understanding (including restricted languages with limited vocabularies); keyboard input; gesture recognition and machine vision; auditory and touch-based output; interfaces that combine multiple modes of input and output; and visual displays, including immersive or virtual reality systems. Because the ECI challenge involves connecting to the information infrastructure, rather than just to stand-alone systems, this chapter reviews the current status of and research challenges for interfaces for systems in large-scale national networks. The chapter ends with the steering committee's conclusions, based on workshop discussions and other inputs, about the research priorities to advance these technologies and our understanding of how to use them to support every citizen.

FRAMING THE INPUT/OUTPUT DISCUSSION—LAYERS OF COMMUNICATION

The interface is the means by which a user communicates with a system, whether to get it to perform some function or computation directly (e.g., compute a trajectory, change a word in a text file, display a video); to find and deliver information (e.g., getting a paper from the Web or information from a database); or to provide ways of interacting with other people (e.g., participate in a chat group, send e-mail, jointly edit a document). As a communications vehicle, interfaces can be assessed and compared in terms of three key dimensions: (1) the language(s) they use, (2) the ways in which they allow users to say things in the language(s), and (3) the surface(s) or device(s) used to produce output (or register input) expressions of the language. The design and implementation of an interface entail choosing (or designing) the language for communication, specifying the ways in which users may express "statements" of that language (e.g., by typing words or by pointing at icons), and selecting device(s) that allow communication to be realized—the input/output devices.

Box 3.1 gives some examples of choices at each of these levels. Although the selection and integration of input/output devices will generally involve hardware concerns (e.g., choices among keyboard, mouse, drawing surfaces, sensor-equipped apparel), decisions about the language definition and means of expression affect interpretation processes that are largely treated in software. The rest of this section briefly describes each of the dimensions and then examines how they can be used to characterize some currently standard interface choices; the remainder of the chapter provides an examination of the state of the art.

Language Contrasts and Continuum

There are two language classes of interest in the design of interfaces: natural languages (e.g., English, Spanish, Japanese) and artificial lan-

BOX 3.1
Layers of Communications

1. Language Layer

   • Natural language: complex syntax, complex semantics (whatever a human can say)
   • Restricted verbal language (e.g., operating systems command language, air traffic control language): limited syntax, constrained semantics
   • Direct manipulation languages: objects are "noun-like," get "verb equivalents" from manipulations (e.g., drag file X to Trash means "erase X"; drag message onto Outgoing Mailbox means "send message"; draw circle around object Y and click means "I'm referring to Y, so I can say something about it.")

2. Expression Layer
   Most of these types of realization can be used to express statements in most of the above types of languages. For instance, one can speak or write natural language; one can say or write a restricted language, such as a command-line interface; and one can say or write/draw a direct manipulation language.

   • Speaking: continuous speech recognition, isolated-word speech recognition
   • Writing: typing on a keyboard, handwriting
   • Drawing
   • Gesturing (American Sign Language provides an example of gesture as the realization (expression layer choice) for a full-scale natural language.)
   • Pick-from-set: various forms of menus
   • Pointing, clicking, dragging
   • Various three-dimensional manipulations—stretching, rotating, etc.
   • Manipulations within a virtual reality environment—same range of speech, gesture, point, click, drag, etc., as above, but with three dimensions and broader field of view
   • Manipulation unique to virtual reality environment—locomotion (flying through/over things as a means of manipulating them or at least looking at them)

3. Devices
   Hardware mechanisms (and associated device-specific software) that provide a way to express a statement. Again, more than one technology at this layer can be used to implement items at the layer above.

   • Keyboards (many different kinds of typing)
   • Microphones
   • Light pen/drawing pads, touch-sensitive screens, whiteboards
   • Video display screen and mouse
   • Video display screen and keypad (e.g., automated teller machine)
   • Touch-sensitive screen (touch with pen; touch with finger)
   • Telephone (audible menu with keypad and/or speech input)
   • Push-button interface, with different button for each choice (like big buttons on an appliance)
   • Joystick
   • Virtual reality input gear—glove, helmet, suit, etc.; also body position detectors

guages (e.g., programming languages, such as C++, Java, Prolog; database query languages, such as SQL; mathematical languages, such as logic; command languages, such as cshell provides). Natural languages are derived evolutionarily; they typically have unrestricted and complex syntax and semantics (assignment of meaning to symbols and to the structures built from those symbols). Artificial languages are created by computer scientists or mathematicians to meet certain design and functional criteria; the syntax is typically tightly constrained and designed to minimize semantic complexity and ambiguity.

Because an artificial language has a language definition, construction of an interpreter for the language is a more straightforward task than construction of a system for interpreting sentences in a natural language. The grammar of a programming language is given; defining a grammar for English (or any other natural language) remains a challenging task (though there are now several extensive grammars used in computational systems). Furthermore, the interactions between syntax and semantics can be tightly controlled in an artificial language (because people design them) but can be quite complex in a natural language.[1,2]

Natural languages are thus more difficult to process. However, they allow for a wider range of expression and as a result are more powerful (and more "natural"). It is likely that the expressivity of natural languages and the ways it allows for incompleteness and indirectness may matter more to their being easy to use than the fact that people already "know them." For example, the phrase, "the letter to Aunt Jenny I wrote last March," may be a more natural way to identify a letter in one's files than trying to recall the file name, identify a particular icon, or grep (a UNIX search command) for a certain string that must be in the letter. The complex requests that may arise in seeking information from on-line databases provide another example of the advantages of complex languages near the natural language end of this dimension. Constraint specifications that are natural to users (e.g., "display the protein structures having more than 40 percent alpha helix") are both diverse and rich in structure, whereas menu- or form-based paradigms cannot readily cover the space of possible queries. Although natural language processing remains a challenging long-range problem in artificial intelligence (as discussed under "Natural Language Processing" below in this chapter), progress continues to be made, and better understanding of the ways in which it makes communication easier may be used to inform the design of more restricted languages.

However, the fact that restricted languages have limitations is not, per se, a shortcoming for their use in ECIs. Limiting the range of language in using a system can (if done right) promote correct interpretation by the system by limiting ambiguity and allowing more effective communication. For instance, the use of domain- and task-specific restricted languages for certain applications of speech recognition systems has produced results, allowing people to use speech to communicate when they cannot see (either because they are limited by the communication device being used, such as the telephone, or because of physical impairment). Radiologists' workstations, for example, allow the use of speech as the primary means of inputting reports on X-rays or other radiographic tests. Direct manipulation languages may be ideal if there is a close match to what the user wants to do (and hence is able to "say"), that is, if the user's needs are anticipated and the user will not need to program or alter what the system does; they can be a robust means of control that limits the risk of system crashes from misdirected user actions.

In short, the design of an interface along the language dimension entails choices of syntax (which may be simple or complex) and semantics (which can be simple or complex either in itself or in how it relates to syntax). More complex languages typically allow the user to say more but make it harder for the system to figure out what a person means.

Expression Contrasts

A natural language sentence can be spoken, written, typed, gestured, or selected from a menu. An artificial language statement also can be spoken, written, typed, gestured, or selected from a menu.

Language expression can take many forms, generally differentiated as being more or less continuous or involving selection from a set of options (e.g., a menu). Speaking can involve isolated words or continuous speech recognition. Writing can involve handwriting or typing; drawing can be free form or can use prespecified options. Gesturing—independently or to manipulate objects—can be free form, can involve a full-scale natural language (e.g., American Sign Language), or can involve a more restricted set of prespecified options (e.g., pointing, dragging, stretching, rotating). Virtual reality and other visualization techniques represent a multimedia form of expression that may involve speech, gesture, direct manipulation, and haptic and other elements.

Thus, the different ways of saying things in a language may also be divided into two structural categories—free form and structured—and several different realization categories: typing, speaking, pointing. Free-form expression is usually more difficult to process than structured expression. For example, a sentence in natural language can be spoken "free form" (this is what we usually think of with natural language), or it might be specified by picking one word at a time out of a structured menu.[3] In the structured form the system can control what the user gets to choose to "say" next, and so it is much easier for a system to interpret and handle. Within a given form, some means of realization may be easier to handle than others (e.g., correctly typed words are easier to interpret than handwritten words; freehand drawings are more difficult than structured CAD/CAM (computer-aided design/computer-aided manufacturing) diagrams). It is also important to note that more structured systems may be preferable for certain applications, such as those involving completion of forms (Oviatt et al., 1994).

Menu/icon systems thus provide an alternative way of expressing command-like languages. They have underlying languages, typically very much like command languages. The commands (natural language verb equivalents) are often menu items (e.g., "select," "edit"); the parameters (natural language noun equivalents) are icons (or open files); and the statements (natural language sentence equivalents) are sequences of select "nouns" and "verbs." The menus and icons provide the structure within which a user can say something in the language.

Devices

The hardware realization of communication can take many forms; common ones include microphones and speakers, keyboards and mice, drawing pads, touch-sensitive screens, light pens, and push buttons. The choice of device interacts with the choice of medium: display, film/videotape, speaker/audiotape, and so on. There may also be interactions between expression and device (an obvious example is the connection between pointing device (mouse, trackball, joystick) and pull-down menus or icons). On the other hand, it is also possible to relax some of these associations to allow for alternative surfaces (e.g., keyboard alternatives to pointers, aural alternatives to visual outputs). Producing interfaces for every citizen will entail providing for alternative input/output devices for a given language-expression combination; it might also call for alternative approaches to expression.

Comparisons Among Graphical User Interfaces, Natural Language, and Speech

The language-expression-device framework can be used to gain perspective on current standard interface types and on the research opportunities and challenges presented by ECIs. For example, it makes clear that natural language processing and speech recognition (and other technologies that may be associated colloquially) introduce different issues and different tradeoffs. A speech-based interface such as AT&T's long-distance voice recognition system, which can recognize phrases such as "collect call" and "calling card,"[4] can combine a restricted language with speech as a means of expression. As this example illustrates, neither speech recognition with unlimited vocabulary nor complete/comprehensive language understanding is necessary to provide natural language-like input to a system within a restricted domain and task. Similarly, it is possible to improve restricted language interfaces by applying principles from natural language communication.

Current graphical user interface/menu/icon systems tightly constrain what one can say, both by starting with a very constrained language and by having a structured way in which one can express things in that language. They are at the opposite end of both the language and the expression spectrum from natural languages. It is thus clear why they are easier to process, but also why they are more constraining (Cohen and Oviatt, 1994).

Ongoing efforts to develop speech interfaces for Web browsers provide a concrete example of the importance of understanding the different tradeoffs of each of these dimensions. Choosing speech on the expression layer rather than pointing and clicking would lead to being able to "speak" the icons and hyperlinks that are designed for keyboard and mouse. Although this may suffice in certain settings—replacing one modality for another can be useful in hands-free contexts and for those with physical limitations—it does not necessarily expand a system's capabilities or lead to new paradigms for interactions. An alternative approach would be to explore how spoken language technology can expand the user's ability to obtain the desired information easily and quickly from the Web, leading to a different, probably more expressive, language. From this perspective, speech would augment rather than replace the mouse and keyboard, and a user would be able to choose among many interface language-expression options to achieve a task in the most natural and efficient manner.

Natural language interaction is particularly appropriate when the information space is broad and diverse or when the user's request contains complex constraints. Both of these situations occur frequently on the Web. For example, finding a specific home page or document now requires remembering a universal resource locator, searching through the Web for a pointer to the desired document, or using one of the keyword search engines available. Current interfaces present the user with a fixed set of choices at any point, of which one is to be selected. Only by stepping through the offered choices and conforming to the prescribed organization of the Web can users reach the documents they desire. The multitude of indexes and meta-indexes on the Web is testimony to the reality and magnitude of the problem. The power of a human/natural language in this situation is that it allows the user to specify what information or document is desired (e.g., "Show me the White House home page," "Will it rain tomorrow in Seattle?" or "What is the ZIP code for

Orlando, Florida?") without having to know where and how the information is stored. A natural language, regardless of whether it is expressed using speech, typing, or handwriting, offers a user significantly more power in expressing constraints, thereby freeing the user from having to adhere to a rigid, preconceived indexing and command hierarchy.

In examining the state of the art of various input/output technologies, it is important to recognize that no single choice is right for all interfaces. In fact, one of the major challenges of interface design may be designing a language that is powerful enough for a user to say what needs to be said, but in as constrained a manner as possible, while still having the power to make processing easier and the possibility of misinterpretation less likely. In looking at input/output options, it will be useful to keep in mind where various options fall on one or another of these scales and the tradeoffs implicit in choosing a given option.

TECHNOLOGIES FOR COMMUNICATING WITH SYSTEMS

Humans modulate energy in many ways. Recognizing that fact allows for exploration of a rich set of alternatives and complements—at any time, a user-chosen subset of controls and displays—that a focus on simplicity of interface design as the primary goal can obscure. Current direct manipulation interfaces with two-dimensional display and mouse input make use, minimally, of one arm with two fingers and a thumb and one eye—about what is used to control a television remote. It was considered a stroke of genius, of course, to reduce all computer interactions to this simple set as a transition mechanism to enable people to learn to use computers without much training. There are no longer any reasons (including cost) to remain stuck in this transition mode. We need to develop a fuller coupling of human and computer, with attention to flexibility of input and output.

In some interactive situations, for example, all a computer or information appliance needs for input is a modulated signal that it can use to direct rendered data to the user's eyes, ears, and skin. Over 200 different transducers have been used to date with people having disabilities. In work with severely disabled children, David Warner, of Syracuse University, has developed a suite of sensors to let kids control computer displays with muscle twitches, eye movement, facial expressions, voice, or whatever signal they can manage to modulate. The results evoke profound emotion in patients, doctors, and observers and demonstrate the value of research on human capabilities to modulate energy in real time, the sensors that can transduce those energies, and effective ways to render the information affected by such interactions.

The state of the art in a range of technologies for communicating with systems is reviewed below. Also addressed are the device and expression layers of the model described in the previous section and summarized in Box 3.1. The choice of language—natural, restricted, or direct manipulation—influences but does not dictate the technologies discussed here. The exception is the subsection, "Natural Language Processing," which also encompasses the language layer of the model and discusses how choices along a spectrum from fully natural languages to relatively restricted languages influence the performance of various expression modes, particularly speech input.

Speech Synthesis

Text-to-speech systems, or speech synthesizers, take unrestricted text as input and produce a synthetic spoken version of that text as output. Most current commercial synthesizers exhibit a high degree of intelligibility, but none sound truly natural. The major barriers to naturalness are deficiencies of text normalization, intonational assignment, and synthesized voice quality. Female speech and children's speech are generally less acceptable than adult male synthetic speech, probably because they have been studied less (Roe and Wilpon, 1994).

In the course of transforming text into speech, all text-to-speech systems must do the following:

- Identify words and determine their pronunciations;
- Decide how such items as abbreviations and numbers should be pronounced (text normalization);
- Determine which words should be made prominent in the output, where pauses should be inserted, and what the overall shape of the intonational contour should be (intonation assignment);
- Compute appropriate durations and amplitudes for each of the words that will be synthesized;
- Determine how the overall intonational contour will be realized for the text to be synthesized;
- Identify which acoustic elements will be used to produce the spoken text (for concatenative synthesizers) or to retrieve the sequences of appropriate parameters to generate synthetic elements (for format synthesizers);[5] and
- Synthesize the utterance from the specifications and/or acoustic elements identified.

While most systems permit some form of user control over various parameters at many of these stages, to fine-tune system defaults, documentation and tools for such control are usually lacking, and most users lack the requisite background to produce satisfying results.

Particularly for concatenative synthesizers, it is difficult and time consuming to produce new voices, since each voice requires that a new set of concatenative units be recorded and segmented. While most research groups are developing tools in an attempt to automate this process (often by using automatic speech recognition systems to produce a first-pass segmentation), none have succeeded in eliminating the need for laborious hand correction of the database. There have also been efforts in recent years to automate the production of other components of synthesis, to facilitate the production of synthesizers in many languages from a single architecture.

We know that synthetic speech should sound better. It is not clear, exactly, how to decide what is better: More natural and more human-like? More intelligible? More intelligible at normal talking speeds or at high speeds? Speech is usually used for conversational modes of interaction. When speech is being used for presenting a Web page, for example, there is additional information that needs to be provided: Which words form links? Which words are italicized? How is this information presented most effectively? How should words be dealt with that have multiple different pronunciations in different parts of the country or to different individuals?

Speech Input/Recognition

The full integration of voice as an input medium, if achievable, could alleviate many of the known limitations of existing human-machine interfaces. People with poor or no literacy skills, people whose hands are busy, people suffering from cumulative trauma disorders associated with typing and pointing (or seeking to avoid them)—could all benefit from spoken communication with systems. While the capabilities envisioned in such a system are well beyond the state of the art in both speech recognition and language understanding at present, the technology has advanced sufficiently to allow very simple voice-based applications to emerge (see below).

Speech recognition research has made significant progress in the past 15 years (Roe and Wilpon, 1994; Cole and Hirschman, 1995; Cole et al., 1996). The gains have come from the convergence of several technologies: higher-accuracy continuous speech recognition based on better speech modeling techniques, better recognition search strategies that reduce the time needed for high-accuracy recognition, and increased power of audio-capable, off-the-shelf workstations. As a result of these advances, real-time, speaker-independent, continuous speech recognition, with vocabularies of a few thousand words, is now possible in software on regular workstations.

In terms of recognition performance, word error rates have dropped by more than an order of magnitude in the past decade and are expected to continue to fall with further research. These improvements have come about as a result of technical as well as programmatic innovations. Technically, there have been advances in two areas. First, a paradigm shift from rule-based to model-based methods has taken place. In particular, probabilistic hidden Markov models (HMM) have proven to be an excellent method of modeling phonemes in various contexts. This model-based paradigm, with its ability to estimate model parameters automatically from training data, has shown its power and versatility by applying the technology to various languages, using the same software. Second, the use of statistical grammars, which estimate the probability of two- and three-word sequences, have been instrumental in improving recognition accuracy, especially for large-vocabulary tasks. These simple statistical grammars have, so far, proven to be superior to traditional rule-based grammars for speech recognition purposes.

Programmatically, the collection and dissemination of standard, common training and test corpora worldwide, the sponsorship of common evaluations, and the dissemination at workshops of information about competing methods have all ensured very rapid progress in the technology. This programmatic approach was pioneered by the Defense Advanced Research Projects Agency (DARPA), which continues to sponsor common evaluations and initiated the establishment of the Linguistic Data Consortium, which has been in charge of the collection and dissemination of common corpora. A similar approach is now being taken in Europe.

Word error rates for speaker-independent continuous speech recognition vary a great deal, depending on the difficulty of the task: from less than 0.3 percent for connected digits, to 3 percent for a 2,500-word travel information task, to 10 percent for articles read from the *Wall Street Journal,* to 27 percent for transcription of broadcast news programs, to 40 percent for conversational speech over the telephone. Although word error rates in the laboratory can be quite small for some tasks, error rates can increase by a factor of four or more when the same systems are used in the field. This increase has various causes: heavy accents, ambient noise, different microphones, hesitations and restarts, and straying from the system's vocabulary.

Speech recognition has begun to enter the mainstream of everyday life, chiefly through telephone-based applications (Margulies, 1995). The most visible of these applications involve directory assistance services, such as the recognition of a few words (e.g., the digits and words such as "operator," "yes/no," "collect") or recognition of the names of cities in a particular area code. Speaker-independent recognition of over-the-phone digit strings (more difficult than single-digit recognition) has been deployed since 1990.[6] Other applications include voice-activated dialing (especially useful for cellular phones), personal assistant services (to manage one's telephone at work), and call router applications (where the caller says the person's full name instead of dialing). Other less prevalent applications include obtaining stock and mutual fund quotes by voice, simple banking services, and bill payment by telephone.[7]

Other operational applications of speech recognition include air traffic control training, dictation, and Internet access. Large-vocabulary dictation systems capable of recognizing discrete speech are available on the market and have been used for years. For continuous speech there are systems that are capable of recognizing a few thousand words in real time; at least one of these systems is now being marketed for the dictation of radiology reports. Systems for using voice for Internet access have recently been announced.

Simply making speech recognition available with machines, however, does not necessarily make it immediately useful; it will have to be interfaced properly with the other modalities so that it appears seamless to the user (Martin et al., 1996). (Several vendors have been shipping speech recognition capabilities with personal computers, but there is little evidence of wide usage.) Optimism for general use of speech technologies comes from the facts that performance levels are continuing to improve and that many applications do not require large vocabulary sizes. However, applications must be designed to take into account the fact that recognition errors will occur, either by allowing the user to correct errors or by designing additional error correction mechanisms, such as proper inclusion of human-machine dialogue capabilities. These include the ability to deal with issues such as how to phrase a system prompt, how to determine if a recognition error has occurred, and how to engage in conversational repair if such a determination is made. Other speech integration issues include habitability (the ability of a user to stay within the system's vocabulary most of the time), portability (the ease with which a speech recognition system can be ported to a new domain), and user experience (different users, depending on their experience, may require different types of interaction).

Looking into the future of the national information infrastructure (NII), speech recognition could have many applications, such as command and control, information access and retrieval, training and education, e-mail and memo dictation, and voice mail transcription. The current state of the art in speech recognition can support these applications at various levels of performance, some quite well (e.g., command and control) and others not well at all (e.g., voice mail transcription). Functions that perform information access, such as making an airline reservation, may require the use of a certain level of language understanding technology. The state of the art in that field only allows for the simplest of such applications at this time (see "Natural Language Processing" below).

Despite significant progress in speech recognition technology in the past decade, the fact remains that machine performance may still not be good enough for many applications. As a barometer of how much progress we may need for certain advanced applications, experiments have shown that human speech recognition performance is still at least an order of magnitude better than that of machines. One optimistic note, however, is that commercialization of the technology is proceeding very vigorously and is lagging the corresponding research capabilities by only a few years, so that any advances in the laboratory can be expected to appear on the market with a delay of only a few years.

Speaker Verification

A related but quite different technology is speaker verification. There has been much concern about private and secure communications over the Internet, especially for business information and financial transactions. Although encryption methods will be used more and more to protect digital data, it will still be necessary to make a more positive identification of customers for certain types of transactions. Speaker verification technology can be used to help provide additional security.

In an initial enrollment phase, each user is enrolled in a system by providing samples of his or her voice. System performance improves over time as the user supplies more voice samples. Using those voice samples, the system creates a model for the voice of each user. Then, when in operation, the system prompts the user to say a (random) phrase and, using the stored model of the user with the claimed identity, computes the likelihood that the speech came from that person. The user is then either accepted or rejected.

The performance of a speaker verification system is often measured by the Equal Error Rate (EER), which is the operating point in a system where the false rejection rate is equal to the false acceptance rate. In the laboratory, an EER of less than 0.5 percent can be achieved. Performance typically degrades to an EER of 2 to 4 percent in the field.

While the current state of the art may be sufficient for low-security applications, it would not, by itself, be adequate for high-security applications. However, if combined with other security measures, such as use of a PIN (Personal Identification Number), speaker verification can provide the added desired security for many applications of interest.

For users with physical disabilities who would like to have voice-only access to devices and systems, speaker verification could be of great benefit. It should be noted, however, that there are a significant number of people who are unable to speak clearly or reliably. For those people, alternate means of verification will be necessary if they are to use systems that rely on voice verification.

Alternate Keying/Typing Approaches: Strategies and Accelerators

As speech recognition becomes accurate and reliable, it will play a much larger role in future interface systems than it does today. It will not, however, ever completely replace or obsolete keyboard or keypad input to systems. Keying information into systems will continue to be a quiet, accurate, noise-immune (and, for some applications, faster) means of inputting data or commands. Furthermore, even as the performance of natural language understanding improves, free-form typing of natural language will remain a viable alternative to spoken input to such systems.

Today, keypads and keyboards range from systems that are as small as a wristwatch and are operated with a pen tip, to large, wall-sized keyboards operated with a light pen. Common keyboards are operated by using all 10 fingers, which push keys one at a time. Other keyboards have been developed that are chordic in nature and involve the pressing of multiple keys simultaneously. Many of these do not require the user to ever remove his or her hand.

In addition to pressing discrete keys, data can also be input using gestures. Finger spelling is one technique. Today, there are gloves that allow the wearer to spell out the desired characters using finger-spelling gestures. Techniques are also being explored that use cameras to take data via both finger spelling and sign language.

Handwriting is another common method for entering alpha-numeric data. There are techniques for recognizing letters formed in the standard way, as well as techniques (such as "Graffiti") that increase the accuracy of handwritten characters by having the user write with letters that are similar to, but different from, the standard characters people are familiar with.

To increase the rate of data entry, a number of abbreviation and prediction techniques have been developed. Abbreviation techniques allow an individual to use a smaller set of letters (which can resemble the target word, such as "abv" for "abbreviation," or be completely arbitrary such as "T1" for "please call home"). Prediction techniques look at what a person has typed and try to guess what the next word or words would be. Prediction techniques are less useful for people who can enter data quickly since the time spent looking at the system's guesses may slow one down to the point where it is faster to just enter the data. However, for individuals who have to enter data very slowly or for those who have difficulty spelling (e.g., because of a learning disability, cognitive impairment, second language), systems that can guess words correctly can significantly increase their rate of communication. If a system always guesses consistently (e.g., when "t" is typed, it guesses "the"; when "th" is typed, it guesses "there"), the user can begin using it for prediction techniques, but very quickly switch over to using it as abbreviation expansion (e.g., the user types "t" and then the confirm button because the user knows that the system will have guessed "the"). Ironically, systems that monitor the context and change their guesses to better match the context prevent an individual from getting into the faster abbreviation expansion mode. If systems can predict whole sentences or phrases, however, their utility would increase. This is usually possible only, however, for stereotypic communication (Vanderheiden et al., 1986).

In some aspects this area is one of the more thoroughly researched ones. However, it is not clear what the best techniques are for combining these input techniques for using keyboard input in connection with speech and other virtual reality and gestural input systems. What is the best way to use a minimalist keyboard with a voice response system either in a key-in/voice-out paradigm or to help handle error correction in voice recognition systems? Also, currently there are no good mechanisms for providing keyboard-based input when people are walking or moving about in virtual reality-like environments.

Natural Language Processing[8]

Natural language—spoken, written, or even signed—is at the heart of human communication. It is key to interaction between humans and the medium for much of the vast amount of information stored in books, newspapers, scientific journals, audio and video tapes, and now Web pages. As a means of interaction with computers, it requires no special training on the part of users, but it remains uncommon because of the difficulties in supporting it technically. To date, there have been a number of successful commercial applications of natural language processing, including grammar- and style-checking programs; text indexing and retrieval systems, particularly for the named-entity task[9] database query products that utilize natural language as input, which are being marketed for targeted applications; abstracting software (for summarizing blocks of text), which has been introduced commercially; and machine-aided translation programs. Access to the NII could be made easier and more productive if people could interact with a computer using natural language and if the computer could better retrieve, summarize, and understand the wealth of linguistic information at its disposal.[10]

Over the years, natural language processing (NLP) has focused primarily on three tasks: (1) database access, from typed or spoken queries; (2) information extraction, or the generation of formatted summaries from texts such as newspaper stories, military messages, and Web pages; and (3) machine translation of typed or spoken utterances from one language to another. The challenge of NLP is to build systems that can distinguish in the input language as many significantly different meanings as are relevant to the applications of interest; to interpret correctly as large a variety of linguistic expressions of these meanings as would naturally occur; and to do so in as many task settings as possible, with the computational resources available.

Until recently, most NLP systems shared the same gross architecture, roughly analogous to that of programming language compilers: a syntactic analyzer, or parser, to identify the lexical category of the words of the input sentence[11] and their hierarchical organization into phrases and clauses; a semantic analyzer, to construct a representation of the meaning of the input sentence, generally independent of the specific task or application domain; and, finally, a domain- and task-specific mapping from the semantic interpretation to a representation suitable to the task at hand, such as a database query for query systems, a filled template for information extraction systems, or an input into a language generation module for a machine translation system.[12] In the current practice, several hundred rules may need to be hand-coded for a new application, even in a limited domain.[13]

In the early 1990s, NLP took several new directions, largely at the instigation of a succession of DARPA program managers. First, after years of working in parallel, researchers in speech recognition and NLP were encouraged to construct integrated speech understanding systems, for which the chosen task was to answer spoken queries to databases (e.g., of air travel information). Second, information extraction was made a major task of interest. Finally, the performance of NLP and speech understanding systems was to be systematically evaluated.

It was thus necessary to reject the then-prevailing assumption that the NLP system needed to understand only syntactically and semantically well-formed utterances or that the entire content of an utterance or text needed to be understood. Spoken language systems had to deal with the inevitable recognition errors of even the best speech recognition systems as well as queries such as "Boston San Francisco after 8 a.m." and "I'd like to go to Boston, ah, to Atlanta, tomorrow." Systems were designed that tolerated not understanding some parts of the utterance, combining partial analyses of other parts, and explicitly correcting certain forms of disfluencies. Even with such difficult input, it now became possible to actually improve the accuracy of even the best speech recognition programs by applying syntactic and semantic constraints, at least in limited domains.

Systematic evaluation of NLP systems is not possible without the collection of large corpora of linguistic data, both raw and annotated, such as with correct transcriptions and correct answers to spoken queries.[14] Although the rule-based paradigm that has dominated computational linguistics so far has produced only a few large-scale systems that have been reused over several different projects (e.g., the CORE Language Engine at SRI), it has been difficult to share large grammars, lexicons, and semantic rules across sites, making it difficult to build on previous results.

The domain specificity of rule-based NLP systems suggests that it would be attractive to be able to automatically train an NLP system, as is done with the hidden Markov models used in speech recognition. Significant effort is being devoted to this direction. The results are promising but still not comparable to what is routinely achievable with rule-based systems. Some of the problems are the amount of training data required, the difficulty of obtaining such data in a wide range of domains, and the cost of annotating the input data with the correct task-specific semantic representation. The annotation problem is exacerbated by the fact that it is much more difficult to get human annotators to agree on correct semantic annotations than on transcriptions of spoken utterances.

Many researchers believe that for some time yet the most effective strategy for the development of NLP systems in new domains will be hybrid systems, based on a core of hand-coded rules but tuned to a domain by automatic training methods. Domain-specific corpora can be used, for example, to assign probabilities to the rules, providing a mechanism by which probabilities can be assigned to rule-based interpretations. This approach, used by most of the currently best-performing systems, can be seen as a way of adapting a set of general rules to a particular domain. Farther down the road are ways of circumventing the data and annotation requirements of fully automatic training methods by dynamically adapting to one domain a system developed in another.

NLP systems vary widely, from those that perform full and deep understanding of an utterance in narrowly construed domains to those that perform partial and shallow understanding of very wide domains. Query systems tend to be at the full and deep understanding end, and information extraction systems at the partial and shallow end.

Several systems have been implemented to answer queries in the DARPA-sponsored Airline Travel Information Service task (DARPA, 1995b), where the user asks information about flights and schedules using speech. The utterance error rate, measured as the percentage of queries for which the system gives the wrong answer, is currently about 6 percent for spoken input and 4 percent for the corresponding text input.

The standards for evaluation of information extraction systems are set by the DARPA-sponsored Message Understanding Conferences (MUCs). For the "named entity" application, where the system must find all named organizations, locations, persons, dates, times, monetary amounts, and percentages, the error rates are below 5 percent. For the "scenario template" application, where the system extracts complex relationships in well-defined domains (such as joint ventures) in an open source (such as the *Wall Street Journal*), the error rate for finding the correct elements of the templates is about 45 percent.

In the area of machine translation, the most significant advances continue to occur in Europe. Recent work in the United States using texts written with an eye toward translation also show promise (Carbonell, 1992). Several speech-to-speech translation systems in limited domains, combining speech understanding, machine translation, and speech generation, have been demonstrated.

Still in their infancy are systems with which a human can conduct a coherent dialogue in service of a complex and extended task. Early examples include the TRAINS system (in use at the University of Rochester), which allows a human to control a system that plans the transport of materials, and the CommandTalk system, which provides a spoken interface to a large military simulator. The approach of Sadek and co-workers, at France Telecom (Bretier and Sadek, 1996; Bretier et al., 1995), offers compelling evidence that spoken language systems can have sophisticated models of dialogue and can benefit from them. Future systems will need to allow for a variety of speech acts (e.g., requests, assertions, questions, rejections) and contain dialogue models that enable the establishment of correlations between occurrence of phrases used to refer to the same entities and events in the discourse. Coreference resolution has been the subject of much research, and systems using it are being evaluated in the MUC benchmarks. Also, there is compelling evidence that spoken language systems can have sophisticated models of dialogue and can benefit from them.

Gesture Recognition

Gesture input can come in many forms from a variety of devices (e.g., mouse, pen, data glove). Its role is to convey information (e.g., identify, make reference to, explain, shift focus) in a manner similar to the other more studied forms of language. Gesture replaces the click of the mouse—the mouse's only word—with a wide range of commands. It eliminates the myriad objects on the screen intended to let the user communicate his or her desires. Rather than having to find the word, duplicate, and click on it, the user can make simpler movements involving only the hand. For example, at the workshop, Bruce Tognazzini's "Starfire" video showed a user separating her fingers to indicate a desire to duplicate an object—leave it here and move it. Gesture can relieve problems of repetitive stresss by varying the user's movements, thereby lowering the repetition of any particular action.

Rimé and Schiaratura (1991) characterize several classes of gesture. Symbolic gestures are conventional, context-independent, and typically unambiguous expressions (e.g., "OK" or peace sign). In contrast, deictic gestures are pointers to entities, analogous to natural language deixis (e.g., "this not that"). Iconic gestures are used to display objects, spatial relations, and actions (e.g., illustrating the orientation of two cars at an accident). Finally, pantomimic gestures display an invisible object or tool (e.g., making a fist and moving to indicate a hammer). Gestural languages exist as well. These include sign languages and signing systems for use in environments where alternative communication is difficult. Early experience with glove interfaces indicates that some users have difficulty remembering the gesture equivalents to commands (Herndon et al., 1994).

Gesture recognition plays a role in immersive environments such as the virtual reality or simulation environments. It also should find widespread application in helping to give directions to computers or computerized agents. Pointing and gesturing with the hand or with other objects are natural communication behaviors and will likely form an important component in a natural intuitive interface. In addition, for individuals who are deaf and who communicate primarily through gestural languages (such as American Sign Language), machine recognition of American Sign Language gestures is the equivalent of speech recognition for those of us who can speak.

Machine Vision and Passive Input

Machine vision is likely to play a number of roles in future interface systems. Primary roles are likely to be:

- Data input (including text, graphics, movement)
- Context recognition (as discussed above)
- Gesture recognition (particularly in graphic and virtual reality environments)
- Artificial sight for people with visual impairments

Experience with text and image recognition provides a number of insights relevant to future interface development, especially in the context of aiding individuals with physical disabilities. In particular, systems that are difficult to use by blind people would pose the same problems to people who can see but who are trying to access information aurally because their vision is otherwise occupied. Similar problems may arise as well for intelligent agents.

Text Recognition

Today, there are powerful tools for turning images of text into electronic text (such as ASCII). Optical character recognition (OCR) is quite good and is improving daily. Driven by a desire to turn warehouses of printed documents into electronic searchable form, companies have been and are making steady advances. Some OCR programs will convert programs into electronic text that is compatible with particular word processing packages, preserving the text layout, emphasis, font, and so on. The problem with OCR is that it is not 100 percent accurate. When it makes a mistake, however, it is not usually a character anymore (since word look-up is used to improve accuracy). As a result, when an error is made, it is often a legal (but wrong) word. Thus, it is often impossible to look at a document and figure out exactly what it did say—some sentences may not be accurate (or even make sense). One company gets around this by pasting a picture of any words the system is not sure about into the text where the unknown word would go. This works well for sighted persons, allows human editors to easily fix the mistakes, and preserves the image for later processing by a more powerful image recognizer. It does not help blind users much except that they are not misled by a wrong word and can ask a sighted person for help if they cannot figure something out. (Most helpful would be to have an OCR system include its guess as to the letters of a word in question as hidden text, which a person who is blind could call up to assist in guessing the word.) Highly stylized or embellished characters or words are not recognizable. Text that is wrapped around, tied in knots, or arranged on the page or laid out in an unusual way may be difficult to interpret even if available in electronic text. This is a separate problem from image recognition, though.

Image Recognition

Despite great strides by the military, weather, intelligence, and other communities, image interpretation remains quite specialized and focused on looking for particular features. The ability to identify and describe arbitrary images is still beyond us. However, advances in artificial intelligence, neural networks, and image processing in combination with large data banks of image information may make it possible in the future to provide verbal interpretation or description for many types of information. A major impetus comes from the desire to make image information searchable by computers. The combination of a tactile representation with feature or texture information presented aurally may provide the best early access to graphic information by users who are blind or cannot use their sight.

Some images, such as pie charts and line graphs, can be recognized easily and turned into raw data or a text description. Standard software has been available for some time that will take a scanned image of a chart and provide a spreadsheet of the data represented in the chart. Other images, such as electronic schematic diagrams, could be recognized but are difficult to describe. A house plan illustrates the kind of diagram that may be describable in general terms and would benefit from combining a verbal description with a tactile representation for those who cannot see to deal with this type of information.

Visual Displays

Visual display progress begins with the screen design (graphics, layouts, icons, metaphors, widget sets, animation, color, fisheye views, overviews, zooming) and other aspects of how information is visualized. The human eye can see far more than current computer displays can show. The bandwidth of our visual channel is many orders of magnitude greater than other senses: ~1 gigabit/second. It has a dynamic range of 10^{13} to 1 (10 trillion to 1). No human-made sensor or graphics display has this dynamic range. The eye/brain can detect very small displacements at very low rates of motion and sees change up to a rate of about 50 times a second. The eye has a very focused view that is optimized for perceiving movement. Humans cannot see clearly outside an ~5-degree cone of foveal vision and cannot see behind them.

State-of-the-art visualization systems (as of 1996) can create images of approximately 4,000 polygons complexity at 50 Hz per eye. Modern graphics engines also filter the image to remove sampling artifacts on polygon edges and, more importantly, textures. Partial transparency is also possible, which allows fog and atmospheric contrast attenuation in a natural-looking way. Occlusion (called "hidden surface removal" in graphics) is provided, as is perspective transformation of vertices. Smooth shading in hardware is also common now.

Thus, the images look rather good in real time, although the scene complexity is limited to several thousand polygons and the resolution to 1,280 × 1,024. Typical computer-aided design constructions or animated graphics for television commercials involve scenes with millions of polygons; these are not rendered in real time. Magazine illustrations are rendered at resolutions in excess of 4,000 × 3,000. Thus, the imagery used in real-time systems is portrayed at rather less than optimal resolution, often much less actually than the effective visual acuity required to drive a car. In addition, there are better ways of rendering scenes, as when the physics of light is more accurately simulated, but these techniques are not currently achievable in real time. A six-order-of-magnitude increase in computer speed and graphics generation would be easy to absorb; a teraflop personal computer would be rather desirable, therefore, but is probably 10 years off.

Visual Input/Output Hardware

The computer industry provides a range of display devices, from small embedded liquid-crystal displays (LCDs) in personal digital assistants (PDAs) and navigational devices to large cathode-ray tubes (CRTs) and projectors. Clearly, desirable goals are lower cost, power consumption, latency, weight, and both much larger and much smaller screens. Current commercial CRTs achieve up to $2,048 \times 2,048$ pixels at great cost. Projectors can do ~$1,900 \times 1,200$ displays. It is possible to tesselate projectors at will to achieve arbitrarily higher resolution (Woodward, 1993) and/or brightness (e.g., video walls shown at trade shows and conventions). Screens with > 5,000-pixel resolution are desirable. Durability could be improved, especially for portable units.[15] Some increase in the capability of television sets to handle computer output, which may be furthered by recent industry-based standards negotiations for advanced television (sometimes referred to as high-definition television), is expected to help lower costs.[16] How, when, and where to trade off the generality of personal computers against other qualities that may inhere in more specialized or cheaper devices is an issue for which there may be no one answer.

Hollywood and science fiction have described most of the conceivable, highly futuristic display devices—direct retinal projection, direct cerebral input, Holodecks, and so on. Less futuristic displays still have a long way to go to enable natural-appearing virtual reality (VR). Liquid crystal displays do not have the resolution and low weight needed for acceptable head-mounted displays to be built; users of currently available head-mounted displays are effectively legally blind given the lack of acuity offered. Projected VR displays are usable, although they are large and are not portable.

The acceptance of VR is also hindered by the extreme cost of the high-end graphics engines required to render realistic scenes in real time, the enormous computing power needed to simulate meaningful situations, and the nonlinearity and/or short range of tracking devices. Given that the powerful graphics hardware in the $200 Nintendo 64 game is just incremental steps from supporting the stereo graphics needed for VR, it is clear that the barriers are now in building consumer-level tracking gear and some kind of rugged stereo glasses, at least in the home game context. Once these barriers are overcome, VR will be open for wider application.

High-resolution visual input devices are becoming available to non-professionals, allowing them to produce their own visual content. Digital snapshot cameras and scanners, for example, have become available at high-end consumer levels. These devices, while costly, are reasonable in quality and are a great aid to people creating visual materials for the NII.[17] Compositing and nonlinear editing software assist greatly as well. Similarly, two-dimensional illustration and three-dimensional animation software make extraordinary graphics achievable by the motivated and talented citizen. The cost of such software will continue to come down as the market widens, and the availability of more memory, processing, graphics power, and disk space will make results more achievable and usable.

As a future goal that defines a conceptual outer limit for input and output, one might choose the Holodeck from the movie *Star Trek*, a device that apparently stores and replays the molecular reconstruction information from the transporter that beams people up and down. In *The Physics of Star Trek*, physicist Lawrence Krauss (1995, pp. 76-77) works out the information needed to store the molecular dynamics of a single human body: 10^{31} bytes, some 10^{16} times the storage needed for all the books ever written. Krauss points out the other difficulties in transporter/Holodeck reconstruction as well.

Auditory Displays

The ear collects sound waves and encodes the spatial characteristics of the sound source into temporal and spectral attributes. Intensity difference and temporal/phase difference in sound reaching the two ears provide mechanisms for horizontal (left to right) sound localization. The ear gets information from the whole space via movement in time.

Hearing individual components of sound requires frequency identification. The ear acts such as a series of narrowly tuned filters. Sound cues can be used to catch attention with localization, indicate near or far positions with reverberation, indicate collisions and other events, and even portray abstract events such as change over time. Low-frequency sound can vibrate the user's body to somewhat simulate physical displacement.

Speakers and headphones as output devices for synthesized sound match the ears well, unlike the case with visual displays. However, understanding which sounds to create as part of the human-computer interface is much less well understood than for the visual case.

About 50 million instructions per second are required for each synthesized sound source. Computing reverberation off six surfaces for four sound sources might easily require a billion-instruction-per-second computer, one that is within today's range but is rarely dedicated to audio synthesis in practice. Audio sampling and playback are far simpler and are most often used for primitive cues such as beacons and alarms.

Thus, the barriers to good matching to human hearing have to do with computing the right sound and getting it to each ear in a properly weighted way. Although in many ways producing sound by computer is simpler than displaying imagery, many orders of magnitude more research and development have been devoted to graphics than sound synthesis.

Haptic and Tactile Displays[18]

Human touch is achieved by the parallel operation of many sensor systems in the body (Kandel and Schwartz, 1981). The hand alone has 19 bones, 19 joints, and 20 muscles with 22 degrees of freedom and many classes of receptors and nerve endings in the joints, skin, tendons, and muscles. The hand can squeeze, stroke, grasp, and press; it can also feel texture, shape, softness, and temperature.

The fingerpad has hairless ridged skin enclosing soft tissues made of fat in a semiliquid state. Fingers can glide over a surface without losing contact or grab an object to manipulate it. Computed output and input of human touch (called "haptics") is currently very primitive compared to graphics and sound. Haptic tasks are of two types: exploration and manipulation. Exploration involves the extraction of object properties such as shape and surface texture, mass, and solidity. Manipulation concerns modification of the environment, from watch repair to using a sledge hammer.

Kinesthetic information (e.g., limb posture, finger position), conveyed by receptors in the tendons, and muscles and neural signals from motor commands communicate a sense of position. Joint rotations of a fraction of a degree can be perceived. Other nerve endings signal skin temperature, mechanical and thermal pain, chemical pain, and itch.

Responses range from fast spinal reflex to slow deliberate conscious action. Experiments on lifting objects show that slipping is counteracted in 70 milliseconds. Humans can perceive a 2-micrometer-high single dot on a glass plate, a 6-micrometer-high grating, using different types of receptors (Kalawsky, 1993). Tactile and kinesthetic perception extends into the kilohertz range (Shimoga, 1993). Tactile interfaces aim to reproduce sensations arising from contact with textures and edges but do not support the ability to modify the underlying model.

Haptic interfaces are high-performance mechanical devices that support bidirectional input and output of displacement and forces. They measure positions, contact forces, and time derivatives and output new forces and positions (Burdea, 1996). Output to the skin can be point, multipoint, patterned, and time-varying. Consider David Warner, who makes his rounds in a "cyberwear" buzz suit that captures information from his patients' monitors, communicating it with bar charts tingling his arms, pulse rates sent down to his fingertips, and test results whispered in his ears, yet allowing him to maintain critical eye contact with his patients (http://www.pulsar.org).

There are many parallels and differences between haptics and visual (computer graphics) interfaces. The history of computing technology over the past 30 to 40 years is dominated by the exponential growth in computing power enabled by semiconductor technology. Most of this new computing power has supported enriched high-bandwidth user interfaces. Haptics is a sensory/motor interaction modality that is just now being exploited in the quest for seamless interaction with computers. Haptics can be qualitatively different from graphics and audio input/ output because it is bidirectional. The computer model both delivers information to the human and is modified by the human during the haptic interaction. Another way to look at this difference is to note that, unlike graphics or audio output, physical energy flows in both directions between the user and the computer through a haptic display device.

In 1996 three distinct market segments emerged for haptic technology: low-end (2 degrees of freedom (DOF), entertainment); mid-range (3 DOF, visualization and training); and high-end (6 DOF, advanced computer-aided engineering). The lesson of video games has been to optimize for real-time feedback and feel. The joysticks or other interfaces for video games are very carefully handled so that they feel continuous. The obviously cheap joystick on the Nintendo 64 game is very smooth, such that a 2 year old has no problem with it. Such smoothness is necessary to be a good extension of a person's hand motion, since halting response changes the dynamics, causing one to overcompensate, slow down, etc.

A video game joystick with haptic feedback, the "Force FX," is now on the market from CH Products (Vista, Calif.) using technology licensed from Immersion Corp. It is currently supported by about 10 video game software vendors. Other joystick vendors are readying haptic feedback joysticks for this low-priced, high-volume market. In April 1996, MicroSoft bought Exos, Inc. (Cambridge, Mass.) to acquire its haptic interaction software interface.

Haptic interaction will play a major role in all simulation-based training involving manual skill (Buttolo et al., 1995). For example, force feedback devices for surgical training are already in the initial stages of commercialization by such companies as Boston Dynamics (Cambridge, Mass.), Immersion Corp. (Palo Alto, Calif.), SensAble Devices (Cambridge, Mass.), and HT Medical (Rockville, Md.).

Advanced CAD users at major industrial corporations such as Boeing

(McNeely, 1993) and Ford (Buttolo et al., 1995) are actively funding internal and external research and development in haptic technologies to solve critical bottlenecks they have identified in their computer-aided product development processes.

These are the first signs of a new and broad-based high-technology industry with great potential for U.S. leadership. Research (as discussed below) is necessary to foster and accelerate the development of these and other emerging areas into full-fledged industries.

A number of science and technology issues arise in the haptics and tactile display arena. Haptics is attracting the attention of a growing number of researchers because of the many fascinating problems that must be solved to realize the vision of a rich set of haptic-enabled applications. Because haptic interaction intimately involves high-performance computing, advanced mechanical engineering, and human psychophysics and biomechanics, there are pressing needs for interdisciplinary collaborations as well as basic disciplinary advances. These key areas include the following:

• *Better understanding of the biomechanics of human interaction with haptic displays.* For example, stability of the haptic interaction goes beyond the traditional control analysis to include simulated geometry and nonlinear time-varying properties of human biomechanics.

• *Faster algorithms for rendering geometric models into haptic input/output maps.* Although many ideas can be adapted from computer graphics, haptic devices require at least 1,000-Hz update rates and a latency of no more than 1 millisecond for stability and performance. Thus, the bar is raised for the definition of "real-time" performance for algorithms such as collision detection, shading, and dynamic multibody simulation.

• *Advanced design of mechanisms for haptic interactions.* Real haptic interaction uses all of the degrees of freedom of the human hand and arm (as many as 29; see above). The most advanced haptic devices have 6 or 7 degrees of freedom for the whole arm/hand. To provide high-quality haptic interaction over many degrees of freedom will continuously create many research challenges in mechanism design, actuator design, and control over many years to come.

Some of the applications of haptics that are practical today may seem arcane and specialized. This was also true for the first applications of computer graphics in the 1960s. Emerging applications today are the ones with the most urgent need for haptic interaction. Below are some examples of what may become possible:

• *1999*: A medical student is practicing the administration of spinal epidural anesthesia for the first time. She must insert the needle by feel (without visual guidance) through the skin, fat, muscle, and spinal dura, and inject the anesthetic without visual guidance. Like all physicians trained before this year, her instructor learned the procedure on actual human patients. Now, she is using a haptic display device hidden inside a plastic model of the human back. The device simulates the distinct feel of each of these tissues as well as the hard bones that she must avoid with the needle. After a few sessions with the simulator and a quantitative evaluation of her physical proficiency, she graduates to her first real patient with confidence and skill.

* *2000:* An automotive design engineer wants to verify that an oil filter that he knows will require routine maintenance can be removed from a crowded engine compartment without disassembly of the radiator, transmission, and so forth. He brings the complete engine compartment model up on the graphics screen and clicks the oil filter to link it to the six-axis haptic display device on his desk next to the workstation. Holding the haptic device, he removes the oil filter, feeling collisions with nearby engine objects. He finds that the filter cannot be removed because coolant hoses block the way. The engine compartment is thus redesigned early in the design process, saving hundreds of thousands of dollars.

The first of these examples is technically possible today; the second is not. There are critical computational and mechatronic challenges that will be crucial to successful implementation of ever-more realistic haptic interfaces.

Because haptics is such a basic human interaction mode for so many activities, there is little doubt that, as the technology matures, new and unforeseen applications and a substantial new industry will develop to give people the ability to physically interact with computational models. Once user interfaces are as responsive as musical instruments, for example, virtuosity is more achievable. As in music, there will always be a phase appropriate to contemplation (such as composing/programming) and a phase for playing/exploring. The consumer will do more of the latter, of course. Better feedback continuously delivered appears to take less prediction. Being able to predict is what expertise is mostly about in a technical/scientific world, and we want systems to be usable by nonexperts, hence the need for real-time interactions with as much multisensory realism as is helpful in each circumstance. Research is necessary now to provide the intellectual capital upon that such an industry can be based.

Tactile Displays for Low- or No-Vision Environments or Users

Tactile displays can help add realism to multisensory virtual reality environments. For people who are blind, however, tactile displays are much more important for the provision of information that would be provided visually to those who can see. For people who are deaf and blind and who cannot use auditory displays or synthetic speech, it is the principal display form.

Vibration has been used for adding realism to movies and virtual reality environments and also as a signaling technique for people with hearing impairments. It can be used for alarm clocks or doorbells, but is limited in the information it can present even when different frequencies are used for different signals. Vibration can also be used effectively in combination with other tactile displays to provide supplemental information. For example, vibratory information can be used in combination with Braille to indicate text that is highlighted, italicized, or underlined, or to indicate text that is a hyperlink on a hypertext page.

Vibrotactile displays provide a higher-bandwidth channel. With a vibrotactile display, small pins are vibrated up and down to stimulate tactile sensors. The most widespread use of this technique is the Optacon (OPtical to TActile CONverter), which has 144 pins (6 × 24) in its array (100 pins on the Optacon II). The tactile array is usually used in conjunction with a small handheld camera but can also be connected directly to a computer to provide a tactile image around a mouse or other pointing device on the screen.

Electrocutaneous displays have also been explored as a way to create solid-state tactile arrays. Arrays have been constructed for use on the abdomen, back, forearm, and, most recently, the fingertip. Resolution for these displays is much lower than for vibrotactile displays.

Raised-line drawings have long been "king of the hill" for displaying of tactile information. The principal problem has been an inexpensive and fast way to generate them "on the fly." Wax jet printers showed the greatest potential (especially for high resolution), but none are currently available. For lower resolution, there is a paper onto which one can photocopy and then process with heat, to cause it to swell wherever there are black lines (although at a much lower resolution). Printers that create embossed Braille pages can also be programmed to create tactile images that consist of raised dots. The resolution of these is lower still (the best having a resolution of about 12 dots per inch), but the raised-dot form of the graphics actually has some advantages for tactile perception.

Braille is a system for representing alphanumeric characters tactiley. The system consists of six dots in a two wide by three high pattern. To do the full ASCII character set, an eight-pin braille (two by four) was developed. Braille is most commonly thought of as being printed or embossed, where paper is punched upward to form Braille cells or characters as raised dots on the page.[19] There are also dynamic Braille displays, where cells having (typically) 8 pins that can be raised or lowered independently are arranged in lines of 12 to 20 or more cells on small portable devices and 20 to 40 cells on desktop displays. A few 80-cell displays have been developed, but they are quite expensive and large. By raising or lowering the pins, a line of Braille can be dynamically changed, rather like a single line of text.

Virtual Page Displays.   Because of the difficulties creating full-page tactile displays, a number of people have tried techniques to create a "virtual" full-page display. One example was the Systems 3 prototype, where an Optacon tactile array was placed on a mouse-like puck on a graphics tablet. As the person moved the puck around on the tablet, he or she felt a vibrating image of the screen that corresponded to that location on the tablet. The same technique has been tried with a dynamic Braille display. The resolution, of course, is much lower. In neither case did the tactile recognition approach that of raised lines.

Full-Page Displays.   Some attempts have been made to create full-page Braille-resolution displays. The greatest difficulty has been in trying to create something with that many moving parts that is still reliable and inexpensive. More recently, some interesting strategies using ferro-electric liquids and other materials have been tried. In each case the objective was to create a system that involves the minimum number of moving parts and yet provides a very high-resolution tactile display.

Ideal Displays.   A dream of the blindness community has been the development of a large plate of hard material that would provide a high-resolution solid-state tactile display. It would be addressable like a liquid-crystal display, with instant response, very high resolution, and variable height. It would be low cost, lightweight, and rugged. Finally, it would be best if it could easily track the position of fingers on the display, so that the tactile display could be easily coupled with voice and other audio to allow parallel presentation of tactile and auditory information for the area of the display currently being touched.

An even better solution, both for blind people and for virtual reality applications, would be a glove that somehow provided both full tactile sensation over the palm and fingertips and force feedback. Elements of this have been demonstrated, but nothing approaching full tactile sensation or any free-field force feedback.

INTEGRATING INPUT/OUTPUT TECHNOLOGIES

Filling out the range of technologies for people to communicate with systems—filling in the research and development gaps in the preceding section—is only part of the input/output requirement for ECIs. Integration of these technologies into systems that use multiple communications modalities simultaneously—multimodal systems—can improve people's performance. (These ideas are discussed in more detail in Chapter 6.) Integration can also ensure that at least one mechanism is available for every person and situation, independent of temporary and/or permanent constraints on their physical and cognitive abilities. Virtual reality involves the integration of multiple input and output technologies into an immersive experience that, ideally, will permit people to interact with systems as naturally as they do with real-world places and objects.

Multimodal Interfaces

People effortlessly integrate information gathered across modalities during conversational interactions. Facial cues and gestures are combined with speech and situational cues, such as objects and events in the environment, to communicate meaning. Almost 100 years of research in experimental psychology attests to our remarkable abilities to bring all knowledge to bear during human communication.

The ability to integrate information across modalities is essential for accurate and robust comprehension of language by machines and to enable machines to communicate effectively with people. In noisy environments, when speech is difficult to understand, facial cues provide both redundant and complementary information that dramatically improves recognition performance over either modality alone. To improve recognition in noisy environments, researchers must discover effective procedures to recognize and combine speech and facial cues. Similarly, textual information may be transmitted more effectively under some conditions by turning the text into natural-sounding speech, produced by an animated "talking head" with appropriate facial movements. While a great deal of excellent research is being undertaken in the laboratory, research in this area has not yet reached the stage where commercial applications have appeared, and fundamental problems remain to be solved. In particular, basic research is needed into the science of understanding how humans use multiple modalities.

Ability-Independent Interfaces

Standard mass-market products are still largely designed with single interfaces (e.g., they are designed to work with a keyboard (only) or they are designed to work with a touchscreen (only)). There are systems designed to work with keyboard or mouse, and some cross-modality efforts have been made (e.g., systems that support both keyboard and speech input). Usually, though, these multiple input systems are accomplished by having a second input technique simulate input on the first—for example, having the speech interface create simulated keystrokes or mouse clicks rather than having the systems designed from the beginning to accommodate alternate interface modalities. This approach is usually the result of companies that decide to add voice or pen support (or other input technique support) to their applications after it has been architected. This generates both compatibility problems and very complicated user configuration and programming problems.

A similar problem exists with media, materials, databases, or educational programs designed to be used in a visual-only presentation format. Companies (and users) run into problems when the materials need to be presented aurally. For example, systems designed for visual viewing often need to be reengineered if the data are going to be presented over a phone-based information system.

The area where the greatest cross-modality interface research has been carried out has been the disability access area. Strategies for creating audio-visual materials that also include time-synchronized text (e.g., captions) as well as audio descriptions of the visual information have been developed. Interestingly, although closed captioning was added to television sets for people who are deaf, it is used much more in noisy bars, by people learning to read a new language, by children, and by people who have muted their television sets. The captions are also useful for institutions wishing to index or search audiovisual files, and they allow "agent" software to comprehend and work with the audio materials.

In the area of public information systems, such as public kiosks, interfaces are now being developed that are flexible enough to accommodate individuals with an extremely wide range of type, degree, and combination of disabilities. These systems are set up so that the standard touchscreen interface supports variations that allow individuals with different disabilities to use them. Extremely wide variation in human sensory motor abilities can be accommodated without changing the user interface for people without disabilities.

For example, by providing a "touch and hear" feature, a kiosk can be made usable by individuals who cannot read or by those who have low vision. Holding down a switch would cause the touchscreen to become inactive (e.g., touching buttons on the screen would cause no action). However, any buttons or text that were touched would be read aloud to the user. Releasing the switch would reactivate the screen. A "touch and confirm" mode would allow individuals with moderate to severe physical disabilities to use the kiosk by having it accept only input that is followed by a confirmation. An option that provides a listing of the items (e.g., text and buttons) down the left edge of the screen can be combined with the talking "touch and confirm" mode to allow individuals who are completely blind to easily and accurately use a kiosk. The use of captions for audiovisual materials on kiosks can allow individuals who have hearing impairments to access a kiosk (as well as anyone else trying to use a kiosk in a noisy mall). Finally, by sending the information on the pop-up list out through the computer's Infrared Data Association (IrDA) port, it is possible for individuals who are completely paralyzed or deaf and blind to access and use a kiosk via their personal assistive technologies.

All of these features can be added to a standard multimedia touch-screen kiosk without adding any hardware beyond a single switch and without altering the interface experienced by individuals who do not have disabilities. By adding interface enhancements such as these, it is possible to create a single public kiosk that looks and operates like any traditional touchscreen kiosk but is also accessible and usable by individuals who cannot read, who have low vision, who are blind, who are hearing impaired, who are deaf, who have physical disabilities, who are paralyzed, or who are deaf and blind. Kiosks with flexible user-configurable interfaces have been distributed in Minnesota (including the Mall of America), Washington State, and other states.

These and similar techniques have been implemented in other environments as well. Since the 1980s, Apple Computer has had options built into its human interface to make it more useful to people with functional limitations (look in any Macintosh control panel for Easy Access). IBM has them built into its hardware and software (AccessDos and OS/2), and UNIX has both options in its human interface and modifications in its underlying structure to support connection to specialized interfaces. Windows 95 has over a dozen adjustments and variations built into its human interface to allow it to be used by individuals with a very wide range of disabilities or environmental limitations, including those with difficulty hearing, seeing, physically operating a keyboard, and operating a mouse from the keyboard.

As we move into more immersive environments and environments that are utilizing a greater percentage of an individual's different sensory and motor systems simultaneously (e.g., VR, multimedia), identifying and developing cross-modal interface techniques will become increasingly challenging. In the techniques developed to date, however, building interfaces that allow for cross-modality interaction have generally made for more robust and flexible interfaces and systems that can better adapt to new interface technologies as they emerge (e.g., allowing WIMP (windows, icons, menus, pointers) systems to accommodate a verbal interface).

Virtual Reality and Artificial Immersive Environments

The past 10 years has brought nearly a complete changeover from command line to WIMP interfaces as the dominant every-citizen's connection to computation. This happened because hardware (memory, display chips) became cheap enough to be engineered into every product. It also happened because the first step to the office of the future required replacing the typewriter with the laser printer, an event neatly handled with the "desktop metaphor" and word processing/spreadsheet software. However, the NII implies a complex of technologies relevant to far more than office work, which is a practical reason not to expect it to be accessed by every citizen with mice and windows interfaces alone (van Dam, 1997).[20] Another transition is now at hand, one that potentially liberates the interface from the desktop, one that presents information more like objects in a shopping mall than printing on a pile of paper. The virtual shopping mall (or museum) is the next likely application metaphor; the parking lots will be unneeded, of course, as will attention to the laws of physics when inappropriate, but as in three-dimensional user interfaces generally, the metaphor can help in teaching users how to operate in a synthetic environment. Such a metaphor helps also to avoid the constraints that may derive from metaphors linked to one class of activity (e.g., desks and white-collar work) at a time when researchers should think about the needs and challenges posed by all kinds of people.

At SIGGRAPH 96, the major conference for computer graphics and interactive techniques, full-quality, real-time, interactive, three-dimensional, textured flight simulation was presented as the next desirable feature in every product. This visual capability, usually augmented with sound and multidimensional interactive controls, presents information as landscapes and friendly/hostile objects with which the user interacts at high speed. Visual representations of users, known as avatars, are one trend that has been recognized in the popular press. Typing is not usually required or desirable. The world portrayed is spatially three dimensional and it continues way beyond the boundaries of the display device. In this context, input and output devices with more than 2 degrees of freedom are being developed to support true direct manipulation of objects, as opposed to the indirect control provided by two- and three-dimensional widgets, and user interfaces appear to require support for many degrees of freedom,[21] higher-bandwidth input and output, real-time response, continuous response and feedback, probabalistic input, and multiple simultaneous input and output streams from multiple users (Herndon et al., 1994). Note that virtual reality also expands on the challenges posed by speech synthesis to include synthesis of arbitrary sounds, a problem that is hampered by the lack of available sound samples analogous to the voice samples used in voice synthesis.

Economic factors will pace the broader accessibility of technologies that are currently priced out of the reach of every citizen, such as high-end virtual reality. Virtual reality technology, deriving from 30 years of government and industry funding, will see its cost plummet as development is amortized over millions of chip sets, allowing it to come into the mainstream. Initially, the software for these new chips will be crafted and optimized by legions of video game programmers driven by teenage mass-market consumption of the best play and graphics attainable. Coupled with the development of relatively cheap wide-angle immersive displays and hundredfold increases in computing power, personal access to data will come through navigation of complex artificial spaces. However, providing the every-citizen interface to this shared information infrastructure will need some help on the design front.

Ten- to 20-Year Challenges for Virtual Reality Systems

Very little cognitive neuroscience and perceptual physiology is understood, much less applied, by human interface developers. The Decade of the Brain is well into its second half now; a flood of information will be available to alert practitioners in the computing community that will be of great use in designing the every-citizen interface. Teams of sensory psychologists, industrial designers, electrical engineers, computer scientists, and marketing experts need to explore, together, the needs of governance, commerce, education, and entertainment. The neuroplasticity of children's cognitive development when they are computationally immersed early in life is barely acknowledged, much less understood.

1. A prioritized list of challenges includes the following:

   a. *Enumerate and prioritize human capabilities to modulate energy.* This requires a comprehensive compilation of published bioengineering and medical research on human performance measurement techniques, filtering for the instrumentation modalities that the human subjects can use to willfully generate continuous or binary output. Modalities should be ranked according to quality/ repeatability of output, comfort, intrusiveness, cost, durability, portability, and power consumption. Note that much is known about human input capacity, by contrast.

   b. *Develop navigational techniques, etc.* This is akin to understanding the functional transitions in moving around in the WIMP desktop metaphor and is critical to nontrivial exploitation of the shopping mall metaphor of VR. Note that directional surround-sound audio and tactile feedback rich enough to assist a vision-impaired person in navigating a mall would also likely help a fully sighted person. Schematic means need to be developed to display the shopping mall metaphor on conventional desktop computers, small video projectors, and embedded displays.

c. *Develop several universal methods for input/output device connectivity.*   Currently, the personal computer clone is the universal input/output adapter because of its open architecture and the availability of cheap mail-order input/output devices, but many personal computers, each doing one filtering task, trying to communicate with one another on serial lines, are not directly adaptable to the ECI set of needs.   Both software and hardware need to be provided in a form that allows "plug and play." Custom chip sets will drive the cost down to consumer level; adapting video game input/output devices where possible will help in achieving similar price performance improvements as computing itself.

d. *Store and retrieve visualization/VR sessions.*   Despite the easily available technology in chip form, it is still clumsy if not impossible for an ordinary user to make and edit a video recording to document a computer session, unless it is a video game! Imagine text editing if you could only cut and paste but never store the results.   One would like to play back and edit visualization/VR sessions in ways akin to the revision mode in word processors.   A key technological development here is extension of the videoserver concept to visualization/VR capture and playback.

e. *Connect to remote computations and data sources.*   This is inevitable and will be driven by every sector of computing and Web usage.

f. *Understand the computer as an instrument.*   This is inevitable and will be market-driven as customers become more exposed to good interfaces. Note that the competition between Web browser companies is not about megahertz and memory size!

g. *Create audio output matched to the dynamic range of human hearing.*   Digital sound synthesis is in its infancy. Given the speed of currently available high-end microprocessors, this is almost entirely a software tools problem from the engineering side and a training problem from the creative side. (Note that flawless voice recognition is left out here!)

2. Controversial: because they seem to be developing for a postliterate society whose members will no longer (!) be able to type and read from screens :

a. *Eliminate typing as a required input technique.*   Many computer applications, of course, already do this (e.g., CAD, video games, touch-screen map displays). Related: provide for typing when necessary in walk-around situations such as VR or warehouse data entry. Possible solutions are wearable chord keyboards, voice recognition, and gesture recognition. Issues include whether training will be essential, ranging from the effort needed to learn a video game or new word processor to that required to play a musical instrument or to drive a bulldozer.

b. *Reduce reliance on reading.* Road signs have been highly developed and standardized to reduce the reliance on reading for navigation in the real world. The controversy here may stem from the copyright (if not patent) protection asserted by commercial developers on each new wrinkle of look and feel on computer screens. A fine role for government here is to encourage public domain development of the symbolism needed to navigate complex multidimensional spaces.

3. Barrier-laden challenges:

a. *Develop haptic devices.* Safe force-feedback devices capable of delivering fine touch sensations under computer control are still largely a dream. Keyboards and mice injure without the help of force feedback; devices capable of providing substantial feedback could do real injury. Some heavy earth-moving equipment designs are now "fly-by-wire"; force feedback is being simulated to give the operator the feel once transmitted by mechanical linkage. The barriers are providing fail-safe mechanisms, finding the applications warranting force feedback, and providing the software and hardware that are up to the task.

b. *Provide enough antialiased image resolution to match human vision* (minimally 5,000 × 5,000 pixels at 50 Hz). CRT technology seems limited by market forces and development to 2,048 × 2,048 this decade. LCD screen sizes and resolutions seem to be driven by market needs for laptop computers. Twenty-twenty vision is roughly 5,000 pixels (at a 90 degree angle of view); less is needed at the angle people normally view television or workstation screens, more for wide-angle VR applications. A magazine advertisement is typically equivalent to 8,000 pixels across, on average, which is what a mature industry provides and is paid for, a suggested benchmark for the next decade or so. More resolution can be used to facilitate simple panning (which is what a person does when reading the *Wall Street Journal*, for example) or zooming in (as a person does when looking closely at a real item with a magnifying glass), both of which can be digitally realized with processing and memory without requiring more resolution from the display device. Certain quality enhancements may be achieved with higher refresh rates (e.g., 100 Hz) including less strobing during panning or the capability of doing stereo visuals by sending two 50-Hz images, one for each eye. Low latency, not currently a feature of LCD displays, is needed for 100 Hz or greater devices. Micromirror projectors show promise in this area.

Desirable, of course, would be wall-sized screens with very high resolution (>20,000 pixels) whose fidelity would be matched to a person's vision even when closely examined. Multiple projectors tiled together may achieve such an effect (Woodward, 1993) where warranted; monitors and LCD screens do not lend themselves to tiling because the borders around the individual displays do not allow seamless configurations. Truly borderless flat displays are clearly desirable as a way to build truly high-resolution displays.

c. *Providing enough computer for the ECI.* (This is probably the least of the problems because the microprocessor industry, having nearly achieved the capability of 1990 vintage Crays in single chips, is now ganging them together by fours and eights into packages.) Gigaflop personal computers are close; teraflop desktop units are clearly on the horizon as massive parallelism becomes understood. Taking advantage of all this power is the challenge and will drive the cost down through mass production as the interfaces make the power accessible and desirable. More futuristic goals such as the petaflop computer and biological "computing" will likely happen in our lifetimes.

d. *Providing adequate network bandwidth to the end user.* Some of the challenges in network infrastructure are discussed in the next section ("The Communications Infrastructure"). With respect to VR specifically, current data transfer rates between disk drives and screens are not up to the task of playing back full-screen movies uncompressed. The 1997 state of the art for national backbone and regional networking is 622 megabits per second. The goal of providing adequate bandwidth depends on the definition of "adequate" and how much computing is used to compress and decompress information. Fiber optics is capable of tremendous information transmission; it is the switches (which are computers) that govern the speeds and capacity now. Assuming that network bandwidth will be provided as demand increases, it seems likely that within 10 years a significant fraction of the population will be able to afford truly extraordinary bandwidth (CSTB, 1996).

THE COMMUNICATIONS INFRASTRUCTURE

Because ECIs must work in a networked environment, interface design involves choices that depend on the performance of network access and network-based services and features. What ramifications does connection to networks have for ECIs? This question is relevant because a user interface for any networked application is much more than the immediate set of controls, transducers, and displays that face the user. It is the entire experience that the user has, including the following:

- Response time—how close to immediate response from an information site or setup of a communications connection;
- Media quality (of audio, video, images, computer-generated environments), including delay for real-time communications and being able to send as well as receive with acceptable quality;
- Ability to control media quality and trade-off between applications and against cost;
- "Always on"—the availability of services and information, such as stock quotes on a personal computer screen saver, without "dialing up" each time the user wants to look;
- Transparent mobility (anytime, anywhere) of terminals, services, and applications over time;
- Portable "plug and play" of devices such as cable television set-top boxes and wireless devices;
- Integrity and reliability of nomadic computing and communications despite temporary outages and changes in available access bandwidth;
- Consistency of service interfaces in different locations (not restricted to the United States); and
- The feeling the user has of navigating in a logically configured, consistent, extensible space of information objects and services.

To understand how networking affects user interfaces, consider the two most common interface paradigms for networked applications: speech (telephony) and the "point and click" Web browser. These are so widely accepted and accessible to all kinds of people that they can already be regarded as "almost" every-citizen user interfaces. Research to extend the functionality and performance of these interfaces, without complicating their most common applications, would further NII accessibility for ordinary people.

Speech, understood here to describe information exchange with other people and machines more than an immediate interface with a device, is a natural and popular medium for most people. It is remarkably robust under varying conditions, including a wide range of communications facilities. The rise of Internet telephony and other voice and video-oriented Internet services reinforces the impression that voice will always be a leading paradigm. Voice also illustrates that the difference between a curiosity such as today's Internet telephony and a widely used and expected service depends significantly on performance:[22] Technological advances in the Internet, such as IPv6 (Internet Protocol version 6) and routers with quality-of-service features, together with increased capacity and better management of the performance of Internet facilities, are likely to result in much better performance for voice-based applications in the early twenty-first century.

Research that would help make the NII as a whole more usable includes making Internet-based information resources as accessible as possible from a telephone; improving the delay performance and other aspects of voice quality in the Internet and data networks generally; implementing voice interfaces in embedded systems as well as computers; and furthering a comfortable integration of voice and data services, as in computer-controlled telephony, integrated voice mail/e-mail, and data-augmented telephony.

The "point and click" Web browser reflects basic human behavior, apparent in any child in a toy store who points to something and says (click!) "I want that." Because of the familiarity of this paradigm, people all over the world use Web browsers. For reaching information and people, a Web browser is actually far more standard than telephony, which has different dial tones and service measurement systems in different countries. Research issues include multimedia extensions (including clicking with a spoken "I want that"), adaptation to the increasing skill of a user in features such as multiple windows and navigation speed, and adapting to a variety of devices and communication resources that will offer more or less processing power and communications performance.

The Network Hierarchy and How It Affects User End-to-End Performance

Among the elements of communications infrastructure that affect performance, the access network is one among several network elements (including networking in the local area of the user and networking within the public network) that have considerable influence on performance. Access network bandwidth is an important parameter affecting performance.

Local-Area Communications

Physical communications networking can be categorized as an interworking of three networking levels: local, access, and core (or "wide area"). Almost any network-based activity of a residential user is likely to use all three.

Local area networks (LANs) are on the end-user's premises, such as a house, apartment or office building, or university campus. Ethernet, the most widely deployed LAN technology, is already appearing in homes for computer access to cable-based data access systems such as Time-Warner's RoadRunner, Com21's access system, and @Home's access system. It could be in millions of American homes by the year 2000. In general, the 10-megabit-per-second (Mbps) Ethernet is the favored communications interface for connecting personal computers and computing devices to set-top boxes and other network interface devices being developed for high-speed subscriber access networks. A properly engineered shared-bandwidth architecture such as Ethernet allows multiple devices to have the high "burst rate" capability needed for good performance, such as fast transfer of an image, with only rare degradation from congestion. It is "always on," allowing devices always to be connected and ready to satisfy user needs immediately, as opposed to a tedious connection setup.

A residence will be able to simultaneously operate not only several human-oriented user interfaces in personal computers, heating/cooling and appliance controls, light switches, communicating pocket calendars and watches, and so on, but also user interfaces used by such devices as furnaces, garage doors, and washing machines. The introduction of IPv6 in the next decade will create an extremely large pool of Internet addresses, allowing each human being in the world to own hundreds or thousands of them. This development will foster the interconnection of a wide range of devices with embedded systems, a phenomenon that underscores the concern not to cast the NII or ECI challenges in overly personal computer-centric terms.

Local networking is not necessarily restricted to one shared wired facility such as Ethernet, which is beginning in the home at 10 Mbps but will likely evolve to "Fast Ethernet" commercial versions or to ATM (asynchronous transfer mode) connection-oriented communications, at 100 Mbps and higher. It can include wireless local networking, generalizations of the cordless phone to cordless personal computers and other devices, with burst rates of at least several megabits per second. Local networking is likely to include assigned (not shared) digital channels in various media for such applications as video programming and other stream or bulk uses, at aggregate data rates of hundreds of megabits per second.

How much bandwidth is enough? Assuming "always connected" and good performance from the other network elements to be described, 10 Mbps symmetric should be adequate for almost all processor-based applications including fast response image transfers (a 5-megabyte image in 0.5 second) and high-quality MPEG-2 or H.323 (conferencing/videophone) video at 4 Mbps. For streaming media such as video, additional requirements of reserved capacity and minimal queuing delay may be needed, requirements for which ATM is well suited. ATM breaks traffic into uniformly-sized "cells" that can be efficiently switched and reassembled with specified quality-of-service guarantees. Forecasts of how soon ATM will be available directly at consumer communicating devices vary, but there is likely to be significant availability in 5 to 10 years. For future applications with very complex immersive environments, multiple high-definition video streams, or other bandwidth-intensive needs, fast Ethernet and ATM should suffice. Additional transmission facilities for program distribution could use these or other technologies.

Both shared-bandwidth networks such as Ethernet and dedicated high-capacity channels could reside in the same physical medium, which might be fiber, coax, or twisted-pair. The cost of a LAN has been falling steadily, with Ethernet cards for personal computers well below $100. The cost of wiring a new house or apartment building with cable for Ethernet is low, but the cost could be substantial for rewiring an old residence. Wireless networking, to bypass the wiring problem, is available now, and it may be priced comparably to Ethernet, for comparable capacity, in 4 to 5 years.

Access Communications

The access network is the set of transmission facilities, control features, and network-based services that sits between a user's premises and the core public network. The twisted-pair subscriber line running from a telephone office to a user's residence is part of the telephone access network, for example. There are four basic paradigms offered (and in development): telephone company services via the twisted-pair subscriber line, cable company services via a coaxial cable (coax) feed, wireless access via higher-powered cellular mobile or lower-powered PCS (personal communications services), and direct broadcast satellite service. There are additional paradigms, such as terrestrial microwave, that are of secondary importance compared with these four. The access network has long been regarded as a performance bottleneck. The telephone channel, restricted to 3-kHz (kilohertz) bandwidth (and data rates of about 30 kbps for reliable transmission) by filters and transmission systems designed for voice, presents both bandwidth limitations and connection delays that seriously degrade performance.

"Access" can be a confusing term. An Internet service provider offers access service to the Internet and some access facilities such as TCP/IP software, but may not provide the physical pipe into the home. For the moment, the discussion is restricted to access networks that include the physical transmission facilities but returns later to Internet service provider facilities because they have a critical influence on the performance of Web browsers and other Internet-oriented user interfaces.

Twisted Pair-based Telephone Company Services.   The first paradigm, access via a twisted-pair subscriber line, is advancing with ISDN (integrated services digital network), ADSL (asymmetric digital subscriber line), VDSL (very-high-speed digital subscriber line), and HDSL (high-speed digital subscriber line).[23]

Cable-based Access Services.   A local cable television (CATV) service company maintains a cable distribution system that is still largely dedicated to broadcasting video programming. The coaxial cable network, now actually combining optical fiber trunks with coaxial branches and "drops" to subscribers, is a "tree and branch" architecture well suited to broadcast and not so well suited to upstream communications from the user. It is not well suited to upstream communications because of noise aggregation problems from many drops and branches coming together and because the capacity of the cable, however large, is being shared with bandwidth-hungry downstream video services and by a great many subscribers.

Nevertheless, the cable industry has succeeded in evolving a promising HFC (hybrid fiber coax) network architecture that can service both video distribution and interactive communications needs.[24] The HFC system provides digital channels with signals produced by cable modems, for which a downstream channel may generate a 30-Mbps signal within a 6-MHz bandwidth. Instead of one analog video signal, this digital transmission can carry seven or eight high-quality MPEG-2 digital video signals or one digital HDTV (high-definition television) signal plus two MPEG-2 ordinary digital video signals. More important for the NII, the digital capacity can be used for an arbitrary mix of signals, supporting medical imaging, language instruction, software downloads, and an infinite array of other applications. A cable system could typically implement up to a few dozen such 30-Mbps channels plus 80 old-fashioned analog channels for subscribers who have not yet purchased the digital TV sets expected to hit the U.S. market in 1998.

Upstream capacity shared among many subscribers is much more constrained. Standards are being developed that will allow a user to share with neighbors a 1.5-Mbps upstream channel (one of about 20 such channels serving a group of 125 to 500 subscribers). Other modem designs allow a pool of users to share a 10-Mbps upstream channel, mimicking the behavior of Ethernet. Here, just as with ADSL, the operator is betting that traffic will be asymmetric and that the user will not have a performance complaint even though the upstream bandwidth is not especially generous.

Above this physical channel level, the cable industry's model usually includes IP services with the same "always on" flavor that professionals enjoy at work. This is an important performance advantage for cable access, supporting broadcast information services that flash the latest bulletin on a computer or TV screen, quick Internet telephony perhaps by touching a miniature picture in the screen directory, and immediate linking to a distant Web site (contingent on performance being good farther upstream). If the service, including getting started and customer premise setup,[25] is done well, the popular conception of Internet service as difficult to get started and unreliable after that could change radically, and the Web browser could indeed become a universal user interface.

Wireless Access Services: Location Transparency and Consciousness and Power/Bandwidth Tradeoffs. Wireless access, currently in cellular mobile networks and soon in PCS networks, supports mobility of persons, devices, and services. It makes possible carrying wearable or pocket devices, doing computing in a car (perhaps with a "heads-up" display on the windshield—used only when it is safe to do so, of course), reading documents and messages on an electronic "infopad" at meetings, and sending "electronic postcards" from digital cameras and camcorders. The new and large unlicensed NII Supernet spectrum authorized by the Federal Communications Commission, in the relatively high 5-GHz band, will give a large boost to interactive multimedia services when mass-produced, low-cost radio modems become a reality. That could happen within 3 to 4 years.

Wireless access can support both location transparency, in which the user's application appears the same regardless of location, and location consciousness, in which the application finds and exploits local resources and can offer location-dependent services, such as giving directions to the nearest drugstore. These two features are not incompatible, and both contribute to the utility and usability of a user interface.

Because of the power constraints imposed by small portable devices, including but not limited to pocket telephones, medical monitoring and alerting devices, communicating digital cameras and camcorders, communicating watches, communicating pocket calendars, and even some laptop computers, it is important for the quality of the user interface that the wireless access system offer appropriate tradeoffs between communications and processing resources. One way this is realized is to concentrate the power of the portable device on display functions, such as a bright sharp display, and leave media processing (such as MPEG and videoconferencing digital video coding/decoding) to processors accessed through the wireless network. However, this balance of function may imply an unacceptable cost for the substantial communications capacity to carry the unencoded video information. Another issue is how to minimize power use on portable systems that are always listening. Further research will be required to identify a reasonable balance between processing and communications power in the system.

The microcellular PCS and Supernet networks are well suited to this need, aiming for burst transmission rates of 25 Mbps or more in small (perhaps 300-meter-wide) microcells. This compares very favorably with present-day telephony-oriented cellular mobile networks, where modems may provide up to about 20 kbps communications rate. Higher rates are possible in the digital cellular mobile systems becoming widely deployed now, but probably not more than 256 kbps, still far below microcellular networks.

The low Earth-orbiting satellite (LEO) systems planned for personal communications from anywhere in the world, which will compete to some extent with terrestrial microcellular PCS systems, could offer the significant user interface advantage of having exactly the same user interface anywhere in the world. This would remove a major anxiety for many users.

Direct Broadcast Satellite Distribution Services. Satellite services could augment wired facilities to improve the performance of the user interface. In particular, downloading of large information files to proxy servers in nearby network offices or in the end-user's equipment itself would reduce the delays of access to information in distant servers. There are cache memories in Web browsers that save Web HTML objects requested by users because there is a high probability that the objects will be requested again, but a proxy server does something else. It caches information when it has been requested by one user, under the assumption that if the material is popular other users may request it as well. This has the effect of improving response time considerably for those users and offering added possibilities for customization. There are many important research questions in selecting material for proxy servers, updating strategies, customization for users, and integrating the satellite facility smoothly with the wired network.

Direct broadcast satellite service in the NII would also include its present function of distributing video programming directly to user TVs. In the future it is possible that continual magazine-style broadcasting of video information clips, captured and displayed immediately by user devices rather than retrieved from cache servers, also will be part of the nation's information infrastructure. This would offer the freshest-possible material, supporting, for example, a customized user information service in which information is updated even as the reader observes it.

Core Network Communications: QoS, Interoperability, and Value-Added Services

The core network interconnects access networks. It aggregates traffic, and is, or should be, designed to provide differing quality-of-service (QoS) treatment for different classes of traffic.[26] Continuous voice and video media should enjoy minimum delay, and data files should be transferred with minimum error rate. ATM is already widely deployed in the core network. Research and development on QoS control is already extensive, and further work, on topics such as renegotiation of offered capacity and dynamic user control over QoS, would improve the performance of future user interfaces. For example, a user with several applications running could trade QoS among them, improving video resolution, for example, at the expense of the rate of transfer of a new software module being downloaded in the background.

There are additional services that either the core network or the access network, or indeed parties other than the network operators, can provide to enhance user interface performance. For example, a multiparty desktop audio/video conference can be displayed on one user's screen as a custom combination of pictures of the other participants with a corresponding spatial distribution of their voices. This can be done either in the user equipment by processing multiple audio/video information streams all coming to that user or by a processing service in the network (or offered by a third party) called a "multimedia bridge" that creates the customized display for the user and supplies that user with only a single audio/video information stream. If access bandwidth is at a premium, the network-based bridging service provides a high-quality user interface at a minimum cost in access bandwidth.

Performance Impacts of Internet Services Architecture

The Internet, which utilizes all of the communications hierarchy outlined above, is considered by many to be the heart of the NII. As the multimedia Internet evolves and assumes much of the quality control (and charge for service!) functionality of the telephone network, this is likely to become true by definition. The Internet is defined by use of IP, which carries packets from one kind of network to another without the application having to directly control any services in those networks.

Although they do not, in general, provide the access transmission facilities, Internet service providers do supply other access facilities that have a large influence on the performance of user interfaces. These include at least the following:

- Adequate modem pools and fast log-on for dial-up service;
- Direct low-level packet interconnection to the Internet, as well as higher-level services such as e-mail, UseNet servers, domain name servers, and proxy Web servers;
- Gateway services between Internet telephony and public network telephony (evolving in the near future to multimedia real-time communications); and
- Documentation and instruction for use of browser applications, e-mail, and various Internet services and resources.

It would require a lengthy report to describe how each of these affects user interface performance. Suffice it to say that a major objective in providing good service is the avoidance of server congestion, by means of the use of proxy Web servers to give users the impression of fast response from uncongested access to a nearby server, when in fact the originating server is far away and highly congested. Fast response time is, as emphasized earlier, an important measure of good performance of the user interface.

We might also reemphasize the importance of being "always connected" to Internet access for applications such as receiving timely information from "push" servers (such as the fast-developing customized current information services producing ever-changing displays in screen savers), immediate delivery of e-mail, fast receipt and initiation of real-time audio/video calls, and participating in the on-line work of a distributed group. An always-connected transmission access facility is required, of course, which must be matched by similar facilities[27] for the Internet service provider.

As with providers of wireless access services, Internet service providers will soon be required to support mobility services, such as locating and characterizing nomadic users. There are significant research questions in coordinating Internet routing and service-class support policies with the movement of individuals, in transferring customer profiles for Internet services, and in other aspects of mobility support.

Software Architecture: Distributed Object Environments and Transportable Software

Management of a mobility environment, particularly location transparency and location consciousness, is complex, and further research is needed. Distributed object environments—a software structure being used more and more in communications as well as applications systems—has a large potential to help resolve the complexities and improve performance.[28] For example, the global availability of a distributed object environment would make abstract service objects available in a consistent format everywhere, with those objects translating user needs into instructions to local systems.

Transportable software is another important object-oriented technology that proceeds from a different assumption, that a common "virtual machine" (a special operating system on top of the real one) can be created on different platforms, so that software in "applets" (and applications) can be moved around from one machine to another.[29] Java is a widely accepted language and virtual machine structure. Web browsers now commonly implement the Java virtual machine, allowing application applets to be downloaded from Web sites and executed in the user's computer. This facilitates animated displays and other features in the user interface, with much better performance than if the software executed in the Web server and large quantities of display information had to be transmitted to the user's browser. It also facilitates customization of the Web browser user interface for users with special needs and constraints.

Transportable software also has great potential for "programmable networks" in which communications protocols and services are not fixed but can be changed on user request by sending the appropriate applets to network elements, such as switches, where they execute. This, too, can improve performance where alternative protocols are better matched to applications needs, making the user interface more responsive and pleasant to use.

NOTES

1. See Gunter (1992), Semantics of Programming Languages, for more extensive discussion.

2. For example, the two sentences below differ only in a single word, but the resulting structure of the preferred interpretation is significantly different (Frazier and Fodor, 1978; Shieber, 1983, gives a computational model that elegantly handles this particular psycholinguistic feature). In the first sentence, "on the rack" modifies "positioned," whereas in the second, it modifies "dress": Susan positioned the dress on the rack. Susan wanted the dress on the rack.

3. Texas Instruments had an early natural language system that did this.

4. This example was discussed by John Thomas, of NYNEX, at the workshop.

5. Concatenative synthesizers achieve synthesis by concatenating small segments (e.g., diphones) of stored digitized speech. Formant synthesizers use a rule-based approach to achieve synthesis, by specifying acoustic parameters that characterize a digital filter and how these parameters change as different phonemes are sequenced.

6. Personal communication, John C. Thomas, NYNEX, December 12, 1996.

7. A system introduced by IBM in 1996 for voice recognition software was designed to enable radiologists to dictate reports into a personal computer. Recognizing 2,000 words and requiring some training, its support for conversational discourse, in a context where certain technical phrases may be used frequently, was contrasted in the press to the need to pause after individual words in older commercial software (Zuckerman, 1996).

8. Candace Sidner, of Lotus Development, and Raymond Perrault, of SRI, contributed much of the content of this subsection.

9. Indexing and retrieval constitute a growing application area, especially with the increased desire to organize and access large amounts of data, much of which is available as text.

10. This section concentrates on the state of the art of complete end-to-end natural language processing systems and does not describe research in individual areas. The steering committee notes that there has been significant progress, ranging from new grammatical formalisms to approaches to lexical semantics to dialogue models.

11. There is much promising research on syntactic models, such as the TAG (tree-adjoining grammars) work (see Joshi et al., 1981, 1983, 1995; Shieber, 1983), which are computationally tractable syntactic formalisms with greater power than context-free grammars, and on lexical semantics.

12. Although space prevents including detailed references here, the interested reader is directed in particular to the recent years' conference proceedings of the Association for Computational Linguistics, the European Association for Computational Linguistics, the international meeting in Computational Linguistics (COLING), the DARPA Spoken Language and MUC workshops, and the journals *Artificial Intelligence, Computational Linguistics,* and *Machine Translation.*

13. For applications involving database query, or for more sophisticated command and control, the mapping between the sequence of words and their meaning can be very complicated indeed. DARPA has funded applications-oriented research in language understanding (Roe and Wilpon, 1994; Cole et al., 1996) in the context of database query, where the user requests the answer to a query by typing or uttering the query. In most language understanding systems to date, a set of syntactic and/or semantic rules is applied to the query to obtain its meaning, which is then used to retrieve the answer. If the query refers to information obtained in previous queries, another set of rules that deal with discourse is used to disambiguate the meaning. Pragmatic information about the specific application is often encoded in the rules as well. Even for a simple application like retrieval of air travel information, hundreds of linguistic rules are hand coded by computational linguists. Many of these rules must be rewritten for each new application.

14. The Linguistic Data Consortium at the University of Pennsylvania, which is sponsored by government and industry, now makes much of this data available, from different sources, for different tasks, and in different languages.

15. Note that portable devices raise the larger issue of data durability: portable devices may be easier to lose or break, which raises questions about ease of backup for the data they contain.

16. Much of the cross-industry disagreement revolved around interlacing, a technique that has long been used in television to increase resolution and that takes advan-

tage of the extremely high line-to-line and temporal coherence of images produced by television cameras. Computer output, especially text and graphics, tends to be hard edged and to flicker badly when displayed on interlace monitors. Although one can convert interlaced broadcast TV to noninterlaced at the receiver end easily enough, there is a cost issue that affects the likelihood of flooding the market with the cheapest sets possible, hence affecting penetration and return on investment. The computer industry (hardware, software, and netware), of course, wants the low-end TVs of the future to handle digital output in a reasonable format; the television industry wants a 16 × 9 interlaced format (which is really a 32 × 9 format non-interlaced).

17. The Web is, of course, a great source for visual input. Copyright concepts of fair use and royalties will necessarily adapt, as they will for text, and audio quotations, samples, and outright theft.

18. Blake Hannaford, of the University of Washington, contributed much of the content of this subsection.

19. In fact, the graphics produced are not Braille but simply dot graphics printed on a Braille printer with the same resolution or dot spacing as Braille. This is a common technique, but it produces relatively low resolution graphics.

20. The WIMP interface will not serve this future, though elements will be involved (keypads, pointing, etc.). In its current form it is arguably dangerous to people susceptible to repetitive stress disorders, unusable by a large segment of the population with disabilities, and far too simple for navigation in complex spaces.

21. As noted in Herndon et al. (1994), a slider or dial for volume control has 1 degree of freedom; the mouse for picking, drawing, or two-dimensional location has 2 DOF, a 6D mouse or head-tracker for docking or view control has 6 DOF, a glove or face device for hand/face animation can have 16 or more DOF, and a body suit for whole-body animation can have over 100 DOF.

22. Many users of today's Internet telephony services experience a long delay, sometimes of the order of a second, in transmission, actually due more to buffering in the user's computer to smooth out arriving packets.

23. "Basic rate" ISDN, providing an aggregate 144-kbps symmetric service to a subscriber, suffered from a too-long development, unattractive rate structure, and general ambivalence on the part of telephone operators, but is now widely available and popular for Internet and "work at home" access needs. The usual access rate is 128-kbps symmetric from tying together 2 64-kbps channels provided within the 144-kbps aggregate service. From the user's point of view, ISDN still suffers from the need to set up a connection, although setup is usually quite fast, and from per-minute charges even for local calls.

ADSL, now focused on the generally asymmetric traffic requirements of computer communications sessions, offers 1.5 to 6 Mbps downstream (network to subscriber) and up to 384 kbps upstream (from the subscriber). A subscriber's ADSL service has the potential to be always connected, permanently linked, for example, through a router in the telephone office into a high-speed data network. It is not yet clear that telephone companies have the "always-connected" paradigm in mind. Telephone companies have wavered in their commitment to ADSL, so it is a very tentative forecast that ADSL service at acceptable cost will be available to millions of telephone subscribers in 5 years.

Although ADSL could vastly improve the performance of multimedia user interfaces, it should be recognized—and this will hold for the other broadband access mechanisms as well—that contention for capacity on networks upstream, and congestion at servers, may also seriously constrain performance.

HDSL, which provides symmetric capacity of 1.5 Mbps and up and usually is designed to work over two twisted pair lines, is not generally associated with residential users but could quickly overtake ADSL if households begin to generate high-capacity traffic. VDSL, at rates of 25 Mbps or higher, requires a distribution point closer to the subscriber than a present-day telephone office. Its potential penetration is difficult to predict and depends a great deal on the success and competitive implications of cable-based data services.

24.   Cable interactive access services are just beginning to be commercially available. It is a fairly safe prediction that by mid-1999 millions of cable subscribers will be offered this service.

25.   It is a challenge to the cable industry to make subscription and service provisioning simple and fast, and some standards interoperability questions discussed later, such as "plug and play" of digital set-top boxes, remain to be resolved.

26.   The conventional "best-effort" IP service does not require any special capabilities from the core network, but the new QoS-conscious IP services and, of course, ATM do. The core network must deploy technologies such as edge switches and access multiplexers that aggregate traffic arriving under various communications protocols, and must closely control QoS parameters for multiswitch routings.

27.   For the modem-based ISPs this implies higher rates, but the cable model may allow "always-on" capability without major increases in hardware investment.

28.   CORBA (Common Object Request Broker Architecture), standardized by the Object Management Group, is a leading candidate for a universally accepted architecture, although there are other distributed object systems proposed by major software vendors, such as Microsoft's ActiveX.

29.   Transportable software and object broker systems such as CORBA are complementary more than competitive. CORBA provides important object location and management services and facilitates use of existing applications software by wrapping applications (written in whatever computer language) in CORBA objects with standard IDL interfaces. The Java virtual machine requires new applications, all in the Java language, and applets may not execute as efficiently as software written for the underlying operating system, but it facilitates the movement of executable software, with appropriate security constraints, with the benefits outlined above. There are many examples now of CORBA-based systems in which CORBA objects are invoked by transportable Java applets.

4

DESIGN AND EVALUATION

Designing any sort of computer-mediated device for ordinary people for effective and pleasant everyday use has proven to be surprisingly difficult. The evidence for this observation comes from the myriad problems cited above in this report and at the workshop organized by the steering committee, from systematic empirical studies cited in this chapter, and from anecdotes involving frequent complaints from ordinary people when they are required to use the currently most common public-oriented application—telephone-based voice response menu systems—as well as from more sophisticated users of World Wide Web concerning the complexities and frustrations that have led as many to abandon the on-line life as to join it. (Consideration of the experiences and needs of people without specific special needs, referred to here as "ordinary" people, is an important complement to discussion of those with special needs (see Chapter 2) for developing ideas for research to support interfaces that work for more, if not most, of the population.)

It is, of course, possible that the greater power, utility, and desirability of computer-based functions as compared to traditional mass-market technologies (e.g., television, telephony) mean that greater difficulty of use is inevitable, worth a high price in human effort and inconvenience, and solvable only by increased education with its concomitant risk of leaving out those with insufficient time, resources, or ability. However, an alternate view is that it should be possible to use the power of the new technologies not only to do more and better things but also to do most of them at least as, or more, easily. Much of the burden of introducing new information technologies to the public can be removed or relieved by better design of the functions and interfaces with which most people will deal.

The steering committee assumes that it is often or usually possible to design more widely useful functions and to make them easier to use through design activities specifically aimed at these goals. Proof of the existence of this opportunity is readily available, beginning with popular knowledge of such consumer devices as cars and television sets, which were very complex initially but became, from the user's perspective, less so through sequences of adjustments over time. *The Handbook of Human-Computer Interaction* (Helander, 1988) contains many examples of prohibitively difficult systems made very much easier and more effective by redesign, and many more recent examples are reviewed by Nielsen (1993) and Landauer (1995). Some of these successes are reviewed in more detail below in this chapter. To set the stage, one is mentioned here that involves comparatively simple store-and-forward (as opposed to more complex multimedia, hypermedia, or collaboration support) technology—a case that has particular relevance to much of the expected uses in the every-citizen interface (ECI) environment.

Gould et al. (1987a) designed an electronic message system for the 1984 Olympics in Los Angeles. The system was to be used by athletes, coaches, families, and members of the press from all corners of the globe. The original design was done by a very experienced team at IBM's J.T. Watson Research Center. When first tested in mock-up with representatives of its intended user population, it was virtually impossible to operate effectively. By the time an extensive program of iterative user testing and redesign was finished, more than 250 changes in the interface, the system-user dialogue, and the functionality were found to be necessary or advantageous. The final system was widely used without any special training by an extremely diverse population. Another example comes from the digital libraries context and relates to the Cypress on-line database of some 13,000 color images and associated metadata from the Film Library of the California Department of Water Resources (Van House, 1996). Iterative usability testing led to improvements for two groups of users, a group from inside the film library and a more diverse and less expert group of outsiders. Both direct user suggestions and ideas based on observing users' difficulties gave rise to design changes that were implemented incrementally.

A central research challenge lies in better design and evaluation for ordinary use by ordinary users and, more basically, in how to accomplish these goals. The future is not out there to be discovered: it has to be invented and designed. The scientific challenge is to understand much better than we do now (1) why computer use is difficult when it is, (2) how to design and ensure a design for easier and more effective use, and (3) how to teach effectively both school children and those past school age to take advantage of what there is to use (a complex topic outside the scope of this report).

Available research and expert opinion point to at least three reasons why many computer-mediated tools (including, especially, communications systems) are currently difficult or ineffective for use by a large part of the population: (1) complexity and power of computer-mediated tools, (2) emphasis on users with unusual abilites, and (3) sophistication of designers and their discipline.

THE PROBLEM

Complexity and Power of Tools

Computer-mediated tools, as compared with traditional technologies, can be extremely powerful and complex, doing a vast array of different things with enormous speed. Of course, this is their advantage and appeal, but it is also their temptation. It means that a communications facility such as e-mail can be designed not only to let a user send an asynchronous text message to another subscriber but also to send multiple messages, create mailing lists, respond automatically, forward, save, retrieve, edit, cut and paste, attach attachments, create vacation messages, fax, and so on. If the design is not handled extremely well, users will have to learn how to negotiate this vast array of options, to know about them and how to operate them if they want to use them, and at least how to ignore them if they do not, and will always be required somehow to choose whether and what. The situation can become analogous to providing the cockpit control panel of an airliner for use by its passengers to turn on their reading lights. The consequences in computing range from the proliferation of features in software products to observations that most amateur spreadsheets contain serious errors, and that employee hand-holding costs as much as hardware for business personal computer users, to additional but seldom-used features on standard computer keyboards.[1] The concept of multimodal interfaces that would accommodate alternative approaches to input and/or output, discussed in Chapters 2 and 3, will introduce considerable complexity into the technology development process, without adding any new functional features.

Great power and complexity also bring the opportunity to make very costly errors. Pressing the wrong key on an ordinary telephone touch-tone pad leads at worst to a wrong number. With a computer-mediated system it can, and often does, lead to hours of lost work or inadvertently sending, for example, a "take me off this mailing list" message to 300 people, many of whom also wish they were not on it. Laboratory studies have found repeatedly that the majority of user time spent with popular applications such as word processors (which will be incorporated into many ECI applications) or spreadsheets is occupied with recovery from errors (see, for example, Card et al., 1983). This is one of two reasons why computer-mediated activities (see below for the second) create very much more variability in task completion times than do traditional technologies (Egan, 1988). Contemporary discussions in the business and personal press about the "futz factor"—extra time and effort to adjust various aspects of a computer-based system—attest to continuing problems resulting from increased complexity and power. The irony is that in some cases (e.g., early cellular phones, personal computer software), a significant amount of complexity appears to derive from software and sometimes hardware added with the intention of "enhancing" usability.[2]

Emphasis on Users with Unusual Abilities

Computer-mediated tools emphasize individual differences in ability more than do traditional technologies. Egan (1988) reviewed a large number of studies of individual differences in the time taken and errors made in using common computer applications. In every case in which comparisons could be made, the variability among different people was much greater when they used computers rather than precomputer approaches to doing the same sorts of operations. An approximate summary of the data from these studies is that while most traditional tasks, such as operating a conventional cash register, calculating a sum (manually), or running around the block, will take about twice as long for the slowest of 20 randomly chosen people than for the fastest, in computer-mediated tasks the range is never that small; typically, it is around 4 or 5 to 1, and may be as high as 20 to 1, even among well-trained and experienced users such as professional programmers.

In several instances a good portion of the greater between-individual differences in computerized tasks has been traced to measurable differences in cognitive abilities. In the aggregate, workshop participants commented, such differences contribute to observations about the concentration of computer use among teenage males; they also contribute to reports in the business press about the frustrations of "information overload."[3] Egan (1988) and Landauer (1995) reviewed studies in which measures of spatial memory, logical reasoning, and verbal fluency, as well as age and interest in mathematics and things mechanical, show greater than two-to-one differences between the highest and lowest quarter of the sampled potential user populations (see Figures 4.1 and 4.2 for examples). The participants in the studies illustrated were mostly noncareer middle-class suburban women with little or no computer experience, fairly representative of the average citizens one might expect to be future network users, although not of their range. How significant a problem is this? One guess comes from studies of the efficiency gains expected for computer applications to common business tasks. From the sparse available data, Landauer (1995) estimated that computer augmentation speeds work by 30 percent on average (with large variations). Combining this with the individual-difference estimates and a normal probability distribution suggests that about a third of the population would usually be better off without computer help as now provided because they do not possess the basic abilities prerequisite to its effective use. This is without consideration of the part of the population ordinarily designated as disabled or disadvantaged.

While education and training can usually reduce individual differences, there are two reasons why computer-mediated tasks may be less susceptible to this solution. One is the aforementioned vastly greater complexity usually offered—the much larger variety of different functions available and alternate means for achieving the same effects (e.g., five or more ways to cut and paste in most recent text editors). This variety often means that it can take longer to acquire high skill, akin on a smaller scale to the greater difficulty of learning to fly a jetliner than to drive a car. It also means, often, that some users will find better ways to operate their system than will others, not because there are large differences in which method serves which person best—such "treatment-aptitude interactions,"despite widespread folk belief in their existence, have virtually never been found in carefully controlled studies—but merely through chance variations in which operations users learn first, make habitual, and thus allow to become dominant over other possibilities that it thereafter takes excessive time to find and retrain for.

The second reason that computer training is less helpful than training for earlier technologies is the much more rapid and challenging changes in the technology itself. The basic automobile, typewriter, and telephone have not changed significantly from the user's perspective in almost half a century, and changes from their very beginning have been few, slow, relatively minor, and learnable without help (nonuse of extra features, such as the clocks on video cassette recorders or cruise control on cars, does not tend to be associated with an inability to use these devices for their essential functions). By contrast, every new model of a personal computing software package, even from the same manufacturer, comes with many new features and functions, new menu arrangements with new labels, and a large instruction book (and built-in help system). Such enhancements can affect even basic tasks. And every few years another new computer-based technology is offered. Thus, there is simply not the time available to consider yearlong high school courses for each computer technology every citizen might want to use—this year e-mail, next year the World Wide Web—as there was for typewriters and accounting machines, or 7-year apprenticeships, as there were for steam shovels and looms; the systems would be obsolete and gone before expertise was gained. The result is that high-functionality computational systems are never completely learned nor is their power fully exploited, and the primary learning strategy is based on learning on demand (Fischer, 1991). The challenge is to design so as to exploit the potential power for ease of learning and use as well as for increased functionality. Discontent with proliferating features contributed to mid-1990s experiments with so-called network computers, with fewer features than conventional personal computers, as well as to periodic articles in the business press about the persistently high costs of owning and using personal computers.[4]

Several members of the steering committee and reviewers of a draft of this report wondered whether the low-efficiency gains and large individual differences found in studies in the 1980s may have been overcome by technological advances in the 1990s. Although market statistics attest to growing use of information technologies, the sparse empirical evaluations of these issues in earlier periods appear to have become no more common in the past 5 years. While it was not possible to mount a systematic search for empirical evidence on trends in usability, the consensus of the usability engineers on the steering committee and among workshop participants was that things have not in general improved: for the most part, technological advances, particularly in software, have increased complexity, and, while some vendors are doing more usability testing, increased competition to be first to market with new features has brought a growing tendency to omit the kinds of early and iterative design and evaluation activities these experts think is essential to ensure ease of learning and use. In addition, what testing is done often generates results that vendors hold closely in the interests of gaining or preserving proprietary competitive advantages.

Market forces alone are unlikely to yield interfaces for every citizen because the rapid pace of the commercial market fosters an emphasis on sales performance as an indirect measure of value or effectiveness rather than direct presale evaluation of interface quality. At the workshop, Dennis Egan suggested several reasons for the lack of attention to interface evaluation by the industry. First, industrial research groups have reoriented themselves toward identifying near-term profit-making products and services, not performing longer-term research to evaluate new interface concepts and technologies and usually not publishing helpfully detailed results when they do. Second, the acceleration of product life cycles—particularly software—leaves little time for interface evaluation studies. Third, information technology products may succeed despite having inferior user interfaces by supporting highly desired functions, reaching the market before their competition and becoming de facto standards. Workshop participants from industry and report reviewers emphasized the commercial dependence on marketplace Darwinism, noting that vendors seem to find fielding their best guesses in products more cost effective than added precommercialization testing. Some went further to suggest that the World Wide Web had provided a mechanism for harnessing market cycles, noting that some vendors are using Web sites for beta testing of products and for eliciting feedback from those users (mostly sophisticated and eager "early adopters" unrepresentative of the average citizen) who opt to try the products. The constant release of beta versions of software over the Web represents a limited kind of software evaluation and user involvement on a massive scale; some of these releases are now reviewed, sometimes even on the basis of modest empirical tests, in trade publications, and usability and other design experts are dedicated by some vendors to some releases. Several companies are using this mechanism for iterative design. However, work by Hartson et al. (1996) suggests that methods for using "the Web as a usability lab" effectively, while promising, are in their infancy and face a number of problems that will be resolved only by considerable research. For example, this approach will require significant innovation in system instrumentation and user sampling techniques because, as outlined later, the untutored opinions of programmers and other power users are usually of little value for detecting the functionality and usability problems that are important for ordinary people (Nielsen, 1993). Tracking such efforts in broad-based user involvement and assessing their effectiveness might provide a productive starting place for research on large-scale participatory design and evaluation methods.

Sophistication of Computer Hardware and Software Designers and Their Discipline

Most of the people involved in the design and implementation of functions and interfaces for computer applications are themselves sophisticated computer users. Feature requests and inventions come primarily from experienced users and are supplemented and implemented by programmers. The situation is unlike that in other consumer-oriented technologies in two important respects. As noted earlier, computers offer and usually provide a larger range of functions and controls and therefore almost always greater complexity in the choices and actions required of the user. Hence, expertise with a computer technology can often play a much greater role in its use. Computer technology started as an aid for a highly technical portion of the population—scientists, engineers, and mathematicians, most of whom were capable of designing at least some software themselves, and often did.[5] To a considerable extent, computer designers have designed for their own use and for that of people like them; the design of computer applications is still primarily in the hands of programmers and other software specialists, albeit now as leaders of large teams and abetted by marketers, physical designers, and managers. Perspectives of other kinds of people—the differently abled, those with low levels of income and education, those resistant to technology merely for its own sake, and so on—have been represented most commonly by proxy or surrogate, if at all.

Not only are software specialists typically more experienced with the technology, but they are also, in general, quite different from the average user in the characteristics and abilities currently needed to deal effectively with computers: youth, mechanical and mathematical interests, good spatial memory, verbal fluency, and logical ability. They also tend to be less socially and pragmatically oriented in personality (Tognazzini, 1992). Although they may attempt to incorporate models of user behavior, behavioral scientists at the workshop noted that in practice designers tend to assume model users—users whose behavior poses fewer problems than actually experienced. As a result, it is extremely difficult for today's computer-based systems designers to have good intuitions about what will and will not be easy and gratifying for all citizens. This situation is illustrated by a press account of a Microsoft consumer product team's visits to five families for 3 hours each, reporting surprise about and better understanding of presumably ordinary households (Pitta, 1995).

The rise of the World Wide Web and experimentation with it by a widening range of people provide many illustrations of the challenge to designers. In a recent e-mail discussion on the topic, it was mentioned that ordinary citizens might experience difficulties in finding e-mail and Web addresses, to which a well-meaning expert replied that there were three universal resource locators (URLs) on the Web that could be searched and that at least one of them would usually locate a person's address. It seems unlikely that this procedure would be very appealing or effective for most citizens who are not already frequent and accomplished users—the suggestion is consistent with an expert rather than an every-citizen interface. True, the availability of these searchable databases means that the possibility of eventually providing a good directory service for every citizen exists, but the necessary next steps need taking. The anecdote suggests that this may be a larger than obvious task, since the difference between usually and always locating a person's address may affect how broad a segment of the population finds the service desirable and how much the Internet can contribute to a truly national information infrastructure (NII). The trends toward supporting do-it-yourself activity that extends to assembly and customization of software systems from components and modules by users appear likely, in the near term, to exacerbate the challenge of serving more of the population. (One of the steering committee members has been told by a major manufacturer that less than 10 percent of office workers ever change the factory configuration of their ergonomically adjustable chairs.)

In short, evidence discussed at the workshop indicates that an organized design and development process that ensures that the needs and abilities of potential average citizen users will be well taken account of has not yet become standard practice in software to nearly the extent that it has in the manufacture of most other mass-market products. Workshop discussions among technical experts and social scientists knowledgeable about specific population segments attested to the diversity of needs, reactions, and other qualities within the population as well as the uneven appreciation for that diversity.

THE POSSIBILITY OF EASIER-TO-USE, MORE EFFECTIVE SYSTEMS

There is ample evidence that computer systems with highly useful functions can be designed and built for easy, pleasant, and effective use by every citizen. Figures 4.1 and 4.2 give two examples. In both cases a function that could be used at an adequate level by only a minority of people was redesigned so that everyone could use it well. Moreover, improving usability for the less capable users did not penalize the more capable. These cases and others like them show that paying attention to the needs of novice users can often be accomplished without undesirable tradeoffs for expert users. Indeed, it is commonly the case that redesigns that help occasional users are even more helpful for frequent users; for example, effective free-form queries such as those provided by Excite and Latent Semantic Indexing will allow both novices and the most sophisticated systems analysts to search the Web more easily and effectively and with fewer frustrating, time-consuming errors than are common with Standard Query Language (SQL) or Boolean search formats.

Two additional examples of success in improving usability through redesign are instructive. In one case, an e-mail system was redesigned for simple text message interchange, e-mail's most popular use. The system was always on (no log-on was required), like a telephone, and had a screen that said "To," a simple backspace and retype editor, a button labeled "Send," and a printer that printed only when a message arrived. A group of elderly women—a segment of the population shown by data and demographics to be especially technophobic and less likely to succeed at computing—learned the system after about 30 minutes of training

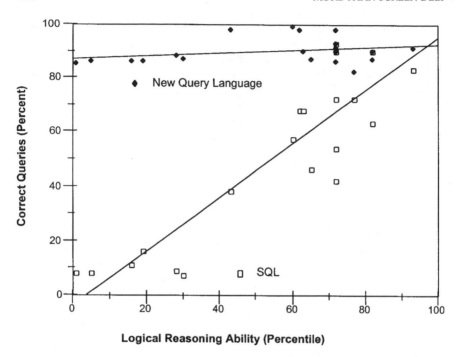

FIGURE 4.1   Using a standard relational query language (SQL) to make simple database searches after a half-day of training required greater-than-average logic-expressing abilities. Based on user studies, a new query language was invented that everyone finds easy to use and effective. SOURCE: Landauer (1995).

and used it eagerly. (The same e-mail system was preferred by several high-level executives of a telecommunications research company, all technical Ph.D.s who had easy access to a much more powerful system.) By contrast, today's typical e-mail systems are usually introduced to business employees in full-day training classes. The second example involves hypertext. In the majority of experiments evaluating how well people can find information in the same large book, manual, or encyclopedia using traditional print versions and on-line hypertext versions, people did significantly better with paper (see, for example, Gould and Grischkowsky, 1984; Gould et al., 1987b[6]). But in a few cases, people using the hypertext systems have greatly outperformed those using the old technology (see Landauer, 1995, for a review). The difference has been attributable to the design of the hypertext system, and especially the methods by which the design was done.

When conflict between ensuring usability for relative novices and providing power for the highly trained is unavoidable, perhaps because

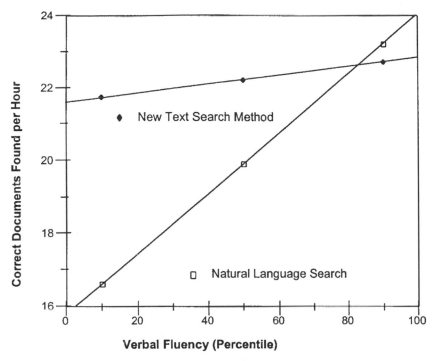

FIGURE 4.2   When people had to compose queries in a natural language to find information, only those with above-average verbal fluency succeeded. When, instead, people could submit examples of documents they wanted, everyone did well. SOURCE: Landauer (1995).

of entrenched development and marketing techniques or the inherent sophistication of some applications, two complementary approaches are possible. One is to provide differing levels of functionality for different users. Several usability specialists at the workshop reported routinely advising designers to provide as many functions, features, and options as will be useful, feasible, and in demand by experts, but to "hide" them from users who want only basic functions—by, for example, retaining the simplicity of short menus that emphasize only the best general functions and offer the option of selecting an "advanced functions" button for access to special features. The second approach is, of course, to increase the sophistication of users through education, training, and access to good guides and manuals (e.g., "training wheels" and "minimal manual" techniques, and scaffolded and staged advancement). Future computing functions of use to many citizens may well require fundamental understanding of concepts and operations that are not now taught in school—iterative and simulation-based problem solving, for example. Some research has been done on speeding the acquisition of such expertise, but the basic issue of what knowledge and skills are most important to teach itself warrants assessment[7]—the history of computing machines and the difference between bytes and bits, RAM and ROM (random access memory and read-only memory), as often taught in "introductory" computer classes may not even be among them.

EXISTENCE OF EFFECTIVE DESIGN METHODS

It is by now well established that iterative test-and-redesign methods almost always result in substantial gains in usefulness and usability. Landauer (1995) summarizes a large number of published reports of comparisons of task performance efficiency before and after a redesign based on some kind of empirical evaluation of the use of a computer-based system. The modal gain is around 50 percent, and new methods and new evidence of their success appear regularly (see, e.g., Sawyer et al., 1996).

Unfortunately, there is almost no discernible commonality to the methods used in the studies surveyed, other than that they all empirically evaluated the performance of users trying to do what the system was designed to help them do and that in all cases the evaluation was formative rather than summative—that is, done early enough and with a view to guiding improvements rather than just certifying adequacy. Sometimes the evaluation was done by systematic experiments in laboratory settings, sometimes by careful examination of the interface and dialogue by two or more experienced usability experts, sometimes by detailed examination of usage logs, sometimes by analysis of videotapes of users working, sometimes by informal observation of users or by asking users to talk about what they were doing. In one telling example, as recounted at the workshop by John Thomas, researchers at NYNEX used a simulation model to estimate and measure the work efficiency of a new graphical user interface intended to improve the efficiency of a computer system for use by thousands of employees. The simulation model, which emulates the perceptual and motion time demands of well-practiced repetitive tasks, predicted a decrease in efficiency. Field results after the system was deployed without revision confirmed the prediction; and at the same time, a revision in the laboratory taking into account the discovered flaws reversed the unfavorable result (Gray et al., 1992).

While there are known ways to ensure improvements, there are two very serious outstanding problems in the design process. The first is that these methods are not applied often enough, well enough, or early enough in design and development cycles to help most systems. In part this results from a persistent myth among technical practitioners and managers that iterative empirical usability engineering methods are too slow and expensive to bring to bear in today's competitive environment. In fact, as has been shown repeatedly, usefulness/usability testing almost always shortens delivery times by removing the need to develop unneeded features and expensively rework designs. Moreover, if done right, it actually takes only about 4 to 12 hours per week during development, a trivial addition in most projects. In addition, even faster and more economical feedback techniques are still evolving (Virzi et al., 1996) and would undoubtedly make even more progress with greater than their present meager support. Indeed, this is the second part of the problem—too little is known about what methods work best for what purposes: which are fastest, most accurate, most cost effective, and what new methods might be even better for some purposes. Workshop participant Dennis Egan, of Bellcore, put it this way:

> Some people have the view that evaluation studies do not matter, that any interface that has to be systematically evaluated and whose obvious superiority does not hit you between the eyes must not be worth much. The idea is to focus on entirely new interface designs and concepts, the "home run" rather than the incremental improvement. Clearly, we need people creating totally novel interface concepts, seeking breakthrough technology. But there are many instances where a creator's intuition about the use of novel technology has proved very wrong. We need to understand how best the new (and older) technology can be harnessed to support work, aid in instruction and training, and provide entertainment. The skeptics and scientists among us often are left wondering whether a new technology really serves well for a particular task or job.

The challenge is compounded with the advance of such innovations as three-dimensional interaction interfaces, which can involve different tasks and metrics than two-dimensional interfaces. Comprehensive usefulness and usability evaluation of entire three-dimensional user interfaces, for example, remains to be undertaken (Herndon et al., 1994).

TOO LITTLE USE OF KNOWN METHODS

While more empirical evaluation of usefulness and usability is being done, especially by large producers on major products, the quantity and intensity of such research is still very slight relative, for example, to the mechanical testing of auto engines, wind tunnel testing of airframes, cycle speed and reliability testing of computer chips, or code correctness and performance testing of computer programs. Often, lessons learned in empirical tests, especially when some features are found to be undesirable and simplification is called for, are ignored in favor of feature-list-driven marketing considerations. Often, testing is postponed until the end of development, when it is both in danger of being omitted entirely and too late to inform revision. Some of this project's industry participants reported that recent reductions in product development times resulting from market pressures have made timely test-and-fix efforts even less common than before.

Evaluation needs to be done very early and at all stages of development—indeed, starting even before invention and development, at the needs analysis, wants identification, and ideas-about-what-to-build stages. A recent study suggests that paper mockups of screens and interaction dialogues are often as effective as full-scale prototype testing (Sawyer et al., 1996). What will cause there to be much more empirical evaluation of whether all citizens can easily use what is provided to do the things they want to do? Ideas proposed at the workshop ranged from encouraging broader education of software engineers (which might be facilitated by federal agency sponsorship of summer schools, workshops, and fellowships) to the creation of a new professional category of computer system designer, separating the design activity from the building activity much as the structural architect job is separated from that of the general contractor, plumber, or carpenter. Professional societies would have a role or at least a position on possible mechanisms. Another suggested approach was to get appropriate evaluation activities better specified in development process standards and their certifications. Consistent with the project objective to identify areas for research were discussions of the need for more interdisciplinary research and suggestions for combining or better linking research on concepts with evaluation of implementations. One idea voiced by several workshop participants was that government (at different levels) might play a leading role by establishing requirements for usability and usefulness testing in procurement processes and by exploring and demonstrating every-citizen usability assurance in the design of public-service-oriented systems offered over the NII.[8] Comments by federal observers at the workshop suggested that the basis for some government activity can already be seen in activities under the aegis of the U.S. Department of Defense (CAPTEC program) and the General Services Administration as well as specific agency projects involving kiosk installations.

Appropriate incentives for better design of what are becoming mass-market products are complicated by the inherent need to balance economic and social interests. At the workshop, industry participants emphasized that additional evaluation, design, and features all have costs. Controversies related to regulatory interventions (e.g., requirements for certain product features) under the aegis of the Occupational Safety and

Health Administration and the Americans with Disabilities Act, for example, illustrate this tension. They raise the question of whether research can make both more usable technology and associated evaluation less expensive. This is one reason why some workshop participants called for research to develop better tools to support design and evaluation.

One of the issues energetically argued at the workshop was the problem of assessing the potential value of a new technology before it exists. Some participants worried that attempts to do so stifle creativity because people cannot be expected to imagine with any accuracy whether they would like or find useful an entirely novel way of doing things. Examples are rife: Alexander Graham Bell did not think the telephone would be useful for interpersonal communication but only for entertainment broadcasting. Early IBM leaders thought a handful of computers would fill the nation's needs. Xerography met long and strong investor resistance because few could see a need. Until recently, large numbers of people who had not tried it, including most telecommunications company executives and marketers, could not see any benefit in e-mail. These examples illustrate that evaluation calls for doing more than simply describing a novel technology and asking people whether they would want it.

Other workshop participants, including especially social psychologists and human factors specialists, were of the opinion that, while such assessments are more difficult and less sure than, for example, comparative evaluation of existing and widely used technologies, methods already exist that can give good early hints. Some methods are associated with scholarly research; some are associated with market research (much of which draws on social science techniques, such as conjoint analysis—using analysis of statistical variance to explore trade-offs—and constant sum point assignment—to assess priorities).

An illustration of the technology-forecasting dilemma is video telephony. On the strength of the technical promise, this technology has been reinvented and tried repeatedly, in approximate 10-year cycles. But from the earliest laboratory and field trials, through many succeeding ones with better and better (and often, because the trials were not constrained by cost, quite excellent) technology, it has been found repeatedly that most people do not choose to use these facilities. Trials accompanied by usage data, observation, and surveys repeatedly find that people—from executives to researchers, engineers, and middle managers, to homemakers—usually prefer not to be seen when conveying a short message. While nonverbal cues can convey information, the amount and validity are much less than is popularly believed. Moreover, what is conveyed is not necessarily relevant to the function at hand and may even detract from it. Studies suggest, for instance, that obscuring information about gender or social status can result in more—and more egalitarian—participation in on-line group activities. On the other hand, the added value of a visual channel for communication is often not for provision of affective cues but rather to enable references to or manipulation of shared visual artifacts (such as photographs, engineering drawings, and proposed budgets). The likely value of these facilities for ordinary citizens and for special populations is among the questions that need answering. These and other examples indicate that, while it is sometimes possible to forecast what technologies will emerge soon in the marketplace with some confidence, more than intuitive hunches are needed to predict whether, how, and why they will be widely used.

Among the methods cited as reasonably effective for predicting the value of a new technology were the following:

• *Task analysis.* Broadly conceived, task analysis means observing people in real-life situations to see what they are trying to accomplish, how well they are succeeding, and what is preventing success, and asking questions about goals, frustrations, and important incidents. This may occur in the context of ethnography, an anthropological approach involving observation of people in their natural environments, or by designers involving themselves as natural participants in the task in its natural setting, sometimes called contextual inquiry. Applied in 1870, a task analysis approach might have discovered that people spent a good deal of time writing letters in order to pass small bits of news or to obtain short answers: reports of sickness, requests for prices, dinner invitations, social maintenance greetings. An analyst might have gone on to count the number of occasions in which circumstances arose that would be well served by different means of communication if they were available and, if clever, would have noted that people often took long periods out of demanding days to walk miles to merely chat with friends, that occasionally runners were sent in all possible haste to fetch midwives or relatives. From such observations would come at least an educated guess that a faster means of interpersonal communication would be useful and desirable. Then the analyst might ask people to imagine talking at a distance, but would do so carefully and with informed interpretation.

Task analysis is implicit in the development of domain-oriented design environments (Fischer, 1994a), which (1) reduce the learning problem by supporting human problem-domain interaction by bringing tasks to the forefront, (2) allow users to learn more about functionality in the context of a task at hand (thereby supporting the integration of working and learning), and (3) assist users through an agent-based critiquing mechanism (Fischer et al., 1991) to reflect and improve the designed artifacts. The use of these systems of domain-oriented design environments has been demonstrated in a variety of different domains, ranging from kitchen design to voice dialogue design, multimedia design, and lunar habitat design.

- *Performance analysis, which goes a step finer.* The word "analysis" is important here and has a meaning not unlike its use in chemistry. Performance analysis involves observation and experimentation to find out what people can do easily and what they can do only with difficulty or not at all. The research that raised the low ends of the curves in Figures 4.1 and 4.2 was of this kind. For example, in the database query research, experimental analysis revealed that the majority of the population cannot form logical expressions to describe an object of search even though they can recognize with high accuracy the things they want (Landauer, 1995). The invention that flowed directly from this was a recognition-based query method (a truth table of possible data).

- *Special forms of focus group discussions.* In these, an analyst takes participants step by step through scenarios of increasingly futuristic technologies, at each step eliciting discussion of possible uses, values, and defects. One variant, known as "laddering," involves interviewing people about what they are familiar with in order to get them to think about newer concepts (Reynolds and Gutman, 1988). The result is not necessarily a prediction of utility and market success but the raising of important and often unanticipated issues.

- *Mock-ups, Wizard-of-Oz experiments, and rapid prototypes.* Very often new interfaces, sometimes new functionality, can be given an informative initial exploration by a mock-up using paper, slides, or video and either walking people through scenarios of using the proposed screens and functions, seeing what they understand, and listening to what they say (statements such as, "What's this for?" or "I wish I could do X") or asking them, where "them" is both ordinary potential users and usability experts, what they think of what the system does and has to offer (Lund and Tschirgi, 1991). At the workshop, Bruce Tognazzini showed the workshop the "Starfire" vision video produced by Sun Microsystems. Similar to Apple Computer's "Knowledge Navigator" video, "Starfire" gives an enactment of a futuristic scenario in which an anticipated or imaginary technology is being used by people. These videos were designed for various purposes; the status of "Starfire" as an engineering project output illustrates the potential value of such vehicles to inform design (e.g., panels of people, both ordinary and expert, could discuss and critique them; see Tognazzini, 1996).

In the Wizard of Oz technique, a human, often assisted by software, performs some of the functions of an imagined system before it can be built. For example, Gould et al. (1987a) used a human to transcribe spoken input to emulate a much better automatic voice dictation transcription machine than could be built at the time (or now) in order to study how useful and desirable it would be and to understand some of the design alternatives and parameters that eventually should be implemented. The technique is only good for functions that humans with computer help can emulate, but with ingenuity this can cover a considerable range.

Finally, there are rapid prototypes, perhaps a more familiar idea. Essentially, the technique is to build a system that does only part of what the invention will call for in actual deployment, using much more easily constructed software and, perhaps, much more expensive hardware so that something like the intended technology can be tried with real users before its design (or attempted production) is settled. One especially appropriate target for the discussion here might be advanced voice recognition, graphics, multimedia, or virtual reality interfaces. Early usefulness and usability trials with approximations to such systems using human participants could reveal what functions and features are and are not promising for every-citizen use before great effort and expense are devoted to their realization. For example, at the workshop, Robert Virzi described how GTE progressed from a 1990 case study of how people shop—identifying unmet needs for information about how to find vendors or special sales and difficulties in communication—through design of a service for which the underlying network technology was not adequate at the time to the 1995-1996 Superpages effort to provide on-line national yellow pages, intended to be a basis for broader services supporting communications and information exchange among vendors and consumers. This anecdote illustrates the blending and balancing of studies of user preferences with judgments about whether and how to address them with available technologies.

BEYOND INDIVIDUAL INTERFACES: COMPUTERS AS SOCIAL MACHINES

Earlier research on interfaces tended to presuppose a view of human-computer interaction as an exchange involving a single individual performing an independent action by means of a computer. This view, perhaps influenced by the "input-process-output" paradigm, has strongly influenced the design and evaluation of user interfaces. Not surprisingly, that orientation yielded a substantial body of information about the significance of individual differences in ability and prior experience for ease of use and judged and measured usefulness of alternative system designs as well as guides for improved research and evaluation (see above). Now, however, advances in information and communications technologies have created a much more complicated context for the design and evaluation of interfaces for everyday use.

The move toward network access, distributed architectures, and open systems has made this medium a social one: computers provide a means for taking part in social activities, doing collaborative work tasks, engaging in educational pursuits with other learners and teachers, doing commerce, playing group games, contributing to and benefiting from shared information stores, and so on (see Chapters 2 and 5). The good news is that these kinds of distributed architectures and tools come much closer to reflecting the ways people learn, work, socialize, and more generally participate in the varied activities that comprise everyday life. The bad news is that "social" computing adds another layer of complexity to the already difficult design and evaluation issues just summarized. Whether interconnected computers are viewed as media for enhancing interactions among individuals in physical communities or for forming information spaces in which people, representations of people (e.g., avatars), and intelligent agents interact in a built environment (or both), it is likely that new or significantly improved design and evaluation methods will be needed to make such interchange accessible to everyday citizens.

Although user-oriented research in this field is relatively new, it is worth reviewing the main findings that can be expected to figure importantly in the design and evaluation of interfaces for computer-based collaborative activities. The term "groupware" was coined to refer to computer-based technologies that primarily target groups as users (Box 4.1).

Roles, Relationships, and Boundaries

As some of the definitions in Box 4.1 indicate, groupware must accommodate many individuals, not all of whom have the same roles (in contrast to individually oriented research, in which humans interacting with a computer application were assumed to be engaging in the same functions). Typically, roles are captured by rules that attempt to express relationships, permissions, and limits. For instance, in collaborative learning environments the teacher role may be accompanied by some options (e.g., annotating student submissions) that students do not have, or students may be allowed to see and comment on one another's term papers, but only after their own papers have been submitted. In health care, more complicated scenarios are envisioned involving, for instance, the roles of patients, health maintenance organizations, expert systems provided by drug companies, and pharmacists (see position paper by Michael Traynor on-line at http://www2.nas.edu/CSTBWEB).

Social applications of the sort citizens might use to support routine aspects of daily life like education and health care complicate underlying system design issues: How much social knowledge of roles and relationships is appropriately incorporated into application development, and

BOX 4.1
Some Definitions of "Groupware"

• Specialized computer aids designed for use by collaborative work groups—Robert Johnson

• Software applications that are designed to support . . . groups—especially software that recognizes the different roles the users of the application have—Jonathan Grudin

• The class of applications arising from the merging of computer plus communications technology. These systems support . . . users engaged in a common task and provide an interface to a shared environment—Clarence Ellis

• Computer-based tools that can be used by work groups to facilitate the exchange and sharing of information (including user adaptations of individual tools to support group functionality)—Christine Bullen and John Bennett

• Loose-bundled collection of multifunction tools in an interactive system . . . that are susceptible to use by all the members of a group, plus the user practices that incorporate them into day-to-day service to accomplish group tasks—Tora Bikson

---

NOTE: The term "groupware," while variously defined, refers to current efforts to make distributed computer technology meet the needs of multiperson groups engaged in varied work or social interactions.

how are such decisions to be made? Whatever decisions are taken, how are the resulting rules and constraints most readily made evident to users in the interface design? Further, besides understanding how the application itself operates, users will require additional information about privacy—when are their communications restricted to authorized others and when is privacy not guaranteed? Creating social context awareness in the interface—so that it is not as easy inadvertently to broadcast personal health status information as it is to spam (flood) a listserv with an "unsubscribe me" message, for instance—is yet another challenge. As this enumeration of issues suggests, the decentralization of computing power that underlies groupware is what differentiates it from telephony, which could be considered a simpler forerunner technology. Realizing the promise of groupware implies aiming to achieve more than is possible through the telephone system, per se.

It is important to underscore that nothing about groupware as a social medium invalidates the prescriptions set out earlier for improving the design of novel technologies. Instead, the inference to be drawn is that taking into account the social nature of most citizens' everyday activities and the range of actors and contexts involved makes advance use of task analysis, performance analysis, focus group discussion, and rapid prototyping both more important and more difficult.

Interdependency and Critical Mass

A second differentiating factor is that, unlike computer applications for individual use, groupware not only presupposes but also requires a multiplicity of users for its functionality to be experienced and evaluated. An example is provided in an early study by Grudin (1988) of why collaborative applications fail. He targeted electronic scheduling as the application of interest because market research had consistently found managers and professionals saying that it would be highly desirable to let their computers handle the tedious task of arranging appointments and meetings automatically, once provided with information about when relevant individuals were available; but when such applications were installed in organizations, they were rarely if ever used.

The reason for the discrepancy between anticipated and actual use is instructive and turns mainly on the interdependent nature of social applications. The payoff from programs that schedule meetings or appointments depends on the proportion of potentially relevant users who in fact use them; if a "critical mass" of people whose calendars are affected do not use the program, others derive no benefit from entering and updating their own schedule information and so they soon stop. The scheduling program thus imposed user costs (in the form of added tasks) without generating the expected benefits. In this way it differs from independent technologies that yield individual benefits to those who adopt them, regardless of whether there are other users.[9]

The same interdependency characterizes shared discretionary databases (Markus and Connolly, 1990) and computer-based communications systems (Anderson et al., 1996). More generally, while the design and development costs are borne up front, the value of interdependent applications is apparent only later, after a substantial portion of the intended user community engages in their actual use. Besides necessitating a more careful understanding of the contexts of use in the design of groupware applications, these considerations underlie the "extreme difficulty" of evaluating them (Grudin, 1988). They also illustrate how broader usability involves not only the user interface per se but also the social context and the overall service and what these imply for interfaces.

Although the more recent growth in sales and apparent use of groupware products such as Lotus Notes suggests that progress has been made, the evolving NII also raises the prospect of far larger numbers of people interacting than has been experienced to date. Sheer numbers, plus variations between groups of people who interact on a sustained basis and those who come together on an ad hoc basis, and variations on what people will do with such facilities beyond the current business environment of their uses, are among the emerging technical challenges that may affect interface design.

Iterative Test and Redesign for Social Applications

Earlier sections of this chapter made it clear that, while there are problems with these methods, iterative test and redesign procedures are effective known ways to improve system usefulness and usability. This thesis holds true for interdependent as well as independent applications, but the deployment of effective test-and-redesign procedures is more complicated for social applications.

In the first place, whatever methods are chosen, they will need to involve trial users playing the interdependent roles relevant to the application in sufficient number and over sufficient time to exercise, assess, and redesign the varied functions that the application is supposed to support. This consideration by itself suggests that iterative test and redesign of groupware may take longer and cost more than the same methods applied to independent applications if sufficient ingenuity is not brought to bear on the evaluation methods, for example, by embedding usefulness and usability analysis in the instrumentation of experimental designs offered over the World Wide Web.

Second, getting good answers to design questions depends on having both realism and control in user trials, and there can sometimes be a tension between them (cf. Mason and Edwards, 1988). Many human-computer interaction studies, for example, have relied on laboratory experiments that presented a computer-based task to individual subjects and measured their performance. While strong on experimental control, such studies are typically weak in realism. In particular, they do not account for the influence of the varied contexts (environmental and social) within which computer-based tasks are usually situated, and they measure performance by means of variables that assume noninterdependency among users. On the other hand, achieving realism means having an adequate scope (enough users and uses) and a realistic time frame as well as an appropriate task context for judging an application's usability and usefulness. Typically, such realism is achieved at the expense of control, in a one-shot field trial (not infrequently, the user group is the development department, as noted above); outcomes do not generalize beyond the unique case. Further, the tensions between realism and control are heightened when social applications are the evaluation focus.

The techniques outlined above for assessing the likely value of a new technology improve evaluation in part by trying to join realism and control, and their extension to social applications is promising (e.g., Olson and Olson, 1995). In addition, better-designed laboratory studies (e.g., Kiesler et al., 1996) and field experiments (e.g., Bikson and Eveland, 1990), as well as innovative approaches to research on the implementation and use of computer-based media over time in nondirected real-world cases (e.g., HomeNet (Kraut et al., 1996); Blacksburg (Va.) Electronic Village project, (http://duke.bev.net)), are helping to address the need for both realism and control in evaluating social applications. However, as the size of user groups increases—as reference to "every citizen" suggests—some participants were not certain about how well any of these approaches would scale up. (These concerns surface above in discussions of social-interest applications of the NII.) Several workshop participants noted that once one moves beyond a focus on personal computers as the access device and considers all manner of devices—telephones, television remote controls, and so on, as well as embedded systems—the problems and opportunities add up to a very large set.

Inherent Unpredictability of Use

For reasons both practical and theoretical, predicting the performance of social applications in real-world use on the basis of prior research is inherently difficult. Practically speaking, cut-and-try or design-and-fix methods—those most likely to yield accurate results—are least likely to be employed for social applications because of the time frame and scope of uses they entail, as suggested above.

In theory as well, groupware uses are hard to anticipate because they are embedded in a social system that exerts effects quite independently of the technology. For instance, the social system of work had a significant influence on the automatic scheduling applications studied by Grudin (1988; see above). Managers, who most often called meetings, were most likely to have secretaries who kept their on-line calendars up to date and handled "workarounds" by phone when others had not put their schedules on-line; so managers benefited from the application but experienced none of its burdens. Lacking secretaries, professional users experienced all of the burdens but few of the benefits and soon gave up on it (Grudin, 1988). There had been several task analysis studies of the problems and promise of schedulers, and many had predicted just the problems Grudin cites, but they were ignored or unknown to proponent designers.

As Markus and Connolly (1990) have pointed out, managers sometimes solve these kinds of problems simply by mandating the use of an application. In turn, however, clever professionals respond by gaming the system so that what appears in the on-line calendar is what is most convenient or most socially desirable, regardless of the actual status of the individual's time commitments. Similar results have been reported for use of shared databases by Patriotta (1996). These outcomes, reflecting interventions by the social system, are even more removed from expectations based on untested designer intuitions. It should be emphasized that social "reinventions" of technology are not necessarily negative; on the contrary, research literature provides a great many instances of user-based improvements (e.g., Bikson, 1996; Orlikowski, 1996). The point, rather, is that unpredictability inevitably characterizes the use of groupware because of the reciprocal adaptations of the technology and the social context in which it is situated.

Implementation as a Critical Success Factor

Implementation, construed as the complex series of decisions and actions by which a new technology is incorporated into an existing context of use, assumes critical importance as a success factor for groupware given the reciprocal influence of social and technical sources of effect cited above. During implementation, the new technology must be adapted to work in particular user settings even as users must learn new behaviors and change old ones to take advantage of it. At the workshop, Sara Kiesler cautioned that experiences related to the performance of specific tasks (e.g., by telephone operators) will not necessarily generalize to the larger NII. Specific tasks tend to be tightly delimited and jobs of the performers in typical studies depend on their use of the system; in the NII, in contrast, there is a huge variety of tasks, a huge variety of users, and the users have more choice in what they do and how. Walter Feurzeig, of BBN, argued that it is nevertheless difficult to consider user interfaces independent of specific activities. Sara Czaja, for example, drew from her work in medical trauma settings to emphasize that real experience in real contexts is necessary to understand interface needs at, for example, physician workstations. Help features of the system and user training as well as modifications of the application and changes in users' behavior, for example, affect the course of implementation.

Current research on work group computing corroborates the conclusion that the effectiveness of the implementation process itself has a substantial impact on the usability and usefulness of social applications somewhat independently of their design features (Mankin et al., 1996; see also the literature reviews in Bikson and Eveland, 1990). The vital role of implementation also emerges as a salient factor in the life of new civic networks, according to their administrators (see Anderson et al., 1995).

Nonetheless, evaluation efforts frequently target technology design as it bears on specific functions, leaving implementation processes and related features (e.g., help screens, on-line tutorials, user manuals) out of account in attempting to predict use. Further, although it is clear that many desirable changes in social technologies cannot be anticipated before their deployment in specific user settings, these applications are not usually designed with a view toward ease of modification either by end users or by service providers who maintain end-user systems. On the contrary, desires on the part of end users or those who provide information technology assistance are usually regarded with suspicion by designers and developers (Ciborra, 1992).

Given the significant variation in uses, users, and user contexts represented by everyday citizens, along with serious questions about how their NII-based interactions can be supported, such implementation issues merit considerable attention.

Directions for Improvement

For reasons like those reviewed here, it is manifest that systems intended for use by communicating social groups—including large populations—raise many kinds of questions that individual applications do not. The design and evaluation techniques appropriate for individual applications need to be extended or supplemented with approaches more suitable for the envisioned NII environment. While there is not a large body of empirical work on which to draw for this purpose, research on computer-supported cooperative work and technologies for collaboration yields suggestive directions for improvement. Some promising approaches are summarized below.

Involve Representative Users in Substantive Design and Evaluation Activity Early and Often

Participatory design is difficult to arrange, as noted above, and so more likely to be slighted. The goal is to understand how interfaces to connected communities may prove more than skin deep, how they may affect how we locate and remain aware of one another and find shared information, as well as how we understand, enact, and track our roles in group activities, recover from errors, merge our work with others, and so on.

An illustrative example comes from an exploration of how new technologies could assist wildlife habitat development by the U.S. Forest Service. To support wildlife habitat protection, forest service teams needed an interface to varied databases (e.g., about soil, vegetation, water quality, forest wildlife) that would permit different experts literally to overlay their views of a geographic territory on a shared map, create and manipulate jointly devised scenarios, and observe the results. The design of such an application required the participation of users with specialized domain expertise from its inception to its evaluation in field trials. NII-based applications envisioned for ordinary use (see Chapter 2) are no less complex and are similarly likely to require participatory design with representative users; offering lifelong learning, continuing education, or targeted training, for instance, or delivering selected health services on-line, are cases in point.

In these and other social applications, methods for design and evaluation that discover and fix problems before they are widely promulgated are especially important. Many workshop participants believe these needs are particularly acute in areas—such as education and health care—that are now being eagerly promoted and anticipated for NII applications. One obvious approach is to conduct field trials with smaller than universal, but still representative, population samples; this procedure is as yet seldom followed. Often, as workshop participants noted, experts—both system designers and such specialists as speech or occupational therapists—may play the role of representative users; sometimes a think-aloud approach is used in which users comment on their experiences as they use a system. A related question is simply how to design and evaluate with the full range of the population in view, rather than drawing on educated middle-class citizens who have constituted the potential or actual computer user samples typically studied in the past.

Expand the Repertoire of Research Methods to Be More Inclusive and Innovative

There is a pressing need for social-psychological, sociological, and organizational research into how innovation, development, and implementation processes should be arranged and managed so that the goal of every-citizen utility is effectively pursued. Issues like those raised above clearly require techniques for research with large populations, for instance, by survey methods or perhaps sampled observations; as yet there is little experience in the use of these techniques for design and evaluation of large networked social applications. In discussing the prospects for instrumenting various systems, an interesting opportunity broached by participants was to use the Internet itself to conduct experiments and surveys, to record usage data (in anonymized ways) stratified by user categories and applications, and to assess the properties of emerging social networks (for examples, see Eveland et al., 1994; Huberman, 1996; Eveland and Bikson, 1987; Dubrovsky et al., 1991; Finholt et al., 1991; and Kraut et al., 1996). Practical issues may relate to protection of user privacy and to the nature of actual user populations (e.g., early adopters of the Internet may not be representative). Thus, consideration of how to get back good information is itself a research issue. Trials and assessments of the suitability of these and other design-and-evaluation techniques for large and widely varying populations would be very worthwhile.

Consider Ways to Minimize the Separation of Design and Evaluation from Implementation and Use

On the one hand, new computer-based technologies continue to emerge in the market at an incredibly rapid pace, and this trend will only be accelerated by population-wide access to the NII. On the other hand, recommendations to use methods for research with representative population samples to ensure the usefulness and usability of social applications before their implementation and use seemingly entail a much more leisurely pace for innovation. This dilemma suggests that it might be worthwhile to reconceptualize as concurrent or overlapping processes the traditional lincar sequence from design, iterative trials, and redesign to implementation, use, and inevitable user "reinvention."

This suggestion draws, in part, on the concurrent engineering model; in bringing together the designing and building stages of technology development, it reduced the total time involved while enabling designers and engineers to learn more from one another in the course of coproduction. It also builds on rapid prototyping approaches that draw no sharp boundaries between prototype trials with representative users, field pilot projects, and early-stage implementation processes (e.g., Seybold, 1994; Mankin et al., 1996). Finally, it takes into account the unfeasibility of "getting it right the first time" as a guiding principle for NII applications. As virtually every study of communicating social applications has shown, these technologies are invariably modified in use in ways that respond to user contexts, changes in skills or task demands, and changes in the suite of applications with which they must be integrated. That is, the application should not be viewed as "finished" or static just because it has left the developer's world (Bikson, 1996).

New back-end technologies (e.g., client-server architectures, middleware) make it possible to keep the infrastructure or platform in place while delivering, updating, and supporting new tools and applications in user environments over a network. This is the principle behind new efforts to conduct product beta-tests via the Web, as noted earlier. Given the desirability of involving greater numbers of representative users in application design and evaluation as well as field trials and implementation, and given the capability of networked systems to enable both the provision of usable prototypes and the collection of user feedback, it would be desirable to explore options for leaving applications intentionally underdesigned, to be adaptively developed as they are implemented in contexts of use (see Box 4.2).

BOX 4.2
Toward Informed Participation

Technology that genuinely supports informed participation will be inherently democratic and adaptable. It will allow us to take advantage of our social diversity and not force us to conform to the limits of our limited foresight.

The philosophical model for understanding knowledge acquisition and the communication of information holds at least three primary lessons for anyone designing or deploying information systems for groups of people, as follows:

1. Focus more on relationships than things. Information technology can and should change relationships among people; that is where its chief value lies. Information technology that changes the nature of relationships can change the fundamental features of a given complex system.

2. Honor "emergent behavior." The new theories of complex adaptive systems hold that the adaptability of any system greatly depends on the "genetic variance"— or pluralism of competing models—within it. Therefore, information technology should allow the emergence of competing agents (or models or schema) and enhance their interrelationships.

3. Underdesign systems in order to let new truths emerge. It is a mistake to set forth some a priori notion of truth or to try to design in totality (which requires an infinite intelligence in any case). Rather, one should underdesign a system in order to assist the emergence of new ideas.

The brilliant logic of an underdesigned information system is well illustrated by the constitutional and cultural principles espoused by Thomas Jefferson, one of the preeminent information architects of all time.

SOURCE: Brown et al. (1994).

Consider the Prospect of Research-based Principles for Design

Regardless of the perspective taken, the bottom line is that what we know now about evaluation and design methods is not good enough to meet the challenges presented by every-citizen applications in an NII context.

Although there are good methods and techniques available for evaluating ideas and systems for individuals at all stages of development and providing tests of usability and guidance for design, none of the workshop participants thought that evaluation methodology was a solved problem. Although a few comparative studies have been made of some of the different methods in use—user testing, heuristic evaluation, cognitive walkthroughs, scenario analysis, ordinary and video ethnography— these studies have not reached any unequivocal conclusions; indeed, there is active controversy about their relative advantages. This is an area in which more and more systematic research would almost certainly have great impact. Some of the current evaluation methods are orders of magnitude more expensive in terms of time and money than others, often prohibiting their use and often inhibiting the use of any evaluation, yet we do not know for sure whether they reliably produce better, or even different, information or result in better or different products. Such research should, of course, also be aimed at finding better methods. In particular, research is needed on what kinds of evaluation give not just summative quality estimates but also useful formative guidance that leads to better design.

These kinds of problems and uncertainties about evaluation techniques and methods lead naturally to reawakened interest in the prospect of research-based principles for design. It has often been hoped by the scientists and technologists involved, and perhaps even more often by their managers, that the design of useful and usable interfaces could be based on theory, engineering principles, and models rather than sheer cut-and-try and creativity. There have been some modest successes along this line. As mentioned earlier, there are models of the perceptual-motor processes involved in operating an interactive device that can predict the times required with useful accuracy. So far, these have had their greatest utility in the design of computer-based work tools where large numbers of people will do the same operations large numbers of times so that small savings in time will add up to large savings in money. In addition, there are some models and means of analyzing and simulating the cognitive operations of users of complex computer-based systems that are often capable of yielding important insights for design or redesign (e.g., Kieras and Polson, 1985; Kitajima and Polson, 1996; Olson and Olson, 1995; Carroll, 1990). And there are a dozen or so basic principles from experimental, perceptual, and cognitive psychology that can be put to work on occasion by insightful experts. However, for everyday guidance about the design of everyday interfaces and functions for every citizen, current science and engineering theory are of little help. One reason is that both the human and the potential computer-based agents involved, and especially their combination, are extremely complex dynamic systems of the sort that are not often reducible to practical closed-form models. They appear to be more like the phenomenon of turbulence that plagues airframe design or the chaos that confronts weather prediction than they are like the design of circuits; they are matters in which test-and try is unavoidable. It is often mystifying to usability professionals that testing is resisted as strongly as it is and that calls for doing principle-based design are so frequent in this arena, when practitioners and managers concerned with other complex dynamic systems (even electronic circuits and software) can easily see the need and strongly support empirical methods.

This hope of avoiding test-and-fix methods is astonishingly persistent. For example, there is a myth in circulation that the Macintosh interface, which for certain basic functions has demonstrated large usability advantages over its predecessors, was accomplished without user testing. The truth could not be more different. At Apple Computer, the Macintosh interface was developed originally for the Lisa computer, building, in turn, on the highly structured design and testing process for the Xerox Star system. During its development, it was subjected to an exemplary application of formative evaluation and involving nearly daily user testing and redesign. Moreover, the graphical user interface (GUI) components of the Macintosh interface can be and have been combined in ways that do not produce superior results, while some old-style command-based applications that have been iteratively designed are just as usable as the comparable Macintosh-style GUI applications (see Landauer, 1995, for a review and examples).

While research on both the fundamental science of human abilities and performance and the engineering principles for better usability certainly could be highly worthwhile in the long run if adequately pressed, progress to date has been slow, and a principle-based approach probably cannot be counted on to underwrite the design of effective every-citizen interfaces in the near term. On the other hand, many of the scientists who have worked on these problems believe that attempting to understand the issues involved in the interaction of people with computer-based intellectual tools and with one another through these tools offers an excellent laboratory for studying human cognition. The problems posed, and the nature of the response of the world to what a human does, can be controlled much better in this environment than, say, in a classroom, and yet are much more realistically complex than in the traditional psychological laboratory. Moreover, the end-result test, making interactions among and between humans and computers go better, requires not just piecemeal modeling but also complete understanding, an especially useful criterion in studying human cognition and communication that can take so many new forms and functions. Thus, more support (of which there is currently very little) of basic human-computer interaction research, especially at the level of the cognitive and social processes involved, could be quite valuable as science.

PROGRESS

In concluding this discussion, the steering committee notes that some technologists, economists, and others have expressed the belief that problems of usefulness and usability are sufficiently solved by market competition and that, in particular, most earlier problems with user productivity have been overcome. There is indeed some anecdotal evidence that large software producers are paying more attention to these matters, and with good effect. For example, a report from Microsoft (Sullivan, 1996) describes iterative user-interface design efforts for Windows 95 that followed prescriptions for interface development suggested by recent research (e.g., Nielsen, 1993; Landauer, 1995; Sawyer et al., 1996). As prior research has found, user test results showed a gain of approximately 50 percent in user task performance efficiency as a direct result of usability engineering activities.

Several lessons can be taken from this and recent, similar reports. First is the encouraging sign that assessment-driven design is being applied to significant projects and that it is working. A more cautionary lesson, however, is the authors' report of how narrowly the Microsoft project escaped neglect of assessment on several occasions, and how important the consequences would have been. In moving the interface design from that of immensely popular Windows 3.1 and 3.11, the team reported, it had originally believed that, because the previous interface was so well evolved and so successful in the marketplace, only small evolutionary changes based on known flaws, user complaints, and bug reports would be needed. However, early direct user tests and observations "surprised" the team into a realization that many critical problems could be solved only by a complete redesign and that many opportunities existed for significant innovative improvements that market response had not suggested. By the time the product was delivered, hundreds of flaws deemed worth remedy had been found and several provably important innovations were incorporated. Throughout the development, the team continued to be surprised both by how poorly features and functions previously thought good actually performed and by how poorly newly proposed fixes often turned out on actual test.

The point here is that the prior interface from the same source, the most "advanced" Windows project, was still, in the mid-1990s, very far from optimized and there was still room for dramatic improvement based on explicit assessment-driven usability engineering. The fact that computer hardware has become much faster and more capacious—and software commensurably larger and more highly featured—does not in the least ensure that usefulness and usability of applications have improved; indeed, the effect is often the opposite. Thus, it seems certain that there will continue to be opportunities for major improvements in the design of interfaces for some time to come, especially in the many new and so far very sparsely evaluated mass network-based applications for social activities.

Meanwhile, another complementary question needs to be answered. Windows 95 got the evaluation attention it needed, but no one knows how many other products are or are not profiting from formative evaluation. One bit of suggestive evidence comes from informal analysis of the same publication in which the Windows 95 results were reported, the *Proceedings of the 1996 ACM Conference on Human Factors in Computing Systems,* CHI96. This is the major organ in which work on interface development and research is first published. Among 67 articles in the 1996 issue, of which over half describe newly developed or modified interface designs, only one of every six articles reports any kind of serious user testing or observation. This small proportion is not significantly different from the numbers reported for relevant publications in the 1980s (Nielsen and Levy, 1993). Thus, it appears that progress toward better interfaces still has plenty of scope for greater application of this well-established methodology. Also of interest, about one-sixth of the papers at CHI96 were directed toward network interface applications, and another sixth were about research on general interface components that might be used in the future—the kind of science research toward principled design many workshop participants thought should be better encouraged.

As mentioned above, it could be hypothesized that greatly increased beta testing made possible by World Wide Web dissemination of software has reduced the need for explicit evaluation. There may be some truth in this hypothesis in that many (but far from all) of the flaws and remedies discovered in usability engineering efforts come from trial user comments. On the other hand, as mentioned, World Wide Web beta testing is suspect as a usability design methodology because it gets information primarily from relatively expert, relatively heavy early-adopter users, those willing and able to try faulty versions (the average untested application interface has 40 flaws, according to Nielsen and Levy, 1993) of unproved things, people who are certainly unrepresentative of the target audience of this report. In addition, the Web has produced an explosion of new software that is often the result of extremely rushed, frequently amateurish, design efforts. Indeed, some usability experts think that much current Web-based software, and most home pages, have reintroduced long-recognized, serious design flaws (e.g., untyped hypertext links, missing escape and backout capabilities, and lengthy processes and downloads about which users are not warned) and that Web dissemination may have promulgated and institutionalized more avoidable problems than it has fixed. Requiring the using public to weed through the technology because of involuntary subjection to a welter of bad applications does not seem a desirable strategy for rapidly bringing every citizen happily on-line. Research is needed to determine whether, in fact rather than impression, recent trends in software development, such as World Wide Web beta testing and increasing speed of development cycles, are making things better or worse.

NOTES

1. According to Cynthia Crossen in the *Wall Street Journal* (1996, pp. B1, B11) "Not even computer industry executives can explain the illogic of the modern keyboard . . . a device jerry-built from technology as old as 1867 and as new as this year. Because there has never been an overarching plan or design, [it] defies common sense. Its terminology is inscrutable (alt, ctrl, esc, home), and the simplest tasks require memorizing keystroke combinations that have no intuitive basis."

2. Today's elegant cellular phone interfaces emerged after a period of what some observers deem excessive feature creep. See Virzi et al. (1996).

3. A Reuters business information survey of 1,300 managers reported complaints about stress associated with an excess of information, fostered by information technology (King, 1996, p. 4).

4. See, for example, Munk (1996). She reports estimates that 27 percent ($3,510) of the $13,000 annual cost of a networked personal computer goes for providing technical support to the user, and writes, "There's a Parkinson's Law in effect here: computer software grows to fill the expanded hardware. This is not to say that all the new software isn't useful; it often is. But not everybody needs it. For mundane uses, the older software may, paradoxically, be more efficient" (p. 280).

5. In addition to instances of software for scientific and engineering applications, current popular examples, such as the World Wide Web and assorted approaches to electronic publishing, derived from efforts of technical users to design systems to meet their own needs.

6. Gould et al. (1987b) notes that equivalent reading speed for screens and for paper depends on high-resolution antialiased fonts, an element of output display (see Chapter 3).

7. A meaningful approach to computer literacy, including essential concepts and skills, is the focus of an anticipated Computer Science and Telecommunications Board project.

8. The Telecommunications and Information Infrastructure Access Program (TIIAP), run by the National Telecommunications and Information Administration, funds diverse public-interest (including government services-related, educational, library, and other) information infrastructure projects that would form a natural platform for evaluation if funding were sufficient. See O'Hara (1996, p. 6).

9. For independent innovations, "early adopters" were regarded as having a competitive advantage over those still using older technologies; for interdependent innovations, early adopters do not achieve full benefits from the new technology until the late adopters come on board (Rogers, 1983).

5

COMMUNICATION AND COLLABORATION

MOTIVATION: WHY COLLABORATION AND COMMUNICATION?

Two trends related to collaboration and communication are fostering useful new conceptions of human-computer interfaces. First, evolving theories of interpersonal collaboration and communication are beginning to be applied to human-machine interactions, demonstrating that thinking about human-machine interactions as communication and dialogue—rather than, for example, a series of isolated commands and responses—can make systems easier to use. Second, the increasing use of computer systems in support of communication and collaboration among groups of people (whether for work, education, or entertainment) highlights the need for understanding interfaces as links among many people and machines, not just one person and one machine. In both of these arenas, better understanding and development of richer theories of collaboration and communication will lead to improvements in the ways people use the national information infrastructure (NII), whether to interact with the NII itself (e.g., to obtain information and services) or to interact via the NII with other people in order to communicate, collaborate, and form communities.

For an individual using a computer system, as Candace Sidner says in her paper in this volume, "interfaces are 'communication engines' to the functionality of software applications; interfaces are how we get our work done." Yet the word "interfaces" suggests a thin veneer (according to the dictionary, "a surface forming a common boundary"), too thin to provide the capabilities for communication and support that people should be getting from computer systems. Most members of the human-computer interface community take the "I" to refer instead to "interaction," but the ability to collaborate ("work with") and not just interact ("act on one another") is becoming increasingly important as people use the NII not just to get individual tasks done, but also to communicate and work with others.

As explained in Chapter 2, the NII's growth is extending civic life and community to include geographically dispersed individuals. It is thus important to expand the conventional conceptualization of interfaces by recognizing that they may involve more than one person and machine and that collaborative systems can either alleviate or exacerbate problems in interactions among individuals with different abilities. As explained by Terry Winograd in his position paper in this volume, the traditional idea of "interface" implies a focus on the person and the machine. In designing interfaces it is important to focus as well on the "interspace" that is inhabited by multiple people and machines in a complex web of interactions. The expanded view this interspace implies adds to—but does not replace—the conventional requirements of interfaces for facilitating communication between person and machine.

With anticipated enhancements in capabilities and reach, the NII may also foster new kinds of collaborations. Recent work on "collaboratories" (Olson et al., 1992) and distance learning over the Web and in multiuser domains (MUDs; Bobrow, 1996) as well as the extensive use that the astronomy and high-energy physics communities make of the Web for large-scale scientific experiments involving widely dispersed people, instruments, and data provide examples of collaborations made possible by networked systems. Graphical interfaces enabling easy access to hyperlinked Web-based documents, for example, have made it much easier for dispersed researchers to share new results, articles, and references within their community than when they had to mail, fax, e-mail, or personally deliver articles to one another. The NII has the similar potential to provide new ways of conducting a range of activities important to every citizen. In health care, for example, there is an increasing emphasis on the construction of large patient care systems that coordinate multiple providers from multiple disciplines and care sites. Network information systems offer the opportunity for new kinds of communication and collaboration and the potential for integrating practices and providers across communities. With the proper support for collaboration and communication, electronic information systems could play a key role in meeting the associated challenges of integrating health care practices, providers, and settings from individuals and families across communities (and individuals with different sensory and cognitive abilities).

The ever-increasing modes of communication and media in which to present information provided by current technology also complicate and enrich the interface challenge. Going beyond a shallow view of interfaces to consider communication and collaboration becomes even more important when we consider combining video, voice, and graphics. Computer systems have become more than machines used to perform isolated tasks. They are now widely used as machines for communicating different kinds of information using a range of media, and they provide possibilities for structuring and interacting that were unavailable previously (traditional print, graphic, and broadcast media). Decisions about what form to use to communicate different kinds of information and techniques for combining different media will require this larger view. There is a wide range of difficult technical problems in making such decisions (Feiner and McKeown, 1991; Roth et al., 1994; Moore et al., 1995; Marks, 1991).

In the resulting complex web of interactions, people's needs for systems to support collaborative activities and to act collaboratively will vary by individual, activity, and situation of use. Thus, it is important to emphasize that this chapter argues not that collaboration is the only type of interaction, but rather that it is an essential element of any system for communication (whether that communication is itself in service of cooperation or, alternatively, competition) and that it is important for the NII to provide support for collaborative activities.

Thus, communication and collaboration affect the design of every-citizen interfaces (ECIs) in two arenas: (1) person-computer interactions (e.g., ECIs may be designed to collaborate with a person) and (2) person-person interactions (e.g., ECIs can provide new ways for people to communicate with one another and support collaboration among groups of people). The former type of support is reflected in software (including interfaces) that applies our theoretical understanding of some aspects of human communication and collaboration to improve people's experiences in working with computer applications. The latter involves software (including interfaces) that facilitates communication among people and collaboration among groups. However, it is important to recognize that for many uses of the NII people may utilize both these types of collaborative support (person-computer and person-person) as several examples in Loren Terveen's position paper (in this volume) illustrate. Identifying optimal ways to integrate the two types of support in ECIs is a major research challenge.

The roles of theories of collaboration and communication differ across these arenas, but the value of a better understanding of what constitutes collaboration and what is needed for effective communication is essential to both of them. For example, the need to have certain capabilities to be able to collaborate on a task or the requirement that particular kinds of information be shared among participants in a collaborative activity affects the design of support tools for group collaborations (e.g., systems like Lotus Notes) as well as the development of interfaces that enable a person and application to work together more collaboratively than most current interfaces. This chapter investigates each of these arenas separately to understand the challenges and opportunities each presents. The recommendations encompass research that will contribute to both arenas as well as research focused on arena-specific needs.

THE NATURE OF COLLABORATION: CRITICAL FEATURES AND CAPABILITIES

Collaboration entails working together toward a common purpose, although the reasons for the collaboration and the ways in which it fits into some larger activity may vary among the participants (Bratman, 1992; Grosz and Kraus, 1996; Searle, 1990). For instance, some authors of a multiauthored report may contribute because the report offers a vehicle for wide dissemination of their ideas, others because they believe the report may help meet a societal need of great concern to them.

Workshop participants generally agreed on the importance of research aimed at answering fundamental questions about the nature of collaboration and its role in ECIs, both for improving the ways in which people and computers interact—the person-computer collaboration arena—and for supporting communication and collaboration among groups of people. However, different specific questions are highlighted by different research communities. Research in artificial intelligence, and computer science more broadly, addresses questions of formalizing the information that must be exchanged (Cohen and Levesque, 1990; Grosz and Kraus, 1996; Kinny et al., 1994), developing negotiation strategies and protocols for reaching agreement on how to divide work (Rosenschein and Zlotkin, 1994; Kraus and Wilkenfeld, 1993) developing languages for communicating or negotiating such information (Sidner, 1994a,b), and measuring the difference in theoretical power or system performance made by adding collaborative capabilities (Bender and Slonim, 1994; Jennings, 1995). Analyses within the paradigms of sociology, organizational behavior, and anthropology examine the ways in which groups function. This diversity makes clear the need for interdisciplinary efforts as we examine the introduction of collaborative capabilities into ECIs.

Appropriately defining the capabilities that systems need and the functionality that can be expected from them as well as developing ways to design collaboration at different levels into systems are major research challenges. From recent research on the modeling of collaboration, it is clear that knowledge about what is being done (the collaborative activity and the goals to which it relates), how to do it, and the capabilities of the participants is essential (Grosz and Kraus, 1996). As a result, for a system to be a collaborator, it needs to "know" what the person using it is trying to do. This knowledge may be implicit in the system design rather than explicit, but it cannot be absent. Another feature of collaboration is the need for participants to negotiate (Sidner, 1994a,b; and others). Negotiation about terms ("semantic alignment"; see below), about means, and about allocation of responsibility are among the ways in which collaboration entails negotiation. Collaboration also requires that participants share both commitment to the common task and knowledge of their shared commitment (see, e.g., Bratman, 1992; Searle, 1990; Grosz and Kraus, 1996; Levesque et al., 1990; Kinny et al., 1994). Establishing the commitments and requisite common beliefs requires communication, but here too the extent to which this information must be explicitly represented by a system and thus the communication requirements may vary.

In examining the possibilities for person-computer collaboration, there was a divergence of opinion among workshop participants about how much collaborative power one should seek to incorporate into ECIs in the near term and more generally how "smart" they might be. Likewise, there was debate about the level at which systems would need to negotiate. For instance, Candace Sidner argued that all collaborators—human and machine—must be "aware of what the task is," with common knowledge about their shared undertaking. Austin Henderson argued that requiring more than minimal ability on the part of systems to understand what people using them are doing sets too high a barrier; he suggested seeking to develop systems that have some knowledge of what they are doing themselves, but not requiring that they understand what a user's purposes are. As he stated, "Maybe it doesn't understand what you are doing, but it surely understands what it is doing in its terms and can talk about those." In his paper (available on-line at http://www2.nas.edu/CSTBWEB), Gary Olson provides some support for the view that machines cannot be expected to meet a human standard by observing that groups of people develop unconscious routines that are hard to specify and therefore hard to represent in a computer system.

Although formal models of collaboration (e.g., Grosz and Kraus, 1996; Flores et al., 1988; Winograd, 1988) make reference to beliefs and intentions, computer systems do not necessarily have to reason explicitly about such mental constructs to behave collaboratively. Ants and other insects have built-in behaviors that lead to their working together (Wilson, 1971). Computer systems that are restricted to specific tasks could incorporate principles of collaboration into their design and work collaboratively without explicitly reasoning about belief or intention. For instance, interfaces can embed task and knowledge implicitly; in effect, automated teller machines (ATMs) do this. Thus, the incorporation of collaborative capabilities does not necessarily entail a requirement that a system have complex reasoning capabilities.

It is useful to consider computer systems falling on a spectrum from very function specific (e.g., ATMs, financial software applications such as Quicken) to general purpose (e.g., personal computers, database systems). People using large-scale information systems will employ systems at all points along this spectrum, and systems across the full spectrum should have capabilities for collaborating. The problems presented by communication and collaboration in general-purpose systems are long term; they entail many of the difficult problems of representation and reasoning that research in artificial intelligence has been addressing. However, the incorporation of capabilities for collaboration into systems for human-computer communication does not have to wait. Models of collaboration can be used to constrain and affect the design of function-specific systems (e.g., Rich and Sidner, 1996). Embodying a set of assumptions into the design of an interface for a function-specific system in the form of a familiar metaphor (e.g., the checkbook-balancing metaphor in Quicken) provides another avenue for incorporating some level of collaboration into a system. Organizing an interface around a particular task domain and cognitive principles related to performing that task (e.g., GLIDE[1]) is another.

The function-specific approach is not, however, an application-specific approach, and misidentifying these two may sacrifice the benefits of consistency in interfaces for different tasks. ECIs must support people's interaction with multiple applications packages when using the NII. As Candace Sidner notes in her paper in this volume, no single interface metaphor is powerful enough for all work, yet a multiplicity of smaller applications, each with its own interface for performing one set of tasks, leaves people with lots of tasks to juggle and creates a need for an interface that communicates and collaborates in terms of the task rather than the application.

It is also important not to confuse collaborative systems with help systems. Systems that have collaborative capabilities should prove helpful, but "help" systems may operate without information that is crucial to collaboration. For example, some current help systems not only offer advice but also take action to help with one's task (e.g., Apple Guide, Microsoft Wizards). These systems exhibit properties of collaboration (e.g., doing things to assist in the user's task without being asked). However, at the workshop, Sidner argued that such systems do not measure up to what is required for collaboration because the missing consensus that collaborators share is critical. For instance, systems with features such as automatic spelling correction are helpful when they get things right, but because they lack knowledge of the task, they can also cause serious problems. One of the lessons of Microsoft's commercially unsuccessful "Bob," which proved not to be as helpful as expected, may be the difficulty of attempting collaboration without adequate built-in models of collaboration.[2]

Collaboration also requires some shared knowledge about the activity or task being done. Because current help systems often lack such information, they are unable to address some critical problems that arise for users. They do well to provide users with additional uncontextualized information (e.g., Microsoft Word's "Tip of the Day," which acquaints users with an arbitrary piece of functionality), and they are able to help users find functionality in cases where users are able to identify their information needs precisely. New generations of help systems are needed, ones that are able to analyze what users are doing and complement information access with information delivery by providing contextualized information that is relevant to the task at hand (Fischer and Nakakoji, 1991). The active help systems currently being explored in research settings (e.g., Fischer et al., 1985) provide examples of such systems.

A major challenge for research on collaborative systems is finding the appropriate level of collaborative capability for a given application. Determining the tradeoffs undoubtedly will require the kinds of iterated design processes described in Chapter 4. A general solution is not likely to be found; one person's ideal level of query may not be another's, and one individual's preferences may vary among tasks. Thus, people's expectations and the qualities they attribute to systems must be taken into account.

An additional risk is that people may attribute greater capabilities to systems that appear to collaborate than those systems that actually have. As Olson observed at the workshop, "People really have a tendency to impute animisms to complicated technical devices, so in the situation of using it, it sure feels like a collaboration even if we, as disembodied researchers, can say it isn't." Lee Sproull noted at the workshop that the ongoing relationship built up in collaborations among people is an important nontask component of their activity. If users impute collaborative abilities to systems, various social aspects of collaborations need to be attended to (Nass and Reeves, 1996). The section "Developing Trust in Systems" below examines several of these.[3]

Semantic Alignment

The ability to communicate clearly with people is a requirement for ECIs. Clear communication requires a shared understanding of the meaning of terms; this understanding is known as semantic alignment (Clark,

1996). ECIs need to accommodate shifts in terminology, not only for people and systems, but also for the multiple systems that may need to be coordinated in a single interaction. At the workshop, Austin Henderson observed that in "all of these situations we have to address the question of how it is that collaborating entities negotiate meaning."[4]

As explained by Terry Winograd in his paper in this volume,

> Whenever two people talk, they have only an approximate understanding of each other. When they speak the same language, share intellectual assumptions, and have common backgrounds and training, the alignment may be quite close. As these diverge, there is an increasing need to put effort into constant calibration and readjusting of interpretations. Ordinary language freezes meanings into words and phrases, which then can be "misinterpreted" (or at least differently interpreted). This problem shows up at every level of computer systems, whenever information is being represented in a well-specified syntax and vocabulary. ... Even simple databases have this problem. If information is being shared between two company databases that have a table for "employee," they are apparently in alignment. But if one was created for facilities planning and the other for tax accounting, they may not agree on the status of part-time, off-site, on-site contract, or other such "employees."

Henderson argued that collaborating entities "start from undefined positions but a common context, and they produce enough alignment for the purposes at hand."

If a computer system is one of the communicating parties, it must participate in establishing the common ground (Clark, 1996). Many current systems work under the presumption that people will learn the system's meaning, but this assumption is a source of misinterpretation and people's difficulties in understanding how to use systems. As wider cross-sections of society use the NII, such assumptions may become untenable.

As Terry Winograd observes in his paper in this volume,

> Ubiquitous networking is leading us to the point where every computer system supports communication and where every term we use will be seen and hence interpreted by others. There are traditional philosophical and linguistic approaches to making sure we have "common understanding," but these tend to be based on highly abstract or idealized examples and settings. We need to develop new theoretical foundations for talking about the kinds of "semantic approximations" that are need-

ed for something as apparently simple as sharing data between two databases and as ubiquitous as the nodes of the Internet.

At the workshop, Craig Knoblock argued that the problem is not one that can be solved simply by imposing standards: "There is going to have to be some kind of distributed solution . . . . [Systems] have to change their model and update things. So there has to be enough information in the underlying structure that it is easy to make those changes. But there is no way that you can anticipate all those changes." Moreover, once obtained, semantic alignment can be undermined over time; this is the well-known problem of semantic drift.

COLLABORATION AND COMMUNICATION

Improving an Individual's Interaction: Person-Computer Collaboration and Communication

The interface is the "face" that meets a person (individual user) who is interacting with the NII. Better systems for human-computer communication are essential if we are to have easy-to-use, large-scale information systems—systems that every citizen can use. If we compare current capabilities for human-machine communication to the ways in which people communicate with one another, it is apparent that current interfaces are severely limited. The example in Chapter 4 of telephone menu confusion problems is evidence of the gulf between person-person communication and person-computer communication. Even more telling is Andries van Dam's table-setting analogy.[5] Bruce Tognazzini's equating of mouse clicks with grunts sheds light on the relative illiteracy of current interfaces, suggesting that direct manipulation interfaces hearken back to the days before language (other than grunting) was used for communication.[6]

Communication and collaboration are interdependent: communication requires collaboration (Grosz and Sidner, 1990; Nass and Reeves, 1996; see also Brown and Duguid, 1992), and collaboration requires communication, though not necessarily linguistic communication, as Terveen's investigations of ways to organize collaboration around shared manipulation of work materials illustrate.

In his position paper in this volume, Terry Winograd notes that people use three primary modes of interacting with others and their environment: manipulation (e.g., grasping, modifying, controlling objects), locomotion, and conversation. Each of these modes of acting must be coordinated with ways of perceiving: we manipulate objects within sight and grasp, sense in various ways as we move among locations, and listen as well as talk when we converse. Direct manipulation interfaces are rooted in the first of these modes, Web travel (and many games) in the second.

Conversations among people have features that have not been captured in either of these classes of interfaces or in the more (human) language-like command-line and query language interfaces. In her paper in this volume, Candace Sidner argues, with reference to research in natural-language dialogue processing, that our conversations are themselves collaborative activities (Lockbaum, 1994, 1995; Stein and Maier, 1995; Nass and Reeves, 1996; Clark, 1996; Clark and Shaefer, 1987). She claims that when we talk to one another, we collaborate not only about what we are doing—whether it is building a chair or trying to design a new interface— but also to make the conversation itself happen. Even when we are disagreeing or competing, for our dialogue to proceed we must collaborate at some level (e.g., that is why we speak to our interlocutors in languages we all understand).

The extended nature of conversations—which are typically more than one sentence, or a question and response, long—and the ways in which they use context are not evident in current interfaces (Moore, 1995). It is worth noting that speech interfaces are likewise single interaction oriented and lacking in these features of conversation. A major deficiency in most systems is the meager or nonexistent model of the ongoing interaction with a user. History lists and "undo" features are sometimes incorporated into interfaces, but they typically capture only a small part of the interaction and encode none of its structure. Such approaches ignore what is known about human discourse and its structure.[7]

In her paper, Candace Sidner notes that "only the user does any modeling or remembering of the interaction and its parts." Capturing some aspects of the structure of a dialogue is required for an interface to track a communication. "While an interface to a given application may have hundreds of so-called dialogue boxes, dialogue in the human sense does not take place." Sidner argues that the inadequacy of current interfaces from the perspective of systems that provide a capability for dialogue with users derives in part from their inadequate models of human communication. For instance, the dialogue is restricted to a single exchange in which the user must respond to a system query (e.g., S: "Replace?" U: "Yes") or statement (e.g., S: "File is too large for editor." U: "OK"), the user's response is strictly delimited by the system choices, and often the user cannot proceed without responding. In contrast, when people carry on a dialogue, it typically comprises multiple exchanges; no one person controls what another may say; and all parties are free to change the topic. Context setting and tracking have been studied widely and modeled by researchers in the natural language processing community, but extensions to other modalities and media are needed.

The Circuit-Fixit-Shoppe system (Smith and Hipp, 1994) and the MINDS system (Young et al., 1989) are examples of prototype systems that integrate dialogue capabilities. Specifically, they can have long sequences of interactions with a user and keep track of the roles of the individual interactions and how they all fit together. They maintain goal structures that show the required steps for realizing a central objective and build dialogue around those necessary steps. They function by selecting unachieved subgoals and carrying out interactions with the user to try to achieve them. Coherence of the dialogue is maintained because of the natural relationship between the top-level goals and their supporting subgoals. A dialogue involves the interactions between the participants as they sequentially address the various subgoals needed to eventually achieve or fail to achieve the top-level goal. The nature of the dialogue may be to jump around the proof tree from subgoal to subgoal in a seemingly random order in an attempt to find subgoals that can lead to high-level success. The associated subdialogues resemble common human-human interactions that similarly jump around from topic to topic in a problem-solving situation. These behaviors are in contrast to typical machine capabilities in which there may be little high-level structure to guide the dialogue and to guarantee a well-formed sequence of interactions.

Communication among people is not error free, misunderstanding free, or perfectly efficient. This fact influences the ways in which models of human communication can be useful for interface design in at least two ways. First, designers will not want to incorporate all characteristics of natural discourse into their systems. Second, as they expand the capabilities of systems to have more of the interaction and context-related characteristics of human dialogue, they will need to provide ways of dealing with errors and misunderstandings. The increased power, naturalness, and flexibility that more true-dialogue capabilities provide will undoubtedly engender situations in which a user or system misunderstand one another. They should also provide a richer base for error recovery techniques.

Because interfaces involve the whole experience of a person using a system (as defined in Chapter 1), they need to fulfill more than simply carrying communications between person and machine. In Austin Henderson's view, interfaces have a fourfold role: (1) to help people do what they are doing, (2) to help people learn how to do what they are doing (e.g., help systems and on-line training), (3) to assist people to manage the resources that go into doing their tasks; and (4) to evolve as the technology and the sociotechnical system in which they are using this technology changes. As he said at the workshop, "That is the domain of the interface. To take it any smaller than that is to simply say you are leaving out most of the job the people have in using a machine."

The communication-collaboration view of interfaces is one that does not expect flawless, errorless execution or fixed sequences of actions. Rather, it requires system designs to provide flexibility and means of changing courses of action when things do not go according to plan, as well as options for recovering. People spend a good deal of the time they are working with computer systems getting in and out of trouble (Suchman, 1987). Modeling of the task or intentional context (why the user is communicating in addition to what he or she is saying) as well as of the structured dialogue history is especially critical to deal with situations in which things do not work out right the first time (Sidner, 1983; Litman and Allen, 1990; Lochbaum, 1994).

Another way of viewing the move toward ECIs that communicate and collaborate with their users is to think of having an "interfaceless system," a system that allows a person to be immersed in what he or she is doing without being sidetracked by irrelevant communication details. Weld (1995) describes the advantages of intelligent interfaces—ones that free users from having to know details of where and how information is stored and describe some of the research needed to move beyond the current state of affairs. As discussed in Chapter 6, some activities of intelligent agents involve collaboration and are relevant as enablers of person-to-machine communication and collaboration.

Another concern in this arena relates to social stratification and variation. Gary Olson notes in his paper (available on-line at http://www2.nas.edu/CSTBWEB), that the dominant user interface metaphors emerged from narrow segments of society: the command-based interfaces of early personal computing came from the world of science and engineering; the popular desktop metaphor emerged from the world of the office and white-collar workers; the hypertext metaphor used in World Wide Web browsers came from the world of experimental document structures; popular interfaces like MUDs (multiuser domains) and MOOs (multiuser domains/object-oriented) emerged from computer games and virtual worlds. A legacy of these plural roots is that designers have not yet figured out how to present the information infrastructure to the broad range of potential users. Even such putative examples of widespread success as automated teller machines turn out to have surprisingly narrow distributions of users (on the order of 10 to 15 percent of the public), while more widely used systems, such as video cassette recorders, are the butt of jokes about the inability of average citizens to make full use of them.

Finally, ECIs should do more than make it possible to do things on the NII; they should make it possible to do things well. At the workshop, Loren Terveen noted that, although some interfaces make it easy to do things, "they don't necessarily make it easy to do the things well. I can design HTML (Hypertext Markup Language) pages easily, I can do all kinds of manipulation in Photo Shop, but I can't necessarily build good HTML pages or do attractive graphical images in Photo Shop. I need expert assistance." He argues further that aiming to have systems that help people do things well is additional motivation for having collaborative systems.

ECIs in Support of Person-Person Communication and Group Activities

ECIs provide support for multiperson activities in two ways: (1) person-person communication—they support communication between individuals and among groups of people, for a range of activities only some of which are collaborative; and (2) group collaboration—they support the collaborative activities of groups, whether formal or informal, that are distributed geographically and with members active at different times of the day (i.e., support of cooperative and collaborative activities that may be carried on asynchronously). These two areas are closely related, but neither subsumes the other. On the one hand, multiperson, multimachine collaborations require communication but also a range of other interface support (e.g., ways of keeping track of the people responsible for various parts of the activity). On the other hand, people use the NII to communicate even when they are not working on a collaborative endeavor; as the social scientists at the workshop observed several times, networks facilitate social communication, and not all communicative uses of the NII are in the service of collaborations.

ECIs for Communication Among People

One of the major uses of the Internet is to enable communication among people (Sproull and Faraj, 1995; Chung and Iacono, 1996; Donath, 1996). We expect that people will similarly use the more enhanced integrated NII for communicating with one another in a variety of ways. Although in some cases they will communicate to get information (here narrowly construed), often the communication will be directed at other purposes.

The impact of networked computer-based communications systems supporting multiple modalities extends beyond those who have their hands on a keyboard. For example, Dourish et al. (1994) in an experiment at Rank Xerox Europarc that involved direct video connections between offices identified four different types of users: people in the wired offices, people who used other people's video links to find someone, the institution that capitalized on members' communications activities, and the surrounding culture that took advantage of those connections to have remote meetings.

People also consult with one another about how to use technology and about where to find information (Constant et al., 1996). At the workshop, Aki Namioka, in discussing the Seattle Community Network, noted that being on the net can be a social activity not only with the community on-line but also with others in the same "room." This same phenomenon appears to be occurring in cybercafes and rooms set up for people to play networked games together. These are very social activities, and the players appear to get a lot out of being colocated. Thus, we should not think of technology as marking the end of face-to-face meetings. It may even lead to meetings that otherwise might not occur. People tackling similar problems want to talk with each other. It is important to understand the ways in which groups pass on information to one another whether they are colocated in the same room or located apart from one other.

This experience is part of a larger pattern, according to Olson, who commented at the workshop on people using technologies in social settings. The telephone is an example, including its history of human operators, and today people commonly get Web URLs (universal resource locators) or help advice from other people (Kraut et al., 1996). He concluded that "the technologies . . . we are studying are themselves embedded in interesting collaborative social situations that we need to take into account when we build these technologies."

Loren Terveen noted in his paper in this volume that such patterns of behavior have seeds for new technology tools. For example, systems might help mediate collaboration between people. They can provide for people to support one another by allowing for asynchronous and geographically remote sharing of information. One set of applications aimed in this direction is work on "social filtering" or "virtual collaboration" (see Reidel and Miller, http://www.sims.berkeley.edu/resources/collab/ for other references). Research in these areas aims to use computational techniques to help people benefit from each other's experience without their having to be aware of, or communicate directly with, each other at all. Hill (http://community.bellcore.com/navigation/) draws the analogy to people establishing and using trails: when walking through the forest, people know where to walk because many people have walked before them. They do not have to decide how to go anew nor do they have to decide about the people who preceded them to benefit from what others have already discovered.

As Lee Sproull explained at the workshop, people attend to social information as well as to task information within an interaction and to community as well as memory across interactions. The result is a need for interfaces to support people as social actors, not just information processors. She cautioned that "a lot of times when people talk with one another, it is not for the purpose of getting information, and if we focus only on that subset of why it is that people communicate, we will have missed an extraordinarily large fraction of what it is that is important to people when they do communicate." Sproull used the example of Usenet groups devoted to topics of physical or mental disabilities or disorders, noting that her research with Sara Kiesler showed them to be used as electronic support groups. "They are places where one can go . . . to get information, but, . . . if what you really want is information, the Usenet group is not the place to get the highest-quality information, or the most efficient way to get information." This is not to say that Usenet groups and the like are never the place to go for high-quality, relevant information (such information can be found, for example, at http://cancernet.nci.nih.gov/ and http://www-med.stanford.edu/CBHP), but to acknowledge that they may not be originators of such information, that people may use them for other reasons, and that establishing the quality of information can be difficult (see Chapter 2).

The use of the NII to facilitate communication among people forces us to consider the social aspects of communication—the ways in which communication supports communities—not just the technological means of getting bits from one party to another. As Lee Sproull explained at the workshop: "When people talk with one another, when people communicate with one another, they are not just exchanging information, they are not just acquiring it, they are not just disseminating it; they are also engaged in social action, social behavior. . . . [W]ithin an interaction, people attend to the messenger and the audience, as well as to the message. . . . [They] attend to social information, as well as to task information. Across interactions, people attend to community as well as to memory. So these new kinds of interfaces that we are thinking about need to be designed and constructed as interfaces for social actors, not just for information processors."

ECIs for Support of Group Activities

The NII needs to support more than individual task-related activity and information gathering in the service of such tasks. Many tasks require coordinated group efforts, and people need to work with one another. In many corporate and governmental settings, group activity is the norm. But work is just the beginning, as the social patterns that have emerged on the Internet show. Groups of fans make extensive use of the Internet to discuss their favorite shows (e.g., "Star Trek," "X-Files," etc.; Clerc, 1994). As Gary Olson noted at the workshop, "The kinds of things that ordinary citizens like to do together—clubs, hobbies, interests of various kinds, civic groups, political action groups, and so on, practical problem solving—[the formal modeling and technology communities] know almost nothing about these kinds of collaborative activities, and I think they have very different kinds of needs than the kinds of intellectual tasks that [these communities] are more familiar with."

Although a substantial body of work and techniques has been developed in the computer-supported collaborative work (CSCW) community,[8] as Terry Winograd notes in his position paper in this volume, "The current state of the art can be described as having a large 'hole in the middle.'" At the theoretical level, there are general abstract theories of how people work together and the role of communication in the process. At the practical level, there are large numbers of specialized applications (including such widely differing ones as retail point-of-sale systems and the National Science Foundation proposal application process) that support organized group activity. Winograd adds,

> But we have not yet developed the conceptual and computational tools to make it easy to bring collaboration into the mainstream of applications. When I work with my research group on a joint paper, we use sophisticated word processors, graphics programs, and the like, but our coordination is based on generic e-mail and calendars, and often fails to help us at the places where breakdowns occur.

Furthermore, there is a need for much greater understanding of the ways in which technology can facilitate (or hinder) community formation, especially in nonwhite-collar work settings. The role of computer support for communication and a better understanding of privacy concerns (and the feasibility of various technical solutions to meet them) are among the challenges presented by this arena. The emerging use of computers to support communities of practice in educational settings (see Charles Cleary's paper in this volume) and networked learning communities provide rich sources on which to base some investigations in this area.

As in the case of person-computer communication and collaboration, in building systems to support group collaborations, a significant issue is the degree to which explicit representations of the interaction are embodied in the software itself. E-mail systems represent very little explicitly; point-of-sale transaction systems have detailed representations of the interaction. As Terry Winograd observed following the workshop (private communication by e-mail), "Some of the most successful software has been at each end of this spectrum (e.g., e-mail and sales terminals). . . . There are few if any examples of systems in this middle area that have had major commercial success. The benefits of the explicit structuring do not always accrue to those who do the work" (Grudin, 1993). Claims in this arena too often run to the extremes: some claim that real work cannot be formalized (Suchman, 1987), others that the design of effective software requires an explicit analysis of work (Keen, 1991; Scherr, 1993; Denning and Dargan, 1996; Medina-Mora et al., 1992; Flores et al., 1988). Workflow systems have been criticized, and there have been recent attempts to design more flexible workflow representations (Glance et al., 1996; Dourish et al., 1996).

Here, too, it is essential to look at intermediate positions, coming to understand both the limitations of formalization and the situations in which it can be effectively deployed to increase system usefulness.

At the workshop, Olson argued that it is critical to look beyond white-collar work. "If you look at the proceedings of CSCW, almost all the studies of collaboration are about white-collar work, professional work of the kind that we all do, and we know almost nothing about what kind of collaborative activities occur in much broader social communities."

Sproull's argument, cited in the previous section, that ECIs must take the social aspects of communication and collaboration into account is quite evident in this setting. Often the kinds of social interactions that must be handled arise subtly. At the workshop, Henderson gave an example: "When Xerox . . . began to put its copiers on-line, it was confronted with a problem that up until then was handled beautifully by the stand-alone machines, which were surrounded by physical space, namely, if you walk up to a machine, you can tell whether it is in use, there is somebody standing there, or it's making noise. When you begin to put them on-line and introduce the potential for people to compete for that resource, suddenly, the machine has willy-nilly created a problem for itself as to how you are going to manage that interaction."

Thus, the design of systems to support collaborative work must address interpersonal as well as task aspects of the work. Although some applications are amenable to fixed a priori solutions, others will require an ability for systems to negotiate with their users. As Henderson added at the workshop, "Trying to figure out . . . a social model for interruption in the use of a copier, say, or any other resource, is probably something which is a little bit beyond us just now." Research on computer agents that negotiate with one another may offer one approach to this problem.[9] In other settings, ECIs might provide support for person-person negotiation.

The setting of many people working together using many machines toward some common end raises social science research issues as well. In particular, the interaction between technology and social effort—effort devoted to participating in a social interaction—needs to be understood. Determining whether technology increases or decreases social effort and why is extraordinarily important. A way to estimate or measure social effort is necessary in order to build ECIs that help people minimize or manage social effort. For example, Lee Sproull argues that we know ways to measure the mental effort that is necessary to use any particular interface but that we need to develop ways to assess the social effort that is necessary to use any interface for communication or collaboration. We need to understand better the effort devoted to participating in the social interaction, attending to the messenger and the audience, as well as to the message. Storck and Sproull (1995) discuss this point in the context of video conferencing; Kiesler et al. (1996) demonstrate it in the context of how people respond to interface agents.

DIVISION OF LABOR

Computers and people have different strengths and different skill competencies. One challenge in designing collaboration into a system is determining the appropriate division of responsibility.[10] The negotiation of responsibility is one component of a complete collaboration. In some settings we might want a system to negotiate with people, but for many applications, and certainly in the short term, there will be a need for the system designer to manage this division.

Two sets of issues are raised by the question of how to divide the work to be done between systems and people. First, there is the question of whether to build into a system a fixed division of labor or to give the system a capability for negotiating the appropriate division with users according to the task at hand. Second, a critical aspect of agreeing to the division of responsibility is having trust in the collaborator to do its part; this raises a range of questions concerning trust in computer systems. In addressing both these problems, there is the question of whether the extent to which systems working with people should emulate what people working together do.

Determining Which Party Will Do What

Sidner argues that in the long-term we should aim to understand collaboration and negotiation sufficiently well that we can build systems that emulate people working collaboratively. Henderson argues that "division is . . . going to be probably a constantly changing matter and therefore needs to be one of the subject matters of the collaboration." The determination of who is in charge cannot be decided "up-front" but must be worked out along the way. "You need to be able to negotiate with the machine when it is doing what it is doing." This is one of the key areas in which ECI designers will have to find a middle ground between giving a system full responsibility and giving it none.

Some recent research on systems for interactive graphic design has produced very interesting exemplars of such a middle ground. These "semiautomated" design systems do not attempt to have the system take over the whole task of designing a presentation (as do various packages that restrict the user to a small number of static designs and some "intelligent interfaces" (e.g., Roth et al., 1994)), nor do they require the user to directly specify all the details (as do direct manipulation drawing packages). For example, in the GLIDE system (Ryall et al., 1996) for network diagrams, the person does global optimization, and the system does local optimization. In the GOLD system (Myers et al., 1994) for business graphics, the user sketches a chart using some of the data and the system completes the diagram for the whole data set. The various SAGE tools (Roth et al., 1994) assist users in creating charts and graphs by providing templates and access to past designs in ways that make them easily modifiable to accommodate new data.

A cautionary note was sounded by some at the workshop with respect to computer systems taking on greater roles. Olson said,

> It seems to me that if you look at examples of technologies that have actually been helpful or useful in human activities, there is a simplicity that runs through them, and there is a real tendency in building technical systems to want to put lots of things in the system, that the system can somehow manage them better than the people can, and I think over and over again, we have gotten burned with that kind of design bias.

One of the key features of the semiautomated systems described above is their attempt to allocate responsibility to person and machine depending on the computational complexity or skill required. This approach presents a challenge to the designer in determining the division of labor and once again leads to questions of design-and-test iterative cycles.

Developing Trust in Systems

For participants in a collaboration to agree on who will do what, they must be able to trust one another. Such trust requires in part being able to rely on others to carry out a job and their commitment to doing so in the current setting (Grosz and Kraus, 1996). At the workshop, Olson argued that simplicity breeds trust and complexity breeds suspicion; this is evident by observation (e.g., people trust paper copies), but little is understood about how trust is established and maintained. Hall (1996) presents a formal approach to showing how a user can gradually come to trust his or her agent more. Hall's sense of trust is basically that the agent will do what the user wants within specified resource constraints.

At the workshop, Lee Sproull related trust to relationships, as did Stephen Kent, who outlined what information security experts refer to as "the web of trust"—social networks in which the parties trust each other to interact. Sproull explained that human collaborators not only solve problems but also build and sustain relationships with one another as part of establishing trust. Her observations speak to the question of how much systems should be like people. For example, Henderson wondered whether collaborating with a system requires a person to worry about maintaining a relationship with it.

At least four different facets of trust arise when considering collaboration and communication in ECIs: trust of a system with information (e.g., privacy), trusting what the system reports about users (authentication), trusting content (credibility), and trusting the system to function (reliability). Privacy concerns arise for individuals using systems but also for developers as they collect data in seeking to evaluate designs. The question of how we negotiate and manage credibility in an on-line environment is an open research question. We trust things we see in hardback volumes in the library more than we trust similar content on a mimeographed circular handed out by an individual. What are the corresponding mechanisms in computer-mediated information?[11]

Another aspect of trust relates to the handling of information shared, stored, transmitted, and processed in computer-based systems. In addition to determining the kinds of information that are needed to inform systems design, we also need to seriously consider the ways in which we handle that data. Because collaborations typically require significant information exchanges, incorporating collaborative capabilities into systems may also raise questions of data confidentiality and associated personal privacy issues. This set of issues is receiving considerable attention in other NII-related contexts and is beyond the scope of this study, but the connection of system trustworthiness vis à vis information that is sensitive is relevant to the broader context of making systems more useful to every citizen, as noted in Chapter 2. Thus, although security may seem to be beyond the scope of ECI design, it will impose some constraints that must be understood for the ECI to be useful. As a result, ECI designers must take security concerns into account. Information security or trustworthiness can affect the kinds of information presumed necessary for a system to collaborate effectively, the way in which it is provided, the ways in which it is used, the granting of access to it, the capacity (and associated mechanisms) for providing anonymity or minimizing records of transactions, and so on—issues that can affect the design and use of interfaces and that should be assessed in the kinds of testing recommended throughout this report. At the workshop, for example, Sproull remarked on autologging:

We now have the ability to do a lot of autologging of data about people when they use systems. We haven't had much public discussion about when or the conditions under which those data should be collected and should be made accessible, and I see this as, in some sense, a division of labor between users and systems, but it is an issue that has to be framed within a larger political and social context, and we don't usually think of it that way.

Designer as Collaborator

One way of achieving the partial level of collaboration Henderson argues for may be to explicitly design into a system ways of obtaining and working with information important for collaboration (e.g., information about what the user is trying to do at a level beyond an individual action or system call). Such systems would have only a limited understanding of a user's goals embedded in their design. They would not understand (in any of the usual senses of the word) what the person wants, but the system designer would have done so. This situation places a spotlight on the skills and abilities of designers—what is the norm, what is the ideal— and what they imply in the context of intrinsically nonordinary design specialists designing systems for use by specific groups or whole populations (every citizen) of people.

Speaking as a successful designer, at the workshop Bruce Tognazzini characterized an ideal as follows:

> As a designer, I feel when I am designing that I am collaborating with my eventual users. It is in the same way that I would collaborate over the telephone with somebody and communicate with them. At the very least, I am communicating with them, and I would claim I am also collaborating with them. The machine is just the medium for what is essentially a time-shifted conversation between the designer and the end user. Now, since many applications are not designed by designers but are designed by engineers, who are weak in communication skills, a lot of software doesn't look like it is very communicative, but my experience has been when you have a design team that collaborates on the design, and part of that collaboration is bringing in users to test it, and so forth, in this very kind of rich iterative environment, you end up with a very communicative and collaborative piece of software.

Some systems aim to gather information while a system is in use to feed back to the designers. Thus, they give substance to the notion that there is an ongoing collaboration between designers and users and provide technological support to make the collaboration more successful (see Girgensohn et al., 1994; also see Hartson et al., 1996).

In the scenario Tognazzini describes in his paper (this volume), systems designers identify and work with people who are representative of the target user community. They collaborate during the design stage so that the resulting systems are able to collaborate with the people who use them. At the workshop, Henderson noted that "as long as you are playing by that tune, everything goes fine; you fit those capabilities into your work, but it is basically you and the designer. The machine isn't changing much." From this we might conclude that if designers take into account the capabilities and properties needed for collaboration (e.g., establishing a common purpose, a way of achieving that purpose, ways of negotiating over the various choices that arise), identify and consult with target users, and tests designs in realistic environments (see Chapter 4 for discussion of relevant design methods), systems can be produced that collaborate with their users. A system's actions and responses will be structured in a way that aligns with what the user is trying to do. There are thus two collaborations: the design team with a sample user population collaborates to yield a system design that will result in a system that is able to collaborate with users. Although this model may represent the best way to proceed for communication between a single user and a system, research on how to extend "iterated design" to systems being used by multiple people and groups will be needed before it can be used for designing systems to support communication or collaboration among groups of people.

The concept of designer as implicit collaborator evoked two sets of concerns among some workshop participants. The first is that of technologist hubris. Lee Sproull cautioned that when designers talk about user models they mean users' models of the technology rather than models of users. The resulting inference is that what designers are doing is imagining model users, yet almost no one behaves like the model user the designer has in mind. As a result, it is important to broaden our understanding of what it is that users are actually about. Austin Henderson, coming to the defense of designers, maintained that many of the techniques of design are pushing designers to understand that the user does not behave as an idealized, trouble-free user and that the model user is, in fact, someone who is prone to all sorts of error. Gary Olson observed that human-computer interface efforts typically focus on individuals in construing model users, whereas there are model social systems and model organizational systems that mostly are invisible to designers.

CONCLUSIONS: RESEARCH ISSUES AND CHALLENGES

- Theories of collaboration should be developed that support the development of systems that collaborate with people and systems that assist group collaborative activities. Various research communities have been developing models and theories of collaboration (e.g., Bratman, 1992; Grosz and Kraus, 1996; Levesque et al., 1990; Cohen and Levesque, 1990; Grosz and Sidner, 1990; Searle, 1990; Olson and Olson, 1995; Flores et al., 1988), but there is much work to be done to extend them to cover the range of behaviors required for ECIs, to use them in developing ECIs, and to experiment with their use in NII settings.

• Methods should be developed to integrate capabilities for person-computer and person-person collaborations.

• Research should investigate what is needed for people to come to trust computer systems. The information that needs to be communicated by the system should be identified. Ethical responsibilities that system designers incur when producing systems that give assurances of trustworthiness to people should be examined.

• The ways in which technology facilitates community formation, the communication capabilities needed to do so, and the privacy concerns raised should be investigated.

• The social effects of different interface choices should be investigated, particularly the ways in which different presentation and communication choices affect people's interactions with media.

Research Issues for Person-Computer Collaboration

• To develop the conceptual and computational tools to make it easy to bring collaboration into the mainstream of application requires a better understanding of the tradeoffs between explicit representations (which may engender more complex computations) and collaborative power (systems that only implicitly embody certain capabilities needed for collaboration may be less general or less powerful). It should focus in part on determining how to derive system design principles from general theoretical results on modeling of collaboration.

• Research should investigate the extent to which human-computer collaborations can be usefully made more like human-human collaborations. This research is necessarily interdisciplinary; for example, it is conceivable that a technical solution could be found that would prove undesirable for sociological reasons. It must consider both the system-sociological problem of human attribution to machines of capabilities greater than they may have and the modeling problem presented by people being less than "ideal" (perfect) collaborators.

• Research should investigate the tradeoffs in presentational power of the full range of modalities for interaction and media in which to present information and the effects of context on choice. The use of systems to support multiperson activities in these different modalities and the kinds of multiperson collaboration we want to support with ECIs introduce challenging questions both technological (e.g., coordination of information presentation at different locations, delivery of video) and sociological (e.g., developing ways of measuring the effectiveness of ECIs for supporting different kinds of interaction).

• Theories of negotiation should be developed that will enable systems to handle the division of labor more flexibly. Principles should be developed for guiding the design time choice of "who will do what" in ECIs. Methods should be developed for measuring/evaluating different approaches to the division of labor.

Research Issues for Computer Support of Person-Person Communication and Group Collaborations

• The design of ECIs to support communication among people and groups should be investigated. The scientific base should be provided and the technologies developed so that interfaces can be designed and constructed as social actors, not just information processors.

• Ways should be provided to support community building and other social aspects of communication. Supporting communication means e-mail, chat, MUDs and MOOs, video links, and so forth for every person, not just for the computer literate (i.e., lots of kids and those of us who have used machines at work) and technically sophisticated (computer science types).

• Ways in which systems can support collaborations among people, perhaps even participating in collaborations with groups, should be determined. In doing so, we must look beyond business and professional work to consider the kinds of collaboration that arise in civic groups, clubs, hobbies, and political action groups.

• An understanding should be developed of negotiation and collaboration sufficient for building into the technology the capability for people to build the social systems that will allow for handling the social interactions that arise (e.g., in a resource competition situation).

• Understanding how different sensory abilities of participants affect multisensory collaborative system design, and understanding how the design is affected by varying interface technologies, which may have different multimedia capabilities (e.g., the implications of someone operating over a voice-only connection in a collaborative interaction with others using other kinds of connection), should be developed.

• Ways should be developed for ECIs to support communication and collaboration among multiple people, each with a personal and organizational background that shapes and guides their interactions with others; within these "interaction spaces" ECIs must support communication structures at all levels, from the generic document structuring of the Web to highly task-specific interactions.

• Understanding of social effort in mediated collaborations should be studied.

• Technologies should be developed to support virtual collaborations.

NOTES

1. GLIDE is a presentation package, like PowerPoint, but optimized for and restricted to drawing network diagrams (Ryall et al., 1996).

2. "Bob" is a software product that guides novice users, via animated characters and settings, in starting up various home computing applications. Customers found the interface cute but lacking in the capability to help them with complex, difficult tasks. See Arar (1996).

3. There are, in fact, a range of social effects inherent in interfaces. Recent research (Nass and Reeves, 1996) has demonstrated that interactive media generate fundamental psychosocial cues regardless of whether the media are explicity designed. The wording of commands and messages and the presentation of images, for example, can also affect an interface in very subtle ways.

4. Although this problem resembles one that arises for distibuted databases in which different databases associate similar terms/data with different meanings, the challenge is much greater in the NII setting than for databases because the world in which the system is operating is both open (in contrast to the "closed-world assumption" that database systems presume) and very dynamic.

5. I want Jeeves (the P.G. Wodehouse butler); I want somebody who has my context, knows how I operate, and can anticipate what I need, and then help execute it in a completely unobtrusive kind of way, and yes, in that sense I do want to collaborate with my machine. If my machine is sufficiently intelligent, then I will call it collaboration. Today's machines don't permit me to do that . . . . [As an analogy] instead of being able to say, "set the table, we are having company for dinner," and have that translate automatically into a whole number of smaller specifications, I have to say, "pick up the dinner plate, put the fork on the left-hand side," and so on. Everything I want to do in my application, I have to do explicitly.

6. This is not to say that direct manipulation is never the right way to communicate. For instance, it works well for many games (e.g., checkers, chess) whether played on a computer or in the physical world. However, not all extensions from the noncomputer to computer-based interactions are straightforward, as a comparison of recent research on semiautomated drawing systems with commercial computer drawing packages makes clear. (See division of labor discussion of SAGE, GLIDE, GOLD systems.)

7. Grosz and Sidner (1990) have pointers to work in this area.

8. See Proceedings of Computer-Supported Cooperative Work Conferences, 1986-1996.

9. Examples of such work may be found in the proceedings of the International Conferences on Multi-agent Systems, the Distributed AI sections of the proceedings of American Association for Artifical Intelligence (AAAI) and International Joint Conference on Artificial Intelligence (IJCAI) conferences, and in Rosenschein and Zlotkin (1994).

10.   Here "responsibility" means "responsibility for doing a job" or "burden," and is not used in the sense of moral or legal responsibility between people and systems.

11.   Cryptography offers mechanisms for authentication and privacy. Various operating systems techniques provide for reliability.

6

AGENTS AND SYSTEMS INTELLIGENCE

SOME PROBLEMS ASSOCIATED WITH THE DELIVERY OF FUNCTION TODAY

Current interfaces to the national information infrastructure (NII) require that the user form a detailed plan to accomplish the tasks he or she desires. Many in both industry and research argue that if ordinary citizens are to use the NII effectively, interfaces must be developed that allow users to specify their needs at a higher level, in terms of their goals. As Maes (1994) has written, "The currently dominant interaction metaphor of direct manipulation . . . requires the user to initiate all tasks explicitly and to monitor all events. This metaphor will have to change if untrained users are to make effective use of the computers and networks of tomorrow." The argument is that we must move away from interfaces that require the user to "micromanage" a system's actions and toward interfaces that allow users to delegate actions to digital proxies (often called software "agents" or "softbots") that use information about users' goals and interests to act on their behalf. Some of these proxies will simply make the networked world more manageable by hiding technical details, much like operating systems and high-level programming languages hide details from users.

An example of the kind of interaction that happens too often with current technologies appears in Box 6.1, which describes a prospective student's attempts to obtain information about scholarships. We can fol-

---

BOX 6.1
A Student Looks for Scholarship Information on the Internet

A reasonable place to start is with one of the well-known indexes. Our user might look for the heading "Education" and do a search on "Scholarship Information." This yields two items: "Loan and Scholarship Programs" and "Science: Mathematics: Organizations: Professional: American Mathematical Society." The latter is not of interest to this student, but the former returns 291 sites where the student can seek further information. Because this flood of information is overwhelming, a reasonable response is to go back to "Education" and follow a link to "Financial Aid." Here the categories are "College Aid Offices" (144), "Companies" (14), "Grants" (35), "Loan and Scholarship Programs" (34), and "Regional Resources" (10). Several of these look attractive, particularly "Loan and Scholarship Programs and Grants." The student does not know where he or she wants to go to college, so the 144 individual offices do not seem to be a good place to look. The prospective student follows a link and finds a site advertising "180,000 scholarships, grants, fellowships, and loans representing billions of dollars." Wow, this is getting interesting! The student is asked to enter a major but does not want to commit to one. Hitting "go" gives an error message. Trying "undecided," "none," and "science" leads to frustration. There is a button labeled "more." Here the student is asked to enter name, address, and more information. But he or she may not want to provide such information. Following a previously discovered link, the user can find a list of special loan and scholarship programs, but they all turn out to be narrowly aimed at such groups as beauty contest winners, specialists in cardiac electrophysiology, and so forth. Following yet another idea, the student looks for military-based scholarship programs, but the maze of paths is similarly extensive and unrewarding.

---

low the student's search on the current Internet and obtain a good idea of the state of existing facilities. The student follows a number of reasonable paths, conscientiously reads the entries, and makes selections. However, the search requires a troublesome number of difficult decisions, takes considerable time, and often results in frustration. The student must enter multiple databases that may be formatted in different ways, must interact with each on its own terms, and may have to restate his or her special interests and constraints again and again in each new environment. Eventually, the student will, in all likelihood, become frustrated and decide to ask a high school teacher or guidance counselor for help. Searches of this kind and with this level of success are more the rule than the exception with present-day facilities. If a person wants to access government services, look for merchandise, or report a downed power line, a multiplicity of choices, an inordinate amount of time, and a lack of satisfaction are common experiences.

The main problems are as follows:

1. *Information overload for the user.* The amounts of information available are astronomical, and any attempt to read the information can lead to an avalanche response. There is no mechanism that prunes the sources for quality or for applicability to the user's need.

2. *System, application, and task complexity.* The functions available on the network may require special command syntax and may have complex facilities not easily accessed by the user. Furthermore, the solution of any given user request could involve calls to many such systems.

3. *Rigidity.* The system may have only very specific ways of receiving input, finding solutions, and returning them to the user.

HOW AGENTS AND SYSTEM INTELLIGENCE CAN HELP

A solution to the above problems is to have a software system between the user and the network that deals with the user in a convenient manner and that interacts with the network and its many facilities in the languages that the network requires. This is analogous to the task of an operating system that may receive a command to "print file1" (either typed or via a direct manipulation command) and that may issue an array of commands to machine facilities to find file1, format it for printing, allocate space for its transfer, open communication to a printer, manage a file transfer to it, receive messages back from the printer as it does its job, and so forth. The user is only aware of the simple command and the fact that the desired file was printed. Yet the complexities involved in servicing the request can be tremendous. In the current situation, however, the job of the intermediary may be considerably more complicated. The facilities on the network may have greater diversity, it may be necessary to decide how many resources can reasonably be invested in a task, there may be a need for common-sense reasoning to decide the relevance of one facility or set of information versus another, and so forth.

The tasks of the agent are (1) to interact with the user to determine the nature of the request, (2) to interact with the network to obtain the best-possible solution, and (3) to present to the user the response that has been obtained in the most useful form. Figure 6.1 shows these functions in a diagram.

Following the flow arrows around the loop, the first step is interaction with the user. This could involve any of the media and/or modalities described in previous chapters: speech, graphic inputs, typing, or others. It could also involve a full dialogue because the user may have a request that is complex. Then the system must translate the results of this interaction to an internal form, which could be an extensive data structure. Next it executes a variety of computations to obtain a response. These may result in a series of additional interactions with the user. Finally, the

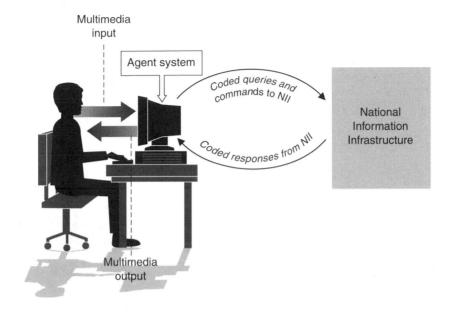

FIGURE 6.1   The intelligent system mediates between the user and the network.

internal form from the computation is translated into user-appropriate terms. Again, one or several of the media and/or modalities could be used, and this could involve more user interactions.

The type of system that delivers these kinds of behaviors is called an agent. Such a system has the properties that it can undertake goals on behalf of its sponsor (presumably the user), and it can act autonomously and initiate actions according to its own agenda. Such a system usually has an ability to undertake responsibility over time, persistently seeking its assigned goals and accounting for significant historical events. It may be designed to handle information searches, communication jobs, educational or recreational functions, commercial buying or selling tasks, or any other function that may be available on the network. It may guide the user through complex information spaces—for example, the way a travel agent guides a customer through the maze of possible itineraries or a research librarian guides a library user through the various reference search facilities. Agents may monitor information sources and inform the user of events that match the user's interest profile or may actively search for new information to call to the user's attention. Agents may look for opportunities to assist the user or to teach the user new things. The definition of an "agent" is, in fact, a controversial issue. Various sources emphasize its ability to perceive and act (Russell and Norvig, 1995), its role in doing a specialized task (Minsky and Riecken, 1994), its network interactive capabilities (Genesereth and Ketchpel, 1994), and its ability to carry out an agenda (Maes, 1994).

The technologies used to deliver these functions may come from traditional computer science with standard programming languages and methodologies or from more contemporary technologies, such as neural networks or rule-based deduction.

Diagnosing the User's Needs

The first convenience a system can offer to a user is some flexibility in the form of the input. The user may wish to make a request by speaking into a telephone, by pointing to items on a displayed menu, by typing a command, by some combination of all of these, or by some other method. It may also be true that the hardware device that is locally available will not allow all media or modes of input. A very attractive feature of an intelligent system is that it may be able to function properly regardless of the input mode or device. Whatever the means of input, the task of such a system is to convert it into an internal form that can be used by the machine.

It is common that a user's input will be inadequate from some point of view. Perhaps the user's syntax cannot be meaningfully parsed, or there may be ambiguity in the request. The system may need to enter into a clarifying dialogue. It must generate a proper internal message to be returned to the user and then translate it into the appropriate media modalities for presentation. Corresponding to the given input, there may be a particularly appropriate output: a menu clarification of some kind for a menu input, a spoken language output for a spoken input, and so forth. The clarification dialogue may continue for several iterations to address various aspects of the request. Some clarifications may come as the task goes forth and problems are encountered.

The agent may have some information about the user. This is called a user model, and it may contain a history of the user's typical requests, any special input/output preferences of the user, and a list of information gathered in the current interaction. The user model may be constructed explicitly by asking the user questions or implicitly by monitoring keystrokes or selections made. All of this information can be used by the system in the interaction to reduce redundancy and to efficiently move toward the goal. The system may be adaptive to improve efficiency. If the user often makes the same request, the interaction might be able to jump over the repetitive parts and move directly to the desired result. If particular interactions with the network prove to be unsatisfactory, the system may vary its behavior to avoid them.

Servicing the User's Request

Upon receiving the user's request, the agent must then undertake a variety of actions such as those described at the beginning of this chapter. This requires an ability to search diverse databases at distant places and to assemble discovered information into a useful form. It could require extensive calculations, calling other agents, and/or resorting to contacting other people and asking them for help. It could also involve making some kind of judgments concerning the reliability of the data being acquired. For example, are data provided by a generic source of scholarship information as reliable as the data presented by the institution making the offer? Simultaneously, the system should be able to inform the user about the nature of the search taking place. The user may want to know what sources are being accessed and where successes and failures have occurred. The user should be informed on the extent of the resources being accessed and the time likely to be required. If the undertaking is not of the nature desired, the user must be able to modify it appropriately.

Presenting the User with a Response

The system response could be a list of 10,000 documents, a complex diagram with extensive annotations, an audio signal, or some other collection of complex objects. Its task on response is to present this in a comprehensible form. The system must undertake content selection and decide which information will best satisfy the user's needs. Then it must do presentation design to structure and format the information in a comprehensible form. This includes media allocation—the decision as to which media will best display which information. Finally, it must realize individual media, ensuring coherency across media (e.g., cross-modal referring expressions, temporal coordination) and a layout that is consistent with the content and intent of the communication.

CURRENT AGENTS

Some Examples

Many types of agents have been developed and tested in recent years. An example is the entertainment ratings agent by Maes (1994), which requires the user to rate a series of items on which he or she has an opinion. The system then compares that local user's responses to many other users' responses who have submitted their own ratings to similar agents and finds groups of users with profiles of likes and dislikes that are similar to those of the local user. Having found such groups, it compiles a list of their average ratings for a variety of items the local user may not have seen and thus provides a group evaluation of items that should be correlated with the local user's own tastes. Such an agent leverages the power of the network to automatically and conveniently deliver to people advice that is personally tuned and would not be easily obtainable any other way, as discussed by Loren Terveen at the workshop.

Lieberman's (1995) Letizia is an agent that recommends Web pages as a user is browsing the Web. It operates in conjunction with a standard browser such as Netscape, tracking the user's behavior and using simple heuristics to form a profile of the user's interests (e.g., if the user saves a bookmark to a document, that document is assumed to be of high interest; if a user follows a link and then returns immediately, that document is assumed to not be of interest). While the user is browsing, Letizia tries to locate other information that may be of interest to the user by performing a resource-bounded best-first search of Web pages starting at the current page. At any time the user may request a list of recommendations and the system will display a page containing its current recommendations, which the user can then follow or ignore. This is another example of a current technology agent in that its main mechanism depends on keyword frequency measurements to represent document content for information retrieval (Salton, 1989).

An example of what can be done with more detailed models of user tasks and more sophisticated processing is Horvitz's Lumiere (http://www.research.microsoft.com/%7Ehorvitz /lum.htm), which monitors a user's actions and determines when the user may need assistance. Lumiere continuously follows a user's goals and tasks as the user works with a suite of software tools (e.g., Microsoft Office), and performs a type of task recognition; individually observed events are combined into higher-level modeled events, which are variables in a Bayesian model. To develop the models, studies were performed to determine how experts in specific software applications came to understand problems that users might be having with software from the user's behaviors and the evidential distinctions that experts used in their reasoning about the best way to assist a user. As a user works, Lumiere generates a probability distribution over topic areas that the user may need assistance with, along with a probability that the user would not mind being bothered with assistance. This research has led to the development of a product, the Office Assistant in Office 97, which monitors user behaviors and assists the user based on underlying models of each of the Office 97 applications.

Another example of an agent that monitors a person's daily behaviors and then can offer help is the Calendar Apprentice (Mitchell et al., 1994). This system enables a user to manage his or her calendar by hand and then it builds rules that attempt to capture the user's typical behaviors. Maes (1994) has described agents that help a user classify and process e-mail and classify news articles based on collections of keywords and nominal information related to author, publication source, and other items. In each case the user's behavior in carrying out daily activities becomes the training data for mechanisms that can later aid the user.

Etzioni and Weld (1994) created the Internet Softbot, which receives a user's request and then employs a goal-oriented controller to seek a solution. It handles network-based problems, such as sending a message to an individual whose address may not be immediately available. The system uses its goal-oriented mechanisms to determine the tasks necessary to satisfy the request; this may involve accessing remote databases and assembling the necessary information to achieve the goal. The Internet Softbot provides a shell in which implementers can embed knowledge to handle a variety of network tasks automatically that can then be used by anyone.

Concerns About Agents

The term "agent" conjures in some critics' minds the picture of a humanoid facade and possibly simulated human-like responses. Individuals with this image may object to agents on the grounds that such an interface is condescending to the user and distracting to the goal of doing the work. While there may be populations or situations where such an interface is desirable, such anthropomorphic interfaces are certainly not a part of the concept of an agent as presented here. The choice of the facade and the interaction style are a design decision and are independent of the decision to build an agent. An agent may exist with menus, keyboard command line, voice, or other input modes and still carry out its function. In fact, one of the goals listed above is to provide the user with the choice of a variety of input/output techniques, any of which will work.

Another concern of some observers is the loss of control implied by having a system that carries out its own "agenda." Will a person "trust" a software system (as discussed in Chapter 5)? The apparent preferred mode for many users is the so-called direct manipulation paradigm that presents the user with a world of objects and methods to control them. Of course, there is a long tradition of automatically handling low-level details for users, as done, for example, by compilers and operating systems. Having a system agenda and automatic processing at such levels is accepted practice, and what is new occurs when the machine offers to carry out tasks automatically that the user might ordinarily do. Here the important thing is to keep the user in charge, either to accept the automatic actions of the system or to reject them and maintain complete step-by-step control.

Another worry relates to the robustness and reliability of a knowledge-based reasoning or learning system that may be a part of an agent. A reasonable policy on this issue is simply that conservative decision making should predominate if such a system is to be used. One can set objective criteria for measuring performance and use experimental or theoretical means to guarantee that standards are met.

Many of these concerns can be addressed by following the guidelines for agents presented by Pattie Maes at the 1997 International Conference on Intelligent User Interfaces:

• Make the user model available (inspectable, modifiable) to the user.

• The agent's method of operation should be understandable to the user.

• The agent should be able to explain its behavior to the user.

• The agent should have the ability to give continuous feedback to the user about its state, actions, and learning.

• The agent should allow variable degrees of autonomy, and the user should decide how much and what type of tasks to delegate to the agent. The user should be able to "program" the agent (e.g., teach it things, make it forget things).

• The user should not have to learn a new language to deal with the agent. A goal is to use the application to communicate between the agent and the user.

SUGGESTED RESEARCH: NEAR AND FAR TERM

Conservative versions of agents exist and are being used today, as described above. The input mode can be restricted to current technology, menus, or a keyboard-oriented command-line language. The computation undertaken for the user can be any traditional computation, mail handling, browsing, information retrieval, and so forth. The output facilities can employ any current technology. An example is the agent mentioned above for providing a person with personally tuned ratings for entertainment events. Such a system is well within the capabilities of current technologies and provides an example of a currently realizable agent. There are many kinds of research projects that begin at this level. For example, one can study human problem solving in the absence of technology and try to determine its characteristics and needs. Or one can study the dynamics of human group behaviors. In each case the goal can be to determine whether and how technology, specifically software agents and networking, might be used to augment or improve what occurs naturally. As a part of this, it is necessary to develop measures of effectiveness in problem solving, for humans or human-machine collaborations, so that comparative studies can be done.

Other important research projects could study or create new architectures for agents. For example, can architectures be found that provide the capabilities called for by Maes and described in the above section? Another area of interest is the development of agent shells that can be created once and then specialized repeatedly to provide a variety of agents that users may need. A part of this research will be the development of common languages for agents to communicate with each other, so that they can pass around requests and answers to requests without regard to which particular agent is being accessed.

More ambitious projects with substantially greater payoff, but with greater risk and longer time periods, involve pushing the state of the art in many areas. An example is the problem of accessing and utilizing diverse sources of information. Data may exist on the net in a variety of standard database formats—free text, tables, or many other forms. Data may be multimodal, time varying, and quality graded. The need of the network user is to input a request in a convenient language and then receive a response regardless of how varied the storage techniques may be. Research is needed into the modeling of knowledge sources and their use and the integration of knowledge from diverse sources. Research is also needed into methods for summarizing data (DARPA, 1992, 1993, 1995a) or enabling a person to peruse large amounts of data in an efficient manner. Clearly, enough progress can be made in these areas to achieve useful results within a 10-year time frame. But there are hard enough problems to keep researchers busy long beyond that.

Another area where progress will come slowly but surely is in the utilization of the input/output technologies described earlier in this report. For example, three-dimensional imaging methodologies will be useful for presenting the "shopping mall" paradigm, where an agent might enable a user to "fly" to a place of interest and make choices among alternatives, as noted by Thomas DeFanti at the workshop. Progress in speech recognition will make it usable, broadening the variety of input techniques available.

The multimedia/multimodal input/output methodologies described above are possible now in primitive forms (Maybury, 1993; Feiner and McKeown, 1991; Wahlster et al., 1993). But advances are required to make progress in fundamental issues such as cross-modal integrated referring expressions, and temporal/spatial synchrony of dynamic media realization. The several decades of language research into formal and natural language theory is needed again for multimedia/multimodal communication. This work is essential if the important goal of media-mode independence is to be approached for ordinary citizens.

Related to these studies is the need for dialogue theory (Grosz and Sidner, 1986, 1990; Lochbaum, 1994; Moore, 1995), which relates individual input/output transactions to an interacter's overall goal. It maintains a model of what has happened and what needs to happen to achieve ultimate success and provides the fundamental mechanisms for successful collaboration. Rich and Sidner (1996, 1997a,b) have demonstrated that there is much to be gained from applying this theory to the design of collaborative agents. Smith et al. (1995) have demonstrated a speech interactive system that utilizes dialogue theory as developed by Grosz and Sidner (1986) to process equipment repair dialogues.

Another area with a less-than-10-year payoff but with more distant ultimate goals is reasoning or inferential systems. Users performing standard tasks such as the scholarship search mentioned above will be helped by inferential capabilities that guide them down logically valid and well-worn paths rather than the plethora that knowledge-free search can find. Expert systems successes of the 1980s provide examples of inference systems that have found use in the real world and similar techniques can be applied immediately in ordinary-citizen applications. More ambitious knowledge-intensive systems will ultimately be needed to provide citizens help on more difficult problems. A reasonable project would be to build a large database of common-sense knowledge for a particular domain that could be used by any system designed to work in that domain. An example of an important and broadly applicable knowledge source is the WordNet system (Miller et al., 1990). Such systems are, in many cases, beyond the 10-year time frame.

A final area of great importance that also will extend beyond the 10-year time frame is user models (Kobsa and Wahlster, 1989) and their utilization. The goal is to enable a system to specialize its actions to account for what the user knows and needs. If a user is entering a system for the first time, he or she should possibly be treated differently from an experienced user. If a user has unsuccessfully followed a given path, perhaps he or she should be encouraged in a new direction. If the user can reasonably be expected to know something, he or she should not be told it again unless specific evidence arises indicating that it has been forgotten. A long-term and very difficult problem is information presentation that accounts for a user model. Thus, if one gives instructions on how to go from point A to point B in a city, the instructions will be very different in nature depending on whether the user is new to town or is a long-time resident. Either individual may be irritated to receive instructions intended for the other.

RECOMMENDATIONS

With respect to agents and systems intelligence, the steering committee makes two recommendations on the basis of its discussions:

Recommendation 1. Agents and intelligent systems technologies should be a priority for research. A major goal of computer science from its beginning has been to build systems that enable people to interact in languages and with paradigms that are comfortable to them and to apply the best current technologies available to deal with the array of details related to the computation. The field of agent technologies is aimed at accomplishing this for users of the NII.

Recommendation 2. A major emphasis should be on the development of technologies for translating between machine internal representations and any of a range of external media or combination of external media for both input and output. Mode and media independence are an important goal for the benefit of ordinary citizens, differently abled and otherwise. This recommendation addresses the technologies that will make such independence possible.

7

CONCLUSIONS AND RECOMMENDATIONS

Assuming that private industry will take the lead in mainstream product development and short-term research, the steering committee presents here recommendations for research that it believes federal research agencies should encourage.[1] Federal initiatives that emphasize long-term goals beyond the horizon of most commercial efforts and that may thus entail added risk have the potential to move the whole information technology enterprise into new modes of thinking and to stimulate discovery of new technologies for the coming century. Of course, work should continue in current areas that have demonstrated promise, but the emphasis here is on opening up new opportunities. Five of the areas elaborated on under recommendations 2 and 3 in this chapter are designated for highest-priority attention because of their potential for contributing to the development of effective every-citizen interfaces.

Recommendation 1: Break away from 1960s technologies and paradigms. Major attempts should be made to find new paradigms for human-machine interaction that employ new modes and media for input and output and that involve new conceptualizations of application interfaces.

Needed in the technical community is a period analogous to the 1960s when a variety of paradigms were tried using emerging technologies of that time. The view then was of a single user interacting with a single terminal using a mouse, menus, and windows to open documents within a local application. The new view should take into account the tasks and technologies of the present and should enable a variety of interactions between humans and machines for communication, information retrieval, and performance of tasks in any of a variety of environments. Moreover, new approaches should enable users to immerse themselves in computer-mediated interactions and should include the option of involving many humans and machines in collaborative activities. New paradigms should emphasize the new role of information technology in society as a mediator among individuals, groups of individuals, and networked machines.

The steering committee's first recommendation is a call not to replace visual interfaces but rather to infuse them with new power and capability through document-centric design, speech, gesture, agents, position-aware and pressure-sensitive input devices, touch screens, and other emerging technologies and techniques. It also emphasizes bringing to fruition equally important new interface strategies, such as speech and voice response, that will carry the power of computing to environments and populations not served today. Today's interfaces often require too much of a user's vision and motor control in situations, such as driving, that present environmental distractions, or they assume physical or other abilities that many potential users may lack.

Coordinated research across several disciplines is necessary to develop new technologies and paradigms that address the psychological, organizational, and societal characteristics of every citizen. This interdisciplinary research should include the testing and evaluation of new interface technologies and paradigms in laboratory or field experiments or other empirical studies involving people who are representative of the citizenry.

The research agenda should acknowledge that the human-machine interface is more than screen deep and should consider every aspect of a person's experience in using computing and communications. People should be able to concentrate on the tasks or purposes for which they are using applications and should experience the interface as an aid rather than an obstacle to achieving success. People should experience a human-problem domain interaction rather than a human-machine interaction.

Several technological and design constraints should be considered in developing a research agenda:

• Architectures are needed for interfaces that have wide spectrum and are easily learnable. Such systems should have simple and semantically obvious commands so that novices can use them immediately. They also should have many levels of increasingly sophisticated capabilities that can be learned incrementally, so that people can move gracefully into more advanced and efficient uses. Such systems could be used in very sophisticated ways by experienced users.

• Systems should support modality and medium independence. Research should be fostered to enable anytime, anywhere, anyone interfaces that enable people to interact with systems using whatever modalities and media are available and convenient at a given time (consistent with the functions being performed). Such interfaces would support the goals of (1) ubiquitous and nomadic access so that a user can communicate on the road, down the hall from the office, calling in via telephone, and so forth; (2) equipment and communications system independence—use of low versus high bandwidth, one medium (e.g., audio, video, text) versus another, and so on; and (3) user ability independence, with special concern for people with disabilities and for the changes in abilities that typically accompany aging.

• Human-machine interfaces should support group (multiperson and multimachine) activities that are work oriented, social, or conducted for other purposes; the groups could be formal, established, or short term and ad hoc. In particular, interfaces should support communities of practice in which many individuals can participate, each contributing incrementally. To build interfaces that provide such support requires further development of theories of dialogue, theories of group behavior, and theories of joint planning and problem solving.

• Interfaces to the national information infrastructure should treat the two directions of communications—to and from individual citizens—more evenhandedly. Historically, with respect to elements of the NII such as broadcast television, citizens have been passive consumers of information. The evolving NII opens prospects for systems and interfaces that provide more flexibility in who can send and receive information, from what locations, and in what manner, as well as more flexibility and ease for people to move between communications- and information-centric activities.

• Information resources should have more attractive means of entry than those available so far. Two possibilities that could merit further research include (1) the concept of hyper-television that enables a viewer to pursue a presented object or event into cyberspace or (2) electronic encyclopedias with ubiquitous pointers into electronic libraries and other sources.

• Methods are needed that enable citizens to achieve the security and privacy they desire. Security-related features can be inconvenient to use; better interfaces could lower the barriers that have deterred their use historically.

Recommendation 2: Invest in the research required to provide the component subsystems needed for every-citizen interfaces. Research is needed that is aimed at both making technological advances and gaining understanding of the human and organizational capabilities these advances would support.

- *Determine the needs of citizens: highest priority.* Apply available sociological, psychological, and human-computer interface methodologies to try to understand the problems and the needs basic to effective human-machine interaction. Undertake studies to find the kinds of functionality and interfaces that will be most important. Such studies may be empirical or historical to determine what was successful in the past. For example, the usefulness and success of existing public information access projects, such as the Library of Congress system, could be examined. Proposed new technologies could be simulated and measurements made of their levels of success in real-life situations. Information so gathered should then guide decisions on what the most important technical areas are for research emphasis.
- *Input technologies—Explore the promise of speech recognition and associated natural language processing: highest priority.* Do the work necessary to open up speech as a viable input for as many new uses as possible. The steering committee is impressed that the range of potential applications for spoken input is tremendous, especially for hands-busy, eyes-busy situations; telephone applications; and differently abled persons. This need, coupled with the rate of progress in speech recognition, points to the importance of continued emphasis on this line of research. An important area that needs more attention is the construction of prototype speech interactive systems and their measurement and refinement in actual use.
- *Improve understanding of computer vision, gesture sensing, and multimodal languages for user input.* Computer vision can be used to gather data a user may wish to transfer to the network and to keep the system updated regarding the user's presence and responsiveness. Gesture recognition could involve the development of gesture languages and gesture support of multimodal languages.
- Measure the effectiveness of all of the above technologies when used by humans in problem-solving situations.
- *Output technologies,* including eyeglass displays; flexible, portable, and compact displays; high-resolution displays; virtual reality; haptic devices; mechanical actuators; voice and artificial sound; and multimodal generation of output. Develop display technologies to match human vision. Create audio output matched to the dynamic range of human hearing. Measure the effectiveness of these technologies in a systematic program to evaluate their relative strengths for human users.

• *Ensure modality and medium independence: highest priority.* Media independence and modality independence are goals that, to this time, have not been extensively researched and, in the new context, should be—for nomadic systems, for low-cost systems, and for people with disabilities. Develop mechanisms that enable translations between internal machine representations of information and various human representations (e.g., visual, audio, haptic). Research in this area will encourage the use of a common machine representation that can be flexibly translated into or from any available modes or media. Determine human multimedia and multimodal communications capabilities. Enumerate and prioritize human capabilities to modulate energy (as described in Chapter 3).

• *Agent technologies.* An important option for delivering services to users will involve agent technologies that interact with people to help determine their needs and then select domain-appropriate mechanisms to respond. The required technologies include traditional computer science mechanisms (such as those needed for database retrieval) and artificial intelligence capabilities (including representation of concepts and reasoning). An array of research topics needs to be addressed, including acquisition of user requests, user modeling, problem solving, and methodologies for summarizing and presenting internally stored data.

• *Network access devices.* A large variety of devices are needed, including mobile terminals, inexpensive minimalist systems, and full multimedia systems with virtual reality capabilities. The steering committee expects that industry will perform most of this work.

Recommendation 3: Encourage research on systems-level design and development of human-machine interfaces that support multiperson, multimachine groups as well as individuals.

• *Develop theories and architectures for collaboration: highest priority.* Develop theories of collaboration and problem solving. Develop architectures for networked people and machines that enable mutual awareness, easy communication across space and time, and individual and joint contributions to common goals. Provide ways to support community building and other social aspects of communication. Theories of collaboration have not been well developed historically, and the advent of networking makes this an important new priority for research.

• *Human-centered design methodologies.* Continue the study of human behavior in the use of technology for problem solving and the design of systems for improved productivity. Investigate the social effects of different interface choices, particularly the ways in which different presentation and communications choices affect people's interactions with media. To obtain feedback and to facilitate efforts at improvement, encourage social science research into how well the public is being served by such technology.

- *Test proposed new designs: highest priority.* Build experimental human-machine systems, for individual users or groups, using proposed technologies or simulations of them. Test, refine, and install them in applications environments, and measure their effectiveness. Industry, under the pressure of competition, has in recent years tended to minimize user testing in favor of quickly getting products to customers. Marketplace success has become the de facto test for usability by humans. Unfortunately, this approach does not lead to the kind of understanding that enables reasoned design of useful devices. Better understanding gained from testing and evaluation is needed to achieve breakthroughs to new paradigms, and to address the needs of differently abled individuals whose market buying power may be inferior to that of majority groups.

NOTE

1. In addition to supporting research, the government can encourage forward-looking approaches to accessibility for every citizen to the national information infrastructure by requiring adequate development processes and evaluation in the procurement and use of systems for public service facilities under government control.

BIBLIOGRAPHY

Anderson, David. 1996. "Diamond Park and Spline: A Social Virtual Reality System with 3d Animation, Spoken Interaction, and Runtime Modifiability," Technical Report Tr96-02, Mitsubishi Electric Research Laboratory. Also available on-line at http://Atlantic. merl/com/reports/index.html.

Anderson, D.B., Tora Bikson, Sally Ann Law, and Bridger M. Mitchell. 1995. "Universal Access to E-Mail: Feasibility and Societal Implications, " RAND, Santa Monica, CA.

Anthes, Gary H. 1993. "New Devices to Propel Technology into Social Fabric, Report Says," *Computerworld*, August 23, pp. 78.

Arar, Yardena. 1996. "Registering Disappointment—Microsoft's Bob Celebrates Lonely First Birthday," *Computer Retail Week*, No. 624, January.

Argyle, M., et al. 1976. *Gaze and Mutual Gaze,* Cambridge University Press, Cambridge, England.

Asia-Pacific Telecommunications Network. 1995. "Conference on Competition in Asia's Telecom Markets," Asia-Pacific Telecommunications Network, IBC Technical Services, Ltd., Singapore.

Austin, J.L. 1962. *How to Do Things with Words,* Harvard University Press, Cambridge, MA.

Badler, N., et al. 1993. "Real-Time Control of a Virtual Human Using Minimal Sensors," Presence, Vol. 2, No. 1.

Bank, David. 1996. "Microsoft Moves to Control the PC Screen," *Wall Street Journal*, December 5, p. B2.

Bates, Joseph. 1994. "The Role of Emotions in Believable Agents," *Communications of the ACM*, Vol. 37, No. 7, pp. 122-125.

Bear, John, John Dowding, and Elizabeth Shriberg. 1992. "Integrating Multiple Knowledge Sources for Detection and Correction of Repairs in Human-Computer Dialog," *Proceedings of the 30th Annual Meeting of the Association for Computational Linguistics*, Newark, DE, ACL, Somerset, NJ.

Bender, Michael A., and Donna K. Slonim. 1994. "The Power of Team Exploration: Two Robots Can Learn Unlabeled Directed Graphs," *Proceedings of the 35th Annual Sympo-*

sium on Foundations of Computer Science, IEEE Computer Society Press, Los Alamitos, CA, pp. 75-85.

Benford, S., et al. 1995. "User Embodiment in Collaborative Virtual Environments," *Proceedings of SIGCHI '95*, ACM, New York, pp. 242-249.

Bertino, E., and L. Martino. 1993. *Object-Oriented Database Systems: Concepts and Architectures*, Addison-Wesley, Reading, MA.

Bikson, T.K. 1996. "Groupware at the World Bank," in *Groupware and Teamwork*, C. Ciborra, ed., John Wiley & Sons, Chichester, England, pp. 145-183.

Bikson, T.K., and J.D. Eveland. 1990. "The Interplay of Work Group Structures and Computer Support," *Intellectual Teamwork*, R. Kraut, J. Galegher, and C. Egido, eds., Erlbaum and Associates, Hillsdale, New Jersey, pp. 245-290. Also available from RAND as N-3429-MF.

Blanchard, C., and S. Burgess. 1990. "Reality Built for Two," *Symposium on Interactive 3D Graphics*, ACM SIGGRAPH, Dallas, ACM, New York.

Boden, Margaret A. 1994. "Agents and Creativity," *Communications of the ACM*, Vol. 37, No. 7, pp. 17-121.

Boff, Kenneth R., and Janet E. Lincoln. 1988. *Engineering Data Compendium, Volume I*, H.G. Armstrong Aerospace Medical Research Laboratory, Wright-Patterson Air Force Base, OH.

Bratman, Michael. 1992. "Shared Cooperative Activity," *Philosophical Review*, Vol. 101, pp. 327-341.

Bretier, P., and M.D. Sadek. 1996. "A Rational Agent as the Kernel of a Cooperative Spoken Dialogue System: Implementing a Logical Theory of Interaction," ECAI-96 Workshop on Agent Theories, Architectures and Language, Budapest, Hungary.

Bretier, P., M.D. Sadek, V. Cadoret, A. Cozannet, P. Dupont, A. Ferrieux, and F. Panaget. 1995. "A Cooperative Spoken Dialogue System Based on a Rational Agent Model: A First Implementation on the AGS Application," *Proceedings of the ESCA/ETR Workshop on Spoken Dialogue Systems*, Hanstholm, Denmark.

Bricken, W., and G. Coco. 1993. "The VEOS Project," Technical Report, Human Interface Technology Laboratory, University of Washington, Seattle.

Brill, Eric. 1993. "Automatic Grammar Induction and Parsing Free Text: A Transformation-Based Approach," *Proceedings of the 31st Annual Meeting of the Association for Computational Linguistics*, Columbus, OH, ACL, Somerset, NJ.

Brown, John Seely, and Paul Duguid. 1992. "Enacting Design for the Workplace," *Usability: Turning Technologies into Tools*, Paul Adler and Terry Winograd, eds., Oxford University Press, U.K., pp. 164-198.

Brown, John S., Paul Duguid, and Susan Haviland. 1994. "Toward Informed Participation: Six Scenarios in Search of Democracy in the Information Age," *Aspen Institute Quarterly*, Vol. 6, No. 4, pp. 49-73.

Bullen, C., and J. Bennet. 1990. "Learning from User Experiences with Groupware," *Proceedings of the Conference on Computer Supported Cooperative Work*, ACM, New York, pp. 291-302.

Burdea, G. 1996. *Force and Touch Feedback for Virtual Reality*, John Wiley & Sons, New York.

Burrows, Peter. 1996. "The Day of the Designer," *Business Week*, June 24, pp. 114.

Buttolo, P., D. Kung, and B. Hannaford. 1995. "Manipulation in Real, Virtual, and Remote Environments," *Proceedings of the IEEE International Conference on Systems, Man, and Cybernetics*, Vancouver, BC, October, IEEE Computer Society Press, Los Alamitos, CA.

Cabinet Minister for Public Service (United Kingdom). "A Prospectus for the Electronic Delivery of Government Services," U.K. Green Paper. Available on-line at http://www.open.gov.uk/citu/cituhome.htm.

Carbonell, J. 1992. "Machine Learning: A Maturing Field," *Machine Learning*, Vol. 9, No. 1, pp. 5-7.

Card, Stuart K., Thomas P. Moran, and Allen Newell. 1983. *The Psychology of Human-Computer Interaction*, Lawrence Erlbaum Associates, Hillsdale, NJ.

Carlsson, C., and O. Hagsand. 1993. "DIVE: A Multi-User Virtual Reality System," *Proceedings of the IEEE Virtual Reality Annual International Symposium*, IEEE Computer Society Press, Los Alamitos, CA.

Carlton, Jim. 1995. "Acer Is Launching Personal Computers Designed to Fit in as Fixture in Homes," *Wall Street Journal*, September 5, p. B2.

Carroll, J.M. 1990. "The Growth of Cognitive Modeling in Human-Computer Interaction Since GOMS," *Human Computer Interaction*, Vol. 5, pp. 221-265.

Chung, Woo Young, and Suzanne Iacono. 1996. "Why Do People Use On-line Services?," working paper, Boston University, Boston, MA.

Ciborra, C. 1992. "From Thinking to Tinkering: The Grassroots of Strategic Information Systems," *The Information Society*, Vol. 8, No. 4, pp. 297-310.

Ciborra, C., and G. Patriotta. 1996. "Groupware and Teamwork in New Product Development: The Case of Consumer Goods Multinational," *Groupware and Teamwork*, John Wiley & Sons, London, pp. 121-144.

Cindio, F.D., and G.D. Michelis. 1986. "Chaos as a Coordinating Technology," *Proceedings of the Conference on Computer Supported Cooperative Work*, ACM Press, New York.

Clark, Don, and Kyle Pope. 1995. "Poll Finds Americans Like Using PCs but May Find Them to Be Stressful," *Wall Street Journal*, April 10.

Clark, Don, and Evan Ramstad. 1997. "Zenith, Thomson Move to Bring Internet to TVs," *Wall Street Journal*, January 8, p. A6.

Clark, Herbert H. 1996. *Using Language*, Cambridge University Press, Cambridge, England, and New York.

Clark, H.H., and E.F. Shaefer. 1987. "Collaborating on Contributions to Conversations," *Language and Cognitive Processes*, Vol. 11, pp. 1-23.

Clerc, S. 1994. "Estrogen Brigades and 'Bit Tits' Threads: Media Fandom Online and Off," *Wired Women: Gender and New Realities in Cyberspace*, L. Cherny and E.R. Weise, eds., Seal Press Feminist, Seattle, WA.

Codella, C., et al. 1993. "A Toolkit for Developing Multi-User, Distributed Virtual Environments," *Proceedings of the IEEE Virtual Reality Annual International Symposium*, IEEE Computer Society Press, Los Alamitos, CA, pp. 401-407.

Cohen, P., and H. Levesque. 1990. "Intention Is Choice with Commitment," *Artificial Intelligence*, Vol. 42, pp. 263-310.

Cohen, Philip R., and Sharon L. Oviatt. 1994. *The Role of Voice Input for Human-Machine Communication*, Department of Computer Science and Engineering, Oregon Graduate Institute of Science and Technology, Beaverton, OR.

Cole, R.A., and L. Hirschman. 1995. "The Challenge of Spoken Language Systems: Research Directions for the Nineties," *IEEE Transactions in Speech and Audio Processing*, Vol. 3, pp. 1-21.

Cole, R.A., et al., eds. 1996. *Survey of the State of the Art in Human Language Technology*, Cambridge University Press, Stanford University, Stanford, CA. Available on-line at http://cse.ogi.edu/CSLU/HLTsurvey/.

Cole, Ron, and Lynette Hirschman. 1992. *The Challenge of Spoken Language Systems: Research Directions for the Nineties*, National Science Foundation, Arlington, VA, February.

Collins, Michael John. 1996. "A New Statistical Parser Based on Bigram Lexical Dependencies," *Proceedings of the 34th Annual Meeting of the Association for Computational Linguistics*, Santa Cruz, CA, ACL, Somerset, NJ.

Computer Science and Telecommunications Board (CSTB), National Research Council.

1994a. *Realizing the Information Future: The Internet and Beyond*, National Academy Press, Washington, DC.

Computer Science and Telecommunications Board (CSTB), National Research Council. 1994b. *Information Technology in the Service Society*, National Academy Press, Washington, DC.

Computer Science and Telecommunications Board (CSTB), National Research Council. 1995. *Evolving the High Performance Computing and Communications Initiative to Support the Nation's Information Infrastructure*, National Academy Press, Washington, DC.

Computer Science and Telecommunications Board (CSTB), National Research Council. 1996. *The Unpredictable Certainty: Information Infrastructure Through 2000*, National Academy Press, Washington, DC.

Conklin, Jeff. 1987. "Hypertext: An Introduction and Survey," *Computer*, September, pp. 17-41.

Constant, David, Sara Kiesler, and Lee Sproull. 1996. "The Kindness of Strangers: On the Usefulness of Weak Ties for Technical Advice," *Organization Science*, Vol. 7, pp. 119-135.

Cortese, Amy. 1996. "Software's Holy Grail," *Business Week*, June 24, pp. 83-92.

Crossen, Cynthia. 1996. "Print Scrn, Num Lock and Other Mysteries of the Keyboard," *Wall Street Journal*, October 22, pp. B1 and B11.

Cross-Industry Working Team. 1995. "Nomadicity in the NII," Corporation For National Research Initiatives, 1895 Preston White Drive, Suite 100, Reston, VA 22091-5434.

Deerwester, S., S.T. Dumais, G.W. Furnas, T.K. Landauer, and R. Harshman. 1990. "Indexing by Latent Semantic Analysis," *Journal of the American Society for Information Science*, Vol. 41, No. 6, pp. 391-407.

DeFanti, T. 1996. "Real-Time Visualization and Virtual Reality as a Future Every-Citizen Interface for the National Information Infrastructure," Toward an Every-Citizen Interface for the National Information Infrastructure Workshop, Washington, DC, August. Available on-line at http://www.nap.edu.

Defense Advanced Research Projects Agency (DARPA). 1992. *Proceedings of the Fourth Message Understanding Conference* (MUC-4), June, San Mateo, Morgan-Kaufmann, Los Altos, CA.

Defense Advanced Research Projects Agency (DARPA). 1993. *Proceedings of the Fifth Message Understanding Conference* (MUC-5), August, San Mateo, Morgan-Kaufmann, Los Altos, CA.

Defense Advanced Research Project Agency (DARPA). 1995a. *Proceedings of the Sixth Message Understanding Conference* (MUC-6), November, Columbia, MD, Morgan-Kaufmann, San Francisco.

Defense Advanced Research Project Agency (DARPA). 1995b. *Proceedings of the Spoken Language Systems Technology Workshop*, January, Austin, TX, Morgan-Kaufmann, San Francisco.

Denning, Peter, and Pamela Dargan. 1996. "Action-Centered Design," *Bringing Design to Software*, Terry Winograd, ed., Addison-Wesley, Reading, MA, pp. 105-120.

DeWitt, D., et al. 1994. "Client/Server Paradise," *Proceedings of the 20th International Conference on Very Large Data Bases*, Santiago, Chile, Morgan-Kaufmann, San Francisco.

Donath, Judith. 1996. "Inhabiting the Virtual City: The Design of Social Environments for Electronic Communities," unpublished doctoral dissertation, Massachussetts Institute of Technology, Cambridge, MA.

Dourish, P., A. Adler, V. Bellotti, and A. Henderson. 1994. "Your Place or Mine? Learning from Long-Term Use of Video Communication," Technical Report, Rank Xerox EuroParc, Number EPC-94-105.

Dourish, P., J. Holmes, A. MacLean, P. Marqvardsen, and A. Zbyslaw. 1996. "Freeflow:

Mediating Between Representation and Action in Workflow Systems," *Proceedings of the Conference on Computer Supported Cooperative Work*, Boston, MA, Nov. 16-20, ACM Press, New York, pp. 190-198.

Dubrovsky, V.J., S. Kiesler, and B.N. Sethna. 1991. "The Equalization Phenomenon: Status Effects in Computer-Mediated and Face-to-Face Decision Making Groups," *Human Computer Interaction*, Vol. 6, pp. 119-146.

Dumais, S., and D. Schmitt. 1991. "Iterative Searching of an On-Line Database," *Proceedings of the Human Factors Society*, Human Factors Society, Santa Monica, CA, pp. 396-402.

Edmonds, Ernest A. 1994. "Support for Collaborative Design: Agents and Emergence," *Communications of the ACM*, Vol. 37, No. 7, July, pp. 41-47.

Egan, Dennis E. 1988. "Individual Differences in Human-Computer Interaction," *Handbook of Human-Computer Interaction*, Martin E. Helander, ed., Elsevier Science, New York.

Elstrom, Peter. 1996. "'Operator, Get Me Cyberspace,'" *Business Week*, June 24, pp. 103-110.

Etzioni, Oren, and Daniel Weld. 1994. "A Softbot-based Interface to the Internet," *Communications of the ACM*, Vol. 37, No. 7, pp. 72-76.

Etzioni, Oren, and Daniel S. Weld. 1995. *Intelligent Agents on the Internet: Fact, Fiction, and Forecast*, Department of Computer Science and Engineering, University of Washington, Seattle, May 30.

Eveland, J.D., and T.K. Bikson. 1987. "Evolving Electronic Communication Networks: An Empirical Assessment," *Office: Technology and People*, Vol. 3, pp. 103-128.

Eveland, J.D., A. Blanchard, W. Brown, and J. Mattocks. 1994. "The Role of 'Help Networks' in Facilitating Use of CSCW Tools," *Proceedings of the Conference on Computer Supported Cooperative Work*, ACM, New York, pp. 265-274.

Feiner, S.K., and K.R. McKeown. 1991. "Automating the Generation of Coordinated Multimedia Explanations," *IEEE Computer*, Vol. 24, No. 10, pp. 31-41.

Finholt, T., L. Sproull, and S. Kiesler. 1991. "Communication and Performance in Ad Hoc Talk Groups," *Human Computer Interaction*, Vol. 6, pp. 291-325.

Fischer, G. 1991. "Supporting Learning on Demand with Design Environments," *Proceedings of the International Conference on the Learning Sciences in 1991* (Evanston, IL), L. Birnbaum, ed., Association for the Advancement of Computing in Education, Charlottesville, VA, pp. 165-172.

Fischer, G. 1994a. "Domain-Oriented Design Environments," *Automated Software Engineering*, Vol. 1, No. 2, pp. 177-203.

Fischer, G. 1994b. "Turning Breakdowns into Opportunities for Creativity, Knowledge-Based Systems," Special Issue, *Creativity and Cognition*, Vol. 7, No. 4, pp. 221-232.

Fischer, G., and K. Nakakoji. 1991. "Making Design Objects Relevant to the Task at Hand," *Proceedings of AAAI-91, Ninth National Conference on Artificial Intelligence*, AAAI-Press/MIT Press, Cambridge, MA, pp. 67-73.

Fischer, G., A.C. Lemke, and T. Schwab. 1985. "Knowledge-Based Help Systems," *Proceedings of the Conference on Human Factors in Computing Systems*, San Francisco, ACM, New York, pp. 161-167.

Fischer, G., et al. 1991. "The Role of Critiquing in Cooperative Problem Solving," *ACM Transactions on Information Systems*, Vol. 9, No. 2, pp. 123-151.

Fish, R.S., et al. 1990. "The Video Window System in Informal Communication," *Proceedings of the Conference on Computer Supported Cooperative Work*, ACM Press, New York, pp. 1-11.

Flohr, Udo. 1996. "3-D for Everyone," *Byte*, October. Available on-line at http://www.byte.com/art/9610/sec6/art1.htm.

Flores, Fernando, M. Graves, Brad Hartfield, and Terry Winograd. 1988. "Computer Systems and the Design of Organizational Interactions," *ACM Transactions on Office Information Systems*, Vol. 6, No. 2, pp. 153-172.

Ford, M., J. Bresnan, and R. Kaplan. 1982. "A Competence-Based Theory of Syntactic Closure," *The Mental Representation of Grammatical Relations*, J. Bresnan, ed., MIT Press, Cambridge, MA.

Frazier, L., and J.D. Fodor. 1978. "The Sausage Machine: A New Two Stage Parsing Model," *Cognition*, Vol. 6.

Freitag, L., et al. 1995. "Remote Engineering Using Cave-to-Cave Communications," *Virtual Environments and Distributed Computing at Supercomputing'95: GII Testbed and HPC Challenge Applications on the I-Way*. Available on-line at http://www.mcs.anl.gov/FUTURES_LAB /CAVE/APPS/SUPER95/BOILER/boiler.html.

Funkhouser, T.A. 1996. "Network Topologies for Scalable Multi-User Virtual Environments," *Proceedings of the IEEE Virtual Reality Annual International Symposium*, IEEE Computer Society Press, Los Alamitos, CA, pp. 222-228.

Gaver, W., et al. 1993. "One Is Not Enough: Multiple Views in a Media Space," *Proceedings of INTERCHI'93*, ACM, New York.

Genesereth, Michael R., and Steven P. Ketchpel. 1994. "Software Agents," *Communications of the ACM*, Vol. 37, No. 7, pp. 48-53.

Georgia Tech Graphics. 1995a. *Visualization & Usability (GVU) Center, 3rd Survey (GVU3)*, April.

Georgia Tech Graphics. 1995b. *Visualization & Usability (GVU) Center, 4th Survey (GVU4)*, October.

Georgia Tech Graphics. 1996a. *Visualization & Usability (GVU) Center, 5th Survey (GVU5)*, April.

Georgia Tech Graphics. 1996b. *Visualization & Usability (GVU) Center, 6th Survey (GVU6)*, October.

Gibbons, Boyd. 1986. "The Intimate Sense of Smell," *National Geographic*, Vol. 170, No. 3, pp. 324-361.

Girgensohn, A., D.F. Redmiles, and F.M. Shipman. 1994. "Agent-based Support for Communication Between Developers and Users in Software Design," *KBSE'94*, September, IEEE Computer Society Press, Los Alamitos, CA, pp. 22-29.

Glance, N.S., D.S. Pagani, and R. Pareschi. 1996. "Generalized Process Structure Grammars for Flexible Representations of Work," *Proceedings of the Conference on Computer Supported Cooperative Work*, ACM, New York, pp. 180-189.

Gomes, Lee. 1997. "Immersion's New Joystick Ensures the Pain of Defeat Is Really Painful," *Wall Street Journal*, January 21, p. A13D.

Gould, J.D., and N. Grischkowsky. 1984. "Doing the Same Work with Hard Copy and with Cathode Ray Tube (CRT) Computer Terminals," *Human Factors*, Vol. 26, pp. 323-337.

Gould, J.D., S.J. Boies, S. Levy, J.T. Richards, and J. Schoonard. 1987a. "The 1984 Olympic Message System: A Test of Behavioral Principles of System Design," *Communications of the ACM*, Vol. 30, pp. 758-769.

Gould, J.D., et al. 1987b. "Why Reading Was Slower from CRT Displays Than from Paper," *Proceedings of the Conference on Computer-Human Interaction + GI*, Toronto, Canada, April 5-9, ACM, New York, pp. 7-11.

Government Information Technology Service (GITS). 1995. *The Kiosk Network Solution: An Electronic Gateway to Government Service*, Interagency Kiosk Committee for the Customer Service Improvement Team of the GITS Working Group, Washington, DC.

Gray, W.D., B.E. John, and M.E. Atwood. 1992. "The Precis of Project Ernestine, or, an Overview of a Validation of GOMS," *Proceedings of the Conference on Human Factors in Computing Systems*, Monterey, CA, ACM, New York, pp. 307-312.

Greene, S., L. Gomez, and S. Devlin. 1986. "A Cognitive Analysis of Database Query Production," *Proceedings of the Human Factors Society*, Human Factors Society, Santa Monica, CA, pp. 9-13.

Greif, Irene. 1994. "Desktop Agents in Group-Enabled Products," *Communications of the ACM*, Vol. 37, No. 7, pp. 100-105.

Gross, Neil. 1996. "Defending the Living Room," *Business Week*, June 24, pp. 96-98.

Grossman, R., et al. 1993. "An Object Manager Utilizing Hierarchical Storage," *Proceedings of the Twelfth Symposium on Mass Storage Systems*, IEEE Computer Society Press, Los Alamitos, CA.

Grosz, B., A. Joshi, and S. Weinstein. 1995. "Centering: A Framework for Modeling the Local Coherence of Discourse," *Computational Linguistics*, Vol. 21, No. 2, pp. 203-225.

Grosz, Barbara, and S. Kraus. 1996. "Collaborative Plans for Complex Group Action," *Artificial Intelligence*, Vol. 86, No. 2, pp. 269-357.

Grosz, Barbara J., and Fernando C.N. Pereira. 1994. *Natural Language Processing*, MIT Press, Cambridge, MA.

Grosz, Barbara J., and Candace L. Sidner. 1986. "Attention, Intention, and the Structure of Discourse," *Computational Linguistics*, Vol. 12, No. 3, pp. 175-204.

Grosz, Barbara, and Candace Sidner. 1990. "Plans for Discourse," *Intention in Communication*, MIT Press, Cambridge, MA.

Grudin, Jonathan. 1988. "Why CSCW Applications Fail: Problems in the Design and Evaluation of Organizational Interfaces," *Proceedings of the Conference on Computer Supported Cooperative Work*, ACM, New York, pp. 85-93.

Grudin, Jonathan. 1989. "The Case Against User Interface Consistency," *Communications of the ACM*, Vol. 32, No. 10, pp. 1164-1173.

Grudin, Jonathan. 1993. "The Next Generation," *Communications of the ACM*, Vol. 36, No. 4, April, pp. 110-120.

Guha, R.V., and Douglas B. Lenat. 1994. "Enabling Agents to Work Together," *Communications of the ACM*, Vol. 37, No. 7, pp. 127-142.

Gunter, Carl. 1992. *Semantics of Programming Languages*, MIT Press, Cambridge, MA.

Hall, R.J. 1996. "Trusting Your Assistant," *KBSE'96*, Syracuse, NY, September, IEEE Computer Society Press, Los Alamitos, CA, pp. 42-51.

Hanson, Wayne, ed. 1994. "Kiosk Realities," *Government Technology*, Vol. 7, No. 9, pp. 1, 50-54, 62.

Haring, Bruce. 1996. "New Home Video Games Really Play with Thoughts, Emotions," *USA Today*, September 18, p. 5D.

Hartson, H.R., J.C. Castillo, J. Kelso, J. Kamler, and W.C. Neale. 1996. "Remote Evaluation: The Network as an Extension of the Usability Laboratory," *Proceedings of the Conference on Human Factors in Computing Systems*, ACM, New York, pp. 228-236.

Harwood, Richard. 1996. "40 Percent of Our Lives," *Washington Post*, November 30, pp. A19.

Health and Welfare Agency Data Center of California. 1993. "INFO/CALIFORNIA: 'A Single Face to Government,'" Health and Welfare Agency Data Center of California, Sacramento, CA, September.

Heeman, Peter, and James Allen. 1994. "Detecting and Correcting Repairs," *Proceedings of the 32nd Annual Meeting of the Association for Computational Linguistics*, Las Cruces, NM, ACL, Somerset, NJ.

Helander, Martin E., ed. 1988. *The Handbook of Human-Computer Interaction*, North-Holland, Amsterdam, The Netherlands.

Helander, Martin G., and Thiagajaran Palanivel. 1992. "Ergonomics of Human-Computer Interaction," *Impact of Science on Society*, Vol. 42, No. 165, pp. 65-74.

Hennecke, Marcus E., et al. 1995. "Visionary Speech: Looking Ahead to Practical Speechreading Systems," in *Speechreading by Humans and Machines*, Vol. 150 of *NATO ASI Series, Series F: Computer and Systems Sciences*, David G. Stork and Marcus E. Hennecke, eds., Springer-Verlag, Berlin.

Herndon, K.P., A. van Dam, and M. Gleicher. 1994. "The Challenges of 3D Interaction, A CHI'94 Workshop," *SIGCHI Bulletin*, Vol. 26, No. 4, pp. 36-43.

Hirschman, Lynette, and Donna Cuomo. 1995. "Evaluation of Human Computer Interfaces: A Report from an ARPA Workshop," *SIGCHI Bulletin*, Vol. 27, No. 2, pp. 28-29.

Hix, D., and H.R. Hartson. 1993. *Developing User Interfaces: Ensuring Usability Through Product and Process*, John Wiley & Sons, New York.

Hof, Robert D. 1996. "These May Really Be PCs for the Rest of Us," *Business Week*, June 24, pp. 76-78.

Hoffman, Donna, W. Kalsbeck, and T. Novak. 1996. "Internet and Web Use in the U.S.," *Communications of the ACM*, Vol. 39, No. 12, pp. 36-46.

Huberman, B. 1996. "Evolution in Cyberspace," in *Future of the Internet*, New York Academy of Sciences Workshop, Xerox Palo Alto Research Center, May 6.

Huff, C., L. Sproull, and S. Kielser. 1989. "Computer Communication and Organizational Commitment: Tracing the Relationships in a City Government," *Journal of Applied Social Psychology*, Vol. 19, pp. 1371-1391.

Interagency Kiosk Committee. 1994. "The Kiosk Network Solution: An Electronic Gateway to Government Service," Government Information Technology Services Working Group, Washington, DC, November 22.

Investor's Business Daily. 1997. "Computers and Technology," January 15, p. A6.

Jennings, Nick R. 1995. "Controlling Cooperative Problem Solving in Industrial Multi-Agent Systems Using Joint Intentions," *Artificial Intelligence Journal*, Vol. 75, No. 2, pp. 1-46.

Joshi, A., I. Sag, and B. Webber. 1981. *Elements of Discourse*, Cambridge University Press, Cambridge, England.

Joshi, A., B. Grosz, and S. Weinstein. 1983. "Providing a Unified Account of Definite Noun Phrases in Discourse," *Proceedings of the 21st Annual Meeting of the Association for Computational Linguistics*, ACL, Somerset, NJ, pp. 44-50.

Junco, Alejandro. 1995. "Digital Monopoly: A New Cloud on Mexico's Horizon," *Wall Street Journal*, June 23, p. A15.

Kalawsky, Roy S. 1993. *The Science of Virtual Reality*, Addison-Wesley, Reading, MA.

Kandel, E., and J. Schwartz. 1981. *Principles of Neural Science*, Elsevier/North-Holland, New York.

Kandogan, E., and Ben Shneiderman. 1996. "Elastic Windows: Improved Spatial Layout and Rapid Multiple Window Operations," *Proceedings of the Advanced Visual Interfaces Conference*, ACM Press, New York, May.

Kautz, Henry A., et al. 1994. "Bottom-Up Design of Software Agents," *Communications of the ACM*, Vol. 37, No. 7, pp. 143-146.

Keen, Peter. 1991. *Shaping the Future: Business Design Through Information Technology*, Boston, Harvard Business School Press, Cambridge, MA.

Ketchpel, S. 1995. "Coalition Formation Among Autonomous Agents," *Proceedings of the 5th European Workshop on Modelling Autonomous Agents in a Multi-Agent World, Lecture Notes in Artificial Intelligence*, Springer, Amsterdam, pp. 73-88.

Kieras, D., and P. Polson. 1985. "An Approach to the Formal Analysis of User Complexity," *International Journal of Man-Machine Studies*, Vol. 22, pp. 365-394.

Kiesler, Sara, Lee Sproull, and Ken Waters. 1996. "A Prisoner's Dilemma Experiment on Cooperation with People and Human-Like Computers," *Journal of Personality and Social Psychology*, Vol. 70, pp. 47-65.

King, Julia. 1996. "Info Overload: A Hazard to Career," *Computerworld*, October 21.

Kinny, D., M. Ljungberg, A.S. Rao, E. Sonenberg, G. Tidhar, and E. Werner. 1994. "Planned Team Activity," *Artificial Social Systems, Lecture Notes in Artificial Intelligence*, C. Castelfranchi and E. Werner, eds., Springer-Verlag, Amsterdam.

Kitajima, M., and P.G. Polson. 1996. "A Comprehension-based Model of Exploration," *Proceedings of the Conference on Human Factors in Computing Systems: Common Ground,* ACM, New York, April, pp. 324-331.

Klavans, Judith L., and Philip Resnick, eds. 1994. *The Balancing Act Workshop: Combining Symbolic and Statistical Approaches to Language,* Las Cruces, NM, Association for Computational Linguistics, Somerset, NJ.

Kobsa, Alfred, and Wolfgang Wahlster. 1989. *User Models in Dialog Systems,* Springer-Verlag, New York.

Koppelman, J., et al. 1995. "A Statistical Approach to Language Modeling for the ATIS Task," *Eurospeech,* Madrid, September, pp. 1785-1788.

Kraus, S., and J. Wilkenfeld 1993. "Multiagent negotiation under time constraints," Technical Report, Number CS 2649, Institute for Advanced Computer Studies, University of Maryland, College Park.

Krauss, Lawrence. 1995. *The Physics of Star Trek,* Basic Books, New York.

Kraut, Robert, J. Galegher, R. Fish, and B. Chalfonte. 1992. "Task Requirements and Media Choice in Collaborative Writing," *Human-Computer Interaction,* Special Issue on Computer-Supported Cooperative Work: Articles, Vol. 7, No. 4, pp. 375-407.

Kraut, Robert, R. Fish, R. Root, and R. Rice. 1993. "Evaluating Video as a Technology for Informal Communication," *Communications of the ACM,* Vol. 36, No. 1, pp. 48-61.

Kraut, Robert, W. Scherlis, T. Mukhopadhyay, J. Manning, and S. Kiesler. 1996. "Internet in the Home, The HomeNet Field Trial of Residential Internet Services," *Communications of the ACM,* Vol. 39, pp. 55-65.

Landauer, Thomas K. 1995. *The Trouble with Computers: Usefulness, Usability and Productivity,* MIT Press, Cambridge, MA.

Lavin, Douglas. 1995a. "Europe's Phone Giants Talk Big, but Changes Are Small," *Wall Street Journal,* June 30, pp. B4.

Lavin, Douglas. 1995b. "On-Line Firms Face Challenge in Europe," *Wall Street Journal,* June 19, pp. B4.

Leduff, Charlie. 1996. "The Web Delivers Light in a Sightless World," *New York Times,* March 28. Available on-line at http://www.nytimes.com/library/cyber/week/0528blind.html.

Lehner, V. 1996. "Caterpillar Collaborative Vehicle Design," Technical Report, National Center for Supercomputing Applications, University of Illinois at Urbana-Champaign. Available on-line at http://www.ncsa.uiuc.edu/VEG/DVR.

Leigh, J., and A.E. Johnson. 1996. "Supporting Transcontinental Collaborative Work in Persistent Virtual Environments," *IEEE Computer Graphics and Applications,* IEEE Computer Society Press, Los Alamitos, CA.

Leigh, J., et al. 1993. "Realistic Modeling of Brain Structures with Remote Interaction Between Simulations of an Inferior Olivary Neuron and a Cerebellar Purkinje Cell," *Proceedings of the SCS Simulations Multiconference,* Arlington, VA, March.

Leigh, J., et al. 1996a. "CALVIN: An Immersimedia Design Environment Utilizing Heterogeneous Perspectives," *Proceedings of the IEEE International Conference on Multimedia Computing and Systems,* IEEE Computer Society Press, Los Alamitos, CA, June.

Leigh, J., et al. 1996b. "Multi-Perspective Collaborative Design in Persistent Networked Virtual Environments," *Proceedings of the IEEE Virtual Reality Annual International Symposium,* IEEE Computer Society Press, Los Alamitos, CA, April.

Lerner, Eric J. n.d. "Talking to Your Computer," VoiceType, IBM. Available on-line at http://www.software.ibm.com/is/voicetype/human.html.

Levesque, H., P. Cohen, and J. Nunes. 1990. "On Acting Together," *Proceedings of the Annual Conference of the American Association for Artificial Intelligence,* MIT Press, Cambridge, MA, pp. 94-99.

Levin, E., and R. Pieraccini. 1995. "CHRONUS: The Next Generation," *Proceedings of the Spoken Language Systems Technology Workshop*, Austin, TX, Morgan-Kaufmann, San Francisco, pp. 269-271.

Levin, Rich. "The Uncommon User Interface," *InformationWeek*, Issue 598, September 23.

Lieberman, Henry. 1995. "Letizia: An Agent That Assists Web Browsing," *Proceedings of the Fourteenth International Joint Conference on Artificial Intelligence*, Morgan-Kaufmann, San Mateo, CA, pp. 924-929.

Litman, Diane. 1985. "Plan Recognition and Discourse Analysis: An Integrated Approach for Understanding Dialogues," No. 170, Department of Computer Science, University of Rochester, Rochester, NY.

Litman, Diane J., and James F. Allen. 1990. "Discourse Processing and Commonsense Plans," *Intentions in Communication*, Philip R. Cohen, Jerry L. Morgan, and Martha E. Pollack, eds., MIT Press, Cambridge, MA.

Lochbaum, Karen E. 1994. "Using Collaborative Plans to Model the Intentional Structure of Discourse," Technical Report TR-25-94, Center for Research in Computing Technology, Harvard University, Cambridge, MA.

Lochbaum, Karen E. 1995. "The Use of Knowledge Preconditions in Language Processing," *Proceedings of the 14th International Joint Conference on Artificial Intelligence*, Morgan-Kaufmann, San Mateo, CA, pp. 1260-1266.

Locke, J. 1995. "An Introduction to the Internet Networking Environment and SIMNET/DIS," unpublished Master's thesis, Naval Postgraduate School, August. Available on-line at http://www-npsnet.cs.nps.navy.mil/npsnet/publications/DISIntro.ps.Z.

Loefler, C. 1993. "Networked Virtual Reality," *Proceedings of ATR Workshop on Virtual Space Teleconferencing*, pp. 108-119.

Lohr, Steve. 1996. "The Network Computer as the PC's Evil Twin," *Washington Post*, November 4, pp. D1 and D6.

Lund, Arnold M. 1994a. "Ameritech's Usability Laboratory: From Prototype to Final Design," *Behaviour & Information Technology*, Vol. 13, Nos. 1-2, pp. 67-80.

Lund, Arnold M. 1994b. "The Evolution of Broadband Work in Ameritech's Customer Interface Systems and Human Factors Department," *Usability in Practice*, Academic Press, Boston, MA.

Lund, Arnold M., and Judith E. Tschirgi. 1991. "Designing for People: Integrating Human Factors into the Product Realization Process," *IEEE Journal on Selected Areas in Communication*, Vol. 9, No. 4, pp. 496-500.

Macedonia, M.R., and M.J. Zyda. 1995. "A Taxonomy for Networked Virtual Environments," *Proceedings of the 1995 Workshop on Networked Realities*, October.

Macedonia, M.R., D.P. Brutzman, and M.J. Zyda. 1995. "NPSNET: A Multi-Player 3D Virtual Environment over the Internet," *Proceedings of the 1995 Symposium on Interactive 3D Graphics*, ACM, New York, pp. 93-94.

Maes, Pattie. 1994. "Agents That Reduce Work and Information Overload," *Communications of the ACM*, Vol. 37, No. 7, pp. 30-40.

Magerman, David. 1995. "Statistical Decision-Tree Models for Parsing," *Proceedings of the 33rd Annual Meeting of the Association for Computational Linguistics*, Cambridge, MA, ACL, Somerset, NJ.

Mandeville, J., and T. Furness. 1995. "GreenSpace: Creating a Distributed Virtual Environment for Global Applications," Human Interface Technology Laboratory, University of Washington, Seattle. Available on-line at http://www.hitl.washington.edu/projects/greenspace.

Mankin, D., S.G. Cohen, and T.K. Bikson. 1996. *Teams and Technology*, Harvard Business School Press, Boston, MA.

Marchionini, Gary, and Catherine Plaisant. 1996. "User Interface for the Library of Congress National Digital Library," Human-Computer Interaction Laboratory (HCIL), University of Maryland, College Park. Available on-line at http://www.cs.umd.edu/projects/hcil/Research/1995/ndl.html.

Marchionini, Gary, et al. 1996. "Users' Needs Assessment for the Library of Congress' National Digital Library," Center for Automation Research, University of Maryland, College Park, May.

Margulies, E. 1995. *236 Killer Voice Processing Applications*, Flatiron Publishing, New York.

Markoff, John. 1994. "Reprogramming the Hacker Elite," *New York Times*, January 2, p. F6.

Marks, J. 1990a. "Automating the Design of Network Diagrams," Technical Report TR 02-90, Harvard University, Cambridge, MA.

Marks, J. 1990b. "A Syntax and Semantics for Network Diagrams," *Proceedings of the 1990 IEEE Conference on Visual Languages*, Skokie, IL, IEEE Computer Society Press, Los Alamitos, CA.

Marks, J. 1991. "The Competence of an Automated Graphic Designer," *Proceedings of the 1991 Long Island Conference on Artificial Intelligence and Computer Graphics*, New York Institute of Technology, New York, pp. 53-61.

Markus, M.L., and T. Connolly. 1990. "Why CSCW Applications Fail: Problems in the Adoption of Interdependent Work Tools," *Proceedings of the Conference on Computer Supported Cooperative Work*, ACM, New York, pp. 371-380.

Martin, Paul, Frederick Crabbe, Stuart Adams, Eric Baatz, and Nicole Yankelovich. 1996. "SpeechActs: A Spoken-Language Framework," *Computer*, Vol. 29, No. 7, pp. 33-40.

Mason, J.A., and J.L. Edwards. 1988. "Surveying Projects on Intelligent Dialogues," *International Journal of Man-Machine Studies*, Vol. 28, Nos. 2, 3, pp. 259-307.

Massaro, Dominic W. 1997. *Perceiving Talking Faces*, MIT Press, Cambridge, MA.

Maybury, Mark. 1993. *Intelligent Multimedia Interfaces*, AAAI/MIT Press, Menlo Park, CA.

Maybury, M. 1994. "Research in Multimedia and Multimodal Parsing and Generation," *Journal of Artificial Intelligence Review*, Special Issue on the Integration of Natural Language and Vision Processing, Vol. 8, No. 3.

McCartney, Scott, and Jonathan Friedland. 1995. "Catching Up: Computer Sales Sizzle as Developing Nations Try to Shrink PC Gap," *Wall Street Journal*, June 29, pp. A1 and A8.

McGrath, J. 1984. *Groups: Interaction and Performance*, Prentice-Hall, Englewood Cliffs, NJ.

McNeely, W.A. 1993. "Robotic Graphics: A New Approach to Force Feedback for Virtual Reality," *Proceedings of the IEEE Virtual Reality International Symposium*, Seattle, WA, September 18-22, IEEE Computer Society Press, Los Alamitos, CA, pp. 336-341.

Medina-Mora, Raul, Terry Winograd, Rodrigo Flores, and Fernando Flores. 1992. "The Action Workflow Approach to Workflow Management Technology," *Proceedings of the Conference on Computer-Supported Cooperative Work*, November, Toronto, ACM, New York.

Miller, Brian. 1994. "Turf Wars," *Government Technology*, Vol. 7, No. 9, pp. 1, 48.

Miller, G.A., et al. 1990. "Five Papers on WordNet," Cognitive Science Laboratory, Princeton University Press, Princeton, NJ.

Miller, S. 1996. "A Fully Statistical Approach to Natural Language Interfaces," *Proceedings of the 34th Annual Meeting of the Association for Computational Linguistics*, Santa Cruz, CA, Morgan-Kaufmann, San Francisco, pp. 55-61.

Miller, S., et al. 1994. "Statistical Language Processing Using Hidden Understanding Models," *Proceedings of the Spoken Language Technology Workshop*, Plainsboro, NJ, Morgan-Kaufmann, San Francisco, pp. 48-52.

Minsky, Marvin, and Doug Riecken. 1994. "A Conversation with Marvin Minsky," *Communications of the ACM*, Vol. 37, No. 7, pp. 23-29.

Mitchell, Tom, Rich Caruana, Dayne Freitag, John McDermott, and David Zabowski. 1994. "Experience with a Learning Personal Assistant," *Communications of the ACM*, Vol. 37, No. 7, pp. 80-91.

Mittal, V.O., S. Roth, J.D. Moore, J. Mattis, and G. Carenini. 1995. "Generating Captions for Information Graphics," *Proceedings of the 14th International Joint Conference on Artificial Intelligence*, Morgan-Kaufmann, San Mateo, CA, pp. 1276-1283.

Moore, Johanna D. 1995. *Participating in Explanatory Dialogues: Interpreting and Responding to Questions in Context*, MIT Press, Cambridge, MA.

Moore, Robert, Douglas Appelt, John Dowding, J. Mark Gawron, and Douglas Moran. 1995. "Combining Linguistic and Statistical Knowledge Sources in Natural-Language Processing for ATIS," DARPA *Proceedings of the Spoken Language Systems Technology Workshop*, January, Austin, TX, Morgan-Kaufmann, San Francisco.

Morningstar, C., and F.R. Farmer. 1991. "Cyberspace: First Steps," *The Lessons of Lucasfilm's Habitat*, MIT Press, Cambridge, MA, pp. 273-302.

Mossberg, Walter S. 1996. "Going On-Line Is Still Too Difficult to Lure a Mass Audience," *Wall Street Journal*, February 22, p. B1.

Munk, Nina. 1996. "Technology for Technology's Sake," *Forbes*, October 21, pp. 280-288.

Myers, Brad A., J. Goldstein, and M.A. Goldberg. 1994. "Creating Charts by Demonstration," *Proceedings of the Conference on Human Factors in Computing Systems*, Active Support for Interaction, Vol. 1, Boston, MA, ACM, New York, pp. 106-111.

Nakatani, Christine, and Julia Hirschberg. 1993. "A Speech-First Model for Repair Detection and Correction," *Proceedings of the 31st Annual Meeting of the Association for Computational Linguistics*, Columbus, OH.

Nass, B., and C. Reeves. 1996. *The Media Equation: How People Treat Computers, Television, and New Media Like Real People and Places*, Cambridge University Press, Cambridge, England, and New York.

National Research Council. 1990a. *Human Factors Research Needs for an Aging Population*, National Academy Press, Washington, DC.

National Research Council. 1990b. *Quantitative Modeling of Human Performance in Complex, Dynamic Systems*, National Academy Press, Washington, DC.

National Research Council. 1995. *Virtual Reality: Scientific and Technological Challenges*, National Academy Press, Washington, DC.

National Science Foundation. 1994. *New Directions in Human-Computer Interaction Education, Research, and Practice*, National Science Foundation, Arlington, VA.

National Science Foundation. 1995. *Survey of the State of the Art in Human Language Technology*, National Science Foundation, Arlington, VA, November 21.

National Science Foundation. 1996. *STIMULATE: Speech, Text, Image and MULtimedia Advanced Technology Effort*, National Science Foundation, Arlington VA, September 1

Nielsen, J. 1993. *Usability Engineering*, Academic Press, San Diego, Calif.

Nielsen, J., and J. Levy. 1993. "Subjective User Preferences Versus Objective Interface Performance Measures," *Usability Engineering*, Academic Press, Boston, MA, p. 36.

Nielsen, Jakob, and Robert L. Mack, eds. 1994. *Usability Inspection Methods*, John Wiley & Sons, New York.

Noack, David. 1994a. "Access Indiana Forming," *Government Technology*, Vol. 7, No. 9, p. 55.

Noack, David. 1994b. "Kansas INK Connects Citizens to Information," *Government Technology*, Vol. 7, No. 9, pp. 22-23.

Norman, Donald A. 1994. "How Might People Interface with Agents," *Communications of the ACM*, Vol. 37, No. 7, pp. 68-71.

O'Hara, Colleen. 1996. "NTIA Funds Model Internet Projects," *Federal Computer Week*, September 23, p. 6.

Olson, G.M., Judith S. Olson, and Robert E. Kraut. 1992. "Introduction to This Special Issue on Computer-Supported Cooperative Work," Editorial, *Human-Computer Interaction*, Vol. 7, No. 3, pp. 251-256.

Olson, J., and G.M. Olson. 1995. "What Mix of Video and Audio Is Useful for Small Groups Doing Remote Real-time Design Work," *Proceedings of SIGCHI'95*, ACM, New York, pp. 362-368.

Orlikowski, W. 1996. "Developing with Notes," *Groupware and Teamwork*, C. Ciborra, ed., John Wiley & Sons, Chichester, England, pp. 31-71.

Oviatt, Sharon L. 1996. "User-centered Modeling for Spoken Language and Multimodal Interfaces," Center for Human-Computer Communication, Oregon Graduate Institute of Science and Technology, Beaverton, OR.

Oviatt, Sharon L., P.R. Cohen, and M.Q. Wang. 1994. "Toward Interface Design for Human Language Technology: "Modality and Structure as Determinants of Linguistic Complexity," *Speech Communication* (European Speech Communication Association), No. 15, pp. 283-300.

Parise, Salvatore, Lee Sproull, Sara Kielser, and Keith Waters. 1996. "My Partner Is a Real Dog: Cooperation with Social Agents," *Proceedings of the Conference on Computer Supported Cooperative Work*, ACM, New York.

Patriotta, G. 1996. "Learning and Appropriating Groupware in the Development of New Products and Processes," *Groupware and Teamwork*, C. Ciborra, ed., John Wiley & Sons, Chichester, England, pp. 138-158.

Perlman, Gary. 1989. *User Interface Development*, Graduate Curriculum Module SEI-CM-17-1.1, Software Engineering Institute, Carnegie Mellon University, Pittsburgh, PA.

Pescovitz, David. 1996. "The Future of the PC," *Wired*, September, p. 80.

Pitta, Julie. 1995. "New Hope for Computer Illiterates?" *Forbes*, January 16, pp. 88-89.

Plaisant, Catherine, et al. 1997. "Bringing Treasures to the Surface: Iterative Design for the Library of Congress National Digital Library Program," *Proceedings of the SIGCHI '97*, March, ACM, New York.

Pope, Kyle. 1994. "Electric Utilities Light Out for Europe's Phone Business," *Wall Street Journal*, December 2, p. B4.

Power, Kevin. 1994. "Neither Rain, Nor Sleet, Nor Darkness of Display . . . ?" *Government Computer News*, October 17, pp. 11-14.

Preece, J., et al. 1994. *Human-Computer Interaction*, Addison-Wesley, Workingham, U.K.

Proceedings of Human Language Technology Workshop. 1993. Plainsboro, NJ. Morgan-Kaufmann, San Mateo, CA.

Proceedings of Speech and Natural Language Workshop. 1992. Harriman, NY. Morgan-Kaufmann, San Mateo, CA.

Proceedings of Speech and Natural Language Workshop. 1991. Pacific Grove, CA. Morgan-Kaufmann, San Mateo, CA.

Proceedings of Speech and Natural Language Workshop. 1990. Hidden Valley, PA. Morgan-Kaufmann, San Mateo, CA.

Proceedings of the Spoken Language Systems Technology Workshop. 1994. Austin, TX. Morgan-Kaufmann, San Mateo, CA.

Raskin, Jef. 1997. "Looking for a Humane Interface: Will Computers Ever Become Easy to Use?," *Communications of the ACM*, Vol. 40, pp. 98-101.

Revzin, Philip. 1995. "Info-Highway Builders Seek to Change African Nation's Development Priorities," *Wall Street Journal*, June 9, p. A5E.

Reynolds, T.J., and J. Gutman. 1988. "Laddering Theory, Method, Analysis, and Interpretation," *Journal of Advertising Research*, Vol. 28, pp. 11-31.

Rheingold, Harold. 1994. *Virtual Communities: Homesteading on the Electronic Frontier*, Addison-Wesley, Reading, MA.

Rich, C., and C.L. Sidner. 1996. "Adding a Collaborative Agent to Direct-Manipulation Interfaces," *Proceedings of UIST*.

Rich, C., and C.L. Sidner. 1997a. "Segmented Interaction History in a Collaborative Interface Agent," *Proceedings of the Intelligent User Interfaces Conference.*

Rich, C., and C.L. Sidner. 1997b. "COLLAGEN: A Toolkit for Collaborative Interfaces," *Proceedings of the First International Conference on Autonomous Agents,* ACM, New York.

Richman, Dan. 1995. "Speech Replaces Point & Click—Boeing and Others Benefit from Voice Recognition, Synthesis," *InformationWeek,* Issue 534, July 3.

Riecken, Doug. 1994a. "A Conversation with Marvin Minsky About Agents," *Communications of the ACM,* Vol. 37, No. 7, pp. 23-29.

Riecken, Doug. 1994b. "Intelligent Agents," *Communications of the ACM,* Vol. 37, No. 7, pp. 20-21.

Riecken, Doug. 1994c. "M: An Architecture of Integrated Agents," *Communications of the ACM,* Vol. 37, No. 7, pp. 107-116, 146-147.

Rigdon, Joan E. 1996. "Testing How Easy 'Easy' Really Is," *Wall Street Journal,* May 10, pp. B1 and B3.

Rimé, B., and L. Schiaratura. 1991. "Gesture and Speech," *Fundamentals of Nonverbal Behaviour,* R.S. Feldmand and B. Rimé eds., New York Press, Syndicate of the University of Cambridge, pp. 239-281.

Roe, D.B., and J.G. Wilpon, eds. 1994. *Voice Communication Between Humans and Machines,* National Academy Press, Washington, DC. Many chapters from this book were revised and published in the October 1995 issue of *Proceedings of the National Academy of Sciences,* Vol. 92.

Rogers, E.M. 1983. *Diffusion of Innovation,* Third Edition, Free Press, New York.

Rosenschein, J., and G. Zlotkin. 1994. *Rules of Encounter: Designing Conventions for Automated Negotiation Among Computers,* MIT Press, Cambridge, MA.

Rossney, Robert. 1996. "Metaworlds," *Wired,* June, pp. 142-146, 206-212.

Roth, S.F., J. Kolojejchick, J. Mattis, and J. Goldstein. 1994. "Interactive Graphic Design Using Automatic Presentation Knowledge," *Proceedings of the Conference on Human Factors in Computing Systems,* Active Support for Interaction, Vol. 1, ACM, New York, April, pp. 112-117.

Roussos, M. 1996. "Constructing Collaborative Stories Within Virtual Learning Landscapes," *Proceedings of the European Conference on Artificial Intelligence in Education,* September.

Roy, T., and C. Cruz-Neira. 1995. "Cosmic Worm in the CAVE: Steering a High-Performance Computing Application from a Virtual Environment," *Presence,* Vol. 4, No. 2, pp. 121-129.

Rubin, Andee. 1996. "Educational Technology: Support for Inquiry-Based Learning," TERC, Cambridge, MA. Available on-line at http://ra.terc.edu/alliance_resources_services/reform/tech-infusion/ed_tech/ed_tech_intro.html.

Russell, Stuart, and Peter Norvig. 1995. *Artificial Intelligence: A Modern Approach,* Prentice-Hall, Englewood Cliffs, NJ.

Ryall, K., J. Marks, and S. Shieber. 1996. "An Interactive System for Drawing Graphs," *GraphDrawing 96.*

Sager, Ira, and Robert D. Hof. 1996. "The Race Is on to Simplify," *Business Week,* June 24, pp. 72-75.

Salton, G. 1989. "ASIS Panel on New Developments and Future Prospects for Electronic Databases," *SIGIR 1989,* ACM, New York, pp. 137-150.

Sandberg, Jared. 1996. "What Do They Do On-Line?" *Wall Street Journal,* December 9, p. R8.

Sawyer, P., A. Flanders, and D. Wixon. 1996. "Making a Difference—The Impact of Inspections," *Proceedings of the Conference on Human Factors in Computing Systems,* ACM, New York, pp. 375-382.

Scherr, A.L. 1993. "A New Approach to Business Processes," *IBM Systems Journal*, Vol. 32, No. 1, pp. 80-98.

Schuler, Doug. 1996. *New Community Networks,* Addison-Wesley, Reading, MA.

Schulzrinne, Henning. 1996. "World-Wide Web: Whence, Whither, What Next?" *IEEE Network Magazine*, March/April, pp. 1-14.

Searle, John. 1990. *Intentions in Communication,* MIT Press, Cambridge, MA.

Selker, Ted. 1994. "Coach: A Teaching Agent That Learns," *Communications of the ACM*, Vol. 37, No. 7, pp. 92-99.

Seneff, S., M. McCandless, and V. Zue. 1995. "Integrating Natural Language into the Word Graph Search for Simultaneous Speech Recognition and Understanding," *Proceedings of Eurospeech,* Madrid, September.

Seybold, P. 1994. "How to Leapfrog Your Organization into the Twenty-first Century: Highlights from Patricia Seybold's 1994 Technology Forum," Patricia Seybold Group, New York, pp. 1-7.

Shaw, C., and M. Green. 1993. "The MR Toolkit Peers Package and Environment," *Proceedings of the IEEE Virtual Reality Annual International Symposium,* IEEE Computer Society Press, Los Alamitos, CA.

Shieber, Stuart M. 1983. "Sentence Disambiguation by a Shift-Reduce Parsing Technique," *21st Annual Meeting of the Association for Computational Linguistics*, Cambridge, MA, ACL, Somerset, NJ.

Shimoga, K.B. 1993. "A Survey of Perceptual Feedback Issues in Dexterous Telemanipulation," *Proceedings of the IEEE Virtual Reality Annual International Symposium*, IEEE Computer Society Press, Los Alamitos, CA.

Shneiderman, Ben. 1988. "Direct Manipulation: A Step Beyond Programming Languages," *IEEE Computer*, Vol. 16, No. 8, pp. 57-69.

Shneiderman, Ben. 1992. *Designing the User Interface: Strategies for Effective Human-Computer Interaction,* Second Edition, Addison-Wesley, Reading, MA.

Shneiderman, Ben. 1994. "Dynamic Queries for Visual Information Seeking," Human-Computer Interaction Laboratory, University of Maryland, College Park, January.

Shneiderman, Ben, Don Byrd, and Bruce Croft. 1997. "Clarifying Search: A User-Interface Framework for Text Searches," *D-Lib Magazine.* Available on-line at http://www.dlib.org/dlib/january97/01contents.html.

Short, J., E. Williams, and B. Christie. 1976. *The Social Psychology of Telecommunications,* John Wiley & Sons, New York.

Shu, L., and W. Flowers. 1992. "Groupware Experiences in Three-Dimensional Computer Aided Design," *Proceedings of the Conference on Computer Supported Cooperative Work,* ACM Press, New York, pp. 179-186.

Sidner, Candace. 1983. "What the Speaker Means: The Recognition of Speakers' Plans in Discourse," *International Journal of Computers and Mathematics,* Vol. 9, pp. 71-82.

Sidner, C. 1994a. "An Artificial Discourse Language for Collaborative Negotiation," *Proceedings of the National Conference on Artificial Intelligence-94*, Seattle, MIT Press, Cambridge, MA, pp. 814-819.

Sidner, C. 1994b. Negotiation in Collaborative Activity: A Discourse Analysis, *Knowledge-Based Systems*, 7(4): 265-267.

Singh, G., L. Serra, H. Ping, and H. Ng. 1994. "BrickNet: A Software Toolkit for Network-Based Virtual Worlds," *Presence: Teleoperators and Virtual Environments*, Vol. 3, No. 1, pp. 19-34.

Smith, David C., et al. 1994. "KIDSIM: Programming Agents Without a Programming Language," *Communications of the ACM*, Vol. 37, No. 7, pp. 55-67.

Smith, Ronnie W., and D. Richard Hipp. 1994. *Spoken Natural Language Dialog Systems,* Oxford University Press, New York.

Smith, Ronnie W., D. Richard Hipp, and Alan W. Biermann. 1995. "An Architecture for Voice Dialogue Systems Based on Prolog-style Theorem Proving," *Computational Linguistics*, Vol. 21, No. 3, pp. 281-320.

Sproull, Lee, and Samer Faraj. 1995. "Atheism, Sex, and Databases: The Net as a Social Technology," *Public Access to the Internet*, Brian Kahin and James Keller, eds., pp. 62-81.

Sproull, Lee, R. Subramani, Jan Walker, Sara Kiesler, and Keith Waters. 1996. "When the Interface Is a Face," *Human Computer Interaction*, Vol. 11, pp. 97-124.

Stansfield, S. 1995. "An Application of Shared Virtual Reality to Situational Training," *Proceedings of the IEEE Virtual Reality Annual International Symposium*, IEEE Computer Society Press, Los Alamitos, CA, pp. 156-161.

Stefik, M., et al. 1987. "Beyond the Chalkboard: Computer Support for Collaboration and Problem Solving in Meetings," *Communications of the ACM*, Vol. 30, No. 1, pp. 32-47.

Stein, A., and E. Maier. 1995. Structuring Collaborative Information-Seeking Dialogues, *Knowledge-Based Systems*, 8(2-3):82-93.

Steinmetz, Greg. 1995. "AT&T and Others Dislike German Deregulation Plan," *Wall Street Journal*, August 10, p. A6.

Stock, Robert W. 1995. "Removing Roadblocks to Computer Use," *Wall Street Journal*, September 14.

Storck, John, and Lee Sproull. 1995. "Through a Glass Darkly: What Do People Learn in Video Conferences?" *Human Communication Research*, Vol. 22, No. 2, pp. 197-219.

Stork, David G., and Marcus Hennecke, eds. 1996. *Speechreading by Humans and Machines: Models, Systems and Applications*, Springer-Verlag, Berlin and New York.

Suchman, Lucy. 1987. *Plans and Situated Actions*, Cambridge University Press, New York.

Sullivan, K. 1996. "The Windows 95 User Interface: A Case Study in Usability Engineering," *Conference on Human Factors in Computing Systems*, ACM, New York, pp. 473-480.

Sycara, K.P. 1987. "Resolving Adversarial Conflicts: An Approach to Integrating Case-Based and Analytic Methods," unpublished Ph.D. thesis, Georgia Institute of Technology.

Tang, J.C., and E. Isaacs. 1993. "Why Do Users Like Video?" *Computer Supported Cooperative Work*, pp. 163-196.

Tognazzini, Bruce. 1992. *Tog on Interface*, Addison-Wesley, Reading, MA.

Tognazzini, Bruce. 1996. *Tog on Software Design*, Addison-Wesley, Reading, MA.

Trace R&D Center. 1996a. *CO-NET: Cooperative Database Distribution Network for Assistive Technology*, 1996-97 Edition, Trace R&D Center, Madison, WI, Spring/Summer.

Trace R&D Center. 1996b. *Trace Resourcebook: Assistive Technology for Communication, Control and Computer Access*, 1996-97 Edition, Trace R&D Center, Madison, WI.

Turkle, Sherry. 1996. "Who Am We?" *Wired*, January, pp. 146-152, 194-199.

University of Udine. 1996. Sixth International Conference on User Modeling, University of Udine, Italy, October.

U.S. Bureau of the Census. 1994. *Americans with Disablities*, U.S. Government Printing Office, Washington, DC. Available on-line at http://www.census.gov/hhes/www/disable.html.

U.S. Bureau of the Census. 1995. *Population Profile of the United States*, U.S. Government Printing Office, Washington, DC.

U.S. Department of Commerce. 1994. "The Information Infrastructure: Reaching Society's Goals," *Report of the Information Infrastructure Task Force Committee on Applications and Technology*, National Institute of Standards and Technology, Gaithersburg, MD, September.

U.S. Department of Education. 1992. *1992 National Adult Literacy Survey*, U.S. Government Printing Office, Washington, DC.

Van Dam, Andries. 1997. "Post-WIMP User Interfaces," *Communications of the ACM*, Vol. 40, February, pp. 63-67.

Vanderheiden, Gregg C. 1996. Reply comments in response to the Federal Communications Commission's Notice of Inquiry 96-198 Regarding Implementation of Section 255 of the Telecommunications Act of 1996 (Access to Telecommunications Services, Telecommunications Equipment, and Customer Premise's Equipment by Persons with Disabilities), WT Docket No. 96-198, submitted by G.C. Vanderheiden, Trace R&D Center, University of Wisconsin-Madison.

Vanderheiden G., et al. 1986. "Human Interface Design and the Handicapped User," *Proceedings of the Conference on Human Factors in Computing Systems*, ACM, New York, pp. 291-297.

Van House, Nancy. 1996. "User-Centered Iterative Design for Digital Libraries: The Cypress Experience,"*D-lib Magazine*, February.

Vaughan-Nichols, Steven J. 1996. "The NC Follies: A Network Computer Is a Small Idea," *Internet World*. Available on-line at http://www.internetworld.com/1996/12/nc_follies.html.

Venture Development Corporation. 1996a. "Five Characteristics of Good Interactive Kiosk Design." Venture Development Corporation, MA, June 14.

Venture Development Corporation. 1996b. "Interactive Kiosks, New Horizons for Advanced Computing Technology: An Executive White Paper," Venture Development Corporation, MA.

Venture Development Corporation. 1996c. "Surging Demand for Interactive Kiosks," Venture Development Corporation, MA, January 19.

Verity, John W., and Paul C. Judge. 1996. "Making Computers Disappear," *Business Week*, June 24, pp. 118-119.

Vince, John. 1995. *Virtual Reality Systems*, Addison-Wesley, Reading, MA.

Virzi, Robert A., and Paul Resnick. 1995. "Relief from the Audio Interface Blues: Expanding the Spectrum of Menu, List, and Form Styles," *ACM Transactions on Computer-Human Interaction*, Vol. 2, June, pp. 145-176. Available on-line at http://ccs.mit.edu/CCSWP184.html.

Virzi, R.A., J.L. Sokolov, and D. Karis. 1996. "Usability Problem Identification Using Both Low- and High-Fidelity Prototype," *Proceedings of the Conference on Human Factors in Computing Systems: Common Ground*, pp. 236-243, ACM Press, New York.

Wahlster, W., E. Andr, W. Finkler, J.J. Profitlich, and T. Rist. 1993. "Plan-Based Integration of Natural Language and Graphics Generation," *Artificial Intelligence*, Vol. 63, Nos.1-2, pp. 378-428.

Waldman, Peter. 1995. "India Seeks to Open Huge Phone Market," *Wall Street Journal*, July 25.

Wang, Q., M. Green, and C. Shaw. 1995. "EM—An Environment Manager for Building Networked Virtual Environments," *Proceedings of the IEEE Virtual Reality Annual International Symposium*, IEEE Computer Society Press, Los Alamitos, CA, pp. 11-18.

Wasser, Judith D. 1996. "Reform, Restructuring, and Technology Infusion," *Technology Infusion and School Change*, TERC, Cambridge, MA. Available on-line at http://ra.terc.edu/alliance_resources_services/reform/tech-infusion/reform/reform_intro.html.

Weiser, Mark. 1993a. "Some Computer Science Issues in Ubiquitous Computing," *Communications of the ACM*, Vol. 36, No. 7, pp. 75-84.

Weiser, Mark. 1993b. "Ubiquitous Computing," *Computer*, October, pp. 71-72.

Weld, Daniel. 1995. "The Role of Intelligent Systems in the National Information Infrastructure," *AI Magazine*,Vol. 3, No. 16.

Wiklund, Michael E., ed. 1994. *Usability in Practice: How Companies Develop User-Friendly Products*, Academic Press, Boston, MA.

Wilson, E.O. 1971. *The Insect Societies*, Belknap/Harvard University Press, Cambridge, MA.

Winograd, T. 1988. "A Language/Action Perspective on the Design of Cooperative Work," *Human-Computer Interaction*, Vol. 3, No. 1, pp. 3-30.

Woodward, P. 1993. "Interactive Scientific Visualization of Fluid Flow," *IEEE Computer Magazine*, Vol. 26, No. 10. October.

Young, S.R., A.G. Hauptmann, W.H. Ward, E.T. Smith, and P. Werner. 1989. "High Level Knowledge Sources in Usable Speech Recognition Systems," *Communications of the ACM*, February, pp. 183-194.

Zuckerman, Lawrence. 1996. "IBM to Market Software That Can Interpret Human Speech," *New York Times*, September 12. Available on-line at http://search.nytimes.com/web/docsroot/library/cyber/week/0912blue.html.

PART II

BACKGROUND PAPER

TRENDS IN HUMAN-COMPUTER INTERACTION RESEARCH AND DEVELOPMENT

H. Rex Hartson
Virginia Polytechnic Institute

INTRODUCTION

Human-computer interaction (HCI) is a field of research and development, methodology, theory, and practice with the objective of designing, constructing, and evaluating computer-based interactive systems—including hardware, software, input/output devices, displays, training, and documentation—so that people can use them efficiently, effectively, safely, and with satisfaction. HCI is cross-disciplinary in its conduct and multidisciplinary in its roots, drawing on—synthesizing and adapting from—several other fields, including human factors (e.g., the roots for task analysis and designing for human error in HCI); ergonomics (e.g., the roots for design of devices, workstations, and work environments); cognitive psychology (e.g., the roots for user modeling); behavioral psychology and psychometrics (e.g., the roots of user performance metrics); systems engineering (e.g., the roots for much predesign analysis); and computer science (e.g., the roots for graphical interfaces, software tools, and issues of software architecture).

Importance of Usability

The entire field of HCI shares the single goal of achieving high *usability* for users of computer-based systems. Rather than being fuzzy and vague as it is sometimes perceived, usability is tangible and can be quantified. Usability can be broadly defined as "ease of use," including such measurable attributes as learnability, speed of user task performance, user error rates, and subjective user satisfaction (Shneiderman, 1992; Hix and Hartson, 1993a). However, an easy-to-use system that does not support its users' needs, in terms of functionality, is of little value. Thus, usability has evolved toward the concept of "usability in the large"—that is, ease of use *plus* usefulness.

Despite many research advances in interactive computer systems, usability barriers still obstruct access to, and blunt effectiveness of, an every-citizen interface for the national information infrastructure—disenfranchising and disenchanting users across society. As a result, the United States fails to accrue the potentially enormous returns of our collective investment in computing technology. These barriers impede human productivity and have a profound impact on computer users in business, government, industry, education, and indeed the whole nation.

In the not-too-distant past, computer usage was esoteric, conducted mostly by a core of technically oriented users who were not only willing to accept the challenge of overcoming poor usability but also sometimes welcomed it as a barrier to protect their craft from uninitiated "outsiders." Poor usability was good for the field's mystique, not to mention users' job security. Now, unprecedented numbers of Americans use computers, and user interface is often the first thing people ask about when discussing software. *To most users the interface is the system.* For the "every citizen" of today, communication with the system has become at least as important as computation by the system.

The goals of most organizations include increased employee and organization productivity, decreased employee training costs, decreased employee work errors, and increased employee satisfaction. These are also exactly the benefits of achieving high usability in user interfaces. Too often, especially in government and large businesses, training is used as a costly substitute for usability, and almost as often it fails to meet its goals. Attention to usability by developers no longer requires justification in most quarters: "Usability has become a competitive necessity for the commercial success of software" (Butler, 1996).

Product and Process

Achieving good usability requires attention to both product and process. The *product*, in this case, is the content of the user interaction design and its embodiment in software. An effective *process* for developing interaction design is also important, and a poor understanding of the process is often responsible for a product's lack of usability. While state-of-the-art user interaction development processes are based on formative usability evaluation in an iterative cycle, much of the state of the *practice* is fundamentally flawed in that remarkably little formal usability evaluation is performed on most interactive systems. This is generally changing now in many industrial settings. However, ensuring usability remains difficult when evaluation, because of real or perceived costs, is not standard practice in interactive software development projects.

User Interaction Versus User Interface Software

Developers attempting to incorporate usability methods into their development environments often refer to their efforts in terms of "evaluating software" or "evaluating user interface software." There are many reasons for evaluating *software*, but usability is not one of them. Usability is seated within the design of the *user interaction component* of an interactive system, not in the *user interface software component*, as shown simplistically below:

Development of the user interface	
Development of user interaction component	Development of user interface software component

Development of the interaction component, toward which most HCI effort is directed, is substantially different from development of the user interface software. The view of the user interaction component is the *user's perspective* of user interaction: how it works; how tasks are performed using it; and its look and feel and behavior in response to what a user sees, hears, and does while interacting with the computer.

In contrast, the user interface software component is the programming code by which the interaction component is implemented. *The user interaction component design should serve as requirements for the user interface software component.* Design of the user interaction component must be given attention at least equal to that given the user interface software component during the development process, if usability in interactive systems is to be ensured.

The overview of HCI topics, issues, and activities that follows is loosely divided into theory, interaction techniques, and development methods. Reflecting its diverse roots, HCI is host to activities in many topical areas, some of which are reviewed here. An attempt has been made to capture a broad, inclusive cross section of a very dynamic field, but this paper is not intended to be an exhaustive survey, and no claims are made for completeness. Emphasis is given to topics of most importance to the usability of an every-citizen interface.

THEORY

HCI theory has its avid proponents. If the proportion of literature devoted to theory is to be taken as an indication, theory plays a strong role in HCI, but in fact theory has not seen broad, direct application in the practice of HCI.

Much theory comes to HCI from cognitive psychology (Hammond et. al., 1987; Barnard, 1993). Norman's (1986) theory of action expresses, from a cognitive engineering perspective, human task performance—the path from goals to intentions to actions (inputs to the computer) back to perception and interpretation of feedback to evaluation of whether the intentions and goals were approached or met. The study of learning in HCI (Carroll, 1984; Draper and Barton, 1993) and Fitts Law (relating cursor travel time to distance and size of target) (MacKenzie, 1992) also have their roots in cognitive theory.

Task Analysis

To design a user interface (or any system) to meet the needs of its users, developers must understand what tasks users will use a system for and how those tasks will be performed (Diaper, 1989). Because tasks at all but the highest levels of abstraction involve manipulation of user interface objects (e.g., icons, menus, buttons, dialogue boxes), tasks and objects must be considered together in design (Carroll et al., 1991). A complete description of tasks in the context of their objects is a rather complete representation of an interaction design. The process of describing tasks (how users do things) and their relationships (usually in a hierarchical structure of tasks and subtasks) is called *task analysis* and comes to HCI primarily from human factors (Meister, 1985). There are various task analysis methods to address various purposes. In HCI the primary uses are to drive design and to build predictive models of user task performance. Because designing for usability means understanding user tasks, task analysis is essential for good design; unfortunately, it is often ignored or given only minimal attention.

Models of Human Information Processing

A significant legacy from cognitive psychology is the model of a human as a cognitive information processor (Card et al., 1983). The Command Language Grammar (Moran, 1981) and the keystroke model (Card and Moran, 1980), which attempt to explain the nature and structure of human-computer interaction, led directly to the Goals, Operators, Methods, and Selection (GOMS) model (Card et al., 1983). GOMS-related models—quantitative models combining task analysis and the human user as an information processor—are concerned with predicting various measures of user performance, most commonly task completion time based on physical and cognitive actions of users, with place holders and estimated times for highly complex cognitive actions and tasks. Direct derivatives of GOMS include NGOMSL (Kieras, 1988) and Cognitive Complexity Theory (CCT) (Kieras and Polson, 1985; Lewis et al., 1990), the latter of which is intended to represent the complexity of user interaction from the user's perspective. This technique represents an interface as the mapping between the user's job-task environment and the interaction device behavior.

GOMS-related techniques have been shown to be useful in discovering certain kinds of usability problems early in the life cycle, even before a prototype has been constructed. Some studies (e.g., Gray et al., 1990) have demonstrated a payoff in a few circumscribed applications where the savings of a small number of user actions (e.g., a few keystrokes or mouse movements) can improve user performance enough to have an economic impact, often because of the repetitiveness of a task.

Nonetheless, these models have not achieved widespread application within the tight constraints of industrial schedules and budgets because of the labor intensiveness of producing and maintaining these relatively formal and structured task representations, the need for specialized skills, and the difficulty in competing with the effectiveness of usability evaluation using a prototype. Furthermore, these techniques generally do not take into account individual differences in user classes and are often limited to expert, error-free behaviors (not representative of "every citizen" as a user). In any case, it is generally agreed that this kind of analytical approach to usability evaluation cannot be considered a substitute for empirical formative evaluation—usability testing of a prototype with users in a lab or field setting (see "User-Based Evaluation" below).

Human Work Activity

Another area feeding HCI theory and practice is "work activity theory" (Ehn, 1990; Bodker, 1991). Originating in Russia and Germany and now flourishing in Scandinavia (where it is, interestingly, related to the labor movement), this view of design based on work practices situated in a worker's own complete environment has been synthesized into several related mainstream HCI topics. For example, "participatory design" is a democratic process based on the argument that users should be involved in designs they will be using, in which all stakeholders, including and especially users, have equal inputs into interaction design. Muller (1991) and others have operationalized participatory design in an approach called PICTIVE, which supports rapid group prototype design using Post-It™ notes, marking pens, paper, and other "low-technology" materials on a large table top.

This interest in design driven by work practices in context has led to the eclectic inclusion in some HCI practice of ethnography, an investigative field rooted in anthropology (LeCompte and Preissle, 1993), and other hermeneutic (concerned with ways to explain, translate, and interpret perceived reality) approaches as qualitative research tools for extracting design requirements. Contextual inquiry/design (Wixon et al., 1990) is an example of an adaptation of this kind of approach, where design and evaluation are conducted collaboratively by users and developers, while users perform normal work tasks in their natural work environment. Much of this collaboration is based on interviews that seek to make implicit work practices more explicit and to draw out structure, language, and culture affecting the work.

The task artifact framework of Carroll and Rosson (1992) and, to some extent, scenario-based design follow an ethnographic focus on task performance in a work context. Scenarios are concrete, narrative descriptions of user and system activity for task performance (Carroll, 1995). They describe particular interactions happening over time, being deliberately informal, open ended, and fragmentary. Scenarios often focus on interaction objects, or artifacts, and how they are manipulated by users in the course of task performance.

Formal Methods

While not theory per se, formal methods have been the object of some interest and attention in HCI (Harrison and Thimbleby, 1990). The objectives of formal methods—precise, well-defined notations and mathematical models—in HCI are similar to those in software engineering. Formal design specifications can be reasoned about and analyzed for various properties such as correctness and consistency. Formal specifications also have the potential to be translated automatically into prototypes or software implementation. Thus, in principle, formal methods can be used to support both theory and practice; however, they have not yet had an impact in real-world system development, and their potential is difficult to predict.

DEVICES, INTERACTION TECHNIQUES, AND GRAPHICS

In contrast to theory, the influence of interaction devices and their associated interaction techniques represents a practical arena of real-world constraints as well as hardware design challenges. "An *interaction technique* is a way of using a physical input/output device to perform a generic task in a human-computer dialogue" (Foley et al., 1990). A very similar term, *interaction style,* has evolved to denote the behavior of a user and an interaction object (e.g., a push button or pulldown menu) within the context of task performance. In practice, the notion of an interaction technique includes the concept of interaction style plus full consideration of internal machine behavior and software aspects. In the context of an interaction technique, an interaction object (and its supporting software) is often referred to as a "widget." Libraries of widgets—software that supports programming of graphical user interfaces (GUIs)—are an outgrowth of operating system device handler routines used to process user input and output in the now ancient and impoverished interaction style of line-oriented, character-cell, text-only, "glass teletype" terminal interaction. At first, graphics packages took interaction beyond text to direct manipulation of graphical objects, eventually leading to new concepts in displays and cursor tracking. Of course, invention of the mouse and advent of the Xerox Star and Lisa Macintosh by Apple accelerated the evolution of the now-familiar point-and-click interaction styles. It is not surprising that many of the computer scientists who developed early graphics packages also introduced GUI interaction techniques as part of their contribution to the HCI field (Foley and Wallace, 1974; Foley et al., 1990). To some extent, standardization of interactive graphical interaction techniques led to the widgets of today's GUI platforms and corresponding style guides intended for ensuring compliance to a style but sometimes mistakenly thought of as usability guides.

This growth of graphics and devices made possible one of the major breakthroughs in interaction styles—direct manipulation (Shneiderman, 1983; Hutchins et al., 1986; Weller and Hartson, 1992)—changing the basic paradigm of interaction with computers. Unlike previous command-line-oriented interaction in which users plan tasks in terms of hierarchies of goals and subgoals, entering a command line for each, direct manipulation allows opportunistic and incremental task planning. Users can try something and see what happens, exploring many avenues for interactive problem solving. This kind of opportunistic interaction is also called *display-based interaction* (Payne, 1991).

DEVELOPMENT METHODS AND SOFTWARE ENGINEERING

The difference between user interaction and user interface software, mentioned in the Introduction, results in a need for separate and fundamentally different development processes for the two components of a user interface.

Development Life Cycles

Studies deriving principles for user interaction development (e.g., Gould et al., 1991) vary, but all agree that interaction development must involve usability evaluation. Just adding some kind of "user testing" to an existing software process is not enough, however. Usability comes from a complete process, one that ensures usability and attests to when it has been achieved (Hix and Hartson, 1993a). Most researchers and practitioners also agree that an interaction development process must be iterative, unlike the phase-oriented "waterfall" method, for example, for software development. Although software can be correctness driven, user interaction design—because of infinite design possibilities and unpredictable, dynamic, and psychological aspects of the human user—must be self-correcting. Thus, interaction development is an essentially iterative process of design and evaluation, one that must, in the end, be integrated with other system and software life cycles. Within this cycle, the interaction design is an iteratively evolving design specification for the user interface software. The star life cycle (Hartson and Hix, 1989) for interaction development explicitly acknowledges these differences from software development, being unequivocally iterative, and allows the process to start with essentially any development activity and proceed to any other activity before the previous one is completed, with each activity informing the others.

Development Activities

Design and Design Representation

Design is closely coupled to, and driven by, early systems analysis activities such as needs, task, and functional analyses. Good interaction design involves early and continual involvement of representative users and is guided by well-established design guidelines and principles built on the concept of user-centered design (Norman and Draper, 1986). Design guidelines address such issues as consistency, use of real-world metaphors, human memory limits, screen layout, and designing for user errors. Additionally, designers are expected to follow style guides (less oriented toward usability than toward compliance with some "standard" style) in their use of widgets.

Although some more recent guidelines enjoy the support of empirical studies, guidelines have typically been scattered throughout the literature, based mostly on experience and educated opinion. In a classic work, Smith and Mosier (1986) compiled guidelines for character-cell, textual interface design. Others (Mayhew, 1992; Shneiderman, 1992) have followed to help cover graphical interfaces.

Many practitioners believe it is enough to know and use interface design guidelines, possibly in addition to an interface style guide (e.g., for Windows). Experience, however, has shown that guidelines and style guides do not eliminate the need for usability evaluation. Experience has also demonstrated that, although guidelines are not difficult to learn as factual knowledge, their effective application in real design situations is a skill acquired only through long experience.

The creative act of design must also be accompanied by the physical act of capturing and documenting that design. Although many *constructional* techniques exist for representing software aspects of interface objects, *behavioral* representation techniques are needed for communicating, among developers, the interaction design from a behavioral task and user perspective. The User Action Notation (UAN) is one such technique (Hartson et al., 1990; Hartson and Gray, 1992). The UAN is a user- and task-oriented notation that describes the behavior of a user and an interface during their cooperative performance of a task. The primary abstraction of the UAN is a user task—a user action or group of temporally related user actions performed to achieve a work goal. A user interaction design is represented as a quasi-hierarchical structure of asynchronous tasks. User actions, interface feedback, and internal state information are represented at various levels of abstraction in the UAN. In addition to design representation, design rationale (MacLean et al., 1991) is captured to record and communicate the history and basis for design decisions, to reason about designs, and to explore alternatives.

Prototyping

Rapid prototypes of interaction design are early and inexpensive vehicles for evaluation that can be used to identify usability problems in an interaction design before resources are committed to implementing the design in software. Much interest has been focused on low-fidelity prototypes (e.g., paper and pencil). Counter to intuition, low-fidelity prototypes have allowed developers to discover as many usability problems as found using interactive computer-based prototypes (Virzi et al., 1996). Paper prototypes are most useful early in the life cycle because they are more flexible in exploring variations of interaction behavior at a cost of less fidelity in appearance. Later in the life cycle, changes made to the behavior of a coded prototype are more expensive than changes made in appearance. Almost all projects eventually move to computer-based rapid prototypes for formal usability evaluation.

User-based Evaluation

Summative evaluation is used to make judgments about a finished product, to gauge the level of usability achieved and possibly compare one system with another. In contrast, *formative evaluation*—the heart of the star life cycle—is used to detect and fix usability problems before the interaction design is coded in software (Hix and Hartson, 1993a,b; Nielsen, 1993), aiding in the improvement of an interaction design while a product is still being developed. For formative evaluation, unlike summative evaluation, statistical significance is not an issue. Formative evaluation relies on both quantitative and qualitative data. The quantitative data are used as a gauge for the process—to be sure usability is improving with each design iteration and to know when to stop iterating. Borrowing an adage from software engineering (and probably other places before that), "if you can't measure it, you can't manage it." The instruments used to quantify usability include benchmark tasks and user questionnaires. Benchmark tasks, drawn from representative and mission-critical tasks, yield objective user performance data, such as time on task and error rates (Whiteside et al., 1988). Questionnaires yield subjective data such as user satisfaction (Chin et al., 1988). In analyzing quantitative data, results are compared against preestablished *usability specifications* (Whiteside et al., 1988)—operationally defined and measurable goals used as criteria for success in interaction design.

Even more valuable than these quantitative data are the qualitative data gathered in usability evaluations. Identification of *critical incidents*— occurrences in task performance that indicate a usability problem—are essential in pinpointing design problems. Verbal protocol (capturing users' thinking aloud) helps designers understand what was going through a user's mind when a usability problem occurred, which may help in ascertaining its causes and in offering useful solutions.

These quantitative and qualitative data typically come from lab-based evaluations involving users as "subjects." While very effective, this process can be expensive. The need for faster, less costly usability methods has led to approaches, such as *discount usability engineering* (Nielsen, 1989), that trade off less-than-perfect and complete results for a lower cost. *Inspection methods* (Nielsen and Mack, 1994) use systematic examinations of design representations, prototypes, or software products. *Cognitive walkthroughs* (Lewis et al., 1990; Wharton et al., 1992) and *claims analysis* (Carroll and Rosson, 1992) are effective inspection methods, especially early in development, but can still be labor intensive and require special training, which is intimidating to developers in search of cost-effective methods. *Heuristic evaluation* (Nielsen and Molich, 1990; Nielsen, 1992), which involves reviewing compliance of an interaction design to a checklist of selected and generalized guidelines, is an even less expensive inspection method but is limited by the scope of guidelines used.

Inspection methods are effective at finding some kinds of usability problems but do not reliably pinpoint all types of problems that can be observed in lab-based testing. In fact, lab-based usability evaluation remains the yardstick against which most new methods are compared in formal studies. Most real-world development organizations continue to be willing to pay the price for extensive lab-based usability evaluation because of its effectiveness in helping them identify and understand usability problems, their causes, and solutions.

Usability Engineering

Many HCI practices, such as the employment of usability specifications and various kinds of evaluation, have been gathered under the banner of *usability engineering* (Nielsen, 1993). This is a good appellation because it includes a concern for cost in the notion of *discount usability methods* (Nielsen, 1989), the practical goal of achieving specifications and not perfection, and techniques for managing the process. The latter is important because iterative processes are sometimes perceived by management as "going around in circles," which is not attractive to a manager with a limited budget and dwindling production schedule.

Usability specifications provide this essential management control for the iterative process. The quantitative usability data are analyzed in each iteration, and the results are compared with the usability specifications, allowing management to decide if iteration can stop. If the specifications are not met, data are assessed to weigh cost and severity or importance of each usability problem, assigning a priority ranking for designing and implementing solutions to those problems that, when fixed, will give the largest improvement in usability for the least cost.

Development Tools

Almost any software package that provides support for the interface development process can be called an *interface development tool,* a generic term referring to anything from a complete interface development environment to a single library routine (Myers, 1989, 1993). New software tools for user interface development are appearing with increasing frequency.

Interface development tools can be divided into at least four types (Hix and Hartson, 1993a). *Toolkits* are libraries of callable routines for low-level interface features and are often integrated with window managers (e.g., X,Windows) *Interface style support tools* are interactive systems that enforce a particular interface style and/or standards (e.g., OSF Motif, Common User Access). *User interface management systems* (UIMs) are development environments that can include both prototyping and run-time support, with the goal of allowing developers to produce an interface implementation without using traditional programming languages. Of these groups, the UIMSs perhaps are the most interesting, have the most potential, and suffer the most difficult technical problems (Myers, 1995).

These first three categories of development tools primarily address user interface software. A fourth category, *interaction development tools*, provides interactive support for user interaction development. Of all the interaction development activities, the one most commonly supported by tools in this group is formative evaluation (Macleod and Bevan, 1993; Hix and Hartson, 1994).

Although tools now exist on many programming platforms to lay out objects of a user interface quickly and easily, usability problems are not necessarily addressed by adding this kind of technology to the process; many interface development tools are potentially a faster way to produce poor interfaces.

COST JUSTIFICATION

Economic justification for usability effort in interactive system development is now beginning to be established (Bias and Mayhew, 1994). Broad acceptance in business and industry requires further demonstration of a return on investment; documented cases and success stories are essential. The bottom line is that usability engineering does not add to *overall* cost, for two reasons: (1) usability does not add as much cost to the development process as many people think, and (2) good usability saves many other costs.

Considering cost added to the process, one must realize that any added cost is confined. Interaction development is a small part of total system development. It occurs early in the process, when the cost of making changes is still relatively low, and mainly impacts only a prototype, not the final system software.

Considering the cost savings attributable to good usability, it is easy to establish that poor usability is costly and that good usability is all about lowering costs. Usability is simply good business. The most expensive operational item in an interactive system is the user. People who develop software are concerned with the cost of development, but the people who buy and use a software application are concerned with the costs of usage. Development costs are mostly one-time costs, while operational costs—such as training, productivity losses, help desks and field support, recovery from user errors, dissatisfied employees, and system maintenance costs (the cost of trying to fix problems *after* release)—accrue for years.

Unless the net of analysis is cast broadly enough, the problem with cost-benefit analysis is that one group pays development costs and another group gets the benefits. People who purchase computer systems are asking which costs more: user-based tasks that are quick, efficient, and accurate or errorprone tasks that take more time? Confused users or confident and competent users?

Beyond this kind of argumentation, used in software engineering for years, substantial measurable economic advantage can be accrued from usability. Case studies have demonstrated that large sums of real money can be saved by increasing user (employee) productivity alone (Bias and Mayhew, 1994). In the end, these are the cases that will make the difference.

THE FUTURE

HCI is a relatively young and broadly diverse field with a rapidly growing impact on the world of computing. Usability, especially in every-citizen interfaces, is becoming recognized as crucial for the national information infrastructure. The future of HCI in this context can be viewed from a perspective of product and process.

Future of HCI in Products

A rich part of the future of HCI is in its application areas, which are growing more rapidly than the HCI methods needed for their development. As an example, it is unlikely that usability methods developed for desktop applications will apply directly to virtual environments, one of the most exciting areas of applications development. Despite intense and widespread research in virtual environments, very little work has been applied toward developing the usability methods that will be required to evaluate this new technology—a necessary coupling if virtual environments are to reach their full potential. Similarly, groupware and computer-supported cooperative work (Baecker, 1993; Grudin, 1994), multimedia (Blattner and Dannenberg, 1992), hypermedia, and interface access for the disabled or impaired persons (Williges and Williges, 1995) will require development of new methods for design and usability evaluation. Educational technology for the classroom, the World Wide Web, and the home is emerging as a giant application area. Perhaps nowhere is usability more important than in the discipline of education, where understanding and communication of concepts and ideas are the stock and trade.

Finally, the Internet, the World Wide Web, and cyberspace are incredibly fast-growing application domains bringing new kinds of usability challenges. The World Wide Web is a technological and sociological frontier with many analogies to the frontier that was the American West over a century ago—lawlessness and disorganization, with exploration and expansion in every direction.

Studies show that users having trouble with an interactive system often cannot find solutions in user manuals or from on-line help; they are more likely to ask a friend, colleague, or co-worker for help. This strategy can work in a local setting where there are other users. However, users of the national information infrastructure will often be remote and distributed, using a network as their work setting. For these isolated users, who are less able to tolerate poor user interfaces and who will abandon applications they find too difficult to learn and use, there is often no one to ask when things go wrong at the computer, and usability will have a large impact on their productivity and satisfaction. For this large-scale environment with its diversity of user types and characteristics, its variety of application types, and potential user isolation, usability takes on special importance.

Additionally, the interaction styles and techniques of future products can be expected to expand beyond the currently ubiquitous WIMP—windows, icons, menus, pointers—or desktop-style interface. While WIMP interfaces have provided a great step forward for interfaces in static situations (e.g., word processing, spreadsheets), innovative interaction techniques that go beyond the WIMP paradigm are necessary to meet user interface needs of demanding, real-time, high-performance applications such as those found in military applications, medical systems, "smart road" applications, and so on. Researchers are promoting a greatly expanded vision of interaction beyond the limited interaction styles now available via just keyboard and mouse, including extensions to current work in graphic and visual displays (Mullet and Sano, 1995), use of hands and feet (Buxton, 1986), eye movement (Jacob, 1993), haptic (touch) feel and force feedback (Baecker et al., 1995), audio and sound (Brewster et al., 1993; Gaver and Smith, 1995), voice (McCauley, 1984), and stylus and gesture (Goldberg and Goodisman, 1995).

Finally, many technology forecasters have predicted that the most significant area of future applications may be computing embedded in appliances, homes, offices, vehicles, and roads. Sometimes called *wearable computers*, these devices can be strapped to one's wrist or embedded in a shoe! A recent television news feature (CNN News, July 1996) described a project at Massachusetts Institute of Technology in which a pair of shoes will, indeed, be instrumented so that, as the wearer gets milk out for breakfast, sensors will note that the milk supply is getting low! Approaching the grocery store on the way home, the system speaks via a tiny earphone to remind the shoe's wearer of the need to pick up some milk.

The requirements for usability of desktop and other familiar systems will pale in comparison to the importance of usability in this new era of computing. That "every citizen" will not tolerate training courses, user manuals, or on-line help to operate everyday objects such as refrigerators and automobiles will compel designers to take seriously their responsibility for usability. Issues of social impact carry high risks if this kind of every-citizen interface is threatening, intimidating, or difficult to use. In successful designs the computing component will be transparent, with users not even thinking of themselves as users of computers. When human factors was first adapted to user interfaces (e.g., Williges et al., 1987), ergonomics was largely filtered out. Interestingly, new devices, combining hardware, software, and firmware as "appliances," will require a reintegration of ergonomics as a part of usability.

Future of HCI Processes

Developers of future HCI processes will struggle to keep pace with these new application areas and interaction styles. One area that is already changing among real-world system developers is the representation of roles and skills in interactive system development teams. Usability specialists, human factors engineers, and HCI practitioners are starting to take their long-overdue places alongside systems analysts and software engineers. These new roles imply the need for new kinds of training in HCI methods. These roles have already begun to be joined by those with technical writing and documentation skills and especially by those with graphics and visual design skills (Tufte, 1983; Mullet and Sano, 1995)—for example, to use color effectively (Shubin et al., 1996) and to design icons, avatars, and rendered images.

It is also expected that a significant increase in future HCI activity will be applied to developing new methods. There is an ongoing need for new high-impact usability evaluation methods. High impact means cost effective, applicable to a wide variety of application types (e.g., World Wide Web applications), applicable to many new interaction styles (e.g., virtual environments), and suitable for gathering usability data from remote and distributed user communities.

Among the approaches to remote evaluation emerging now, most are either limited to subjective user feedback (Abelow, 1993) or require expensive bandwidth to support video conferencing as an extension of the usability lab (Hammontree et al., 1994). A method based on user-assisted critical incident gathering (Hartson et al., 1996) has been proposed to bypass the bandwidth requirements for full-time video transmission and to cut analysis costs.

Methods and software support tools are also in demand for boosting return on investment of resources committed to usability evaluation. Koenemann-Belliveau et al. (1994, p. 250) have articulated this need: "We should also investigate the potential for more efficiently *leveraging* the work we do in empirical formative evaluation—ways to 'save' something from our efforts for application in subsequent evaluation work." Most of the time results from usability evaluation are applied only to specific usability problems in a single design. Database tools for information management of the results would accrue immediate gains in effective usability problem reporting (Jeffries, 1994; Pernice and Butler, 1995). More significantly, a usability database tool would afford some "memory" to the process, amortizing, through reuse of analysis, the cost of results across design iterations and across multiple products and projects. Beyond organizational boundaries, a collective usability database could serve as a commonly accessible repository of a science base for the HCI community and as a practical knowledge base for exemplar usability problems, solutions, and costs.

The future of HCI is both exciting and challenging. In moving beyond GUIs and in developing new methods, problems continue to increase. But the promise of these new products and processes will come to fruition in an every citizen interface for the national information infrastructure.

ACKNOWLEDGMENT

Many thanks to Dr. Deborah Hix, of Virginia Tech, for her help in providing inputs and in reading this paper.

REFERENCES

Abelow, D. (1993). Automating Feedback on Software Product Use. *CASE Trends*, 15-17.

Baecker, R. M. (Ed.). (1993). *Readings in Groupware and Computer-Supported Cooperative Work: Assisting Human-Human Collaboration*. San Francisco: Morgan-Kaufmann.

Baecker, R. M., Grudin, J., Buxton, W. A. S., and Greenberg, S. (1995). Touch, Gesture, and Marking. In R. M. Baecker, J. Grudin, W. A. S. Buxton, and S. Greenberg (Eds.), *Readings in Human-Computer Interaction: Toward the Year 2000*. San Francisco: Morgan-Kaufmann, 469-482.

Barnard, P. (1993). The Contributions of Applied Cognitive Psychology to the Study of Human-Computer Interaction. In R. M. Baecker, J. Grudin, W. A. S. Buxton, and S. Greenberg (Ed.), *Readings in Human Computer Interaction: Toward the Year 2000*. San Francisco: Morgan-Kaufmann, 640-658.

Bias, R. G. and Mayhew, D. J. (Eds.). (1994). *Cost Justifying Usability*. Boston: Academic Press.

Blattner, M. M. and Dannenberg, R.B. (Eds.). (1992). *Multimedia Interface Design*. New York: ACM Press.

Bodker, Susanne. (1991). *Through the Interface: A Human Activity Approach to User Interface Design*. Hillsdale, NJ: Lawrence Erlbaum Associates.

Brewster, S. A., Wright, P. C., and Edwards, A. D. N. (1993). An Evaluation of Earcons for Use in Auditory Human-Computer Interfaces. *Proceedings of INTERCHI Conference on Human Factors in Computing Systems*. New York: ACM Press, 222-227.

Butler, K. A. (1996). Usability Engineering Turns 10. *Interactions* (January), 58-75.

Buxton, W. (1986). There's More to Interaction than Meets the Eye: Some Issues in Manual Input. In D. A. Norman and S. W. Draper (Ed.), *User Centered System Design*. Hillsdale, NJ: Lawrence Erlbaum Associates, 319-337.

Card, S. K. and Moran, T. P. (1980). The Keystroke-Level Model for User Performance Time with Interactive Systems. *Communications of the ACM*, 23, 396-410.

Card, S. K., Moran, T. P., and Newell, A. (1983). *The Psychology of Human-Computer Interaction*. Hillsdale, NJ: Lawrence Erlbaum Associates.

Carroll, J. M. (1984). Minimalist Design for Active Users. *Proceedings of Human-Computer Interaction—Interact '84*, September, Amsterdam: North-Holland, 39-44.

Carroll, J. M. (Ed.). (1995). *Scenario-Based Design: Envisioning Work and Technology in System Development*. New York: John Wiley and Sons, Inc.

Carroll, J. M., Kellogg, W. A., and Rosson, M. B. (1991). The Task-Artifact Cycle. In J. M. Carroll (Ed.), *Designing Interaction: Psychology at the Human-Computer Interface*. Cambridge, England: Cambridge University Press, 74-102.

Carroll, J. M. and Rosson, M. B. (1992). Getting Around the Task-Artifact Cycle: How to Make Claims and Design by Scenario. *ACM Transactions on Information Systems*, 10, 181-212.

Chin, J. P., Diehl, V. A., and Norman, K. L. (1988). Development of an Instrument Measuring User Satisfaction of the Human-Computer Interface. *Proceedings of CHI Conference on Human Factors in Computing Systems*, May 15-19, New York: ACM, 213-218.

Diaper, D. (Ed.). (1989). *Task Analysis for Human-Computer Interaction*. Chichester, England: Ellis Horwood Limited.

Draper, S. W. and Barton, S. B. (1993). Learning by Exploration and Affordance Bugs. *Proceedings of INTERCHI Conference on Human Factors in Computing Systems (Adjunct)*. New York: ACM, 75-76.

Ehn, P. (1990). *Work Oriented Design of Computer Artifacts* (2nd Ed.). Hillsdale, NJ: Lawrence Erlbaum Associates.

Foley, J. D. and Wallace, V. L. (1974). The Art of Natural Graphic Man-Machine Conversation. *Proceedings of the IEEE*, 63(4), 462-471.

Foley, J. D., van Dam, A., Feiner, S. K., and Hughes, J. F. (1990). *Computer Graphics: Principles and Practice*. Reading, MA: Addison-Wesley.

Gaver, W. W. and Smith, R. B. (1995). Auditory Icons in Large-Scale Collaborative Environments. In R. M. Baecker, J. Grudin, W. A. S. Buxton, and S. Greenberg (Eds.), *Readings in Human-Computer Interaction: Toward the Year 2000*. San Francisco: Morgan-Kaufmann, 564-569.

Goldberg, D. and Goodisman, A. (1995). Stylus User Interfaces for Manipulating Text. In R. M. Baecker, J. Grudin, W. A. S. Buxton, and S. Greenberg (Eds.), *Readings in Human-Computer Interaction: Toward the Year 2000*. San Francisco: Morgan-Kaufmann, 500-508.

Gould, J. D., Boies, S. J., and Lewis, C. (1991). Making Usable, Useful, Productivity-Enhancing Computer Applications. *Communications of the ACM*, 34(1), 74-85.

Gray, W. D., John, B. E., Stuart, R., Lawrence, D., and Atwood, M. (1990). GOMS Meets the Phone Company: Analytic Modeling Applied to Real-World Problems. *Proceedings of INTERACT '90—Third IFIP Conference on Human-Computer Interaction*, August 27-31, Amsterdam: North-Holland Elsevier Science Publishers.

Grudin, J. (1994). Groupware and Social Dynamics: Eight Challenges for Developers. *Communications of the ACM*, 37(1), 92-105.

Hammond, N., Gardiner, M. M., Christie, B., and Marshall, C. (1987). The Role of Cognitive Psychology in User-Interface Design. In M. M. Gardiner and B. Christie (Eds.), *Applying Cognitive Psychology to User-Interface Design*. Chichester: Wiley, 13-53.

Hammontree, M., Weiler, P., and Nayak, N. (1994). Remote Usability Testing. *Interactions* (July), 21-25.

Harrison, M. and Thimbleby, H. (Ed.). (1990). *Formal Methods in Human-Computer Interaction*. Cambridge, England: Cambridge University Press.

Hartson, H. R. and Gray, P. D. (1992). Temporal Aspects of Tasks in the User Action Notation. *Human-Computer Interaction*, 7, 1-45.

Hartson, H. R. and Hix, D. (1989). Toward Empirically Derived Methodologies and Tools for Human-Computer Interface Development. *International Journal of Man-Machine Studies, 31*, 477-494.

Hartson, H. R., Siochi, A. C., and Hix, D. (1990). The UAN: A User-Oriented Representation for Direct Manipulation Interface Designs. *ACM Trans. Inf. Syst., 8*(3), 181-203.

Hartson, H. R., Castillo, J. C., Kelso, J., Kamler, J., and Neale, W. C. (1996). Remote Evaluation: The Network as an Extension of the Usability Laboratory. *Proceedings of CHI Conference on Human Factors in Computing Systems.* New York: ACM, 228-235.

Hix, D. and Hartson, H. R. (1993a). *Developing User Interfaces: Ensuring Usability Through Product and Process.* New York: John Wiley and Sons.

Hix, D. and Hartson, H. R. (1993b). Formative Evaluation: Ensuring Usability in User Interfaces. In L. Bass and P. Dewan (Eds.), *Trends in Software, Volume 1: User Interface Software.* New York: Wiley, 1-30.

Hix, D. and Hartson, H. R. (1994). IDEAL: An Environment for User-Centered Development of User Interfaces. *Proceedings of EWHCI'94: Fourth East-West International Conference on Human-Computer Interaction*, 195-211.

Hutchins, E. L., Hollan, J. D., and Norman, D. A. (1986). Direct Manipulation Interfaces. In D. A. Norman and S. W. Draper (Eds.), *User Centered System Design.* Hillsdale, NJ: Lawrence Erlbaum Associates, 87-124.

Jacob, R. J. K. (1993). Eye-Movement-Based Human-Computer Interaction Techniques: Toward Non-Command Interfaces. In H. R. Hartson and D. Hix (Eds.), *Advances in Human-Computer Interaction.* Norwood, NJ: Ablex, 151-190.

Jeffries, R. (1994). Usability Problem Reports: Helping Evaluators Communicate Effectively with Developers. In J. Nielsen and R. L. Mack (Eds.), *Usability Inspection Methods.* New York: John Wiley and Sons, Inc., 273-294.

Kieras, D. E. (1988). Towards a Practical GOMS Model Methodology for User Interface Design. In M. Helander (Ed.), *Handbook of Human-Computer Interaction.* Elsevier Science Publishers B. V., 135-157.

Kieras, D. and Polson, P. G. (1985). An Approach to the Formal Analysis of User Complexity. *International Journal of Man-Machine Studies, 22*, 365-394.

Koenemann-Belliveau, J., Carroll, J. M., Rosson, M. B., and Singley, M. K. (1994). Comparative Usability Evaluation: Critical Incidents and Critical Threads. *Proceedings of CHI Conference on Human Factors in Computing Systems.* New York: ACM, 245-251.

LeCompte, M. D. and Preissle, J. (1993). *Ethnography and Qualitative Design in Educational Research* (2nd Ed.). San Diego: Academic Press.

Lewis, C., Polson, P., Wharton, C., and Rieman, J. (1990). Testing a Walkthrough Methodology for Theory-Based Design of Walk-up-and-Use Interfaces. *Proceedings of CHI Conference on Human Factors in Computing Systems*, April 1-5, New York: ACM, 235-242.

MacKenzie, S. (1992). Fitts' Law as a Research and Design Tool in Human-Computer Interaction. *Human-Computer Interaction, 7*, 91-139.

MacLean, A., Young, R. M., Bellotti, V. M. E., and Moran, T. P. (1991). Questions, Options, and Criteria: Elements of Design Space Analysis. *Human-Computer Interaction, 6*, 201-250.

Macleod, M. and Bevan, N. (1993). Music Video Analysis and Context Tools for Usability Measurement. *Proceedings of INTERCHI Conference on Human Factors in Computing Systems*, April 24-29. New York: ACM, 55.

Mayhew, D. J. (1992). *Principles and Guidelines in Software User Interface Design.* Englewood Cliffs, NJ: Prentice-Hall.

McCauley, M. E. (1984). Human Factors in Voice Technology. In F. A. Muckler (Ed.), *Human Factors Review.* Santa Monica, CA: Human Factors Society, 131-166.

Meister, D. (1985). *Behavioral Analysis and Measurement Methods.* New York: Wiley.

Moran, T. P. (1981). The Command Language Grammar: A Representation for the User Interface of Interactive Computer Systems. *International Journal of Man-Machine Studies, 15*, 3-51.

Muller, M. J. (1991). PICTIVE—An Exploration in Participatory Design. *Proceedings of CHI Conference on Human Factors in Computing Systems*, April 27-May 2. New York: ACM, 225-231.

Mullet, K. and Sano, D. (1995). *Designing Visual Interfaces*. Mountain View, CA: SunSoft Press.

Myers, B. A. (1989). User-Interface Tools: Introduction and Survey. *IEEE Software, 6* (1), 15-23.

Myers, B. A. (1993). State of the Art in User Interface Software Tools. In H. R. Hartson and D. Hix (Eds.), *Advances in Human-Computer Interaction*. Norwood, NJ: Ablex.

Myers, B. A. (1995). State of the Art in User Interface Software Tools. In R. M. Baecker, J. Grudin, W. A. S. Buxton, and S. Greenberg (Eds.), *Readings in Human-Computer Interaction: Toward the Year 2000*. San Francisco: Morgan-Kaufmann, 323-343.

Nielsen, J. (1989). Usability Engineering at a Discount. In G. Salvendy and M. J. Smith (Eds.), *Designing and Using Human-Computer Interfaces and Knowledge-Based Systems*. Amsterdam: Elsevier Science Publishers, 394-401.

Nielsen, J. (1992). Finding Usability Problems Through Heuristic Evaluation. *Proceedings of CHI Conference on Human Factors in Computing Systems*, May 3 - 7. New York: ACM, 373-380.

Nielsen, J. (1993). *Usability Engineering*. San Diego: Academic Press. Inc.

Nielsen, J. and Mack, R. L. (Ed.). (1994). *Usability Inspection Methods*. New York: John Wiley and Sons.

Nielsen, J. and Molich, R. (1990). Heuristic Evaluation of User Interfaces. *Proceedings of CHI Conference on Human Factors in Computing Systems*, April 1-5. New York: ACM, 249-256.

Norman, D. A. (1986). Cognitive Engineering. In D. A. Norman and S. W. Draper (Eds.), *User Centered System Design*. Hillsdale, NJ: Lawrence Erlbaum Associates, 31-61.

Norman, D. A. and Draper, S. W. (Eds.). (1986). *User Centered System Design: New Perspectives on Human-Computer Interaction*. Hillsdale, NJ: Lawrence Erlbaum Associates.

Payne, S. J. (1991). Display-based action at the user interface. *International Journal of Man-Machine Studies, 35*, 275-289.

Pernice, K. and Butler, M. B. (1995). Database Support for Usability Testing. *Interactions* (January), 27-31.

Shneiderman, B. (1983). Direct Manipulation: A Step Beyond Programming Languages. *IEEE Transactions on Computers, 16*(8), pp. 57-69.

Shneiderman, B. (1992). *Designing the User Interface: Strategies for Effective Human-Computer Interaction* (2nd Ed.). Reading, MA: Addison-Wesley.

Shubin, H., Falck, D., and Johansen, A. G. (1996). Exploring Color in Interface Design. *Interactions* (July/August), 36-48.

Smith, S. L. and Mosier, J. N. (1986). *Guidelines for Designing User Interface Software* (ESD-TR-86-278/MTR 10090). MITRE Corporation.

Tufte, E. R. (1983). *The Visual Display of Quantitative Data*. Cheshire, CT.: Graphics Press.

Virzi, R. A., Sokolov, J. L., and Karis, D. (1996). Usability Problem Identification Using Both Low- and High-Fidelity Prototypes. *Proceedings of CHI Conference on Human Factors in Computing Systems*. New York: ACM, 236-243.

Weller, H. G. and Hartson, H. R. (1992). Metaphors for the Nature of Human-Computer Interaction in an Empowering Environment: Interaction Style Influences the Manner of Human Accomplishment, *8*(3), 313-333.

Wharton, C., Bradford, J., Jeffries, R., and Franzke, M. (1992). Applying Cognitive Walkthroughs to More Complex User Interfaces: Experiences, Issues, and Recommendations. *Proceedings of CHI Conference on Human Factors in Computing Systems*, May 3 - 7, New York: ACM, 381-388.

Whiteside, J., Bennett, J., and Holtzblatt, K. (1988). Usability Engineering: Our Experience and

Evolution. In M. Helander (Ed.), *Handbook of Human-Computer Interaction*. Amsterdam: Elsevier North-Holland, 791-817.

Williges, R. C. and Williges, B. H. (1995). Travel Alternatives for the Mobility Impaired: The Surrogate Electronic Traveler (SET). In A. D. N. Edwards (Ed.), *Extra-Ordinary Human-Computer Interaction: Interfaces for Users with Disabilities*. New York: Cambridge University Press, 245-262.

Williges, R. C., Williges, B. H., and Elkerton, J. (1987). Software Interface Design. In G. Salvendy (Ed.), *Handbook of Human Factors*. New York: John Wiley and Sons, 1416-1449.

Wixon, D., Holtzblatt, K., and Knox, S. (1990). Contextual Design: An Emergent View of System Design. *Proceedings of CHI Conference on Human Factors in Computing Systems*, April 1-5. New York: ACM, 329-336.

ADDITIONAL READING

Representative supplementary references here are chosen for breadth. Cited references also are representative but not all are repeated here.

ACM. (1990). *Resources in Human-Computer Interaction*. New York: ACM Press.

Baecker, R. M. and Buxton, W. A. S. (Eds.). (1987). *Readings in Human-Computer Interaction: A Multidisciplinary Approach*. San Francisco, Morgan-Kaufmann.

Baecker, R. M., Grudin, J., Buxton, W. A. S., and Greenberg, S. (Eds.). (1995). *Readings in Human-Computer Interaction: Toward the Year 2000*. San Francisco: Morgan-Kaufmann.

Carroll, J. M. (Ed.). (1987). *Interfacing Thought: Cognitive Aspects of Human-Computer Interaction*. Cambridge, MA: The MIT Press.

Carroll, J. M. (Ed.). (1991). *Designing Interaction: Psychology at the Human-Computer Interface*. Cambridge, England: Cambridge University Press.

Hartson, H. R. and Hix, D. (1989). Human-Computer Interface Development: Concepts and Systems for Its Management. *ACM Comput. Surv.*, 21(1), 5-92.

Helander, M. (Ed.). (1988). *Handbook of Human-Computer Interaction*. Amsterdam: North-Holland.

Monk, A. F. and Gilbert, N. (1995). *Perspectives on HCI—Diverse Approaches*. Cambridge, England: Cambridge University Press.

Olson, J. R. and Olson, G. M. (1990). The Growth of Cognitive Modeling in Human-Computer Interaction Since GOMS. *Human-Computer Interaction*, 5, 221-265.

Preece, J., Rogers, Y., Sharp, H., Benyon, D., Holland, S., and Carey, T. (1994). *Human-Computer Interaction*. Reading, MA: Addison-Wesley.

Rubin, J. (1994). *Handbook of Usability Testing*. New York: John Wiley and Sons.

Thimbleby, H. (1990). *User Interface Design*. New York: ACM Press/Addison-Wesley.

POSITION PAPERS

ON INTERFACE SPECIFICS

AN EMBEDDED, INVISIBLE, EVERY-CITIZEN INTERFACE

Mark Weiser

Xerox Palo Alto Research Center

The nation's information infrastructure is a vast, loosely connected network of informing resources found mostly in people's everyday lives. When considering interfaces to new electronic information sources, and especially when replacing old information sources with new electronic sources, it is crucial to consider how the existing infrastructure really works. Two examples will help.

Consider how you would find a grocery store in a new town. How do you solve this problem on first driving in? Most likely, by looking around, watching the people and the streets, and making a couple of guesses, you could find one in no time. The information infrastructure is everyday knowledge of towns (including economic and practical constraints on layout, walking distances, etc., that are embedded in that knowledge), and physical clues that map that general knowledge into this particular town. Information infrastructure can be physical (see www.itp.tsoa.nyu.edu/~review/current/focus2/open00.html).

More conventionally, our national information infrastructure today includes tens of thousands of public and school libraries all across the country. These libraries are in nearly every elementary, junior high, and high school; and they are in nearly every community, even the very small. Of course, many of these libraries are connected to the Internet. But it is very important to consider the other resources provided by these libraries. Thirty-five percent of all library visitors never use the catalog, and 12 percent use no library materials at all, but bring in their own materials. Clearly, libraries do something more than just supply data that could be gotten over the Web (see www.ubiq.com/weiser/SituationalAspectsof ElectronicLibraries.html).

As the above examples illustrate, the existing information infrastructure often functions without calling itself to our attention. It stays out of sight, effectively not even noticed. So the first challenge for every-citizen interface is to be invisible (what I have called "calm technology" elsewhere; see www.ubiq.com/weiser/calmtech/calmtech.htm).

As the above examples also illustrate, the existing information infrastructure is extremely widespread, found in every nook and cranny of our lives. The second challenge for the every-citizen interface is to be ubiquitous (see www.ubiq.com/ubicomp).

Finally, not addressed by the above examples but presumably clear to everyone, the current Internet is just the beginning. I like to think of it by analogy to television channels. Once upon a time we fretted about how we would manage a TV with 500 channels. How could we ever view them all? The Internet will give us 5 billion channels, one for every person on the planet—only about 30 million so far, but more are coming. And soon these channels will be multimedia, multiway video and sound using the Mbone. This kind of interconnection is a deep technical challenge to the current Web infrastructure, which cannot begin to support even a few multiway Mbone connections, much less 5 billion. I consider this to be a user interface issue because it is just this infrastructure that opens up the Web to use by anyone who can point a camera or talk on the phone. The third challenge for the every-citizen interface is to support billions of multiway real-time interactive connections.

Of these three challenges I believe that the first is currently the most promising of progress, the one most susceptible to interdisciplinary attack, and the one least well addressed by existing projects. How does a technology become invisible? To some degree, anything can, given enough practice. Invisibility is a property of people, technology, and the situation in which we find ourselves (a tiger invisible in the tall grass stands out at the zoo).

Some suggested challenges for developing a "science of invisibility" for a every citizen interface are as follows:

- Human information processing includes operations at many different levels, the vast majority of them invisible to our conscious thought at any given moment. As we learn a skill, operations that formerly required attention ("turn the steering wheel") become automatic and are replaced by higher level directions ("turn left," "drive to Cincinnati"). Invisible interfaces are those that connect "below" the conscious level, through both learning and natural affinity. What computer interfaces are most appropriate for coupling into a large amount of unconscious information processing? Which ones take a long time to learn but are worth the effort (analogous perhaps to piano playing)? Which ones fit our brain's affinity for information (information browsing as a walk in the woods)?

• The difference between something being effectively invisible because it is being processed below conscious thought and something being managed for us (e.g., by a computerized agent) is profound. A key advantage of effective invisibility is the quick refocus from peripheral inattention to center attention. For instance, while ordinarily unaware of engine noises in our car, we suddenly become very aware if the noise should change unexpectedly. We can then focus our attention on the noise and make decisions about its danger, the distance to the nearest expressway exit, what lane to be in, and so on. (A silent car with an intelligent agent monitoring engine condition would keep us from any knowledge at all.) Which computer interfaces do well at keeping something invisible most of the time, but allowing quick recentering when appropriate? Which interfaces let the same information be either in the center of our attention or in the periphery without even clicking a button but simply changing our attention?

• The concept of an intelligent agent can be a very powerful one if it does not take over the function of human judgment and our ability to control the focus of our attention. Can we design intelligent agents in our computers that preserve our ability to refocus? If something has been taken over for me, is there a presentation of what has been taken over that I can bring to the fore whenever I like, including retroactively? Can I have agents that filter for me without losing all of the context of the information after the filter? For instance, if I use a computerized newspaper clipping service, can it show me one or two lines of articles that were physically near the ones it clipped for me in the physical newspaper? What kind of context helps, and what doesn't help, when dealing with a computerized agent?

INTELLIGENT MULTIMEDIA INTERFACES FOR "EACH" CITIZEN

Mark T. Maybury
Mitre Corporation

Future interfaces will take advantage of knowledge of the user, task, and discourse and exploit multiple input/output media and associated human sensory modalities to enable intuitive access to information, tools, and other people (see Figure 1). The more effectively computers can process heterogeneous information and automatically acquire knowledge about users, the more efficient they will become at supporting users' frequently changing tasks, particularly information-seeking ones. Information-seeking tasks range from directed search to casual browsing, from looking up facts to predicting trends. Each of these goals can be achieved more or less effectively by the content, form (i.e., media), and environment that support the user. Our emphasis at Mitre Corporation has been on investigating technologies and tools that enable more effective and efficient information interfaces for a variety of application areas, including command and control, intelligence analysis, and education and training. As a consequence of our experience, we believe we should aim not to

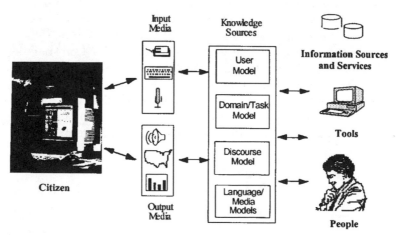

FIGURE 1   Intelligent interfaces.

build a one-of-a-kind interface for every citizen, but rather common interfaces that can be tailored to each citizen in accordance with his or her goals, knowledge, skills, and preferences.

CHALLENGES

Achieving an intelligent interface vision requires addressing some fundamental technology limitations, including:

- Lack of a scientific approach to device and user interface design, development, and evaluation.
- Lack of interface standards that make it easy to pull out one device and plug in a similar one.
- Lack of general mechanisms for (1) interpreting input from multiple devices (e.g., mouse gesture and speech, as in "put that there <click>") and (2) automatic generation of coordinated multimedia output.
- Lack of general mechanisms for constructing dialogue-based interaction that supports error detection and correction, user models, and discourse models to ensure tailored and robust communication.
- Few tools or procedures that facilitate porting language-enabled interfaces to new domains (and/or languages); it remains a time-consuming and knowledge-intensive task.

We believe there exist fundamental tasks associated with communication that underlie all interface activities. These can be viewed as a hierarchy of communicative acts, which can be formalized and computationally implemented and by their nature can be realized in multiple modalities (e.g., linguistic/auditory, gestural, visual). The choice among modalities itself is an important, knowledge-based task, as is the broader task of presentation planning.

In supporting information access, our efforts have focused on multimedia analysis (in particular, message understanding and video analysis), including its segmentation into atomic units, extraction of objects, facts and relationships, and summarization into compact form. New requirements have arisen (e.g., resulting in multimedia query mechanisms that raise issues such as how to integrate visual and linguistic queries). Multimedia information-seeking tasks remain perhaps the most important but least well understood area. We believe that careful experimental design, use of instrumented environments, and task-based evaluation (e.g., measuring at least time and accuracy (false positives, false negatives)) will yield new insights.

248

TABLE 1 Research Recommendations

Area	State of the Art	Near-Term Research	Long-Term Research
Text processing	Commercial named entity extraction (SRA, BBN); many hand-crafted, domain-specific systems for event extraction; large cost to port to new domains; incremental sentence generation, limited document generation.	Demonstrate portability of TIPSTER technology to support multilingual information extraction and spoken language; incremental text generation; text summarization; topic detection and tracking.	Scaleable, trainable, portable algorithms; document-length text generation.
Speech processing	Commercial small-vocabulary recognizers (Corona, HARK); large-vocabulary (40,000+ words) recognizers exist in research labs (BBN, SRI, Cambridge University).	Speaker, language, and topic identification; prosodic analysis; natural-sounding synthesis.	Large-vocabulary, speaker-independent systems for speech-enabled interfaces; large-vocabulary systems for video and radio transcription, for example.
Graphics processing	Graphical User Interface Toolkits (e.g., object-oriented, reusable window elements such as menus, dialogue boxes).	Tools for automated creation of graphical user interface elements; limited research prototypes of automated graphics design.	Automated, model-based creation and tailoring of graphical user interfaces.
Image/video processing	Color, shape, texture-based indexing and query of imagery.	Motion-based indexing of imagery and video; video segmentation.	Visual information indexing and extraction (e.g., human behavior from video).
Gesture processing	Two-dimensional mice; eyetrackers; tethered body-motion tracking.	Tetherless, three-dimensional gesture, including hand, head, eye, and body-motion tracking.	Intentional understanding of gesture; cross-media correlation (with text and speech processing); facial and body gesture recognition.

Multimedia integration	Limited prototypes in research and government.	Content selection, media allocation, media coordination, media realization for multimedia generation.	Multimedia and multimodal analysis; multimedia and multimodal generation; investigation of less-examined senses (e.g., taction, olfaction).
Discourse modeling	Limited prototypes in research and government.	Error handling (ill-formed and incomplete input/output), two-party conversational model, discourse annotation schemes, discourse data collection and annotation, conversation tracking.	Context tracking/dialogue management; multiuser conversation tracking, annotation standards; model-based conversational interaction.
User modeling	Fragile research prototypes available from academia; one-user modeling shell (BGP-MS).	Track user focus and skill level to interact at appropriate level; empirical studies in broad range of tasks in multiple media.	Hybrid stereotypical/personalized and symbolic/statistical user models.
Visualization	Some commercial tools (e.g., NetMap), text-based, limited semantics; computationally intensive, often difficult to use.	Improve information access interfaces; visualization generation from extracted (semantic) information; automated graphical encoding of information properties.	Multidimensional visualization; multimedia (e.g., text, audio, video) visualization.
Collaboration tools	Multipoint video, audio, imagery; e-mail-based routing of tasks.	Instrument environments for data collection and experimentation; multiparty collaborative communication; investigate asynchronous, distant collaboration (e.g., virtual learning spaces).	Field experiments to predict impact of collaborative technology on current work processes; tools for automated analysis of video session recordings; flexible, workflow automation.
Intelligent agents	Agent communication (e.g., KQML) and exchange languages (e.g., KIF).	Mediation tools for heterogeneous distributed access.	Shared ontologies; agent integration architectures and/or control languages; agent negotiation.

A PLAN OF ACTION

There are several important recent developments that promise to enable new common facilities to be shared to create more powerful interfaces. A strategy to move forward should include:

• Creating architectures and services of an advanced interface server that are defined in the short term using open standard distributed object middleware, namely the Object Management Group's Common Object Request Broker Architecture (CORBA), and that investigate higher-risk architectures, such as agent-based communication and coordination.

• Fostering interdisciplinary focused science that investigates the nature of multiple modalities, with an aim to understanding the principles of multiple modalities in order to provide insight into such tasks as multimedia interpretation and the generation of coordinated multimedia output.

• Utilizing, refining, integrating, and extending (to additional media) existing architectures for single media, including (1) the TIPSTER architecture (for document detection and information extraction) and associated tag standards (e.g., Penn Treebank part-of-speech tags, proper name tags, coreference annotations) for language source markup and (2) leverage evolving applications programming interface (API) standards in the spoken language industry (e.g., SRAPI, SAPI).

• Via an interdisciplinary process, defining common interface tasks and associated evaluation metrics and methods; creating a multimedia corpora and associated markup standards; and fostering interdisciplinary algorithm design, implementation, and evaluation.

• Fostering emerging user modeling shells (e.g., BGP-MS) and standards.

• Focusing on creation of theoretically neutral discourse modeling shells.

• Applying these facilities in an evolutionary fashion to improve existing interfaces, supporting a migration from "dumb" to "smart" interfaces (S. Bayer, personal communication, 1996).

• Performing task-based, community-wide evaluation to guide subsequent research, measuring functional improvements (e.g., task completion time, accuracy, quality).

Because they affect all who interact with computers, user interfaces are perhaps the single area of computing that can most radically alter the ease, efficiency, and effectiveness of human-computer interactions.

RECOMMENDED RESEARCH

Table 1 indicates several functional requirements and associated key technologies that need to be investigated to enable a new generation of human-computer interaction, indicating near-term and far-term research investment recommendations. Key areas for research include:

- processing and integrating various input/output media (e.g., text, speech and nonspeech audio, imagery, video, graphics, gesture);
- methods to acquire, represent, maintain, and exploit models of user, discourse, and media; and
- mechanisms that can provide information visualization, support multiuser collaboration, and intelligent agents.

REFERENCE

Maybury, M.T. (Ed.) 1993. *Intelligent Multimedia Interfaces.* Menlo Park, Calif: AAAI/MIT Press.

INTERFACES FOR UNDERSTANDING

Nathan Shedroff
vivid studios

Over the next 15 years the issues facing interface designers, engineers, programmers, and researchers will become increasingly complex and push farther into currently abstract and, perhaps, esoteric realms. However, we are not without guidance and direction to follow. Our experiences as humans and what little history we have with machines can lead us toward our goals.

Computers and related devices in the future will need to exhibit many of the following qualities:

• Be more aware of themselves (who and what they are, who they "belong" to, their relationships to other systems, their autonomy, and their capabilities).

• Be more aware of their surroundings and audiences (who is there; how many people are present or around; who to "listen" to; where and how to find and contact people for help or to follow directions; who is a "regular"; how to adapt to different people's preferences, needs, goals, skills, interests, etc.).

• Offer more help and guidance when needed.

• Be more autonomous when needed.

• Be more able to help build knowledge as opposed to merely process data.

• Be more capable of displaying information in richer forms—both visually and auditorially.

• Be more integrated into a participant's work flow or entertainment process.

• Be more integrated with other media—especially traditional media like broadcast and print.

Funding for research and development, therefore, should concentrate on these issues and their related hardware, software, and understandings. These include research into the following:

• Display and visualization systems (high-resolution, portable, and low-power displays; HDTV (high-definition television) and standards in related display industries; integration with input/output devices such as scanners, pointing devices, and printers; fast processing systems for n-dimensional data models; standards for these models, display hardware, and software; software capable of easily configuring and experimenting with visualizations and simulations; etc.).

- Perceptual systems (proximity, sounds, motion, and electronic "eyes" for identification and awareness; standards for formating instructions and specifications to help systems "understand" what they are, what is around them, what and who they can communicate with, and what they are capable of; facilities for obtaining help when necessary; ways of identifying participants by their behavior, gestures, or other attributes; etc.).
- Communications systems (standards, hardware, and software to help participants communicate better with each other—as well as with computers; natural-language interfaces—spoken and written—and translation systems to widen the opportunities of involvement to more people; hardware and software solutions for increasing bandwidth and improving the reliability, security, privacy, and scalability of existing communications infrastructure; etc.).
- Understanding of understanding (information and knowledge-building applications; understandings about how people create context and meaning, transform data into information, create knowledge for themselves, and build wisdom; software to help facilitate these processes; standards to help transmit and share information and knowledge with connections intact; etc.).
- Understanding of interaction (a wider definition of interaction used in the "industry," how participants define and perceive "interactivity"; what they expect and need in interactivity; historical examples of interaction; lessons from theater, storytelling, conversation, improvisation, the performing arts, and the entertainment industry; etc.).
- Increased education (of both participants and audiences, as well as professionals, and the industry).
- Better resources for understanding cultural diversity (in terms of gestures, languages, perceptions, and needs of different age, gender, cultural, and nationality groups).

In addition, there are some procedural approaches to these undertakings that can help the overall outcomes to be more valuable:

- Reduced duplication of research and development by government-sponsored grants and institutions (requiring the disclosure, sharing, and reporting of research efforts, problems, and solutions).
- More means of coordination and knowledge sharing of research and development scholars and professionals (whether government-sponsored or not).

• More adventurous spending in "esoteric" research (such as the nature of understanding and the meaning of "interactivity").

• Grant proposal templates and procedures that are easier to complete (simplified and clarified requirements, less paperwork, less process-specific "inside" information that requires professional grant writers so that more adventurous people can apply more easily).

WHERE DID THE "USER" GO?

Although the word "user" is, admittedly, easy to say and use and has some history, it is important that our understanding of those using computers is broadened to emphasize growing participatory aspects of computer use. While historically, people input, managed the processing, and output data and information, the building of knowledge requires more participation and interaction of the type most closely experienced with other people. People are becoming active audiences and participants instead of merely users. They are increasingly communicating with others and creating meaningful things rather than merely "viewing" and watching.

The next 100 million computer users (who may begin using computers over the next 3 years) have different needs and understandings than current users. Their needs are different not because of their capabilities (all of these people are *capable* of learning to use existing systems) but mostly because of differences in their perceptions, interests, and understandings of computers. One important reason why these people are not now buying or making use of current computers is that, in their minds, computers don't do much that they are interested in doing. Existing computers are not capable of or equipped for helping these people enjoy, expand, or make meaning of their lives. This is the reason why home computer sales have traditionally been dismal and are currently confined to home-office purchases and for kids' educations. Fifteen years ago the best use that computer marketers could come up with for people to buy their own computers was to balance their checkbooks and store recipes. Today, while computers have evolved significantly, many people's perceptions have not, and they understand precious few reasons why computers might enhance the lives of this next "user group." Part of this is an education issue (and, perhaps, a marketing one), but mostly it is a failure of computer systems (hardware and software) to respond to the needs and interests of the general public.

The interface starts much before a computer is turned on. Consider an analogy to shopping. The shopping experience does not start the moment a transaction is made (perhaps an item is bought or ordered). It doesn't even start when someone walks into a store or browses a catalog.

The shopping experience starts when people perceive the need for some-thing, at least, and often before they encounter others shopping, products and services they do not currently need, and even celebrity athletes sport-ing brand names on their outfits. Likewise, the interface to a computer begins at the fulfillment of life needs and interests and the education of the participants about the capabilities and possibilities of computers and interfaces. Automobiles are often held up as examples of easy-to-learn, universal interfaces, but in reality they are neither. They take months—sometimes years—to master, are not standardized, and are sometimes never learned sufficiently well. Yet our understanding of driving a car and its fulfillment of our needs make us persevere.

WHAT IS A COMPUTER?

What I mean when I use the word "computer" is a specific device for processing, storing, and transmitting information, aiding the building of knowledge, and/or facilitating communications more sophisticated than a current telephone. To be sure, many objects around us will evolve to be more sophisticated and many already include computers whether this is evident to their users or not. To what extent computers will disappear as distinct de-vices is not a question that can yet be answered. However, it does not really matter either. The needs and interests of people have changed very little over the past 100 years and will likely change only slightly over the next 15 to 20. Most people will still need to work, create, love, interact, communicate, and be entertained (as well as entertain each other). Interfaces should concentrate on the activities, not the technologies—nor should they be immediately con-cerned with the nature of a device itself (is it distinct or embedded?). These interfaces may show up in computers, televisions, telephones, door knobs, or devices not yet invented. What will remain fairly constant, however, are the needs themselves.

WHAT IS INTERACTIVITY?

When I use the word "interactive" I do not mean what has become the standard industry definition of dynamic media or the ability to make choices when using computer programs. Most "interactive media" is nothing more than multimedia presentations (usually with video and animation) with the ability to click to the next screen of material in a nonlinear way. In this sense interactivity has become bad television where the audience must click for more in order to keep the stream coming. To me interactivity is much richer and includes the abilities to create, share, and communicate rather than merely watch. Interactive experiences should change over time and between different people. Sadly, few products or experiences do this now, which is the main reason why the CD-ROM industry fell apart over the past few years (the products offered little to do that was interesting).

However, this is merely the starting point. As an industry (academics and professionals alike), we understand this word "interactivity" very little and need to explore greatly what it means to people, what it can be, and how to create it. This is one of the points that grants and funding can apply. Unfortunately, the commercial end of the interactive media industry offers little chance of exploring and experimenting with the whole notion of interactivity, as the demands of an overhyped market, sky-rocketing costs, too much publicity, and too many expectations prevent most companies from asking these questions. Likewise, on the academic end of the spectrum, demands to produce work-ready students, lack of interdisciplinary programs, and the history of computer science studies (emphasis on software, programming, engineering, and computer languages) prevent students and professors from asking these questions because they seem esoteric and "light" in the phase of other research.

About the only people who are explicitly trained in the skills of interaction are those in the performing arts: dancers, actors, singers, comedians, improvisational actors, and musicians. However, these fields are hardly seen as complementary or valid courses of study in computer science, multimedia, and even design programs. Yet the experience and knowledge that performers can bring to these disciplines are exactly the answers to the questions that should be asked. Grants for programs that try to explore these issues with the help of many different disciplines would help speed the development of answers badly needed in this industry.

COMPUTERS THAT ARE AWARE

Interfaces need to become more aware of themselves and those around them. This is true in both a physical sense (where am I, where are you, and who else is here?) and a cognitive sense (who am I, what can I do, and how can I communicate with others?). While computers won't have truly "cognitive" capabilities for a long time—if ever—they already have a few elements of these capabilities and information and need even more. What features these capabilities will eventually create are mostly unpredictable right now, but we can count on the facilities to respond to people in a more adaptable and individual manner to make a major improvement in interfaces. Developing processes, standards, and technologies to build these capabilities upon will prove mandatory.

Other technologies that will be needed to develop these more intuitive and adaptive interfaces include perceptual technologies to support computer perception in sound, vision, touch, gesture, environment, temperature, airborne particles, and so forth.

INTERFACES TO KNOWLEDGE

Most interfaces and applications today have sped the transmission, storage, and processing of data but have hardly changed the accumulation, creation, or quantity of either information or knowledge. Certainly, we cannot say that computers have made us more "wise," but the interactions computers offer *do* give us more chances to communicate our thoughts and build wisdom if we only knew better how to. Our understanding of knowledge and wisdom and its processes is inadequate but also critical to our continued development as a culture and a species. Research into the components of these processes, of our minds, and of our thoughts is needed to advance not only our tools—of which the computer is one of our best—but ourselves. This research is needed not only in terms of software and hardware (perhaps finding form in file formats, applications, operating systems, and products), but in the underlying processes and understandings of how we think—upon which all of the aforementioned are based. This must be coordinated with the fields of education, psychology, and communications, as well as computer science. It may even be helpful—and necessary—to include those in philosophy.

These are the most esoteric and unpredictable of questions—indeed, they have kept us busy for our entire histories—but this should not deter us from seeking their answers. Even if we will never truly answer these questions completely, each part of the answer gives us new insights into building more valuable interfaces that meet more of our needs.

Another aspect of interfaces that facilitate knowledge are the technologies involved with representing and displaying data and information. Present tools commonly available on the market such as spreadsheets, word processors, databases, and graphics programs are hardly adequate for representing or visualizing complex relationshipships and informing communications. The hardware required for better-performing visualization systems includes displays that are high resolution, portable, and low power so that they are more easily used where needed. Standards for evolved displays will need to be established, adopted, and made prevalent so that engineers, programmers, and audiences can come to count on their capabilities and availability. Integration with input/output devices such as scanners, pointing devices, and printers will need to be advanced as well. Devices that enable more direct interaction between display and control are more learnable and more evident to use—in essence, an evolution of what is commonly understood as direct manipulation today. Systems for processing and working with these devices will need to rely on more powerful and faster CPUs (central processing units) and hardware as well.

Software for representing and manipulating more complex data visualizations will need to build on new understandings of how people think and work with data. These applications will need to explore new paradigms in representation and manipulation in order to offer the kinds of flexibility and understandability required by more complex processing and less "professional" audiences.

INTERFACES ACROSS MEDIA

Where possible, new interfaces should translate well across media and devices, whether portable, stationary, shared, public, private, networked, or personal, and should strive to encompass and integrate traditional media, such as broadcast and print media, where possible—not merely electronic and on-line media. This is not to say that interfaces shouldn't take advantage of their unique capabilities—indeed, they need to do so more than currently—but they also need to relate to each other where possible and it should be recognized that printed interfaces such as newspapers, classifieds, catalogs, documentation, and directories are in just as dire need of evolution as technological ones. I am certainly *not* calling for computer screens to look like little notebooks of paper with spiral binds nor print paper to look like current computer interfaces with pull-down menus. However, our interfaces to printed information and knowledge have evolved little (outside of stylistic appearances) in the past 100 years, and, since this still represents a huge proportion of information dissemination and interaction (and will likely continue to be), some funding for the evolution of these critical interfaces should be allocated.

INTERFACES ACROSS CULTURES

As interfaces become more complex and deal with more abstract issues, how they address people from different backgrounds and cultures will become more critical. We have been able to achieve a certain amount of standardization and utilization so far with present interfaces, but this is due mainly to the nature of tasks currently completed with computers. As computers become more involved with knowledge building, communications, and community and as interfaces facilitate these more social purposes, they will need to address how differences between people change their understanding of how to use these devices and of the processes themselves. These differences may be based on age, gender, culture, language, or nationality. Interfaces in the future will not have the luxury of requiring the same amount of capitulation on the part of the audience since the next level of computer users (the next 100 million users) will not be as willing to change their approach to problems and their interaction with devices as the enthusiasts and professionals who comprise the present base of computer users. Issues of language, gesture, understanding, privacy, approach, civility, and "life" are not consistent throughout the world—and wonderfully so—and must be discovered and documented. Also, systems, standards, and interfaces must be developed that are sensitive to these differences. Lastly, the knowledge of these difference must be made available to researchers and developers.

Automatic language translation is one of the most critical—and most difficult—problems to solve. It is such a complex problem that it is probably not solvable by conventional programming means. Efforts to "grow" or "evolve" complex software for pattern recognition and processing are probably the best hope for tackling problems of this complexity, and it will probably require several efforts in coordination.

Lastly, greater education is needed to inform researchers, professionals, participants, and the industry of these issues, their importance, the state of their progress, and their details. We cannot merely rely on the media to inform people about computers or their capabilities since the messages usually get dissolved to the lowest common denominator—but one of cynical expectations and far lower than actual capabilities to understand. Movies, news, books, and other instruments of culture often create unrealistic understandings, expectations, and often fears of computers and their uses. We must address these and reverse them ourselves—as no one else will—if we expect future interfaces for everybody to be more effective.

INTERSPACE AND AN EVERY-CITIZEN INTERFACE TO THE NATIONAL INFORMATION INFRASTRUCTURE

Terry Winograd
Stanford University

With the sudden emergence of widely used Internet-centered applications, it has become glaringly obvious that the computer is not a machine whose main purpose is for a person to pursue a task. The computer (with its attendant peripherals and networks) is a machine for communicating all kinds of information in all kinds of media, with layers of structuring and interaction that could not be provided by traditional print, graphic, or broadcast media.

The traditional idea of "interface" implies that we are focusing on two entities—the person and the machine—and on the space that lies between them. But a more realistic view recognizes the centrality of an "interspace" that is inhabited by multiple people, workstations, servers, and other devices in a complex web of interactions. The hardest task in creating an every-citizen interface will be the design of appropriate theories, models, and representations to do justice to the potential richness of this interaction space.

As a simple example, consider the Web. Today we talk of surfing from place to place on the Web, touching home pages, and following links. These metaphors of spatial locomotion are engaging. They opened up new ways of thinking and doing that had not been explored in the predecessor desktop metaphor. But the Web is not the answer to the future of interfaces any more than the desktop was in its day. Each metaphor is another stepping stone, which in turn creates a way of thinking that creates a blindness to new possibilities.

New research and development activities need to enhance our ability to understand, analyze, and create interaction spaces. The work will be rooted in disciplines that focus on people and communication—such as psychology, communications, graphic design, and linguistics—as well as in disciplines that support computing and communications technologies. The work will start from an assumption that a computer system provides a shared space for multiple people, each in a personal and organizational background that shapes and guides interaction with others. The systems we can build based on new research will support communications structures at all levels—from the generic document structuring of the Web to highly task-specific interactions, like those that go on in an airport control tower.

Some sample areas for research are discussed below.

COLLABORATION STRUCTURES

There is a body of research on the structure of collaborative work, sponsored under previous National Science Foundation (NSF) initiatives on collaboration and developed by commercial software developers under labels such as "workflow." The current state of the art can be described as having a large "hole in the middle." At the highest level there are very general (and hence very abstract) theories of how people get work done through communication. At the low level, there are thousands, even millions, of specialized applications—from the order system at a fast food restaurant to the NSF proposal application process—that support organized group activities. But we have not yet developed the conceptual and computational tools to make it easy to bring collaboration into the mainstream of applications. When I work with my research group on a joint paper, we use sophisticated word processors, graphics programs, and the like, but our coordination is based on generic e-mail and calendars and often fails to help us at the places where breakdowns occur.

SEMANTIC ALIGNMENT

Whenever two people talk, they have only an approximate understanding of each other. When they speak the same language, share intellectual assumptions, and have common backgrounds and training, the alignment may be quite close. As these diverge, there is an increasing need to put effort into constant calibration and readjusting of interpretations. Ordinary language freezes meanings into words and phrases, which then can be "misinterpreted" (or at least differently interpreted).

This problem shows up at every level of computer systems, whenever information is being represented in a well-specified syntax and vocabulary. Even simple databases have this problem. If information is being shared between two company databases that have a table for "employee," they are apparently in alignment. But if one was created for facilities planning and the other for tax accounting, they may not agree on the status of part-time, off-site, on-site contract, or other such "employees." This difference may be nowhere explicit in what is stored on the computer but is a matter of background and context.

Ubiquitous networking is leading us to the point where every computer system supports communication and where every term we use will be seen and hence interpreted by others. There are traditional philosophical and linguistic approaches to making sure we have "common understanding," but these tend to be based on highly abstract or idealized examples and settings. We need to develop new theoretical foundations for talking about the kinds of "semantic approximations" that are needed for something as apparently simple as sharing data between two databases and as ubiquitous as the nodes of the Internet.

BUILDING NEW "VIRTUALITIES"

In designing new systems and applications, we are not simply providing better tools for working with the objects in the previously existing world. Computer systems and software are a medium for the creation of virtualities—the worlds in which users of the software perceive, act, and respond to experiences. Software is not just a device with which the user interacts; it is also the generator of a space in which the user lives. Software design is like architecture: when an architect designs a home or an office building, a structure is being specified. More significantly, though, the patterns of life for its inhabitants are being shaped. People are thought of as inhabitants rather than as users of buildings.

The creation of a virtual world is immediately evident in computer games, which dramatically engage the player in exploring the vast reaches of space, fighting off the villains, finding the treasures—actively living in whatever worlds the game designer can imagine and portray. But the creation of worlds is not limited to game designers. There is also a virtual world in a desktop interface, in a spreadsheet, and in a use of the World Wide Web. Researchers in human-computer interfaces have used other terms, such as conceptual model, cognitive model, user's model, interface metaphor, user illusion, virtuality, and ontology, all carrying the connotation that a space of existence, rather than a set of devices or images, is being designed. The term *virtuality* highlights the perspective that the world is virtual, in a space that is neither a mental construct of the user or a mental construct of the designer.

Today, we are all familiar with the virtuality of the standard graphical user interface, with its windows, icons, folders, and the like. Although these virtual objects are loosely grounded in analogies with the physical world, they exist in a unique world of their own, with its special logic and potentials for action by the user. The underlying programs manipulate disk sectors, network addresses, data caches, and program segments. These underpinnings do not appear—at least when things are working normally—in the desktop virtuality in which the user works.

There is little theoretical grounding today on which to base the design of new virtualities. Obviously, there are considerations from psychology about how people perceive new kind of objects and activities. There are philosophical discourses about how we divide the world up into constituent things and properties and how we can formulate our interactions with them. There is also a more common-sense level of understanding how people think about familiar domains and how their expectations from their experiences in life will shape their interactions with computer systems.

As a simple example, consider the three primary modes of interacting with a virtuality that are learned by every normal person in infancy:

- *Manipulation.* Perceiving, grasping, modifying, and controlling objects that are in front of the person. This is a "hand-eye" modality that fills much of our daily life (from the kitchen to the cash register). It is at the heart of the current desktop metaphor and most of what has been done with graphic user interfaces.
- *Locomotion.* Observing location and moving from place to place. This is an "eye-foot" modality in which the world is primarily stable and the user moves within it. This is the basis for the Web's place-and-link-following metaphor, as well as many popular computer games (where the manipulative aspects are reduced to "shoot weapon").
- *Conversation.* Using a language to communicate with another person in a two-sided discourse. This is an "ear-mouth" modality that comes from our experience in encountering other people. It is the basis for the traditional command-line interface as well as speech interaction with machines.

What can be said at a theoretical level about the nature of these modalities and the problems that arise in using—and especially in mixing—them? Are there other conceptual modalities that are fundamentally different from these three that will be understandable and practical for people to use? How does the finer-grained analysis of interaction structure fit into this larger picture? And, finally, what is the difference in the nature of multi-person activity in these different modalities, and how does that map onto the kinds of multiperson collaboration we want to support in an every-citizen interaction space? (See <http://www-pcd.stanford.edu/winograd> and <http://www-pcd.stanford.edu/winograd/book.html>.)

BIBLIOGRAPHY

On Coordination

Denning, Peter and Pamela Dargan, Action-Centered Design, in Terry Winograd (ed.), *Bringing Design to Software*, Reading, MA: Addison-Wesley, 1996, pp. 105-120.

Holt, Anatol, Diplans, A Formalism for Action, *ACM Transactions on Office Information Systems* 6:2 (April 1988).

Malone, Thomas W. and Kevin Crowston, What Is Coordination Theory and How Can It Help Design Cooperative Work Systems?, MIT CCS report 112, 3402/3183, Cambridge, MA: Massachusetts Institute of Technology, April 1990.

Medina-Mora, Raul, Terry Winograd, Rodrigo Flores, and Fernando Flores, "The Action Workflow Approach to Workflow Management Technology" in *The Information Society*, Volume 9, Number 4, October-December 1993, p. 391.

Verharen, Egon, Nardo van der Rijst, and Jan Dietz (eds.), *Proceedings of the Language/Action Perspective: International Workshop on Communication Modeling*, Economisch Institut Tilburg, Tilburg, *the Netherlands*, 1996. <http://infolabwww.kub.nl:2080/infolab/lap96/>

Winograd, Terry (1988), Introduction to the Language/Action Perspective, *ACM Transactions on Office Information Systems* 6:2 (April 1988), pp. 83-86.

On Semantic Alignment

There are papers on this topic from the point of view of artificial intelligence ("ontology" matching), databases ("schema" matching), and information retrieval ("attribute set" matching). I have not put together a good list or found an integrative article that cuts across them. Some general considerations are presented in the following:

Winograd, Terry and Fernando Flores, *Understanding Computers and Cognition: A New Foundation for Design*, Norwood, NJ: Ablex, 1986, 220 pp. Paperback issued by Addison-Wesley, 1987.

On the Design of "Virtualities"

Hutchins, Edwin, James Hollan, and Donald Norman, Direct Manipulation Interfaces, in D. Norman and S. Draper (eds.), *User-Centered System Design*, Hillsdale, NJ.: Erlbaum, 1986, pp. 87-124.

Lakoff, George, and Mark Johnson, *Metaphors We Live By*, Chicago: University of Chicago Press, 1980.

Winograd, Terry, with John Bennett, Laura De Young, and Bradley Hartfield (Eds.), *Bringing Design to Software*, Reading, MA: Addison-Wesley, 1996. Available on-line at <http://www-pcd.stanford.edu/winograd/book.html>. See, especially, Introduction, Chapter 2 (David Liddle, "Design of the Conceptual Model"), and Chapter 4 (John Rheinfrank and Shelley Evenson, "Design Languages").

MOBILE ACCESS TO THE NATION'S INFORMATION INFRASTRUCTURE

Daniel P. Siewiorek
Carnegie Mellon University

INTRODUCTION

The focus of this position paper is mobile access to the nation's information infrastructure (NII). The goal should be to provide "the right information to the right person at the right place at the right time." In order for the NII to reach its potential, the average person should be able to take advantage of the information on or off the job. Even while at work, many people do not have desks or spend large portions of time away from their desks. Thus, mobile access is the gating technology required to make the NII available at any place at any time.

The next section describes the time rate of change of computer technology, indicating what might be expected in the form of technology from the computer industry as well as defining a new class of computers—the wearable computer. The third section describes the importance of a variety of modalities of interaction with wearable computers. The paper concludes with some research challenges.

TIME RATE OF CHANGE OF COMPUTER TECHNOLOGY

Computer systems are typically compared using two classes of metrics: capacity and performance. Capacity is how large a component may be or how much information it may store. Performance is measured in functions per unit of time (often referred to as bandwidth or throughput) or, conversely, the time needed to complete a specific function (referred to as latency). Recently, ease of use has become a major differentiating characterisitic between computer systems and hence represents a third class of metrics.

Because they directly reflect the state of technology, hardware capacity and performance metrics are the easiest to determine or derive. These measures are usually associated with individual components in a computer system. There are six basic functions in a computer system. In addition, attributes such as energy consumption and physical size gain increasing importance as computers become more mobile. Table 1 sum-

TABLE 1   Examples of Computer System Capacity and Performance

Components	Units	Workstation	Laptop	Palmtop/Personal Digital Assistant
Processor	Instructions/second	100M	10M	1M
Random access memory	Bytes	64M	8M	1M
Disk memory	Bytes	600M	100M	—
Display	Pixels	1M	0.18M	0.045M
Network communications	Bits/second	10M	2M	0.02M
Distance	Meters	—	100	10
Energy	1/kW	5	100	500
Physical size	(Weight × volume) $1/\text{kg} \times \text{m}^3$	1	16	2,000

marizes eight metrics for a computer system, including their units of measurement. Capacity is usually measured in the number of information units such as bytes or pixels. Bandwidth/throughput is measured in operations per second for the processor and bits per second for communications. Energy is measured as the reciprocal of kilowatts, while physical size is summarized as the reciprocal of the product of the weight times the volume of space occupied. Notice that for all these metrics the larger the number the better. The three columns in Table 1 include a contemporary workstation (an anchored, unmovable system), a contemporary laptop computer (a luggable system), and a palmtop/personal digital assistant (a portable pocketable system).

Since ease of use is so closely associated with human reaction, it is much more difficult to quantify. There are at least three basic functions related to ease of use: input, output, and information representation. Box 1 summarizes several points for each of these basic functions. Note that, unlike the continuous variables for capacity and performance, the ease-of-use metrics are discrete.

Siewiorek et al. (1982) considered the concept of the computer class. A computer class attempts to integrate many computer system details into an overall evaluation, grouping similarly evaluated systems together. Thus, the workstation, laptop, and palmtop in Table 1 can each be considered representative of a computer class. These researchers also observed that computer classes differ in physical dimensions and price by roughly 1.5 orders of magnitude (e.g., approximately a factor of 30). In addition, it was observed that, as each computer class evolves, new members of the class are expected to have increased capacity and functionality. The increases in technology serve to increase the capacity and functionality of a

---

BOX 1
Ease-of-Use Metrics

Input	Output	Information Representation
• Keyboard	• Alphanumerical display	• Textual
• Mouse	• Graphical display	• Ionic desktop
• Handwriting recognition	• Speech synthesis	• Multimedia
• Speech recognition		
• Gesturing		
• Position sensing		

---

class. Thus, the boundary of various attributes can be considered to be increasing with time.

On the other hand, technological changes can be used to initiate new computer classes with the same functionality offered by the next higher class several years before. It is extremely important to remember that all classes of computers have followed approximately the same evolutionary paths as their capacity and functionality have increased. The newer computer classes benefit from the evolutionary process of older classes, adapting to proven concepts quickly, where the older classes required a trial-and-error process. Siewiorek and co-workers also observed that computer classes tend to lag each other by approximately 5 years. Thus, the palmtop computer of today could be considered to have approximately the functionality of a laptop 5 years ago or a workstation 10 years ago. Thus, we can expect the palmtop of the year 2006 to have the attributes of today's workstation.

One can speculate on the emergence of a new class of computers called "wearable computers." Wearable computers will weigh less than a few ounces, operate for months or years on a single battery, and have esthetically pleasing shapes that can adorn various parts of the body. Pagers and electronic watches (complete with calculator and memory to store phone numbers/memos) represent the first examples of the wearable class of computers. Thus, the wearable computer of the year 2006 will have at least the functionality of today's laptop (as depicted in Table 1).

As with the capacity and performance metrics in Table 1, the ease-of-use metrics in Box 1 are also moving out with time. For example, the keyboard with an alphanumerical display using textual information is representative of time-sharing systems of the early 1970s. The keyboard and mouse, graphical output, and iconic desktop are representative of personal computers of the early 1980s. The addition of handwriting recognition input, speech synthesis output, and multimedia information is emerging in the early 1990s. It takes approximately one decade to completely assimilate new input, output, and informational representations. By the early part of the next decade, speech recognition, position sensing, and eye tracking should be common inputs. Heads-up projection displays should allow superposition of information onto the user's environment.

MODALITIES OF INTERACTION WITH WEARABLE COMPUTERS

The objective of wearable computer designs is to merge the user's information space with his or her work space. The wearable computer should offer seamless integration of information-processing tools with the existing work environment. To accomplish this, the wearable system must offer functionality in a natural and unobtrusive manner, allowing the user to dedicate all of his or her attention to the task at hand with no distraction provided by the system itself. Conventional methods of interaction, including the keyboard, mouse, joystick, and monitor, all require some fixed physical relationship between user and device, which can considerably reduce the efficiency of the wearable system. Among the most challenging questions facing mobile system designers is that of human interface design. As computing devices move from the desktop to more mobile environments, many conventions of human interfacing must be reconsidered for their effectiveness. How does the mobile system user supply input while performing tasks that preclude use of a keyboard? What layout of visual information most effectively describes system state- or task-related data. To maximize the effectiveness of wearable systems in mobile computing environments, interface design must be carefully matched with user tasks. By constructing mental models of user actions, interface elements may be chosen and tuned to meet the software and hardware requirements of specific procedures.

The efficiency of the human-computer interface is determined by the simplicity and clarity of the mental model suggested by the system. By modeling the actual task as well as the human interface, a linkage can be constructed between user and machine that can be examined to improve the overall efficiency of the wearable system. We begin with the assertion that for wearable systems to be efficient the mental model of the interface design must closely parallel that of the user task; there must be minimal interference or obstruction posed by the computer in completing jobs. Although the number of quantifiable metrics suited for interface evaluation is small, a series of basic observations provide a means for comparison. One characteristic of an application interface is the number of user actions required to perform a given subtask. We define a subtask as an

TABLE 2   Comparison of Number of Steps to Retrieve Information Using Selection Buttons and Speech

	Buttons/Menu Selection	Speech
Get information	4	1
Get photograph	5	1
Navigate to location	3	2

operation, possibly consisting of multiple inputs, that a user completes in the process of performing a larger coherent task. For example, in the course of performing an inspection, a user might wish to return from his or her present location in an application to the main menu. This subtask may require a single input (perhaps a voice command or an on-screen button) or multiple inputs (backing out through a hierarchy of categories to reach the top or main level). We assert that an application requiring few inputs will allow a user to dedicate more attention to the job at hand, while a larger number of inputs will require more concentration on the computing system. A comparison of equivalent subtasks in two wearable computers (Smailagic and Siewiorek, 1996) is shown in Table 2. The speech recognition engine accepts complex commands that allow some subtasks requiring a series of manual inputs to be executed with a single phrase. However, the response time to a spoken input is longer and the accuracy is lower. For these reasons the quantitative aspect of system latency and accuracy must be factored into evaluations of usability.

RESEARCH CHALLENGES

There are several challenges that research must address to make mobile access to the NII effective. Following is a partial list of those challenges:

- *User interface models.* What is the appropriate set of metaphors for providing mobile access to information (i.e., the next "desktop" or "spreadsheet")? These metaphors typically take over a decade to develop (i.e., the desktop metaphor started in the early 1970s at Xerox PARC and required over a decade before it was widely available to consumers). Extensive experimentation working with end-user applications will be required. Furthermore, there may be a set of metaphors each tailored to a specific application or a specific information type.
- *Input/output modalities.* While several modalities mimicking the

input/output capabilities of the human brain have been the subject of computer science research for decades, their accuracy and ease of use (i.e., many current modalities require extensive training periods) are not yet acceptable. Inaccuracies produce user frustrations. In addition, most of these modalities require extensive computing resources, which will not be available in low-weight, low-energy wearable computers. There is room for new, easy-to-use input devices, such as the dial developed at Carnegie Mellon University for list-oriented applications.

• *Quick interface evaluation methodology.* Current approaches to evaluating a human computer interface require elaborate procedures and scores of subjects. Such an evaluation may take months and is not appropriate for use during interface design. These evaluation techniques should focus especially on decreasing human errors and frustration.

• *Matched capability with applications.* The current thought is that technology should provide the highest performance capability. However, this capability is often unnecessary to complete an application, and fancy enhancements such as full-color graphics require substantial resources and may actually decrease ease of use by generating information overload for the user. For example, one informal survey of display requirements for military planning estimated that 85 percent of the applications could be performed with an alphanumerical display and 10 percent with simple graphics and that only 5 percent required full bitmap graphics. Interface design and evaluation should focus on the most effective means for information access and resist the temptation to provide extra capabilities simply because they are available.

REFERENCES

Siewiorek, D., C. G. Bell, and A. Newell. 1982. *Computer Structures: Principles and Examples,* McGraw-Hill, Inc., New York.

Smailagic, Asim, and D.P. Siewiorek. 1996. Modalities of Interaction with CMU Wearable Computers. *IEEE Personal Communications,* Vol. 3, No. 1, February.

ORDINARY CITIZENS AND THE NATIONAL INFORMATION INFRASTRUCTURE

Bruce Tognazzini
Healtheon Corporation

The original working title for this workshop was "Toward an Ordinary-Citizen Interface to the National Information Infrastructure." It was then altered to "Every-Citizen" to be inclusive of all of our citizens. While I support that change, we did lose something quite important in the transition, for of all the people whose lives have been affected by the computer revolution, perhaps none has received as scant attention as our ordinary citizens.

Today, we face the prospect of millions of have-nots shut out of cyberspace, a threat that has little to do with economic status, country of origin, race, creed, color, or physical ability. Instead, it has everything to do with age, gender, education, culture, aptitude, and attitude. If cyberspace today were to have a dead-honest advertising slogan, it would read: Built by Boys, for Boys!

As Margie Wylie (1995) says: "Far from offering a millennial new world of democracy and equal opportunity, the coming Web of information systems could turn the clock back 50 years for women." The 18- to 39-year-old males with technological talent and above-average intelligence and education who built today's cyberspace built it for themselves. Large parts of it reflect the delicate ambiance of an automobile junkyard. We must make fundamental changes in the direction of computer design if the true have-nots of cyberspace are not to be those rare individuals who do not feel instantly comfortable clattering over mounds of twisted metallic wreckage—in other words, ordinary people.

Somewhere along the line, many technology designers lost track of the real goal: empowering users. From video cassette recorders to clock radios, designers are adding every button, switch, and other power-user doodad they can in the mistaken belief that the true power of technology is to be measured in the number of features and controls rather than the impact on people's lives. Our computer software has tracked this trend. Systems and applications today are festooned with every "wangdoodle" imaginable, offering users plenty of power to blow themselves up while at the same time inhibiting them from accomplishing their task.

If the desktop computer is a dark and mysterious closet, the Internet is a positively terrifying, sucking black hole. The advent of the World

Wide Web is helping to address part of the problem by making at least the waystations on the Internet visible, but just the sheer immensity of today's Cyberspace is frightening to all but a small group of people. Sure, the kinds of tasks users attempt on their computers have become more complex, but something else is leading to the increased difficulty of using our machines, something we need to address: we are designing our systems for power users, to the exclusion of everyone else.

POWER USERS VERSUS EXPERT USERS

Most people want to be seen as power users, but then we have the real thing. Power users typically consist of bipedal, testosterone-soaked life forms between the ages of 18 and 39. Yes, I said testosterone-soaked life forms. At the risk of offending certain politically correct parties, there does appear to be a difference, however minor, between boys and girls. And the overwhelming majority of power users I've come across are definitely male.

Let me explain what I mean by power user. A "power user" is a person driven by hormones to want complete and utter control of every function of his or her computer, even if having such control seriously degrades efficiency and productivity. Tim Allen's character on "Home Improvement," the ABC comedy series, is the prototypical power user. He's the only guy in the neighborhood with a 120-horsepower lawn mower that will do 0 to 60 in less than 7 seconds. It's not much use on his suburban lawn, but it makes a really neat noise when he starts it up.

I knew several guys at Apple who had so many weird public-domain extensions in their system folder that virtually none of their applications ran properly. Accomplishing the smallest task was like walking through a mine field. So what? As far as they were concerned, it merely increased the challenge! They wouldn't have thought of paring down their systems.

Most women see their machines as serious productivity tools, there for the express purpose of helping them accomplish their task. Women want to do their work, not "play computer" (Bulkeley, 1994). They are not alone: A high percentage of men don't want to "play computer" either; they just don't dare complain about it.

Many people across the board become expert users. Expert users understand their craft and are competent at using the tools that will help them succeed. They may have no interest in tearing apart their tools, either to understand them or to "improve" them. It's the difference between someone who is an expert at driving a car and someone who looks forward to Saturday morning because that is when he can tear the car apart and perhaps get it back together. The Saturday-morning power user may very well not be particularly expert at driving the car (although he will claim to be).

CHANGING TIMES

Thirty years ago computer users consisted of two classes: young male programmers and operators and powerless, minimum-wage females who endlessly keypunched 80-column cards. (Of course, not all keypunch operators were female. I was one of the few powerless male keypunch operators in those days. My cohorts and I quickly escaped, but the women were generally not so lucky.)

Today, two-thirds of personal computer users are women, according to a Logitec Inc. poll (1992), and millions of those female users are now in higher technical and management positions. Those who are not wandering the labyrinths of cyberspace today will be in the very near future.

The majority of users, according to the same poll, are now more than 36 years old. Most of us above the age of 36—male or female—have abandoned changing our own motor oil. And we are no longer quite as amused by the prospect of spending 10 hours tracking down the reason why our World Wide Web connection has become unresponsive ever since we installed our new tax planner.

THE ECONOMIC PENALTY FOR "BOYTOYISM"

A 1992 survey by Nolan, Norton and Company pegged the annual cost of ownership for a standard business personal computer at as much as $21,500 per year. That's a lot of money for a $5,000 computer. Where's the money going? A disproportionate percentage can be traced to direct and indirect training costs. The study found that the known visible costs per computer ranged from $2,000 to $6,000 annually. These direct costs cover hardware, software, initial installation, scheduled maintenance, and people taking time from their regular jobs to attend training classes.

The indirect costs are more complex: users waste time pressing buttons and flailing through manuals trying to figure out what went wrong with their machine, when the problem is that they inadvertently triggered some unknown and less-than-obvious system state. They waste time wandering around looking for a warm body in another office to ask for help. Finally, when they find someone who can help, the other party ends up wasting their own time, too. This peer-to-peer training is expensive. The study pegged the cost at $6,000 to $15,000 per year.

According to Bulkeley (1992):

"We all just about fell out of our chairs when we saw the amount of mutual support," says David J. Baker, a process consultant for Sprint who participated in organizing the study. "Everyone knew [peer-to-peer training] was taking place, but when we guessed what the amount would be beforehand, we missed by a factor of 65."

SUPPORTIVE FAMILY AND FRIENDS

The effect of interface complexity can be felt beyond the workplace. Ordinary people's access to cyberspace is a direct function of their access to a family member or friend who can carry out informed peer-to-peer activities. Should the knowledgeable family member die, divorce, or grow up and move out, the other family members may lose their access to cyberspace with the first disk problem or mandatory upgrade. Even if their hardware and software systems continue to function, they may well be unable to gain the full benefit of services offered, just because they do not have the technical skills to access them.

Ordinary citizens who do not live in a high-tech area of the country, who had no one to lean on from the beginning, are just as effectively disenfranchised from the cyber revolution as those who are economically disadvantaged.

RESEARCH ISSUES

While the solution to the problem of today's excessive complexity will involve applied technology, the problem has not arisen from a lack of technology, and it will not be solved by blindly throwing more technology at it. The solutions, I believe, lie more in the areas of sociology and psychology.

Macintosh used to have the slogan, "the computer for the rest of us." Macintosh was not. From the beginning, the Macintosh was designed to be "the computer for the rest of *them*." The Macintosh team, like the Lisa team, Alan Kay's Xerox PARC Altos team, and Doug Engelbart's original SRI team before them, was keenly aware that they were designing not for themselves but for others. All these teams held a common understanding of who their users were and chief in that understanding was a rock-solid belief that users were not like themselves.

Ten years later we are expecting ordinary citizens traveling on the World Wide Web to follow a naming convention so foreign to human experience as to be completely incomprehensible: http://www.goliath. com/~grandma.

We need research projects that will enable us to form a bridge between the needs of ordinary people and the inventiveness of our young technological minds. Several studies have shown startling differences between software engineers and ordinary citizens on Jungian psychological-type tests (Sitton and Chmelir, 1984; Tognazzini, 1992). These tests need to be repeated and expanded on, using larger populations and varied and more exacting instruments, answering the question: How are engineers different from ordinary citizens? Those engineers who do want to make technology accessible to ordinary people have little to go by since we still know remarkably little about our ordinary citizens. What are the capabilities, needs, and wants of ordinary citizens?

Today, software engineers master systems of amazing complexity during the course of their education and often graduate with the attitude that others can and should experience the same complexity they have: In what ways can we improve the education of our engineers so they are better able to understand and provide for the needs and wants of ordinary citizens?

Much of the complexity our computer science students face is necessary—they are doing complex things. However, much of it is just bad design, bad design they often end up emulating in their own products. How prevalent is bad design in the systems that computer science students use? What can be done to improve those systems? What can be done to sensitize our students to bad design and its consequences, so they will cease emulating it?

We need case studies of projects that resulted in approachable products or services versus those that only an engineer could love. What makes a project result in a system that people can use? What caused that project to succeed? What changes could have been made early on in projects that resulted in difficult-to-use systems that would have made them more approachable?

While many organizations have embraced the idea of human interaction design as a profession, many still see human interaction design as something to be done by engineers in the normal course of their work. What are the comparative outcomes of projects done in conjunction with human interaction designers versus engineers acting alone? Is the investment in human interface specialists worth it? Does that investment result in designs that are more approachable by ordinary citizens?

Our interfaces to the national information infrastructure must be accessible to ordinary people. The Star-Lisa-Macintosh interface made a fundamental shift in design away from the earlier "black cave" interfaces. People had previously been expected to navigate blindly through cyberspace, leaping from menu to menu, building in their mind's eye an image of what their cyberspace looked like. The new interfaces swept all of that aside. The "lights were turned on," with cyberspace objects and actions represented by icons, menu selections, and other visible objects in the interface. People no longer navigated at all: everything was brought to the user, with the user staying always in one place—seated before the desktop.

The Web represents a step backward to the old black cave metaphor. True, people can see one home page at a time, but they are back to navigating their way around cyberspace and, once again, can see no visual evidence of their movement. It's like the tunnel of love: you see a lot of objects jumping out at you, but you don't really know where you are.

In the early days of the personal computer, we were attempting to sell an unproven technology to a skeptical world. We could not depend on people investing weeks or months of self-education in a system they did not yet know would improve their lives. We had to make things easy. However, sometimes, what was easy in that first 20 minutes was not necessarily the right solution for maximum efficiency over the long haul.

People now recognize the value of the personal computer or workstation. They are willing to make a reasonable commitment toward learning. The interface of today does not necessarily need the training wheels that the Star, Lisa, and Macintosh provided, but we need research to find out how much we can increase the difficulty of the learning experience in an effort to further empower users. We need to establish the relevance today of the principles that drove the design of the original graphical user interfaces, as embodied in such lists as the Principles of Macintosh Design (Apple Computer, Inc., 1986). Which of the design principles for early graphical user interfaces represented "training wheels," and which represented needs, wants, and limitations of ordinary citizens that are just as important today as they were then?

Since the advent of those early graphical user interfaces, users have faced increasing complexity. What are the areas of today's technology that act as a barrier to ordinary citizens? What seeming complexities are not acting as barriers but are in fact embraced by ordinary citizens?

It takes 16 years to learn how to drive, with a lot of formal and informal education along the way. How much education should our ordinary-citizen children be receiving in school? What form should this education take? Based on an understanding that our children would be formally educated in information retrieval and other complex computer tasks, how far can we increase the learning burden for such tasks in our aim to improve overall efficiency and productivity?

Finally, we need to explore what, if anything, government or industry needs to do to bring simple power to our systems. Will competition by itself eventually result in approachable systems, or will we need an "Underwriters' Laboratory" type of institution that can certify our technological efforts? Will we need fast-moving standards organizations that can stay abreast of developments? If so, could there ever be any such thing as a fast-moving standards organization?

We have recently seen the result of the computer industry "putting its foot down" on the issue of the digital versatile disk (DVD, nee digital video disk). Instead of two competing systems being thrown on the market, there will be only one, and that one is better than either of the two that would have arrived. The DVD was also designed, rather than just kind of evolving. It had input from marketers, as well as engineers, marketers who actually went out and spoke to clients. Industry cooperation can work.

On the other hand, industry has had a miserable overall record of cooperation and consistency, from the VHS versus Beta wars to the Windows versus Macintosh wars, with ordinary citizens not only paying the price along the way but often ending up with an inferior alternative in the end. We know governmental supervision can work. We've seen it with the standards for NTSC video, for "compatible color," and, more recently, for HDTV (high-definition television) standards. The question always is whether any of us will live long enough to see the results. How can we achieve the certainty of governmental supervision with the mercurial speed of industry cooperation?

SUMMARY

Many of the above explorations could be carried out by a variety of agencies—industry, government, or academia. Who does what study is probably relatively unimportant. What is critical is that it become a matter of public policy that we make our national information infrastructure accessible to ordinary citizens as well as the technologically gifted. What is critical is that people drop the belief that the realm of cyberspace should rightly be the exclusive province of those boys who worked on cars, that cyberspace is by nature, not by design, a dark, dangerous, and forbidding place.

Today, every aspect of computers, from the out-of-the-box experience to surfing the Internet, is a joy to "technoguys" and an unpleasant challenge to ordinary citizens. We have the technology to make the national information infrastructure accessible and attractive to the vast majority of our citizens. The time has come to make the investment in research and education that will enable all of our citizens to participate in the future.

REFERENCES

Apple Computer, Inc. (1986). *The Apple Human Interface Guidelines,* Addison-Wesley, Reading, Mass.

Bulkeley, William M. (1992). Study Finds Hidden Costs of Computing, *Wall Street Journal*, November 2.

Bulkeley, William M. (1994). A Tool for Women, A Toy for Men, *Wall Street Journal*, March 16.

Logitec Inc. (1992). PC's and People Poll, A National Compatibility Study of the Human Experience with Hardware, sponsored by Logitec Inc., 6505 Kaiser Drive, Fremont, CA 94555, (510) 795-8500.

Nolan, Norton and Company (1992). *Managing End-User Computing*, Nolan, Norton and Company, Boston.

Sitton, Sarah, and Chmelir, Gerard (1984). The Intuitive Computer Programmer, *Datamation*, October 15.

Tognazzini, Bruce (1992). *Tog on Interface*, Addison-Wesley, Reading, Mass.

Wylie, Margie (1995). "No Place for Women: Internet Is a Flawed Model for the Infobahn," *Digital Media: A Seybold Report*, Vol. 4, No. 8, pp. 3-6, January 2.

SPOKEN-LANGUAGE TECHNOLOGY

Ronald A. Cole

Oregon Graduate Institute of Science and Technology

Spoken-language systems allow people to communicate with machines by using speech to accomplish some task. The development of spoken-language systems is a true multidisciplinary endeavor, requiring expertise in areas of electric engineering, computer science, statistics, linguistics, and psychology. The technologies involved in spoken-language systems include speech coding, speech recognition, natural language understanding, and dialogue modeling and may optionally include speaker recognition, language identification, and speech-to-speech language translation.

Advances in speech technology are of critical importance to the goal of an every-citizen interface to the national information infrastructure (NII). To be sure, speech technology cannot by itself achieve this goal. Many people are unable to speak or hear. Some information (e.g., paintings) is not in a form that can be appreciated using speech. Nevertheless, the vast majority of people in the United States speak and understand a language, and speech is an obvious means for them to access information. As spoken-language technologies mature, we can imagine spoken-language systems performing as cooperative agents, not unlike helpful human operators, to support a wide variety of transactions. For this to take place, significant advances in the technology must occur through fundamental research.

A significant advantage of using speech as an interface modality is that it can be transmitted by existing communications networks using common and inexpensive devices such as telephones and televisions. Today, use of the Internet is limited to people with access to computers and the skills to use them. These requirements exclude a great many Americans: computers are too expensive for many of us to own, and about one-third of our citizens are functionally illiterate (National Center for Education Statistics, 1993). In the future, computers are unlikely to be the major appliance for accessing the NII; telephones, cellular phones, televisions connected to cable networks, and inexpensive information appliances are likely to become the preferred means of access.

The state of the art in human language technology was summarized recently in an international survey entitled State of the Art of Human Language Technology, sponsored by the National Science Foundation

(NSF) and the European Community (Cole et al., 1996). Each of the 92 authors who contributed to the survey was asked to define a specific area of human language technology, review the state of the art in that area, and identify key research challenges. The survey is available on the World Wide Web at http://cse.ogi.edu/CSLU/HLTsurvey/ HLTsurvey.html. A second source of information on the state of the art of speech technology is the report of a workshop sponsored by the NSF in 1992 and published subsequently as a journal article (Cole et al., 1995). The workshop participants identified eight areas in which research advances are essential to the development of spoken-language systems and the infrastructure needed to support research in those areas: (1) robust speech recognition, (2) automatic training and adaptation, (3) spontaneous speech, (4) dialogue models, (5) natural language response generation, (6) speech synthesis and speech generation, (7) multilingual systems, and (8) multimodal systems.

Given the importance of speech technology to an every-citizen interface and to U.S. economic competitiveness, it is important to ask if the activities of the research community will produce the desired technology in the shortest period of time. In the remainder of this note, I offer my opinions about the major stumbling blocks to the development of spoken-dialogue systems for an every-citizen interface. These are (1) an insufficient focus on interactive systems by speech researchers, (2) limitations of statistical modeling approaches, and (3) lack of tools for research and technology transfer.

INSUFFICIENT FOCUS ON INTERACTIVE SYSTEMS

The defining feature of a spoken-dialogue system is the interaction between human and machine. It follows that progress in developing these systems requires the continued study of how people interact with machines using speech. Such studies will highlight the limitations of speech recognition technology in the context of system use and focus research efforts on ways to overcome these limitations.

Today, the primary focus of speech recognition research in the United States is not interactive systems but the transcription of words in continuous speech. Large-vocabulary continuous speech recognition (LVCSR) is a priority of the defense establishment, which plays a major role in defining the priorities of the speech research community. For the past 12 years, progress in speech recognition research has been measured by recognition performance on benchmark tasks in annual competitions. Current benchmark tasks include recognition of articles read from newspapers, recognition of speech in news broadcasts, and recognition of speech in telephone conversations.

Transcription of words in continuous speech is both important and challenging, but the challenges are different from those needed to produce spoken-dialogue systems. For example, research in LVCSR does not focus on such issues as how to phrase a system prompt, how to determine if a recognition error has occurred, or how to engage in conversational repair if such a determination is made.

LIMITATIONS OF CURRENT TECHNOLOGY

There is growing evidence that current statistical modeling approaches to speech recognition, which treat speech as a sequence of independent time frames, will not scale to acceptable levels of performance on difficult tasks. For example, current systems are able to recognize about 50 percent of words in telephone conversations. This level of performance is achieved by gathering statistics on the frequency of occurrence of word sequences; performance drops to below 20 percent when word sequence constraints are disabled and word recognition is based solely on acoustic information. Significant effort has been devoted to this task in recent years, with only minor improvements in performance. The ability of statistical modeling techniques to recognize words in natural conversations is not encouraging.

A serious limitation of frame-based statistical modeling techniques is the difficulty of incorporating linguistic knowledge into the recognition paradigm. The IBM speech group, one of the pioneers of speech recognition using hidden Markov models, worked with linguists for several years to incorporate syntactic and semantic knowledge into IBM's systems, always with the same result—an increase in word recognition error rates. This led Bob Mercer, then of the IBM speech group, to assert in a keynote address to a speech recognition workshop that the most effective technique IBM has found for decreasing error rates is to fire a linguist.

The difficulty of incorporating linguistic knowledge into the dominant research paradigm stands as a major stumbling block to progress. Accurate speech recognition requires the integration of diverse acoustic cues, such as stop bursts, format movements, changes in pitch and comparison of acoustic features across segments. Similarly, speech understanding requires the integration of these acoustic cues with syntactic, semantic, pragmatic, and situational knowledge. No paradigm exists today that allows these information sources to be combined in a principled way that improves system performance. The result is that those with the most knowledge about human communication and spoken-language are largely excluded from the research process. New paradigms are needed that enable psychologists and linguists to become vital contributors to the development of human language technology.

LACK OF TOOLS FOR RESEARCH AND TECHNOLOGY TRANSFER

A final obstacle to progress in spoken-dialogue systems is the lack of available tools to support research and technology transfer. The development of spoken-language systems is a complex activity, requiring significant computer resources, integration of sophisticated signal processing, training and recognition algorithms, and language resources such as speech corpora and pronunciation dictionaries. Because of the resources and expertise required, spoken-language systems research is localized in a few specialized laboratories, which produce only five or six Ph.D. students each year. The result is that all but a few of the most fortunate students are denied the opportunity to participate in this exciting area of research, and we are not training enough researchers in an area of great strategic importance.

Without tools to create and manipulate spoken-dialogue systems and to support technology transfer, progress will be limited to the efforts of relatively few researchers at elite laboratories. For progress in spoken-language systems to occur, researchers need tools to rapidly design working systems and manipulate system parameters to test experimental hypotheses.

Despite these obstacles, I see great hope for the future. This workshop recognizes the importance of interface technologies, as do an increasing number of NSF initiatives in human language technology sponsored jointly by the Defense Advanced Research Projects Agency and other defense agencies. The growing support for interface research is bringing new researchers and new ideas into the field. Some of these researchers will focus their efforts on spoken-dialogues systems, and some will produce more powerful recognition techniques that will limit the amount of engineering required for each new task. There are also efforts under way to develop and distribute tools to support research and development of spoken-language systems. One such toolkit has been released by the Center for Spoken-language Understanding at the Oregon Graduate Institute (Sutton et al., 1996).

REFERENCES

Cole, R.A., L. Hirschman, et al. 1995. The Challenge of Spoken-language Systems: Research Directions for the Nineties, *IEEE Transactions on Speech and Audio Processing*, Vol. 3, No. 1, pp. 1-21.

Cole, R.A., J. Mariani, H. Uszkoriet, A. Zaenen, and V. Zue (Eds.). 1996. *Survey of the State of the Art in Human Language Technology,* Cambridge University Press, Stanford University, Stanford, Calif.

National Center for Education Statistics. 1993. *Adult Literacy in America*, U.S. Department of

Education, technical report no. GPO 065-000-00588-3, U.S. Government Printing Office, Washington, DC, September.

Sutton, S., D.G Novick, R. Cole, P. Vermeulen, J. de Villiers, J. Schalkwyk, and M. Fanty. 1996. Building 10,000 Spoken-Dialogue Systems, to appear in *Proceedings of the 1996 International Conference on Spoken-Language Processing*, Philadelphia, Pa. (Information on the availability of the toolkit is provided on-line at http://www.cse.ogi.edu/CSLU/toolkit/toolkit.html.)

TOWARD AN EVERY-CITIZEN INTERFACE

Steven K. Feiner

Columbia University

INTRODUCTION

Building user interfaces to the national information infrastructure (NII) that can fulfill the needs of all users, rather than just a privileged subset, will be a difficult task. In this position paper, I state my understanding of what the NII will be, lay out a set of goals for future NII user interfaces, and describe some research issues and projects associated with these goals.

I take the NII to be the public medium supporting all forms of interaction between people and machines that do not require the transport of physical matter. A user's interactions with the NII are accomplished through displays, interaction devices, and controlling software, which together comprise a user interface. I expect that an interface's displays and interaction devices would in most cases be the property of an individual or private company, as would the facilities needed to communicate and store information within a home, office, car, or pocket. The NII would include public networks that carry information between these private facilities and public sources of information and computation. Moreover, it would also include public displays and interaction facilities (e.g., the global positioning system (GPS) position tracking infrastructure), and software and standards needed to make communication and interaction possible.

GOALS

I have tried to capture the properties that I believe user interfaces to the NII should ideally have in the following list of high-level characteristics.

Multimedia

Interactions should be multimedia and multimodal, taking maximal advantage of all our senses to communicate information effectively. I intend this to go beyond the combination of graphics, video, text, sound, and voice typically implied by popular usage of the term *multimedia* to encompass the goals of research in virtual environments and visualization.

Adaptive

User interfaces should adapt to the needs and abilities of the individual user and situation, interactively tailoring both the form and content of the material being presented and providing customized help when necessary. An adaptive user interface would take into account factors as diverse as the user's education, skills, previous experience, and physical capabilities or disabilities. Recognizing that many activities are long lived, it should accommodate fluid and frequent changes in all aspects of the environment: who, what, where, when, why, and how.

Integrated

Interaction through the NII should be integrated smoothly and naturally into our daily activities, rather than being, as it is now, a compartmentalized special-purpose activity accomplished only when sitting in front of a workstation running special software. That is, the goal is not just to get the NII into our homes but rather to get it into our lives. In part this means mobility and wearability but without the compromises that are built into current PDAs.

Collaborative

Many of the tasks we perform are group activities, not solitary endeavors. NII user interfaces should support collaborative work and play, regardless of whether users are collaborating in the same place or at the same time.

Instructable

A user should be able to describe tasks that are to be carried out through the NII. Assuming that the lowest-level steps are within the capability of the resources available, the tasks should ideally be as rich and complex as those that the user could describe to other people. I hesitate to use the word "programmable" here to avoid the implication that this should involve a conventional programming language, such as Java, or even the simpler languages provided by current systems for end-user programming.

Responsive

Large enough quantitative differences in performance can make for qualitative differences in how a user interface feels and how it is used.

Sufficient resources must be available to all users to allow certain baseline tasks to be accomplished comfortably.

Empowering

Independent of a system's style (e.g., "invisible," "intelligent agent," or "direct manipulation tool"), its users should be able to accomplish more with it than without it and should feel a sense of satisfaction in doing so.

RESEARCH ISSUES AND PROJECTS

Each subsection below provides a background overview, followed by a selected set of issues and projects, keyed to the list of characteristics presented above.

Multimedia

Background

Interpreting "multimedia" broadly, I see two major research subgoals here: developing user interfaces that support real-time interaction with true three-dimensional (3D) input/output devices (i.e., virtual environments or virtual worlds) and learning how to use these devices to present information effectively, a task known in the graphics community as visualization. I am partial to the term *information visualization* (Card et al., 1991), which is rapidly gaining currency (e.g., see Gershon and Eick, 1995) and which stresses the diversity of domains and users that can benefit beyond those targeted by research on scientific visualization. While visualization research embraces work that appeals to senses other than the visual, the term *sonification* has been used to refer explicitly to the ways in which information can be presented through sound (Kramer, 1994).

Most state-of-the-art commercial user interfaces emphasize the use of 2D Windows, with which users interact using 2D devices such as mice. Increasing CPU (central processing unit) power, combined with the popularization of VRML (Virtual Reality Modeling Language; VRML, 1996) and the introduction of low-priced sound, video, and 3D graphics cards, is transforming personal computers into 3D multimedia workstations. The results thus far are evolutionary: 3D graphics appear in 2D windows and are manipulated under mouse control. Research in 3D user interfaces extends beyond this to address the use of interactive 3D graphics, audio, and haptics, presented with true 3D stereo displays and 3D interaction devices that monitor the user's actions in three-space. The goal is to harness the physiological capabilities and training that enable us to perform physical tasks effectively in 3D, and apply them to develop effective user interfaces for visualizing and accomplishing computer-based tasks.

Issues

We must develop real-time operating systems support for highly parallel asynchronous input (from large numbers of 3D trackers) and output (to multiple-display modalities). We need to build effective "augmented realities" (Caudell and Mizell, 1992; Bajura et al., 1992; Feiner et al., 1993b) that enrich the user's existing environment with additional information, merging synthesized material with what the user normally sees, hears, and feels—overlaying or replacing it, as appropriate. We need to develop display and interaction device hardware that matches our abilities better than the current offerings do, including high-quality, high-resolution, wide-field displays (e.g., graphics, sound, force, temperature) and tracking (e.g., hand, body, eye). For example, there is a need for lightweight, comfortable, high-quality, "see-through" displays for use in augmented realities. A general-purpose see-through display technology would allow differential visual accommodation, corresponding to real and virtual objects at different distances in the same image. It would also perform full visible-surface determination with all objects, real and virtual: virtual objects should be able to occlude real objects, and real objects should be able to occlude virtual ones.

How can we map abstract task domains effectively to a 3D environment in which we can visualize and manipulate objects in the domain? How can we take advantage of the richness of 3D gesture to reduce our reliance on icons to express actions in current user interfaces? For example, rather than moving an item to the trash can, could we dispose of it by using an appropriate gesture?

In a world of whole-body computer interaction, there may no longer be any distinction between human factors in general and the human factors of computer interfaces. The existing hardware that limits our capabilities (and that also limits our mistakes) will be gone, making it possible to create user interfaces that are both far better and far worse than anything we can create now. How can we ensure that 3D user interfaces are usable, especially in an environment that supports end-user programming and customization?

Projects

Much of this work is and should be multidisciplinary. For example, the design of display and interaction device hardware and software should be informed by research in human psychophysics. The design of user interface software should draw on disciplines that have long explored the design and use of 3D space, such as architecture, industrial design, theater (Laurel, 1993), and dance.

Adaptive

Background

This goal is to develop approaches that make it possible for user interfaces to adapt interactively to the needs of the current user, situation, and hardware. Adaptive multimedia user interfaces should be able to design and present information to people through multiple output media and understand user input provided through multiple input media. They should be able to adapt to the user's work mode, be it direct manipulation and exploration or passive observation.

Issues

To design high-quality adaptive multimedia user interfaces, we must first be able to design ones that function well in a single medium. We must be able to perform high-quality automated generation and understanding of individual media, ranging from those that have long been explored by artificial intelligence researchers (e.g., written text and speech) to less well-charted terrain (e.g., graphics, audio, haptics).

How can we predict and evaluate presentation quality? A system should be able to predict the quality of a presentation in the course of designing it. Based on these predictions, it should be able to refine the presentation until it is adequate. This requires the ability to evaluate the presentation (estimating how it will affect the user) and evaluating the user's response (estimating how it has affected the user). The ability to evaluate the presentation makes possible time-quality tradeoffs. For example, if our time is limited, we might prefer a "rush job" now over a higher-quality presentation later.

Temporal media are those in which information content is presented over time in a way that is controlled explicitly by the producer (Feiner et al., 1993a), such as animation, speech, and audio. We must develop generation and understanding capabilities for temporal media. Issues include how to "phrase" information (e.g., for maximal comprehension). For example, we must develop the ability to generate output and understand input that communicates complex temporal relationships. If a system can convey the relative order of actions, information need not be provided in chronological order (e.g., presenting the most important information first, as in a newscast).

We must develop facilities for coordinated generation and understanding of multiple media. The key challenge is to assure that material in different media reinforce, rather than interfere with, each other. Multimedia presentations must be temporally coordinated (especially when using temporal media such as animation and speech), so that information presented in all media is synchronized.

Given the ever-increasing amount of information bombarding us, automated multimedia generation offers the potential for automated summarization, selecting the material most relevant to a user's needs and presenting it in a way that meets their time constraints.

We must develop models that can be used as a basis for customizing the interaction between users and systems so that information is presented and obtained as effectively as possible. These models must represent:

- *Users.* Including general human cognitive and physical abilities, individual abilities and preferences, and individual users' knowledge and skills.
- *Dialogue history.* Track and maintain a history of the interaction between users and systems. This information makes possible references to things that happened in the recent or distant past.
- *Resources.* Model the generation and input resources available to the system, making it possible for the system to choose between different ways of providing or obtaining information, based on what displays and interaction devices are or will be available.
- *Activities.* The application knowledge per se, both general and specific to what the users are doing.
- *Situations.* Model current situations (e.g., routine versus crisis, individual work versus multiuser interaction).

Rather than requiring that these models be static, they should be able to be updated on the fly. Difficult problems here include being able to determine how a user is affected by a presentation. For example, can the system determine whether a user has actually learned the material that an explanatory presentation is intended to communicate? Ideally, it should be able to do this based on the user's normal interactions with the system, without requiring explicit testing.

We need to develop the facilities to model the rhetorical structure of multimedia dialogues for real, complex multiuser tasks. This includes what a user tells the system, what the system tells the user, and what users tell other users, in addition to what the user(s) and system(s) each believes the others have communicated. By studying current multimedia interactions and developing cognitive models that account for how information is being communicated among participants, we can lay the groundwork for developing rules for generating and understanding multimedia.

Projects

This research would center in the artificial intelligence and human-computer inferface communities, especially in the fields of multimedia generation and understanding (Sullivan and Tyler, 1991; Maybury, 1993) and modeling of users (Kobsa and Wahlster, 1989) and how they perform tasks (Card et al., 1983).

Integrated

Background

Integration of the NII into our lives will mean, in part, accommodating users who are mobile, and who use the NII as they move about. As displays of all sizes proliferate, this will also spell the end of the one-user, one-display metaphor that underlies so many current systems. We need to support interaction in a world in which there are many displays and interaction devices: handheld, head-worn, desktop, and wall-mounted. Some will be private, others public (or at least shared). As users walk about, they will move into and out of the presence of some of these peripherals and of other users. We need to build user interfaces that exploit this rich and constantly changing combination of peripherals.

Issues

Drawing an analogy to window management, the term *environment management* has been used (MacIntyre and Feiner, 1996) to describe the idea of managing large numbers of objects on large numbers of displays. This is a difficult task: unlike the one or two displays that most window managers typically control, the environment may be continually changing as users and resources move and may include displays and devices that are shared, such as a wall-mounted hallway display. From the user's standpoint, however, environment management should ideally be easier than the current task of window management. This could be possible if environment management were to be carried out through systems that used knowledge of the user's needs and effective information presentation approaches to determine how to structure the surrounding information environment.

Projects

Research projects should build on ongoing research in mobile computing, wearable computing, ubiquitous computing (Weiser, 1991), and augmented reality.

Collaborative

Background

User interfaces should support collaborative problem solving and interaction among multiple people and computers cooperating in the same task or in coordinated tasks.

Issues

We must design systems that account for the personal presentation needs of individual users while allowing for communication among users based on material they have been presented in common. An important problem here is how is to accommodate users who have been presented with different information and who would like to refer to the presentation as they interact with each other. The system might serve as an intelligent "go-between" that mediates between users so that references made by one user to what she has been presented are translated into references to what another user has been presented.

The NII has the potential to help create a strong sense of national (and global) community. Consider the information infrastructure provided by a residential street, town square, or college dorm hallway. By encouraging citizens to interact with others across the country and providing information about our country's workings on the NII, we could foster a better understanding of how people depend on each other and ultimately provide more opportunity for an informed populace to participate in government. Imagine, for example, a multimedia SimCity-like virtual environment that modeled the country's economy and supported collaborative attempts to see how it responded to different situations and assumptions.

Projects

There are separate communities of researchers in computer-supported cooperative work (many of whom concentrate on the design of multimedia systems in the popular sense of the term) and in distributed multiuser virtual environments. Joint research projects could be especially fruitful here.

Instructable

Two key research areas for the creation of instructable systems are programming by demonstration and agents.

Programming by Demonstration

Background. Research in end-user programming attempts to develop ways for end users to "program" an application's behavior without the overhead of learning or using a conventional programming language. One promising line of research is "programming by demonstration," in which users demonstrate the tasks to be performed using the application's interface (Cypher, 1993). A simple example is the keyboard macrofacility in e-macs: the user can specify that a series of keystrokes issued in the course of editing should be saved (and optionally named and bound to a key), so that it can be applied again, typically at another place in the document being edited. Since the demonstration is a specific example, if it is to be applied to other situations, it must be generalized. In the case of the e-macs keyboard macro, generalization is usually achieved solely by using keystroke commands that operate relative to the current position in the file.

An allied notion is that of having the system learn patterns in the user's behavior and volunteer to complete some recognized pattern when it guesses that the user has begun to perform it. Existing research systems monitor the user's interactions during a session, can present "graphical histories" of a session, allow the creation of macros using about-to-be-executed (or previously executed) commands, and can perform primitive inferencing to support simple generalization.

Issues. Most existing end-user programming facilities rely on simple straight-line flow of control (or escape into conventional programming syntax to perform all but the simplest conditionals and loops). How can end-user programs allow complex flow of control without looking and feeling like conventional programming? How can they incorporate multimodal interaction into the programming user interface itself?

How can we generalize demonstrational programs in a way that minimizes the amount of end-user involvement while maximizing the places where the system guesses right? When should generalization be performed—at program creation time, at execution time? What sources of information can be used?

If large numbers of user-developed programs exist, how can the user find the ones that are relevant to some specified task? How can the user determine what each does (without necessarily having to execute it)? Note that this is a particularly difficult example of on-line search: the user isn't looking for a match on a text string but rather on a set of capabilities, which may be implicit in the program.

How can a user-developed program be modified? How can one develop an end-user programming capability that intrinsically supports cooperation among multiple users and systems?

Projects. Most work in this domain has concentrated on 2D user interfaces. I think there is much to be gained in trying to take advantage of interactive multimedia and 3D in the design of the language itself.

Agents

Background. One kind of instructable interface is based on the metaphor of an "agent" that carries out a task on the user's behalf, often using knowledge and abilities that the user may not have herself. There has been a fair amount of heated debate in the human-computer interface community, pitting proponents of agent-based user interfaces against those who favor direct-manipulation user interfaces. Among the arguments against agents are claims that people may prefer interfaces over which they feel they have direct control and that agent-based interfaces are being unfairly touted as having some responsibility for their actions beyond that of their programmer or user.

Issues. I believe that much of the controversy is due to the popular conception of the agent as a busy-body anthropomorphic assistant, in the manner of the nattering bow-tied helper in Apple's "Knowledge Navigator" videotape. While the argument has been made that users will not want to sacrifice control to such agent-based systems, people willingly give up control in other matters that do not involve computers. For example, although it is common to compare the relative ease of using cars and computers, consider instead the car's predecessors: horses, mules, and donkeys. Environmental issues aside, would you really send even an experienced driver hurtling down the Grand Canyon's trails on a motorcycle? Yet each year thousands of folks with no previous riding experience travel those same trails safely on mules. A mule's rider exerts only discretionary high-level control with regard to general speed and direction, especially so for inexperienced riders. Riders are even told that, if acrophobia sets in, they should just close their eyes, hold on, and let the mule find its way—the original intelligent user interface. Mules are hardly anthropomorphic (although the reverse is sometimes true), yet they are possessed of skills and abilities that we don't have. While we may be amazed at how much more surefooted they are than us, we find this reassuring, not intimidating. Instead of asking why computers can't be more like cars, perhaps we should ask why computers can't be more like mules.

Projects. There is already overlap between the programming-by-demonstration and agent-based systems communities, particularly in addressing how agents can be instructed to perform tasks. Coordinated projects could address how users would determine what these systems can do (including what they can learn and what they already know). There is also potential for joint research with the multimedia generation community.

Responsive

Background

The goal is to build systems that can utilize the power available throughout the NII in a way that doesn't compromise the responsiveness of the user interface.

Issues

Resources needed to make a responsive system include not only network bandwidth and computational power but also appropriately sized and sited storage. While we can assume that users will have personal storage space at home, permanent or temporary mirroring of material at additional sites throughout the NII might be able to significantly decrease network load and response time. For example, we might have a system of large public storage caches located throughout the country to provide users with relatively local copies of frequently referenced material. This could include both conventional "mirror" sites and caches of currently accessed material controlled by some automated paging strategy. This could be the next tier in a caching system that would include the individual local memory and disk caches of current Web browsers.

Projects

Many of the issues here build on research being done in the systems

(OS and distributed systems) and multimedia storage/transport communities.

Empowering

Background

Plainly put, we need to study the kinds of things that people do and determine how the NII can best assist in doing them. In part, this will involve building the models of activities mentioned previously.

Issues

I trust that falling prices will ultimately put any technology that has the potential to be popular within the reach of all. This has happened with television, microwave ovens, Walkman-style tape players, digital watches, and compact-disc changers. It is about to happen with computers, be they net-tops, set-tops, palm-tops, or something else. Unlike fixed-function devices, however, computers (in particular, computer programs) have an essentially unlimited potential to confuse and intimidate. While much of this potential can be mitigated through better user interface design, there is no substitute for users having the right skills and mindset. Even if we can build powerful systems that are truly "self-teaching," users will still need time to learn how to use them effectively. We need to ensure not only that computer skills (whatever that might mean in the future) are taught in school but also that there is ample opportunity and time for people who are not in school to acquire them.

Projects

Experimental studies and model building by academic and industrial researchers address only one part of the problem. Enlightened social and governmental policies also will be key.

REFERENCES

Bajura, M., Fuchs, H., and Ohbuchi, R. 1992. Merging Virtual Objects with the Real World: Seeing Ultrasound Imagery Within the Patient. *Computer Graphics* 26(2):203-210.

Card, S., Moran, T., and Newell, A. 1983. *The Psychology of Human-Computer Interaction.* Lawrence Erlbaum Associates, Hillsdale, N.J.

Card, S.K., Robertson, G.G., and Mackinlay, J.D. 1991. *Proceedings of the Computer Human Interactions: Human Factors in Computing Systems,* pp. 181-188. The Information Visualizer, An Information Workspace. New Orleans, La., April 28-May 2.

Caudell, T., and Mizell, D. 1992. Augmented Reality: An Application of Heads-Up Display

Technology to Manual Manufacturing Processes, *Proceedings of the Hawaii International Conference on System Science,* January.

Cypher, A. (Ed.). 1993. *Watch What I Do: Programming by Demonstration,* MIT Press, Cambridge, Mass.

Feiner, S., Litman, D., McKeown, K., and Passonneau, R. 1993a. Towards Coordinated Temporal Multimedia Presentations. *Intelligent Multimedia Interfaces,* M. Maybury (Ed.), pp. 139-147. AAAI/MIT Press, Menlo Park, Calif.

Feiner, S., MacIntyre, B., and Seligmann, D. 1993b. Knowledge-Based Augmented Reality. *Communications of the ACM* 36(7):52-2.

Gershon, N., and Eick, S. (Eds.). 1995. *Proc. Information Visualization '95.* IEEE Computer Society Press, Los Alamitos, Calif.

Kobsa, A., and Wahlster, W. (Eds.). 1989. *User Models in Dialogue Systems.* Springer-Verlag, Berlin.

Kramer, G. (Ed.). 1994. *Auditory Display: Sonification, Audification, and Auditory Interfaces.* Addison-Wesley, Reading, Mass.

Laurel, B. 1993. *Computers as Theatre.* Addison-Wesley, Reading, Mass.

MacIntyre, B., and Feiner, S. 1996. Future Multimedia User Interfaces. *Multimedia Systems.*

Maybury, M. (Ed). 1993. *Intelligent Multimedia Interfaces.* AAAI/MIT Press, Menlo Park, Calif.

Sullivan, J., and Tyler, S. (Eds.). 1991. *Intelligent User Interfaces.* Addison-Wesley, Reading, Mass.

VRML (Virtual Reality Modeling Language). 1996. The VRML Forum (available on-line at http://vrml.wired.com/).

Weiser, M. 1991. The Computer for the 21st Century. *Scientific American* 265(3):94-104.

NOMADICITY, DISABILITY ACCESS, AND
THE EVERY-CITIZEN INTERFACE

Gregg C. Vanderheiden
University of Wisconsin-Madison

THE CHALLENGE

With the rapid evolution of the national information infrastructure (NII) and the global information infrastructure (GII), attention has turned to the issue of information equality and universal access. Basically, if information systems become as integral to our future life-styles as electricity is today, access to these systems will be essential for people to have equal access to education, employment, and even daily entertainment or enrichment activities.

Although the goal of equal access seems noble, it can seem somewhat less achievable when one considers the full range of abilities or disabilities which must be dealt with to achieve an every-citizen interface. It must be usable even if people

- cannot see very well—or at all;
- cannot hear very well—or at all;
- cannot read very well—or at all;
- cannot move their heads or arms very well—or at all;
- cannot speak very well—or at all;
- cannot feel with their fingers very well—or at all;
- are short, are tall, use a wheelchair, and so forth;
- cannot remember well;
- have difficulty learning or figuring things out;
- have little or no technological inclination or ability; and/or
- have any combination of these difficulties (e.g., are deaf-blind;

have reduced visual, hearing, physical, or cognitive abilities, which occurs in many older individuals).

In addition, the products and their interfaces must remain equally efficient and easy to use and understand for those who (1) have no problems seeing, hearing, moving, remembering, and so forth; and (2) are power users.

Is It Possible?

A list like this can bring a designer up short. At first blush, it appears that even if such an interface was possible it would be impractical or inefficient to use for people with all of their abilities intact. Packages such as the EZ Access approach developed for kiosks (http://trace.wisc.edu/world/kiosk), PDAs (personal digital assistants), and other touchscreen devices, however, demonstrate how close we can come to such an ideal, at least for some types of devices or systems. Using a combination of Talking Fingertip and Speed List technologies, the EZ Access package (for information, see http://trace.wisc.edu/TEXT/KIOSK/MINIMUM.HTM) provides efficient access for individuals with low vision, blindness, and poor or no reading skills. A ShowSounds/caption feature provides access for individuals with hearing impairments or deafness, as well as access for all users in very noisy locations. An infrared link allows the system to be used easily with alternate displays and controllers, so that even individuals who are deaf-blind or paralyzed can access and use the system. Thus, with a relatively modest set of interface variations, almost all the needs listed above can be addressed.

Is It Practical?

Practicality is a complex issue which involves cost, complexity, impact on overall marketability, support, and so forth. To use the EZ Access approach as an example, the hardware cost to provide all of these dimensions of accessibility to a standard multimedia kiosk is less than 1 percent of the cost of the kiosk. Addition of this technique does not affect the standard or traditional mode of operation of the kiosk at all. At the same time, it makes the system usable by many visitors as well as new citizens whose native language is not English, and who may have some difficulty with words. Implementing cross-disability interface strategies can take only a few days with the proper tools. EZ Access techniques are currently used on commercial kiosks in the Mall of America and other locations. Other examples of built-in accessibility are the access features that are built into every Macintosh- and Windows 95-based computer.

Thus, if done properly, interfaces that are flexible or adjustable enough to address a wide range of individuals can be very practical. There are, however, approaches to provide additional access or access for additional populations that are not currently practical (e.g., building $2,000 dynamic braille displays into every terminal or kiosk). In these cases, the most practical approach may be to make the information and control necessary for operation of the device available on a standard connector so that a person who is deaf and blind can connect a braille display and keyboard. Practicality also is a function of the way the access features relate to and reinforce the overall interface goals of the product.

HOW DOES AN EVERY-CITIZEN INTERFACE RELATE TO NOMADIC SYSTEMS?

The devices of tomorrow, which might be referred to as TeleTransInfoCom (tele-transaction/information/communication) devices, will operate in a wide range of environments. Miniaturization, advances in wireless communication, and thin-client architectures are rapidly eliminating the need to be tied to a workstation or carry a large device in order to have access to computing, communication, and information services and functions.

As a result, we will need interfaces for use while driving a car, sitting in an easy chair, sitting in a library, participating in a meeting, walking down the street, sitting on the beach, walking through a noisy shopping mall, taking a shower, or relaxing in a bathtub, as well as sitting at a desk. The interfaces also will have to be usable in hostile environments—when camping or hiking, in factories or shopping malls at Christmas time.

Many of us will also need to access our information appliance (or appliances) in very different environments on the same day—perhaps even during the same communication or interaction activity. These different environments will place constraints on the type of physical and sensory input and output techniques that work (e.g., it is difficult to use a keyboard when walking; it is difficult and dangerous to use visual displays when driving a car; speech input and output, which work fine in a car, may not be usable in a shared office environment, a noisy mall, a meeting, or a library). Systems designed to work across these environments will therefore require flexible input/output options to work in different environments. The interface variations, however, must operate in essentially the same way, even though they may be quite different (visual versus aural). Users will not want to master three or four interface paradigms in order to operate their devices in different environments. The metaphor(s) and the "look and feel" must be continuous even though the devices operate entirely visually at one point (e.g., in a meeting) or entirely aurally at another (e.g., while driving a car). Many users will also want to be able to move from one environment to another, one device to another (e.g., workstation to hand-held), and one mode to another (e.g., visual to voice) in the midst of a task.

DOES NOMADICITY EQUAL DISABILITY ACCESSIBLE?

It is interesting to note that most of the issues regarding access for people with disabilities will be addressed if we simply address the issues raised by the range of environments described above:

• When we create interfaces that work well in noisy environments such as airplanes, construction sites, or shopping malls at Christmas, and for people who must listen to something else while they use their device, we will have created interfaces that work well for people who cannot hear well or at all.

• When we create interfaces that work well for people who are driving a car or doing something that makes it unsafe to look at the device they are operating, we will have created interfaces that can be used by people who cannot see.

• As we develop very small pocket and wearable devices for circumstances in which it is difficult to use a full-sized keyboard or even a large number of keys, we will have developed techniques that can be used by individuals with some types of physical disabilities.

• When we create interfaces that can be used by someone whose hands are occupied, we will have systems that are accessible to people who cannot use their hands.

• When we create interfaces for individuals who are tired, under stress, under the influence of drugs (legal or illegal), or simply in the midst of a traumatic event or emergency (and who may have little ability to concentrate or deal with complexity), we will have interfaces that can be used by people with naturally reduced abilities to concentrate or deal with complexity.

Thus, although there may be residual specifics concerning disability access that must be covered, the bulk of the issues involved are addressed automatically through the process of developing environment/situation-independent (modality-independent) interfaces.

WHAT IS NEEDED?

Interfaces that are independent of the environment or the individual must have the following attributes:

• *Wide variability in order to meet the diversity of tasks that will be addressed.* Some interfaces will have to deal only with text capture, transmission, and display. Others will have to deal with display, editing, and manipulation of audiovisual materials. Some may involve VR (virtual reality), but basically be shop-and-select strategies. Others may require full immersion, such as data visualization and tele-presence.

• *Modality independence.* Interfaces have to allow the user to choose sensory modalities appropriate to the environment, situation, or user.

Text-based systems will allow users to display information visually at some times and aurally at others, on high-resolution displays when available and on smaller low-resolution displays when necessary.

• *Flexibility/adaptability.* Interfaces will be required that can take advantage of fine motor movements and three-dimensional gestures when a user's situation or abilities allow but can also be operated by using speech, keyboard, or other input techniques when this is necessary because of the environment, the user's activities, or any motor constraints.

• *Straight forwardness and ease of use.* As much of the population as possible must be able to use these interfaces and to master new functions and capabilities as they are introduced.

SOME COMPONENTS NECESSARY TO ACHIEVE EVERY-CITIZEN INTERFACES

Although this section does not address all possible interface types, particularly freehand graphic production interfaces (e.g. painting), it does address the majority of command-and-control interfaces.

1. *Modality Independence.* For a device or system to be modality independent or alt-modal (i.e., the user can choose between alternate sensory modalities when operating the device), two things are necessary:

a. All of the basic information must be stored and available in either modality-independent or modality-redundant form.

Modality independent refers to information that is stored in a form that is not tied to any particular form of presentation. For example, ASCII text is not inherently visual, auditory, or tactile. It can be presented easily on a visual display or printer (visually), through a voice synthesizer (aurally), or through a dynamic braille display or braille printer (tactually).

Modality redundant refers to information that is stored in multiple modalities. For example, a movie might include a visual description of the audio track (e.g., caption) and an audio and electronic text description of the video track so that all (or essentially all) information can be presented visually, aurally, or tactually at the user's request based on need, preference, or environmental situation.

b. The system must be able to display data or information in different modalities. That is, it should provide a mechanism for displaying information in all-visual, or all-auditory, or mixed audiovisual form as well as in electronic form.

2. *Flexibility/Adjustability.* The device must also offer alternate selection techniques that can accommodate varying physical and sensory abilities arising from the personal environment or situation (e.g., walking,

wearing heavy gloves), and/or personal abilities. Suggested alternate operating modes follow:

• *Standard mode.* This mode often uses multiple simultaneous senses and fine motor movements. It would offer the most effective device for individuals who have no restrictions on their abilities (due to task, environment, or disability).

• *A list mode.* In this mode, the user can call up a list of all the information and action items and use the list to select items for presentation or action. It would not require vision to operate. It could be operated using an analog transducer to allow the individual to move up and down within a list, or a keyboard or arrow keys combined with a confirm button could be used. This mode can be used by individuals who are unable to see or look at a device.

• *External list mode.* This would make the list available externally through a software or hardware port (e.g., infrared port) and accept selections through the same port. It can be used by individuals who are unable to see and hear the display and therefore must access it from an external auxiliary interface. This would include artificial intelligent agents, which are unable to process visual or auditory information that is unavailable in text form.

• *Select and confirm mode.* This allows individuals to obtain information about items without activating them (a separate confirm action is used to activate items after they are selected). It can be used by individuals with reading difficulties, low vision, or physical movement problems, as well as by individuals in unstable environments or whose movements are awkward due to heavy clothing or other factors.

• *Auto-step scanning mode.* This presents the individual items in groups or sequentially for the user to select. It can be used by individuals with severe movement limitations or movement and visual constraints (e.g., driving a car), and when direct selection (e.g., speech input) techniques are not practicable.

• *Direct text control techniques.* These include keyboard or speech input.

EXAMPLE: USING A UNI-LIST-BASED ARCHITECTURE AS PART OF THE INTERFACE

One approach to device design that would support this type of flexibility is the Uni-List architecture. By maintaining a continually updated listing of all the information items currently available to the user, as well as all the actions or commands available, it is possible to provide a very flexible and adjustable user interface relatively easily. All the techniques listed above are easy to implement with such an architecture, and it can be applied to a range of devices or systems.

Take, for example, a three-dimensional (3D) virtual reality-based shopping mall. In such an application, a database is used to provide the information needed to generate the image seen by the user and the responses to user movements or actions on objects in the view. If properly constructed, this database could also provide a continually updated listing of all objects in view as well as information about any actionable objects presented to the user at any time. By including verbal (e.g., text) information about the various objects and items, this 3D virtual shopping system can be navigated and used in a variety of ways to accommodate a variety of users or situations.

- Individuals who are unable to see the screen (because they are driving their car, their eyes are otherwise occupied, or they are blind) can have the information and choices presented vocally (or via braille). They can then select items from the list in order to act on them, in much the same that an individual can pick up or "click on" an object in the environment.
- Individuals with movement disabilities can have a highlight or "sprite" step around to the objects, or they could indicate the approximate location and have the items in that location highlighted individually (other methods for disambiguating also could be used) to select the desired item.
- Individuals who are unable to read can touch or select any printed text presented and have it read aloud to them.
- Individuals with low vision (or who do not have their glasses) can use the system in the same way as a fully sighted individual. When they are unable to see well enough to identify the objects, they can switch into a mode that lets them touch the objects (without activating them) and can thereby have them named or described.
- Individuals who are deaf-blind could use the device in the same fashion as an individual who is blind. Instead of the information being spoken, however, it could be sent to the individual's dynamic braille display.

ADDITIONAL BENEFITS OF FLEXIBLE, MODALITY-INDEPENDENT ARCHITECTURES AND DATA FORMATS

The two key underlying strategies for providing more universal access are input and display flexibility and the companion availability of information in sensory/modality-independent or parallel form.

Both input and display flexibility and presentation independence have additional benefits beyond the every-citizen interface. These include the following:

- *Nomadicity support* (discussed above).
- *Searchability.* Graphic and auditory information that contains text streams can be indexed and found by using standard text-based search engines, which not only can locate items but also can jump to particular points within a movie or a sound file.
- *Alternate client support.* The same information can be stored and served to different types of telecommunication and information devices. For example, information could be accessed graphically over the Internet, via a telephone by using a verbal form, or even by intelligent (or not so intelligent) agents using electronic text form.
- *Display flexibility.* Presentation-independent information also tends to be display size independent, allowing it to be more easily accessed using very small, low-resolution displays. (In fact, some low-resolution displays present exactly the same issues as low vision.)
- *Low bandwidth.* The ability to switch to text or verbal presentation can speed access over low-bandwidth connections.
- *Future Support.* Modality-independent servers will also be better able to handle future serving needs that may involve access to information using different modalities. Creating a legacy system that cannot handle or serve information in different modalities may necessitate a huge rework job in the future as systems evolve and are deployed.

LIMITATIONS

Today, most of the universal access strategies are limited to information that can easily be presented verbally (in words). However, although the Grand Canyon could be presented in three dimensions through virtual reality, its full impact cannot be captured in words, nor can a Picasso painting or Mahler symphony easily be made sensory modality independent. Also, although planes could be designed to fly themselves, we do not as yet know how to allow a user who is blind to control directly flight that currently requires eye-hand coordination (or its equivalent). There are also situations in which the underlying task requires greater cognitive skills than an individual may possess, regardless of the cognitive skills required to operate the interface. It may be a while before we resolve some of these limitations to access.

On the other hand, we also have many examples where interfaces that were previously thought to be unusable by individuals with a particular disability, were later made easily accessible. The difference was simply the presence or absence of an idea. The challenge, therefore, is to discover and develop strategies and tools that can make next-generation interfaces accessible to and usable by greater numbers of individuals and easier for all to use.

SUMMARY

Through the incorporation of presentation-independent data structures, an available information/command menu, and several easy-to-program selection options, it is possible to create interfaces that begin to approximate the anytime-anywhere-anyone (AAA) interface goal. Some interfaces of this type have been constructed and are now being used in public information kiosks to provide access to individuals with a wide range of abilities. The same strategies can be incorporated into next-generation TeleTransInfoCom devices to provide users with the nomadicity they will require in next-generation Internet appliances.

Before long, individuals will look for systems that allow them to begin an important communication at their desk, continue it as they walk to their car, and finish it while driving to their next appointment. Similarly, users will want the ability to move freely between high- and low-bandwidth systems to meet their needs and circumstances. They will want to access their information databases by using visual displays and perhaps advanced data visualization and navigation strategies while at a desk, but auditory-only systems as they walk to their next appointment. They may even wish to access their personal rolodexes or people databases while engaged in conversations at a social gathering (by using a pocket keypad and an earphone to ask, What is Mary Jones' husband's name?).

The approaches discussed will also allow these systems to address issues of equity such as providing access to those with disabilities or those with lower-technology and lower-bandwidth devices and providing support for intelligent (or not-so-intelligent) agent software. The AAA strategies discussed here do not provide full cross-environment access to all types of interface or information systems. In particular, as noted above, fully immersive systems that presented inherently graphic (e.g., paintings) or auditory (e.g., symphonies) information will not be accessible to anyone who does not employ the primary senses for which this information was prepared (text descriptions are insufficient). However, the majority of today's information and most services can be made available through these approaches, and extensions may provide access to even more.

Finally, it is important to note that not only do environment/situation-independent interfaces and disability-accessible interfaces appear to be closely related, but also one of the best ways to explore environment/

situation-independent nomadic interface strategies may be the exploration of past and developing means for providing cross-disability access to computer and information systems.

CHALLENGES AND RESEARCH AREAS

For a system to be more accessible to and usable by every citizen, it must be (1) perceivable, (2) operable, and (3) understandable.

The following areas of research can help to address these needs:

- Data structures, compression, and transport formats that allow the incorporation of alternate modalities or modality-independent data (e.g., text embedded in sound files or graphic files);
- Techniques and architectures for partial serving of information, (such as the ability to fetch only the visual, the auditory, the text, or any combination of these tracks from a multimedia file or to fetch one part of a file from one location and another part from a second location (e.g., fetching a movie from one location and the captions from another);
- Modality substitution strategies (e.g., techniques for restructuring data so that ear-hand coordination can be substituted for eye-hand coordination);
- Natural language interfaces (e.g., the ability to have information presented conversationally and to control products with conversation, whether via speech or "typed" text);
- Alternate, substitute, and remote interface communication protocols (e.g., robust communication protocols that allow sensory- and presentation-independent alternate interfaces to be connected to and used with devices having less flexible interfaces);
- Voice-tolerant speech recognition (ability to deal with disarthric and deaf speech);
- Dynamic tactile displays (two- and three-dimensional tactile and force feedback 3D);
- Better random access to information/functions (instead of tree walking); and
- Speed-List (e.g., EZ Access) equivalent access to structured VR environments.

ON FUNCTIONS

COMPUTER-MEDIATED COLLABORATION

Loren Terveen
AT&T Research

INTERFACE . . . INTERACTION . . . COLLABORATION

A narrow view of the human-computer interface focusing on superficial "look-and-feel" issues is unproductive. It offers neither deep understanding nor practical design guidance. Even simple interface decisions may require significant knowledge about people's interaction with a system. Three interfaces provide practical examples: the popcorn button on microwave ovens, the VCR (video cassette recorder)+ system, and the ATM (automated teller machine) fast cash withdrawal button. Each of these interfaces was added years into the product cycle in response to people's actual use of the products. At a theoretical level, Hutchins et al. (1986) couched their seminal analysis of direct manipulation interfaces in terms of users' cognitive situation and resources, a general model of tasks, and the coupling between user goals and interface features. Their analysis shows why interface design decisions cannot be made on the basis of look and feel alone.

Indeed, we also begin to see that people may require even more from systems, namely help with tasks they don't know enough about to do on their own. Norman (1986) observed that the Pinball Construction Set makes it easy to design computerized pinball games but not good games; this takes knowledge about pinball design. More generally, Schoen (1983) discussed how skilled professionals can interpret the state of their work objects to make good decisions; they act and the situation "talks back." The problem is that less skilled people may not be able to understand what the situation is "saying." Fischer and Reeves (1992) studied interactions between customers and sales agent in a large hardware store. They identified crucial knowledge only the sales agents possessed, which they used to help customers. The knowledge included knowing that a tool existed, how to find a tool, the conditions under which a particular tool should be used, and how to combine tools for a specific situation.

People often work together on tasks. Thus, in addition to collaborating with users, another appropriate role for systems is to support human collaboration. The field of computer-supported cooperative work (CSCW) seeks to understand the nature of joint work and design technologies to support it. Important technologies include shared editors, group discussion support tools, and awareness systems.

Even when people do not work together explicitly, they still can benefit from the prior experience and opinions of others. Computational techniques for mining such information and turning it into a reusable asset raise the potential for a form of "virtual collaboration," with some of the benefits of collaboration without the costs of communication or personal involvement.

To summarize, there are three fundamental motivations for collaborative systems and a research approach built on each one:

- Tasks require specialized skills and knowledge → Intelligent collaborative agents
- Work is inherently social → Computer-supported cooperative work
- People can reuse the experience of others → Virtual collaboration

Next I discuss the prospects for collaboration in common tasks supported by the national information infrastructure (NII).

THE NII—WHAT PEOPLE USE IT FOR, WHERE COLLABORATION IS NEEDED

The change from stand-alone to networked computers is transforming computers from desktop tools into windows on the world, from information containers and processors into communication devices. The

World Wide Web is the primary innovation ushering ordinary citizens into this new world, so much of my discussion focuses on the Web.

The World Wide Web was designed expressly to support communication and collaboration among geographically distributed colleagues (Berners-Lee et al., 1994). Specifically, it supports information sharing, with the dual aspects of publishing and finding information. As the Web has expanded to embrace a diverse population of users and a broad range of uses, more activities have become important:

- Person-person communication (e.g., through e-mail or "newsgroups"; entertainment, arts, and advertising; from Web sites for the latest movies to high-quality on-line magazines to serious (or not-so-serious) artistic sites).
- Commerce—offering items for sale, finding items that match one's interests; brokering between buyers and sellers.
- Education—for example, on-line course materials, interactive tutorials, and distributed science experiments.

Let us next consider the role of collaboration in these activities:

- *Information sharing.* Information seekers need assistance in finding high-quality, relevant information in the vast, ever-changing sea of Web sites. Information publishers need assistance in designing functional and attractive interactive applications.
- *Person-person communication.* All the major CSCW issues arise here (e.g., shared document access, discussion support, awareness aids).
- *Entertainment, arts, and advertising.* There is great potential for computational agents in interactive fiction, social role-playing environments, and games (Lifelike Computer Characters Conference—http://www.research.microsoft.com/lcc.htm; Maes, 1995).
- *Commerce.* Computational match-making agents can bring together buyers and sellers. Support for communication protocols such as auctions also is important.
- *Education.* Computational agents can engage learners. Teachers and students need support for communicating and working together (e.g., to complete assignments and carry out experiments).

COMPUTER-MEDIATED COLLABORATION: A UNIFYING PERSPECTIVE

A unified research framework offers two main benefits: (1) it advances communication and understanding among researchers by helping them to share and compare methods and results, and (2) it makes it easier to explore designs that integrate different types of collaboration. I propose a perspective of "computer-mediated collaboration"—people collaborating with people, mediated by computation.

A given instance of computer-mediated collaboration can be characterized by using the following dimensions:

- roles and responsibilities of the human participants;
- nature of the computational mediation, including;
  —how information is acquired, processed, and distributed;
  —whether the information evolves during (and in response to) system usage;
  —temporal properties of the mediation (e.g., synchronous vs. asynchronous, time delays); and
  —nature of the human-computer interaction.

This framework is adequate for describing CSCW and virtual collaboration; both of these explore computational techniques for mediating human collaboration. As applied to collaborative agents, it highlights the involvement of the people who create the agents, both domain experts whose knowledge is modeled in the agents and knowledge engineers (or artificial intelligence researchers) who work with the experts to articulate the knowledge and develop representations and algorithms for using it. It also reminds us of the time and resource costs of the design process.

More deeply, the framework guides us to consider combinations of various types of collaboration. For example, users of a computational agent may not think about its designers when things work; however, when the user-agent interaction breaks down, an effective remedy may be to provide the user access to a knowledgeable human expert, such as the domain expert involved in designing the agent (Terveen et al., 1995). Or when an agent has inadequate knowledge to perform a task on behalf of its user, it might be able to obtain assistance from other agents (Lashkari et al., 1994).

RESEARCH ISSUES

Dividing Responsibility Among People and Computational Agents

People and computers have fundamentally different abilities. Thus, a basic issue is creating divisions of responsibility that maximize the strengths and minimize the weaknesses of each (Terveen, 1995). "Critics" (Fischer et al., 1993) represent a well-known approach that responds to this issue. Critics are agents who observe users as they work in a computational environment and offer assistance from time to time. Users are responsible for the overall course of the work, while critics use domain expertise to help users solve problems and evolve their conception of the problem. While much interesting work has been done in this area, most of it still consists of proof-of-concept explorations. The next step is to develop robust generalizations that can be embedded in toolkits.

Collecting and Evaluating Data Necessary for Virtual Collaboration

Two major approaches to virtual collaboration have been explored. Systems like the Bellcore Recommender (Hill et al., 1995) and Firefly (http://www.firefly.com) ask users to rate objects of interest, such as movies or music. The systems maintain a database of raters and their ratings, compute similarities among raters, and recommend objects to people that were rated highly by other people with similar tastes. Data-mining approaches (Hill and Hollan, 1994; Hill and Terveen, 1996) attempt to extract useful information automatically from people's normal activities, such as reading and editing documents or discussing topics on netnews. (One goal is to require little or no extra data entry from users.) Abstracted versions of this information are then made available to other people engaged in the same activity.

One of the major issues for both types of approaches is obtaining the necessary information. For ratings systems the question is: Will enough people rate? For data-mining systems, the questions include: Can useful information be extracted automatically? Can it be extracted efficiently (important since quality often comes from aggregating over large amounts of data)? Can it be extracted and reused without violating the privacy of the people who produced it?

Once data—recommendations or ratings—are available, the problem is to evaluate them. One good way to do this is to consider the source; some people are more credible for any given topic. Therefore, computing a person's credibility from available data is a second major problem. One complication is that most interaction on the World Wide Web is anonymous; if one cannot even attribute particular actions or opinions to a person, it is hard to compute his or her credibility. This again raises a potential conflict in values between the privacy of on-line interaction and the attempt to mine information that could be used to enhance interaction.

The credibility problem can be further refined into that of determining good sources (raters/recommenders) for a specific person. Developing effective algorithms for this is precisely what the ratings approach does. However, the problem is harder for data-mining approaches: they operate only on already-available data, and existing data may not always be an adequate source for computing similarities among people.

Introducing Computational Agents into On-line Communities

When an agent participates in an on-line community, such as a newsgroup or text-based virtual reality (e.g., a MUD or MOO), interesting issues arise beyond those faced in single-user human-computer collaboration. I illustrate these issues using PHOAKS (Hill and Terveen, 1996), which serves as a group memory agent that maintains recommended Web pages for a group.

• Will the community accept the agent's participation? Every community has behavioral norms. An agent ought not violate these norms (the norms for an agent may well be different than those for people). Some concern has been expressed that the PHOAKS ranking of Web resources by frequency of mention might distort community behavior (e.g., inducing people to post many spurious messages recommending their favorite resources). Thus, one must consider not only whether an agent respects community norms but also whether its participation may cause others to violate the norms.

• Does the agent make a useful contribution to the community? In Foner's (http://foner.www.media.mit.edu/people/foner/Julia/Julia.html) discussion of the interesting social characteristics of the "Julia" agent, he points out that "she" serves useful functions, including taking and delivering messages, giving navigation advice, and sharing gossip. We also should consider to whom an agent is to be useful (e.g., community insiders, newcomers, or outsiders), especially since their interests may be different. For example, PHOAKS could make it easy to contact community participants by e-mail (or even by telephone). While outsiders might find this an attractive way to get information, presumably the community participants would be displeased.

• Will the community help make the agent smarter? An agent begins its participation in a community with some knowledge. If the agent has the capability to learn, and the community will offer necessary input the agent can improve over time. For example, PHOAKS maintains a ranked set of Web pages for each newsgroup based on its categorization of URL mentions in messages. However, it will miscategorize some URLs, and some important URLs may not be mentioned or may be mentioned infrequently, perhaps because they are so well known (e.g., they may be in the FAQ). Therefore, PHOAKS contains forms that allow people to give opinions on the Web pages it links to and to add additional links. The general problem is to create techniques that let the system obtain performance-enhancing feedback and that people are willing and able to use. Or machine learning techniques may be used that let agents learn on their own.

• Who stands behind the agent? Sometimes community members want to talk to the people behind the agent. Maybe they want more information, or maybe the agent has done something that makes them angry. We have seen both in PHOAKS. People ask questions about the topic of a newsgroup, like where to find a bagpiper. People complain about the way PHOAKS has categorized Web pages; for example, in rare cases a condemnation of a Web page (e.g., from a hate group) is categorized as a recommendation. Sometimes, we have manually changed the PHOAKS databases, and less frequently we have modified the categorization algorithms or interface. The general problem is how to provide needed human backup for agents who may be participating in many (e.g., thousands of) different communities at once.

CONCLUSION

I would like to conclude with two claims. First, if we take the argument of this paper seriously, we need not one but many every-citizen interfaces to the NII. It is specific appropriate types of computer-mediated collaborations that have the potential to increase the access and power of ordinary citizens, not a standard look-and-feel. Second, research must move into the real world. Many of the PHOAKS issues discussed here are ones not anticipated, but discovered only by wading into the uncontrolled, unpredictable, messy World Wide Web. We have been able to formulate issues, hone our tools, and evaluate our results in ways that we could not have done if we had stayed in our laboratories. At some stage, all promising new research ideas will have to take the same plunge to prove their benefits to the ordinary citizen engaging in life on the NII.

ACKNOWLEDGMENTS

I thank Will Hill for our collaboration on PHOAKS and for our many conversations developing and exploring the issues mentioned here.

REFERENCES

Berners-Lee, T., Cailliau, R., Luotonen, A., Nielsen, H.F., and Secret, A. (1994) The World-Wide Web. *Communications of the ACM*, 34(12), 321-347.

Fischer, G., and Reeves, B. (1992) Beyond Intelligent Interfaces: Exploring, Analyzing, and Creating Success Models of Cooperative Problem Solving. *Applied Intelligence*, 1, 311-332.

Fischer, G., Nakakoji, K., Ostwald, J., Stahl, G., and Sumner, T. (1993) Embedding Critics in Design Environments. *The Knowledge Engineering Review Journal*, 4(8), 285-307.

Hill, W.C., and Hollan, J.D. (1994) History-Enriched Digital Objects: Prototypes and Policy Issues. *The Information Society*, 10, 139-145.

Hill, W.C., Stead, L., Rosenstein, M., and Furnas, G. (1995) Recommending and Evaluating Choices in a Virtual Community of Use. Pp. 194-201 in *CHI'95*. ACM Press, New York.

Hill, W.C., and Terveen, L.G. (1996) Using Frequency-of-Mention in Public Conversations for Social Filtering. *CSCW'96*. ACM Press, New York. (See also http://www.phoaks.com/phoaks/)

Hutchins, E.L., Hollan, J.D., and Norman, D.A. (1986) Direct Manipulation Interfaces. Pp. 87-124 in Norman, D.A., and Draper, S.W., Eds., *User Centered System Design*. Erlbaum, Hillsdale, N.J.

Lashkari, Y., Metral, M., and Maes, P. (1994) Collaborative Interface Agents. In *AAAI'94*. AAAI Press, Seattle, Wash.

Maes, P. (1995) Artificial Life Meets Entertainment: Interacting with Lifelike Autonomous Agents. *Communications of the ACM*, 38(11), 108-114.

Norman, D.A. (1986) Cognitive Engineering. Pp. 31-61 in Norman, D.A. and Draper, S. W., Eds., *User Centered System Design*. Erlbaum, Hillsdale, N.J.

Schoen, D. (1983) *The Reflective Practitioner*. Basic Books, New York.

Terveen, L.G. (1995) An Overview of Human-Computer Collaboration. *Knowledge-Based Systems*, 8(2-3), 67-31.

Terveen, L.G, Selfridge, P.G., and Long, M.D. (1995) Living Design Memory: Framework, System, and Lessons Learned. *Human-Computer Interaction*, 10(1), 1-37.

CREATING INTERFACES
FOUNDED ON PRINCIPLES OF DISCOURSE
COMMUNICATION AND COLLABORATION

Candace Sidner
Lotus Development Corporation

Today's user interfaces are just too hard to use: they are too complex even for the narrow range of users for whom they were designed. At the same time, they also are impoverished in the range of modalities which they provide to users. While new modalities are becoming available, they could make interfaces even harder to use. What's the solution to this dilemma? Principles of human discourse communication and of human-to-human collaboration are two critically overlooked sources for simplifying interfaces. They offer a means of integrating various modalities and of extending the range of computer users.

Until recently user interface technology has not made use of what is now understood about the principles of discourse that govern human communication or the principles of collaboration that model joint work. This may seem surprising because interfaces are "communication engines" to the functionality software applications; interfaces are how we get our work done. While the field of computer-supported cooperative work has directed the majority of its concerns at understanding how computers can be used to help people work together, the computer has not been seen as a full-fledged partner in the human collaboration. Interfaces are designed to make collaboration between people better and to some extent they succeed, but the computer is not a collaborator with any of the people.

The current model of communication in interfaces is rudimentary at best. It is the "interaction" model, which is to say the user invokes a command and gets some, perhaps expected, performance by the computer, rather like when one's dog does a trick on the basis of a command such as "roll over." To communicate, users must choose one- or two-word commands from a menu with a mouse or incant a line of mumbo-jumbo that is meant to command the computer to run a program. Any clarification with the user results from the user responding to "dialogue boxes."

This interaction model of communication is, in the weakest sense, a dialogue: some information flows between two agents who are capable of acting on that information. While an interface to a given application may have hundreds of so-called dialogue boxes, dialogue in the human sense does not take place. There is no structure to the overall dialogue between user and interface from one dialogue box to the next and no memory of past dialogues or commands. Each command and action pairing is taken as completely independent of the next, so that there is no overall organization around the purposive intent of the overall set of "interactions" between the user and the machine.

Just as a dog doesn't always do what you tell it to, computers don't either. The interface is meant to inform users about what the computer can do, but, as we all know, short phrases are especially ambiguous in human language. Users have little means to resolve this ambiguity. If the meaning of a command is not obvious to them, they can at best try it out and hope that it does what they want, or they can make their way through a help system to determine if they are on the right track. All the while, they are required to be very explicit about every reference to objects, such as a files, that they make. While the user bears the burden of being explicit, the interface often communicates with ambiguity back to the user. For example, what should the user conclude is the meaning of the "ok" button in a dialogue box? "Yes, that's fine with me, I agree," or "I understood the words," or "well, I read the words" are possible, though in human discourse, these uses of "ok" convey very different responses to the content of utterances in the dialogue. Because users cannot communicate these distinctions, it becomes clear to them that the computer interface does not really know what it is doing. It's just a dumb machine.

Being able to be a collaborator is three steps up on the ladder of communication and work. The first is minimal interaction. Today's interfaces do not pass the "minimality test" because they do not know enough to do so. Only the user does any modeling or remembering of the interaction and its parts. Whatever role the machine has played in the interaction it completely forgets when it completes the action requested. It also is completely unaware of any difficulty the user may have had in determining the meaning of a command. Capturing this level of interaction provides a bare minimum of interactive understanding—the interface would have a more complete model of the back-and-forth nature of the communication than it does now even if it did not know why the user wanted to communicate in the first place.

The second step on the ladder of communication and collaboration is slave-like interaction. To perform this way, the interface must have a model of what the user wants to do. Current interfaces do not have such a model. The user's goals and tasks lie completely outside of interface, and there is no means to say anything about them. No part of the user's goals and tasks is recorded or even recognized.[1] Instead, all of this information must reside only in the head of the user. None of it can be found in the application and its interface.

Some interfaces seem to be useful and quite satisfying to users. The metaphors on which they are based are highly predictive for users in determining what to do next. One such example is the interface for checkbook activities. I believe this is because the metaphor has been used to build in a model of the task the user is doing and to represent aspects of the task. The metaphor has also been used to keep the user narrowly focused on the task at hand—to balance a checkbook, write checks, or produce reports based on the checkbook information. As a result, the interface metaphor helps users work and also helps them predict what the interface is likely to do. While the interface is not aware of the task the user is doing, it is designed to do that task and to keep the user highly focused.

While it would be wise to continue to design interfaces carefully using well-thought-out metaphors, it will not solve the larger problems concerning interactivity, communication, and collaboration. No one metaphor is powerful enough for all work. Furthermore, lots of smaller applications each with an interface for performing one set of tasks leaves the user with lots of tasks to juggle. We still need an interface that communicates and collaborates, one that's at step three on the ladder. How do we get there from here? There is a great deal more known about human discourse communication that could be used in interfaces today. Recent work in linguistics, natural language processing, and psychology offers principles of communication that can be embodied in interfaces, even when they do not speak full human language. All discourse, of which dialogue is an example, is purposive behavior, and the structure of the discourse is organized and segmented according to purpose. The focus of attention of the discourse is used, among other things, to provide context, which means creating locality in the segments of the discourse for interpreting recent references and to help discourse participants assure that each of them is paying attention to the same items in the discourse (Grosz and Sidner, 1986). Grounding of utterances in the human-computer dialogue[2] makes conversation more efficient by allowing people to leave out what is truly obvious to both participants, as well as to slow the conversation down in order to reestablish focus, correct for unwanted ambiguity, and determine the next participant who has the floor.

It is possible to build interfaces that make use of these principles (and associated algorithms, which I will not discuss here) while at the same time simplifying the interface itself. We are doing that in our current work on collaborative interface agents (Rich and Sidner, 1996). To do so, designers will need to think in terms of user purposes (not just what actions the interface permits), the structure of purposes, and the relationship between what the user must communicate and the purposes of the communication. Maintenance of focus of attention will provide users with a local context in which to complete their subpurposes and may even make it possible to introduce implicit means of referring to the objects of the application.

Far more research is needed. Most linguistics and natural language processing work is directed at progress in natural language/speech understanding and generation, in machine translation, or at more applied concerns such as language-based information retrieval. Uncovering the principles of human communication requires considerably more effort than has been undertaken so far. Applying those principles to interfaces is a largely untouched area of research. Little of this work is likely to occur in industrial research settings, as it is not near enough term for the needs of applied research now typical in industrial labs.

Recent work in understanding human collaboration and user modeling offers two sources of value to the interface: (1) the near-term ability to ground the interface in the users' goals and tasks and (2) the more futuristic ability to make the machine a collaborator with the user once those goals and tasks are available. What is known about collaboration makes it clear that collaborators come to share mutual beliefs about their ways of doing something (called the recipe), about their ability and intentions to do things, and about their commitment to completing the goal. The models of collaboration can also be linked to discourse not simply by saying that collaborators must communicate their beliefs to others, but through much more detailed models of the relationship of belief and intention as purposes for segments of discourse (cf. Lochbaum, 1995).

Recent work in modeling collaboration and discourse in interfaces (Biermann et al., 1993; Stein and Maier, 1995; Rich and Sidner, 1996; cf. Terveen, 1995, for an overview of human-computer collaboration) indicates this is a promising direction for research. While industrial groups as well as some university work has been directed at these problems, only the first steps have been taken in modeling interfaces after human collaboration. However, to extend this work to applications that real users would use on an everyday basis would require further research on human collaboration and more system experimentation in building interfaces. Two critical issues in human collaboration are more exploration of the means by which humans negotiate in collaboration (cf. Guinn and Biermann, 1993; Sidner, 1994a; Chu-Carroll and Carberry, 1995) and human collaboration in task domains that are richer than the simple ones (e.g., building simple physical equipment, gathering simple information) considered so far.

A new technology, which after long delay, is about to splash on the scene: speech. While I will confine my comments to speech input (recognition and understanding), similar comments apply to speech output. Speech will force issues about communication and collaboration. At the same time, if applied wisely, speech offers a valuable modality to many users who do not fit the profile of use for current interfaces. To use speech adequately, researchers must continue to address a number of technical problems in speech recognition and understanding. There are many technical problems in using speech well in interfaces. Some are related to speech recognition per se; others concern how interfaces are designed to use speech as the communication medium. Concerning the first set of problems, one must consider modeling the speech of small dialect populations. This is possible to do but may be overlooked because the cost may seem too high for market return for industrial labs to concern themselves with such populations. Yet small dialect groups make up part of the citizenship of our nation.

Having good speech recognition/production and understanding/generation technology is only the tip of the interface iceberg. A great deal more research is needed in understanding users and their interaction needs in the presence of speech.

Speech technology for desktop and telephony interfaces offers the potential of using computers in ways that users interact with other people. It also opens up a host of metaphorical uses[3] that could enhance computer use or exacerbate our current use of metaphors in interfaces. Careful studies of users and applications with speech (such as the SpeechActs work of Martin et al., 1996) will provide speech interfaces that make use of communication principles. Special attention must be paid to the needs of users who communicate with special limitations. Research on the use of speech interfaces by visually or motor-impaired users and linguistically limited users[4] is not likely to come from industry (as is evident from the current problems with recent operating systems providing interfaces for the blind) and will require industry/university/government collaboration to be feasible. Finally, user populations never considered before, such as the multiple millions of semiliterate and illiterate Americans, will require careful study in speech interfaces; this research is also not likely to occur in industry and will require joint research between industry and universities under government funding.

Speech as a modality naturally suggests speaking to someone. The speaking face is compelling not only because it is so imprinted on us from birth, but because it appears quite valuable to users in communicating. Recent research on faces, human or otherwise, has now captured the imagination of some interface researchers (e.g., Ball et al., 1996; Nagao and Takeuchi, 1994; Waters and Levergood, 1995). While much of the associated research concerns believable agents, that is, research on representing agents visually that are generally designed to have some effect on users (e.g., being persuasive, friendly, or entertaining), faces have inherent value for communication. While little is understood at the computational level about these matters, faces provide a locus for spoken communication and a means of introducing efficiency in the grounding aspects of dialogue. However, these issues are poorly understood, as are the means by which we find faces natural in terms of their micro-level changes (but see work by Thorisson, 1994, and Walker et al., 1994, for some directions to pursue). Research in these areas will require the combined efforts of researchers in a number of disciplines, including psychology, computational linguistics, linguistics, computer science, and media arts. Those aspects that apply to media and believable agents will probably be heavily funded because of their potential payoff in the new entertainment/computer industry. Communication-related matters will require some government funding to keep industrial applied research focused on this matter.

While current interfaces are hard to use and give few choices of modality, we are on the brink of having available many new technologies that can change the nature of interfaces. We must bring to bear our knowledge of human collaboration and discourse communication on these interfaces so that they serve a wider range of users. We must extend our knowledge of collaboration and communication so that our interfaces can grow into better collaborative partners as our work needs change.

NOTES

1. Although interface product groups are now aware of many of the micro-actions that users perform in a given software application, the only method they have come up with to help users is bottom-up recognition of micro-actions. They will never be able to do more because extending this solution to "higher-level" actions is computationally too hard.

2. By this I mean the process by which dialogue participants establish that the message was understood and determine who speaks next in the conversation and when (cf. Clark and Shaefer, 1987; Sidner, 1994a,b; Traum and Heeman, 1996).

3. A near-term example is name-dialing, which is the ability to call a person on the phone by simply saying the name to a telephone prompt.

4. By "linguistically limited," I mean people who have less-than-perfect knowledge or use of the majority culture language because they are nonnative speakers, have some cognitive/physical handicap, or have not yet been trained in the full range of the language owing to age or economic circumstances.

REFERENCES

Ball, Gene, Dan Ling, David Kurlander, John Miller, David Pugh, Tim Skelly, Andy Stankosky, David Thiel, Maarten Van Dantzich, and Trace Wax. 1996. Lifelike Computer Characters: The Persona Project at Microsoft Research. In *Software Agents*, Jeffrey M. Bradshaw (Ed.). AAAI/MIT Press, Cambridge, Mass.

Biermann, Alan W., Curry I. Guinn, D. Richard Hipp, and Ronnie W. Smith. 1993. Efficient Collaborative Discourse: A Theory and Its Implementation. *Proceedings of the ARPA Human Language Technology Workshop*. March. Princeton, NJ.

Chu-Carroll, Jennifer, and Sandra Carberry. 1995. Response Generation in Collaborative

Negotiation. Pp. 136-143 in *Proceedings of the 33rd Annual Meeting of the Association for Computational Linguistics.* ACL, Somerset, N.J.

Clark, H.H., and E.F. Shaefer. 1987. Collaborating on Contributions to Conversations. *Language and Cognitive Processes,* 11(1):1-23.

Grosz, B., and C.L. Sidner. 1986. Attention, Intention and the Structure of Discourse. *Computational Linguistics,* 12(3).

Guinn, Curry, and Alan W. Biermann. 1993. Conflict Resolution in Collaborative Discourse. *Proceedings of the 1993 International Joint Conference on Artificial Intelligence Workshop: Computational Models of Conflict Management in Cooperative Problem Solving,* August. Chambery, France.

Lochbaum, Karen, E. 1994. Using Collaborative Plans to Model the Intentional Structure of Disclosure. Technical Report, Harvard University. Available on http:// liinwww.ira.uka.de/ searchbib/index.

Lochbaum, Karen E. 1995. "The Use of Knowledge Preconditions in Language Processing," *Proceedings of the 14th International Joint Conference on Artificial Intelligence,* Morgan-Kaufmann, San Mateo, CA, pp. 1260-1266.

Martin, P., F. Crabbe, S. Adams, E. Baatz, and N. Yankelovich, 1996. SpeechActs: A Spoken Language Framework. *Computer,* 29 (7):33-40.

Nagao, K., and A. Takeuchi. 1994. Speech Dialogue with Facial Displays: Multimodal Human-Computer Conversation. Pp. 102-109 in *Proceedings of the 32nd Annual Meeting of the Association for Computational Linguistics.* Morgan-Kaufman. San Francisco.

Rich, C., and C.L. Sidner. 1996. "Adding a Collaborative Agent to Direct-Manipulation Interfaces," *Proceedings of UIST.*

Sidner, C. 1994a. An Artificial Discourse Language for Collaborative Negotiation. Pp. 814-819. in *Proceedings of the National Conference on Artificial Intelligence-94,* Seattle. MIT Press, Cambridge, Mass.

Sidner, C. 1994b. Negotiation in Collaborative Activity: A Discourse Analysis. *Knowledge-Based Systems,* 7(4): 265-267.

Stein, A., and E. Maier. 1995. Structuring Collaborative Information-Seeking Dialogues. *Knowledge-Based Systems,* 8(2-3):82-93.

Terveen, L.G. 1995. An Overview of Human-Computer Collaboration. *Knowledge-Based Systems,* 8(2-3).

Thorisson, K.R. 1994. Face-to-Face Communication with Computer Agents. Pp. 86-90 in *AAAI Spring Symposium on Believable Agents,* March 19-20, Stanford University, Palo Alto, Calif.

Traum, D., and P. Heeman. 1996. Utterance Units and Grounding in Spoken Dialogue. *ICSLP,* October.

Walker, J., L. Sproull, and R. Subramani. 1994. Using a Human Face in an Interface. Pp. 85-91 in *Proceedings of the Human Factors in Computing Systems Conference.* ACM Press, New York.

Waters, K., and T. Levergood. 1995. DECface: A System for Synthetic Face Applications. *Journal of Multimedia Tools and Applications,* 1(4):349-366.

DIGITAL MAPS

Lance McKee and Louis Hecht
Open GIS Consortium Inc.

GOAL: INTEGRATE THE NATIONAL SPATIAL DATA INFRASTRUCTURE AND THE NATIONAL INFORMATION INFRASTRUCTURE

The National Spatial Data Infrastructure (NSDI), when opened up through geoprocessing interoperability interfaces based on the Open GIS Consortium's (OGC) OpenGIS™ specification, will expand out of the domain of geographic information system (GIS) experts into the day-to-day lives of the general population. OGC's research and development goal is the development of the OpenGIS specification.

One goal of others in the national information infrastructure (NII) research and development community ought to be to examine the ways in which digital spatial data (geodata) can be most effectively used by citizens in their everyday way finding and transportation, electronic consumer purchasing, education, and interactive entertainment and also in the many existing and future jobs that will involve geodata and geoprocessing. Another research goal ought to be to seek new ways in which designers of virtual environments and visualization tools can make use of humans' spatial visualization abilities, including our almost innate ability to understand maps and aerial views.

Taking a longer psychological, social, and historical view of every citizen, we should also research the various "media effects" of digital maps. Maps of all kinds powerfully condition our thinking about the world beyond our immediate viewspace. GISs, which enable interactive viewing and intersection of multiple spatially coincident maps representing diverse cultural and natural themes, promote holistic, cross-disciplinary thinking. Widespread viewing and use of geographic information potentially promote broad public global awareness in the same way that views from orbiting spacecraft expand the world views of astronauts, as reported by astronauts. If we assume that human-machine interfaces and interactions affect consciousness, and if we care about the evolution of consciousness, we ought to study and characterize these effects with an eye toward developing high-level design principles that support the development of interfaces and uses that nudge us toward greater awareness of our relationships with each other and our planet.

MARKET AND TECHNOLOGY DRIVERS

Various market and technology drivers are converging to make geodata and geoprocessing a more important part of the NII.

Current producers of geoprocessing software have long looked for an expansion of their markets commensurate with the benefits their technology has to offer in many segments of society. That expansion has been inhibited by noninteroperability and difficulties in sharing data held in diverse proprietary formats. Open GIS interfaces will remove those barriers.

Society has a growing need for geoprocessing owing to growing population and worsening environmental problems; geographically distributed government and business activities; rapid globalization of many markets and activities; and increasing pressure on businesses, governments, and individuals to operate more efficiently.

There is a growing realization that much data (70 percent to 85 percent of data in all databases) has a spatial component that can be exploited in a variety of ways for more effective analysis and display.

Faster CPUs (central processing units) and high-performance image processing and graphics processing finally provide a base capable of supporting distributed geoprocessing, which often involves intense computation and large data files. Wider-bandwidth networks and distributed computing infrastructure (OLE/COM, CORBA, Java, etc.) and middleware and componentware architectures are important because so many geoprocessing applications benefit from transparent access to remote geodata stores and remote specialized geoprocessing functions and from integration of geoprocessing functions into other workflow. "gIS" with a lowercase g expresses the potential for open systems architectures and object technology to enable integration of geoprocessing as one (increasingly cost-effective) subordinated component of applications and decision support systems. Growth in the use of geoprocessing will occur as middleware and componentware approaches release geoprocessing from the confines of large, expensive, complex monolithic software systems.

Geoprocessing technology is proceeding as rapidly as the general computing and telecommunications technologies and not only in the area of geoprocessing interoperability interfaces. All of the following support the wider use of geodata and geoprocessing by every citizen: powerful spatial database technologies introduced by major database vendors; smaller and cheaper geographic positioning systems (GPSs); sophisticated, inexpensive, and abundant commercial earth imaging data products; advances in digital orthophotogrammetry for satellite earth imaging and aerial still and video imaging; continuing specialization and product differentiation in the areas of GIS, CAD (computer-aided design), and digital cartography; distributed interactive simulation; and three-dimensional spatial data visualization techniques (including interactive virtual reality approaches). These technologies hybridize in many ways. For example, high-resolution satellite images and digital orthophotogrammetry permit quite precise automatic generation of three-dimensional views of the earth's surface.

GEODATA AND GEOGRAPHIC INTERFACES

Simple geodata accumulation is also a driver. There is only one earth, and the set of all geodata is referenced to this one finite spherical volume, like a rapidly growing onion of thematic maps of cultural and natural phenomena. As network-accessible geodata accumulate in tens of thousands of archives around the world, it becomes an ever-richer, ever-more-significant basis for an ever-growing number of local and global activities. It becomes one of the foundations of the new world culture of the information age.

NETWORK-BASED GEOSPATIAL INFORMATION

Below are some examples of how network-resident geodata and geoprocessing resources will be used by every citizen. Most will involve simple, specialized, stylized interactive map displays. A set of research issues can be derived by examining the user interface requirements of categories of applications, such as simplicity, information density, and interactivity modes.

Citizens will use the NII to help them get from A to B. GPSs in car and cell phones will provide the coordinates of A, and a car's map display and the cell phone's multimedia yellow pages will show the way to B. The necessary geodata will be stored remotely and downloaded on demand, transparently to the user.

Geoprocessing middleware and componentware will compare the distances to multiple possible destinations. The multimedia yellow pages, for example, will show driving time or walking time to a selected set of nearby restaurants. The software need not be stored permanently in the information appliance.

Not just car drivers, but hikers, boaters, and visitors to a city will see on a little screen where they are and how to get to where they want to go. A numbered package en route from A to B will show up on a digital map display, showing where it is now on its route. (Some shippers already provide this service.) People waiting for buses and airplanes will see where the bus or airplane is, on a digital map, with estimated minutes till arrival.

More than 70 percent of database records contain spatial information. Every database and spreadsheet, and the compound documents and work environments in which these functions are embedded, will be able to make maps based on spatial information (usually street addresses) in data records. Spatial display and analysis will be important in many workflow scenarios.

Listed below are other geographic applications used by every citizen during daily life. Each has particular user interface requirements:

- Education/training, distance learning, research collaboration
- Electronic libraries, electronic museums and galleries
- On-line government geographic information for informed citizens
- Maintenance of the individual's information context and connection (personal logical network) as the individual moves through space, bridging media and modality; mapping electronic locations of devices (addresses) to their physical locations; using concepts of reach space, colocation, and nearby
- Virtual reality landscapes from earth images for interactive entertainment
- Security monitoring and intrusion response
- Special way finding for elderly and disabled people
- Product distribution/warehousing optimization
- Intelligent vehicle highway systems (IVHSs) and parking place location
- Traffic/weather information
- Route guidance and planning, multimodal trip planning, traveler services
- Locale-specific resources and recommendations for small farms and gardens
- City information services
- Finding jobs and clients available locally.

Some geographic applications used by citizens in various jobs are as follows:

- Emergency road services and 911 emergency response systems
- Virtual reality landscapes from earth images for military, disaster relief, and rescue preparedness; civil engineering and landscape architecture
- Agriculture and forestry
- Climate research, agronomy, biology, ecology, geology, other sciences

- Urban and regional planning
- Automated mapping and facilities management
- Military surveillance
- Natural resource discovery, exploitation, and management
- Water resource management
- Parolee tracking
- Global and local environmental monitoring, advance of environmental sciences
- Support for "green" standards, local waste-as-resource arrangements
- Cable, microwave, and cellular transmission installation planning
- Telemedicine, better care for rural trauma victims
- Global maritime information and rescue system, air traffic control
- Commercial vehicle operations
- Business siting, market research, and other business geographics applications
- Geographic matching of prospective employees with available jobs or prospective service providers with prospective clients
- Public administration networks
- Land tenure systems
- Precision farming (GPS-guided controlled delivery of nutrients and chemicals based on earth imagery or automated GPS-located soil or crop sampling).

The number of applications for geodata is growing rapidly and will continue to grow as the national and global spatial data infrastructures develop.

MAPS

Maps are a part of most cultures because spatial thinking is an essential part of people's relationship with their physical and cultural environments. Even in simpler cultures that do not pass down written records, individuals make temporary maps to remind themselves or to show others how to find their way in unfamiliar territory. All birds and mammals form mental maps, and, as cooperative hunter-gatherers, humans developed sophisticated spatial awareness and spatial communications abilities that came to support other cultural activities besides physical way finding. For example, we say in a figurative sense that "we are on our way" to making the NSDI an integral part of the NII. User interfaces are collections of symbols and metaphors, and the map metaphor is inherently important in cyberspace. Basic research in spatial reasoning, spatial memory, and spatial communication would support development of better user interfaces that employ spatial display and manipulation.

Virtual reality will also help geodata users evaluate data sources. Because so many geodata are available, and because geodata are often complex, we will often be concerned about geodata quality, content, and lineage. A system of geometric shapes could be used to represent certain content parameters, and their shape, color, and motion could represent quality parameters. A human-computer interface could be a map or an image. Once you center on a spot you can call up various basic icons that represent data objects. It is easy on the Internet to find lots of data but hard to sift through all the data. The interface ought to be able to tell every citizen easily and intuitively about the "goodness" of the data. For example: How does software communicate to a skier who wants to see the snow pack at eight Rocky Mountain ski resorts? The skier finds imagery, but it is summer data, not winter data, so an error signal intervenes. Through user configuration of simple preference files, the computer system knows that skiing requires winter data.

DIGITAL MAPS

Paper maps are a special form of printed communication, important to motorists, subway riders, explorers, scientists in many disciplines, historians, municipal service agencies, shippers, travelers, property owners and managers, and marketers. The utility of maps is amplified in several ways by computers and networks. A GIS, for example, is like multiple same-region overlaid thematic maps drawn on clear film, a visual-interface spatial database. You can query a GIS to meld thematic maps into a new map showing, for example, all the areas 3,000 feet or higher in elevation, within 50 meters of a standing body of water, within 1,000 meters of a road, where most of the trees are pines, where the slope of the ground is less than 10 percent, and where the population density is less than 1 person per square mile. (More spatial temporal reasoning research needs to be done on how to articulate the conditions of a spatial search.) Digital technology allows storage of (and network access to) huge quantities of geodata; zooming, panning, and other kinds of interactive manipulation that overcome the limitations of paper space and human visual acuity; real-time tracking; input from GPS and earth observation satellites; and instant display of nonspatial data (text, pictures, graphs, etc.) associated with selected map features or locations.

Through paper maps every citizen is familiar with graphic abstraction of large terrestrial spaces. Digital maps apply this helpful information presentation convention to vastly greater information domains. Digital maps and three-dimensional virtual fly-overs and fly-throughs will be an important part of many graphical user interfaces because everyone intuitively understands maps and aerial views and many kinds of information have a spatial component that makes spatial representation and visualization appropriate.

The new media are "massaging," in Marshall McLuhan's term, our individual minds and collective culture away from text-induced linear sequential thinking toward nonlinear thinking characterized by multiple simultaneous modalities. Spatial display and analysis offers a visual, intuitive, and effective means for solving a wide range of complex problems. Visualization of geographic information, or visualization of information geographically, helps people cope with information glut. Virtual reality applications will employ spatial representations of real spatial phenomena, but they will also employ spatial representations of nonspatial phenomena simply because our brains are hardwired for solving problems in three-dimensional space. Important parts of the software and data for configuring and populating cyberspace will be borrowed from geoprocessing applications and geodata archives and data feeds. Similarly, research into spatial thinking will ultimately benefit both "real space" and cyberspace applications.

RESEARCH ISSUES

Several research issues are identified in the text above. OGC's research and development in the area of geoprocessing interoperability is primary in the sense that spatial data will have a much greater role in the NII when diverse systems can exchange diverse kinds of data and access other systems' geoprocessing resources. Many applications will then be using geodata, and application developers will be looking for ideas and guidance concerning geoprocessing user interface development. Useful research will draw inspiration from traditional cartography and from general ideas about user interfaces.

Over the next 20 years we will learn more about how people function while immersed or partially immersed in virtual environments. We will learn what problem simulation schemes work best and what kinds of problems are most fruitfully addressed by these schemes. Many of these environments, certainly, will include extended landscapes representing real or imaginary spaces, and the role of spatial reasoning, spatial memory, and maps will be of interest.

Everyone views the world differently. This is an issue for Open GIS specification developers because different geodata producers and users give the same geographic feature different names and sets of descriptive parameters and different metadata. Part of the specification proposes semantic translators that domain experts from two different domains will configure to enable semiautomatic translation and integration of geodata. The problem is a difficult one and is much broader than geodata integration because computer users involved with other computer users need common interfaces to enable effective communication and collaboration. Map interface developers as well as other kinds of interface developers need to address the issue of standard symbology and usage.

Undoubtedly, commercial research and development projects and market activity will generate many of the dominant productizable ideas and standard graphical and conceptual approaches. Academia should take a longer view; it should (1) address the cognitive and broader social effects of developments in the spatial subdomain of the multimedia world and (2) look in very basic ways at how user interface design can layer most elegantly on our legacy wetware and cultural firmware and leverage most powerfully a positive vision for the future. The government has a role in cataloging and tracking evolving research topics of all kinds and supporting those that best serve the nation and the world community. By participating as technology users in industry consortia (such as OGC) that include users in technology planning and specification efforts, government agencies can ensure that the technology provider community meets agency needs and can influence the direction of technology that will become part of the larger economy and culture.

GATHERING AND INTEGRATING INFORMATION IN THE NATIONAL INFORMATION INFRASTRUCTURE

Craig A. Knoblock
University of Southern California

GOALS AND ISSUES

A critical and unsolved problem for the World Wide Web is how to gather and integrate the huge amount of available information in an automated fashion. Web browsers and search engines are an enormous step forward in providing access to the available information. Yet they rely heavily on hypertext links, which require a human to navigate. I believe an important goal for the national information infrastructure (NII) is to develop the infrastructure, technology, and tools to provide automated gathering and integration of data. Consider an example from the financial domain, where the ability to integrate the large amount of available data would make that information much more accessible and useful. Someone might be interested in investing in the airline industry but is undecided about which airline stock to buy and wants some additional information. Some of the information they might like to have includes the annual report, one-year price history, and current trading price for all U.S. airline stocks, and they might want them presented in order of increasing PE (price/earnings) ratios. All of this information is publicly available, but knowing where to look and integrating the information is not a simple task.

Assuming that users knew where to look (and that is a strong assumption), they could put together this information using the following steps. First, they must determine what all of the airline stocks are. This could be done by examining the prospectus of each publicly traded stock to see if it falls into the SIC (Standard Industrial Classification) category of Scheduled Air Transportation, but that would be very time consuming. Another approach would be to find an information source that contains a list of airlines, such as the EAASY SABRE page that includes all of the airlines for which it provides reservations. This information could then be used on another page to input the name of a company and get back the ticker symbol (the symbol by which the stock is listed in one of the stock exchanges) for that company. Using that information, they can then go to another page and enter the ticker symbol to get the current trade price and PE ratio. They would go to yet another page to find the one-year price history in a graphical form. And they could go to the Securities and Exchange Commission (SEC) EDGAR Archives to find the annual report filed with the SEC but in this case accessed using the company name. Even within the EDGAR Archives, they would need to know that the code for an annual report is 10K in order to extract it from the 20 or 30 reports available for each company. This entire process would have to be repeated for each airline, and they would not know how to order them until they had the data for each company.

Ideally, instead of going through this tedious process, a user could simply issue the query to a software agent for the financial domain and that agent would know where to retrieve the relevant information and how to process it to produce the data requested by the user. The goal then is to develop the infrastructure and tools required to easily construct and maintain software agents for querying and integrating information in any domain of interest. One could laboriously construct and maintain such software agents by writing specialized software applications. In fact, that is the current state of the art. The limitation of this approach is that such specialized applications are difficult to maintain and extend. If a new source becomes available, a programmer must modify the program in order to exploit that information. Also, each new application domain requires constructing a whole new program.

RESEARCH PROBLEMS TO BE ADDRESSED

There are a number of research issues that must be addressed in order to realize the goal described in the previous section:

- *Modeling the contents of sources.* To automate the access to sources requires both a precise syntactic description (e.g., a grammar) of the organization of the data as well as a detailed description of the semantic content of the source. The latter can most naturally be described using a knowledge representation language.
- *Construction of domain ontologies.* To describe the information provided by each source such that it can be integrated with other sources requires a comprehensive set of shared terminology.
- *Planning to access and integrate information sources.* Given a query and the models of the available sources, we need a system that can automatically select an appropriate set of sources and generate a plan to efficiently integrate the required information.
- *Machine learning of source structure and source contents.* The problem of modeling all of the currently available information sources on the Web is far too large to be done manually. Thus, we need to develop

machine learning technology to automate as much of this process as possible. Of course, the hope is that eventually the added information would be so critical that information providers would provide it just as they currently format their data.

  • *Data mining for patterns and relationships in sources.* A critical aspect of this problem is how to efficiently process queries, since some sources may be very expensive to access (in either time or money). Data mining can be used to learn relationships in the data for optimizing access to sources.

  • *Natural language querying.* Ideally, users would be able to write natural language queries. This requires developing natural language systems that can be used to formulate valid queries.

PROPOSED RESEARCH PROJECTS

The various issues described above can be broken down into four possible research projects. The first two projects would provide the core work, and the other two projects would be important in making the resulting research useful to everyday users.

Representation and Ontologies

The problem of representing both the syntax and semantics of sources is central to addressing the entire problem. The goal of the first project is to develop approaches to describing the syntax and semantics of Web pages. Given the size of the task, I would expect that this would be a fairly large, long-term problem. The hope is that this would eventually lead to standards for marking up pages with semantic information and to the development of domain-specific ontologies that can be used for information integration.

Planning Information Gathering and Integration

Given a description of the available sources, the problem still remains as to how to select and integrate the most relevant information. There are a number of challenging aspects to this problem, such as handling semantic discrepancies, resolving syntactic differences, and evaluating reliability and recency. In addition, another critical aspect to this problem is performing the processing efficiently, since access to many Web-based sources can be very slow, and plans that require access to many sources can require hours or days.

Machine Learning and Data Mining of Sources

Because of the need for large amounts of information about sources and how they relate, machine learning and data mining will play a critical role in simplifying the task of the first two projects. Machine learning can be used to help build grammars for parsing sources as well as for building models that describe the contents of sources. Data mining can be used to find relationships in individual sources and between sources, which can then be used to optimize the query processing.

Natural Language Processing and User Interfaces

Natural language querying and/or graphical interfaces are needed to provide user-friendly access to information. In addition, user interfaces are important for displaying various types of multimedia data and for providing tools to help build models of sources.

POTENTIAL IMPACT

The overall project has the potential to make a dramatic impact. If the work is done right, it could change the nature of the NII. Instead of using browsers and search engines, users would have access to a wide range of specialized agents that could quickly locate and integrate the huge amount of available data. Instead of being a data repository, the NII could be a knowledge repository.

INTEGRATING AUDIENCES AND USERS

John Richards
Turner Le@rning Inc.

LIFELONG LEARNING

The National information infrastructure (NII) is designed—from a technological perspective—to integrate a wide range of communication and information systems including video delivery, telephony, computer networks, and on-line services. These are, for the most part, known technologies, and the technological integration is a matter of time and money. In contrast, we have not yet begun to think about the integration of diverse media from a human perspective. People relate to even a single medium in very different ways, determined by the context of use and by the individual's understanding of the situation. The development of functional multiple media learning environments is not simply the result of combining different media types—an additive process—but consists of creating a brand new kind of media, a transforming process. The development of interfaces for these new media types depends on coming to understand the ways in which people will come to use the media for learning. As real video and truly interactive networking are integrated, television audiences do not simply become network users or vice versa. Instead, there are qualitatively different experiences in store. In this paper I consider some issues that we should try to anticipate in the construction of a voice, video, and data infrastructure that provides the opportunity for just-in-time learning throughout life.

ANALOG VS. DIGITAL

Our analog modes of communication by voice, print, and video are gradually being replaced by digital modes. Ultimately, most of human knowledge will be stored in a common digital library

—Kaufman and Smarr [1993] (p. ix)

This transformation from analog to digital will have deep implications for human knowledge, and, in my judgment, even deeper implications for human communication and relationships. Kaufman and Smarr argue that the fundamental idea of replacing the continuous world of nature with a model of that world, formed of discrete units, has transformed the pursuit of science. They argue that the digital perspective provides a controllable, imaginable representation that, ultimately, provides the key to a more comprehensible world.

How, then, does our understanding of the content of media differ as we move from analog to digital? This is not an arcane question pertaining to the relevance of simulations on supercomputers; rather, it affects all of our interactions with voice video and data technologies. For example, in the most developed of these digitizations, consider how writing e-mail messages differs from writing letters. It certainly seems that only yesterday we were seeing paeans to letter-writing as a dying medium. The commonly accepted explanation was that writing was the problem—culture was deteriorating, and the literacy required for letters was a lost art. In retrospect, given the success of e-mail, the delays in letter delivery were simply not tolerable, especially when contrasted with the immediacy of telephones. But e-mail did not change the nature of letter writing—it replaced letter writing with a full panoply of alternatives. Not only did a new, more informal genre evolve, but entirely new forms of written communication also evolved with entirely new rules for participation. E-mail evolved into bulletin boards and "listservs" that do not have straightforward analogs in the letter-writing or, more generally, precomputer culture. And even more distinct forms of communication are only now appearing. As argued by Sherry Turkle [1995], chats, MUDs, and MUSEs are developing unique, and unprecedented, participation structures. How will these conversations change with the easy availability of voice on the Internet? How will putting telephone (or video-telephone) on the Internet change the nature of a phone call? What new forms will evolve?

In my judgment, though, the most profound differences will occur with video. The control added to video through the digitization process changes the nature of the video—more importantly the digitization inherent in the NII brings together television and computers, two technologies that have been distinct in development and production. More significantly, these technologies are culturally quite distinct. As we talk about an infrastructure that integrates voice, video, and data, we must consider the power of the cultural differences of these technologies and their complex contexts of use.

CABLE MODEMS VS. CABLE BOXES

Prior to coming to Turner, I lived in Newton, Massachusetts, and had cable television installed. The cable came into the basement of my home and was routed up to my bedroom, into a cable box, through my VCR and into my television—my "entertainment center." In March of 1996, I became part of an early trial of cable modems by Continental Cablevision and BBN. The cable into the basement was split and part of it routed into my home office, into a cable modem, and then into my computer, providing ethernet-speed access to the Internet—my "work center." The two setups were separated by a thin wall, two different boxes, and two different monitors.

What separates these worlds? Why aren't they going to the same box or the same monitor? When will I see a picture within a picture? While watching TV the 2" square picture in the corner is the Internet. When surfing the Web the 2" square picture is the television signal. What separates these worlds are the viewers/users and the industry standards and expectations.

This is a temporary division. The cable industry has promised a free cable modem to every U.S. school they pass as they provide this service to the community. These will be 5 to 10 feet from television cable boxes. What will the interface be when these are a single box connected to a single monitor? How are we to think of television as an inset in software—and conversely? Are the two streams of data to be integrated for interactive television or video-enhanced software? Once all the technologies are digitized, there is no functional delivery difference between television, e-mail, phone, radio, movies, or even the networked alarm systems in people's homes. From a human perspective, this convergence will represent remarkable transformations in the nature of the media.

PARTICIPATION VS. DELIVERY

Networking has been dominated by a philosophy of participation and user constructibility. From the beginning of the ARPANET, for national security reasons networking has been distributed with no central locus of control.[1] The removal of any node would have no effect on the rest of the system. Moreover, the wild success of the World Wide Web is precisely because it so adeptly fits the underlying participatory philosophy of networking.

Television and cinema, in contrast, have been dominated by centralized delivery models. Beginning with Hollywood domination of moviemaking, and continuing with the "big three" U.S. broadcast companies, television and cinema content has been tightly controlled, produced, and distributed. Even as television audiences are being analyzed as "active meaning producers of texts and technologies . . ." (Ang [1996], p. 8), this is seen as a postmodern development that is only now being taken into account. In particular, as the plethora of programs provides choice, the audience is seen as being freer to construct meaning through participating in these choices. Television itself is evolving as the surrounding technologies change:

> The VCR disrupted the modern entanglement between centralized transmission and privatized reception because it displaced the locus of control over the circulation of cultural texts to more local contexts.
>
> —Ang [1996] (p. 12)

Thus, there is a different experience when the same movie is shown in a cinema, on TV, or as a tape played at home on your VCR. In fact, the audience is different, with different expectations regarding interruptions—a movie theater is continuous and commercials are resented, television presentations are "geared" toward the interruptions, and only with a rented tape can the bathroom break be at the discretion of the audience. Replays are possible with the VCR. In short, the nature of the medium is changing because of the role of the active audience.

AUDIENCE VS. USERS

Each of the media carries with it different relationships with its users/audiences. And these relationships are not dependent solely on the media in isolation. Consider the distinctions John Ellis [1982] draws between the audience of cinema and the audience of television. The cinema spectator is a voyeur. The television viewers are "uninvolved in the events portrayed" and ". . . are able to see 'life's parade at their fingertips,' but at the cost of exempting themselves from that parade for the duration of their TV viewing" (Ellis [1982], pp. 169-170). The spectator pays for the cinema, and resents any commercial intrusion during the showing. The viewer accepts television commercials as a part of the basic structure of watching.

How does this compare with the audience for video in software? Or video on the Web? As software developers we have naively assumed that the introduction of the new media types fit in with the nature of the software—videos, pictures, and sounds are included for motivational purposes, or as illustrations of some concept, and have little or no fundamental effect on the user.

Moreover, the deep distinctions between viewers and spectators suggest that the computer/user relationship may, and probably does, change with the introduction of the Web. Typically the computer/user relationship is one-to-one (or two or three at best), essentially an individual participation structure. The Web is somewhat different without many precursors. It is essentially a social structure. The underlying metaphor is that when we are connecting with other individuals there is a dynamic, changing, unstructured, cluttered world.

There are different educational philosophies that have grown up around the technologies. There are two cultures in technology and education—perhaps this is parallel to the C.P. Snow observation. These two cultures—digital (computers/networking and education) and analog (TV/cable video)—know little of each other.

VIDEO IN SOFTWARE VS. SOFTWARE IN VIDEO

There is a small stream of research and development that has evolved in the intersection of video and computing. Kristina Hooper Woolsey and Bob Mohl produced the Aspen project. The user drove through the town of Aspen by manipulating a touch-sensitive screen. The branching structures themselves are sufficiently constrained that it is possible to anticipate all choices (at an intersection in the road you can stop or go forward, backward, right, or left). It is possible to film alternatives. The mapping metaphor provided the basis for the more successful commercial product, Palenque. Other early attempts to tie TV and computing were Sam Gibbon's and Bank Street's *The Voyage of the Mimi*, and John Bransford's Cognition and Technology Group at Vanderbilt's The Jason Project (Cognition [in press]). Another interesting attempt by Woolsey and the Apple Multimedia Lab is the Watson and Crick DNA story, based on a BBC production.

More recently, at Turner, we have experimented with several qualitatively different attempts to integrate the two cultures. CNN Newsroom is broadcast by CNN at 4:30 a.m. for taping by teachers. Traditionally, teachers would receive teachers' guides by fax or through a centralized distribution within a state. More recently, the teachers' guides may be downloaded from cnn.com/newsroom on the World Wide Web. We are working together with researchers at the Center for Educational Computing Initiatives at MIT who have set up a system to automatically digitize the broadcast, separate it into meaningful segments, and make it available through streaming video on the Web. The teachers' guides are also separately available for each segment. This qualitatively changes what teachers can access. They can choose particular segments from the day's broadcast, and they have access to an indexed history.

Turner Le@rning has also been experimenting with electronic field trips. Students participate in two to four weeks of curriculum activities involving videotapes, data disks, electronic chat groups, and print materials. The midpoint of the curriculum is marked by two live broadcasts where experts at the field trip location respond to students' questions, submitted to an 800 number or over the Web by students. The student's act of asking a question changes the presumption of the broadcast. Moreover, the variety of media is specifically designed to foster active participation on the part of the teacher and student in the construction of their learning.

As the broadcast and cable media become more involved in the Internet, the nature of television is also changing. CNN networks (CNN, *CNN Headline News, CNN Airport News, CNN fn*) download feeds from CNN bureaus worldwide. In each network a team of editors and writers produce stories that are then televised. *CNN Interactive* is a Web site that is produced and distributed in much the same way. It is this unique television-oriented model, with constant news-based updates, that accounts for its immense popularity (over 5 million page-views per day). How will television-based concepts translate onto the Web? Currently, Web sites change weekly, if you are fortunate, and daily at the very best sites—CNN's timely updates are very much an anachronism—requiring over 140 programmers/writers. At what point will we be programming the Web as we program television, with sites changing according to the time of day? And how will this be modified by the Web's ability to adjust for your interests and history?

CONCLUSION

The rise of image in communication is more than a matter of educating ourselves to analyze and interpret visual experiences. Rather, as argued by Taylor and Saarinen [1994], the incorporation of images in presentations has changed the very nature of communication. Text by its very nature is linear, sequential. A picture or video allows for an infinite series of branches.

This may not be a new stage of meaning but a return to an old one. McLuhan [1964] argues that prior to Gutenberg, story telling relied on images and metaphors that were much more generative—taking into account the multiplicity of the audience and the individual construction of meaning.

What I am suggesting in this paper is that the integration of video media with computer technology is not a quantitative difference but a qualitative difference that requires that we begin to rethink learning in this digital world.

BIBLIOGRAPHY

Ang, Ien [1996]. Living room wars: Rethinking media audiences for a postmodern world. London: Routledge.

Cognition and Technology Group at Vanderbilt (in press). The Jason series: A design experiment in complex, mathematical problem solving. In J. Hawkins and A. Collins (Eds.), Design experiments: Integrating technologies into schools. New York: Cambridge University Press.

Ellis, John [1982]. Visible Fictions. London: Routledge and Kegan Paul.
    Kaufman, William J. and Smarr, Larry L. [1993]. Supercomputing and the transformation of science. New York: Scientific American Library.

McLuhan, Marshall [1964]. Understanding media: The extensions of man. New York: New American Library.

Taylor, Mark C. and Saarinen, Esa [1994]. Imagologies: Media philosophy. London: Routledge.

Turkle, Sherry [1995]. Life on the screen. New York: Simon and Schuster.

NOTE

1. To understand that this is not necessarily true of the technology but has arisen as a deliberate design decision, notice the "star-nets" that MIS departments always try to establish. This design emphasizes the collection of data (attendance and grade information, or inventories, or bank accounts) in one central location, and the distribution of centralized resources or information (paychecks, reports, decisions).

INTELLIGENT AGENTS FOR INFORMATION

Katia P. Sycara
Carnegie Mellon University

GOALS AND ISSUES

The overall goal of the every-citizen interface research program is to provide fundamental research and enabling technologies for the development of computer interfaces that allow easy access to the national information infrastructure (NII) by many citizens, ranging from software experts to physically or mentally handicapped persons. Given the current nature of computer technology and current characteristics of the NII, there are many issues that must be addressed.

CURRENT PROBLEMS

Effective use of the Internet by humans or decision support machine systems has been hampered by some dominant characteristics of the infosphere. First, information available from the Net is unorganized, multimodal, and distributed on server sites all over the world. Second, the number and variety of data sources and services are increasing dramatically every day. Furthermore, the availability, type, and reliability of information services are constantly changing. Third, information is ambiguous and possibly erroneous owing to the dynamic nature of the information sources and potential information updating and maintenance problems. Therefore, information is becoming increasingly difficult for a person or machine system to collect, filter, evaluate, and use. Current interface technology, dominated by the Web browser paradigm, besides being slow, lets users do the access, filtering, interpretation of raw data through point and click, and text/graphic cognitive processing. Current NII technology has a number of limitations, including the following:

- It does not flexibly support information, access, and filtering.
- It does not easily adapt to user interaction style and information-seeking goals and preferences.
- It does not flexibly transfer task performance from user to system.
- It is not user friendly to many people with disabilities.

- It is not suitable for easy perusal of continuous-time multimedia (e.g., video, audio).
- It is not easily portable across different display devices.
- It does not flexibly support user mobility.

Addressing the above set of current interface technology limitations can constitute a list of requirements for short-term (2 to 3 years) and medium-term (3 to 5 years) research requirements. Additional longer-term requirements include supporting the flexible physical realization of "action-at-a-distance" capabilities and making the computer a real collaborative partner of the user.

RESEARCH ISSUES

To address the above-mentioned goals and requirements, researchers from different disciplines, such as computer science, cognitive science, human factors, physiology, psychology, design, and engineering, will need to collaborate.

The paradigm of intelligent agents has shown initial promise for handling some of the above problems, especially information location, filtering, and integration. Although a precise definition of an intelligent agent is still forthcoming, the current working notion is that intelligent software agents are programs that act on behalf of their human users in order to perform laborious information-gathering tasks, such as locating and accessing information from various on-line information sources, resolving inconsistencies in the retrieved information, filtering away irrelevant or unwanted information, integrating information from heterogeneous information sources, and adapting over time to their human users' information needs and the shape of the infosphere.

To make intelligent agents a reliable part of interface technology, some important research issues must be addressed. They include the following:

- *Development of intelligent agents that locate and retrieve information from distributed multimedia and multimodal information sources according to a user specification.* To what extend should agents hide information complexity from users? Agent audit trails and behavior explanation also should be investigated. How can agents determine information trustworthiness, so they can give some credibility estimate to users? Is this desirable?
- *Development of intelligent agents that unobtrusively and reliably learn user information goals and preferences as well as display preferences.* To what extend should agents be proactively presenting information? How au-

tonomous should they be in terms of initiating information searches that their learned user model tells them might be useful at this time?

- *What "face and personality" should intelligent agents present to users?* Utility and trade-offs of anthropomorphizing agents—does anthropomorphization create particular expectations on the part of users?
- *Adaptive function allocation and coadaptation.* Is adaptation always good? Development of methodology and techniques to manage resulting changes in roles and tasks to avoid undermining system reliability and performance. Identification of characteristics of agent design and presentation that facilitate helpful adaptation and flexibility in use.
- Because of the vastness of the infosphere, *investigation of protocols for collaboration of distributed intelligent agents also is necessary.*
- *Development of ontologies and transformation techniques to support semantic interoperation of distributed agents.* Can these ontologies be standardized? Are there "ontology czars"?
- *Investigation of the trade-offs associated with agent mobility in support of interface technology.*

Additional research issues include:

- *How to display information on different appliances* (e.g., workstations, personal digital assistants, wearable computers). While static and mobile telephones present the same interface to users, this is not true for computer displays. Issues of maintaining consistency of interface over appliances with significant differences in display real estate need to be researched.
- *How to deal with temporally continuous data modalities*—for example, how to let users quickly skim video objects to locate sections of interest and how to aid users in the analysis and reuse of digital video information. In the hands of a user, every medium has a temporal nature. It takes time to read (process) a text document or a still image. However, in traditional media each user absorbs the information at his or her own rate. One may even assimilate visual information holistically—that is, come to an understanding of complex information nearly at once. Solutions to these problems require an intimate understanding of digital video and digital audio and development of new modes of interfaces based on this model.
- *Research in matching modality to task* (e.g., speech is unsuitable for describing information that has a lot of spatial content, such as maps, or mechanical parts).
- *Research in seamless integration of different input* (e.g., speech to retrieve a map) *and output* (e.g., graphic display of the retrieved map) *modalities for the same information object.*

• *Research in supporting users in specification of information requests* (e.g., through visual retrieval specification cues) *and development of principles for ecological interface design.*

• *Searching and skimming video and audio large-scale information:* Just viewing digital video, while useful, is not enough. Once users identify video objects of interest, they will need to be able to manipulate, organize, analyze, and reuse the video. Whether proffered by a computer or human agent, users would like to peruse video much as they flip through the pages of a book. Unfortunately, today's mechanisms are inadequate. Scanning by jumping a set number of frames may skip the target information completely.

PROJECTS

To make progress along these issues, a variety of projects should be instituted. Small projects to investigate circumscribed issues (e.g., how to structure agents, interaction protocols, how to determine information credibility) and larger projects that should involve collaboration between academic institutions, government, and industry. For the moment, industry seems to lead in the NII. The smaller projects should involve only academia and should investigate fundamental longer-term issues, so that the longer-term goals (e.g., computer systems becoming real collaborators and partners of humans) should be addressed.

INTELLIGENT INFORMATION AGENTS

Johanna D. Moore
University of Pittsburgh

INTRODUCTION

The evolving national information infrastructure (NII) has made available a vast array of on-line services and networked information and networked information resources in a variety of forms (text, speech, graphics, images, video). At the same time, advances in computing and telecommunications technology have made it possible for an increasing number of households to own (or lease or use) powerful personal computers that are connected to this resource. Accompanying this progress is the expectation that people will be able to more effectively solve problems because of this vast information resource. Unfortunately, development of interfaces that help users identify the information that is relevant to their current needs and present this information in ways that are most appropriate given the information content and the needs of particular users lags far behind development of the infrastructure for storing, transferring, and displaying information. As Grosz and Davis (1994) put it, "the good news is that all of the world's electronic libraries are now at your disposal; the bad news is that you're on your own—there's no one at the information desk." In this paper I provide desiderata for an interface that would enable ordinary people to properly access the capabilities of the NII. I identify some of the technologies that will be needed to achieve these desiderata and discuss current and future research directions that could lead to the development of such technologies. In particular, I focus on ideas related to agents and system intelligence and ways in which advances in these areas could enhance eventual interfaces to the NII.

DESIDERATA FOR AN EVERY-CITIZEN INTERFACE TO THE NII

As I envision it, an every-citizen interface would consist of intelligent information agents (IIAs) that can:

- work with users to determine their information needs;
- navigate the NII to identify and locate appropriate data sources from which to extract relevant information;

- present information in ways that are most appropriate to the type of information being conveyed, as well as users' goals, time constraints, and current context (i.e., what other information resources are they currently accessing?); and
- adapt to changes in users' needs and abilities as well as to changes in information resources.

INTELLIGENT INTERACTIVE QUERY SPECIFICATION

Database query languages allow users to form complex queries that request information involving data entities and relationships among them. Using a database system, users can typically find the information they require or determine that the database does not contain such information. However, to use a database system, users must know which data resource(s) to access and must be able to specify a query in the appropriate language. That is, the users must essentially form a plan to identify and access the information they require to achieve their information-seeking goals. In contrast, keyword-based search engines for the World Wide Web allow users to search many information resources at once by specifying their queries using combinations of keywords (and indications of whether or not the keywords are required to occur in the document, whether they must occur in sequence, etc.). Such search engines do not require users to form a detailed plan, but they often turn up many irrelevant documents and users typically do not know what data resources have been examined. Moreover, keyword-based search engines provide users with a very crude language for expressing their information-seeking goals. To provide the kind of interface I envision, IIAs must be able to work with users to help them express their information-seeking goals in terms that the system understands and can act on. The IIA should then form a plan to find information that may help users achieve their goals. That is, we would like to provide technology that would allow users to tell their systems what information-related tasks they wish to perform, not exactly what information they need, and where and how to find it. For example, as an associate editor for a journal, I often need to find reviewers for papers on topics outside my area of expertise. I know that information is out there in the NII that could help me identify appropriate reviewers, but finding it is a difficult task. What I'd like is an IIA that could accept a goal such as "find me highly qualified, reliable reviewers for a paper on parsing using information compression and word alignment techniques" and perhaps a preference on the ranking of solutions, such as "and disprefer reviewers who have recently written a review for me." An interactive agent that did not know how to determine whether a researcher is "highly qualified" could engage in a dialogue with its user to determine how to assess this. For example, the user may tell the agent to assess this by counting articles in well-respected journals or by counting citations in the citation index. Again, if the agent did not know how to determine what the user considered well-respected journals for this particular situation, it would work with the user to define this term and so on.

As a more "every-citizen" example, imagine a patient who has just been prescribed a drug and then catches the tail end of a news story suggesting that several people have become critically ill after taking the drug. This user would likely have a goal such as: "tell me about the side effects of Wonderdrug" and "show me the serious side effects first." If no information on "serious side effects" were found, the agent should work with the user to define the term more precisely. For example, the agent could provide the user with a list of the types of side effects it encountered and ask the user which type(s) he or she considers serious.

PLANNING FOR INFORMATION ACCESS

Once the agent has worked with the user to identify his or her goals, it must be able to form a plan to acquire the information that will aid the user in achieving those goals. IIAs must be equipped with strategies that tell them how to form such plans and must also be able to trade off the urgency of the request against the cost of accessing different information sources and the likelihood that a particular plan will be successful. In the journal editor example I gave earlier, the agent may need to be capable of determining which information sources would be most likely to help find an appropriate reviewer before the end of the day. In the drug example the agent may need to take into account the cost of accessing databases put out by pharmaceutical companies. Agents must also reason about how much advance planning to do before beginning to act and how much information they should acquire before planning or acting in order to reduce uncertainty.

Making progress on these issues will require integrating several ideas coming out of the planning community, including planning under uncertainty (Kushmerick et al., 1995); reasoning about the trade-off between reactive and deliberative behavior (Bratman et al., 1988; Boddy and Dean, 1994); planning for contingencies (Pryor and Collins, 1996); and techniques that integrate planning, information gathering, execution, and plan revision (Draper et al., 1994; Zilberstein and Russell, 1993).

To support agents in forming such plans, new types of automatic indexing schemes must be devised. Data may need to be indexed in multiple ways—for example, reflecting different purposes the data may serve or different levels of detail. In the World Wide Web, links going into and out of a document characterize that document and may be useful in forming indexes to it (as is done in citation search systems). In addition, automatic indexing schemes that work across modalities are needed.

INTELLIGENT MULTIMEDIA PRESENTATION OF INFORMATION

IIAs will be able to acquire information from many different information sources in a variety of media. These systems will need to be able to plan multimedia presentations that most effectively communicate this information in ways that support users in achieving their goals and performing their tasks. For example, an IIA helping a visitor to the Washington, D.C., area identify good Thai restaurants may provide a *Consumer Reports*-like chart rating the 10 best restaurants on a variety of features, a city map showing where the restaurants are located relative to the user's hotel, and spoken excerpts from restaurant reviews that are coordinated with highlighting of the row in the chart and dots on the map that correspond to the restaurants being described. We would also like such multimedia presentations to be tailored to the user's background and preferences, the task at hand, and prior information displays the user has viewed. In the restaurant example, if the system can determine that the user is not familiar with the D.C. area, specific directions to the various restaurants may be given, whereas for a D.C. native an address may be sufficient. If the user has previously requested detailed directions to one restaurant and then requests directions to another restaurant nearby, the system may describe the location of the second restaurant relative to the location of the first.

Owing to the vast information resources that are now available, improved networking infrastructure for high-speed information transfer, and higher-quality audio, video, and graphics display capabilities, intelligent multimedia presentation is an active area of research. As Roth and Hefley (1993) define them, intelligent multimedia presentation systems (IMMPSs) take as input a collection of information to be communicated and a set of communicative goals (i.e., purposes for communicating information or the tasks to be performed by the user requesting the information). An IMMPS typically has a knowledge base of communicative strategies that enable it to design a presentation that expresses the information using a combination of the available media and presentation techniques in a way that achieves the communicative purposes and supports users in performing their tasks. Roth and Hefley argue that IMMPSs will be most effective in situations where it is not possible for system developers to design presentation software because they cannot anticipate all possible combinations of information that will be requested for display. This is clearly the case for an every-citizen interface to the NII.

IMMPSs must perform several complex tasks. They typically consist of a presentation planner, a number of media generators, and a media coordinator. The presentation planner uses presentation design knowledge to select content to be included in a display intended to achieve a set of goals for a particular user in a given context. It uses its knowledge of techniques available to the various media generators to apportion content to media and generate a sequence of directives for individual media generators. Media generators (e.g., for natural language text, speech, and graphics) must determine how to convey the content given the directives they receive from the planner and then report back their results to the presentation planner and media coordinator. The coordinator must manage interactions among individual media generators, resolve conflicts, and maintain presentation consistency.

Considerable progress has been made toward systems that perform these tasks for limited domains, user tasks, data, and presentation types. For example, extant prototype systems can coordinate text and graphical depictions of devices for generating instructions about their repair or proper use—for example, Comet (Feiner and McKeown, 1991) and WIP (Wahlster et al., 1993). These systems generate multimedia presentations from a representation of intended presentation content and represent progress toward some of the functionality desired in an every-citizen interface. For example, these systems can effectively coordinate media when generating references to objects (e.g., "the highlighted knob"; McKeown et al., 1992; Andr and Rist, 1994) and can tailor their presentations to the target audience and situation (McKeown, 1993; Wahlster et al., 1993). In addition, it generates its presentation in an incremental fashion. This allows it to begin producing the presentation before all of the input is received and to react more promptly if the goals or inputs to the generator are changed. These are important features for an IMMPS that will be used in an interface that is presenting information from the NII. Another important area of recent research is in coordinating temporal media (e.g., speech and animation), where information is presented over time and may need to be synchronized with other portions of the presentation in other media (Feiner et al., 1993; Andr and Rist, 1996).

Ideally, an IMMPS would have the capability to flexibly construct presentations that honor constraints imposed by media techniques and that are sensitive not only to characteristics of the information being presented but also to user preferences and goals and the context created by prior presentations. Researchers working in text generation have developed systems that are capable of using information in a discourse history to point out similarities and differences between material currently being described and material presented in earlier explanation(s), to omit previously explained material, to explicitly mark repeated material so as to distinguish it from new material (e.g., "as I said before, 1dots"), and to use alternative strategies to elaborate or clarify previously explained material (Carenini and Moore, 1993; Moore, 1995; Moore et al., 1996).

This prior research requires rich representations of the information that is presented, as well as models of the user's goals, tasks, and preferences. Extending this work for an interface to the NII will require research on standardized data modeling languages and/or translation kits and reusable models of common tasks. In addition, IMMPSs capable of operating with shallower representations must be developed.

Finally, we cannot expect and may not even want IMMPSs to be monolithic systems that completely design presentations according to their own criteria. Thus, systems must be devised that can provide many levels of assistance to users in the presentation design process. Users cannot be expected to fully specify presentation design choices; it is more natural for them to learn a language for expressing their tasks and goals than to learn a language for describing presentation techniques. In some cases, users will have preferences about presentation design in advance of display generation. In other cases they will want the ability to alter the way information is presented once they have seen an initial presentation. Research is needed to develop natural, flexible interfaces to support interactive design, such as those described by Roth et al. (1994, 1995).

USER INTERFACE ENVIRONMENTS FOR INFORMATION EXPLORATION

Even if IIAs can be provided that accept the type of queries I envision, users will want the capability to browse or explore the NII. This may be because they could not articulate a query (even interactively) until they saw some of what was available or because the information they received led them to want further information. In addition, users may want to see some of the information in more detail or see it presented in a different manner. For example, a user who is relocating to a new area might request a visualization that shows several attributes of a set of available houses and relationships between them (e.g., number of rooms, lot size, neighborhood, and asking price). Once this display is presented, the user may then want to select some subset of the particular houses contained in the original display, pick up this set, and drag-and-drop it on a map tool to see more precisely where the houses in the set are located.

To provide these kinds of capabilities, software environments need to be developed for exploring and visualizing large amounts of diverse information. As Lucas et al. (1996) argue, this requires moving from an application-centric architecture to an information-centric approach. The distinction hinges on differences in the basic currency through which users interact with a system. In application-centric architectures the basic currency is the file, and users must rely on applications to fetch and display information from files. Each application has its own user interface that defines the types of files people can manipulate and what they can do with them. With the introduction of graphical user interfaces and the desktop metaphor, files became concrete visual objects, directly manipulated by the user, stored on the desktop or in folders, and, to a limited extent, arranged by users and software in semantically meaningful ways. But the contents of those files is still out of direct reach of the user.

In their Visage system, Lucas et al. (1996) take an information-centric approach in which the basic currency is the data element. Rather than limiting the user to files (or documents) as targets of direct manipulation, Visage permits direct drag-and-drop manipulation of data at any level of granularity. A numerical entry in a table, selected bars from a bar chart, and a complex presentation graphic are all first-class candidates for user manipulations, and all follow the same "physics" of the interface. Users can merge individual data items into aggregates and summarize their attributes or break down aggregated data along different dimensions to create a larger number of smaller aggregates. These capabilities form the foundation for a powerful interface for data navigation and visualization.

ADAPTIVE INTERFACES

Although the Visage approach has proven successful for the simple graphics implemented in the Visage prototype (i.e., text in tables, bars in charts, symbols in maps), continued research is needed to handle the wide range of data and presentation types that populate the NII. In particular, new approaches that allow richer analysis of the information contained in hypertext documents are needed. One area that is developing technology relevant to this need is research on adaptive hypertext and hypermedia systems, which exploit information about a particular user (typically represented in the user model) to adapt both the hypermedia displays and the links presented to the user. Adaptive hypermedia is useful in situations where the hyperspace is large or the system is expected to be used by people with different knowledge and goals. This is clearly the case for the NII.

Researchers in text generation (Moore and Mittal, 1996) are working on interfaces in which system-generated texts are structured objects. During the generation process, the system applies abstract rules to determine which text objects should be selectable in the final presentation (i.e., which text objects will have "hyperlinks" associated with them). To pose questions, the user moves the mouse over the generated text, and those portions that can be asked about become highlighted. When the user selects a text object, a menu of questions that may be asked about this text appears. Question menus are generated on the fly using a set of rules that reason about the underlying concepts and relationships mentioned in the selected text (as represented in a knowledge base). Because the system has a record of the plan that produced the text as well as a user model, it can reason about the context in which the selected text occurs and provide a menu of follow-up questions that are sensitive to both the discourse context and the individual user. In this system, texts are synthesized from underlying knowledge sources by the system in response to the user's question or the system's need to communicate with the user. Because the text is generated dynamically, the system cannot in advance identify the particular text objects that should have associated links or links to other texts. Indeed, in this framework, traversing a link corresponds to asking the system to generate another text. Moreover, the follow-up questions, which correspond to the links in traditional hypertext systems, cannot be precoded and fixed in advance but are generated dynamically using heuristics that are sensitive to domain knowledge, the user model, and the discourse context. As with many other artificial intelligence approaches, this technology depends on the system having a rich underlying representation of the domain content described in the generated text as well as a model of the textual structure. But we can easily imagine adapting this technology for use with the NII. Techniques exist for automatically generating indexes from unrestricted text for information retrieval (Evans and Zhai, 1996), so we can expect that such indexes will (or could) be available for many, if not all, documents on the NII. In addition, parsers and part-of-speech taggers can robustly identify the constituents of sentences (Brill, 1993). Building on these existing technologies would allow an interface in which, say, all noun phrases in a document become mouse sensitive, and the hyperlinks to other documents are determined on demand by using the noun-phrase (synonyms, etc.) as an index to find related documents. Techniques developed in the area of adaptive hypermedia may also be employed to allow the selection of links to be sensitive to the user's knowledge and goals.

REFERENCES

Andr, E., and T. Rist. 1994. Referring to World Objects with Text and Pictures. Pp. 530-534 in *Proceedings of the 15th International Conference on Computational Linguistics.*

Andr, E., and T. Rist. 1996. Coping with Temporal Constraints in Multimedia Presentation Planning. *Proceedings of the National Conference on Artificial Intelligence.* Menlo Park, Calif.: AAAI Press.

Boddy, M., and T.L. Dean. 1994. Deliberation Scheduling for Problem Solving in Time-Constrained Environments. *Artificial Intelligence,* 67(2):345-385.

Bratman, M.E., David J. Israel, and M.E. Pollack. 1988. Plans and Resource-Bounded Practical Reasoning. *Computational Intelligence,* 4(4):349-355.

Brill, E. 1993. Automatic Gammar Induction and Parsing Free Text: A Transformation-Based

Approach. Pp. 259-265 in *Proceedings of the 31st Annual Meeting of the Association for Computational Linguistics*.

Carenini, G., and J.D. Moore, 1993. Generating Explanations in Context. Pp. 175-182 in W.D. Gray, W.E. Hefley, and D. Murray, Eds. *Proceedings of the International Workshop on Intelligent User Interfaces*. New York: ACM Press.

Draper, D., S. Hanks, and D. Weld. 1994. Probabilistic Planning with Information Gathering and Contingent Execution. Pp. 31-36 in K. Hammond, Ed., *Proceedings of the 2nd International Conference on Artificial Intelligence and Planning Systems*. Menlo Park, Calif.: AAAI Press.

Evans, D.A., and C. Zhai. 1996. Noun-Phrase Analysis in Unrestricted Text for Information Retrieval. Pp. 17-24 in *Proceedings of the 34th Annual Meeting of the Association for Computational Linguistics*. Somerset, NJ: ACL.

Feiner, S.K. and K.R. McKeown. 1991. Automating the Generation of Coordinated Multimedia Explanations. *IEEE Computer*, 24(10):33-41.

Feiner, S.K., D.J. Litman, K.R. McKeown, and R.J. Passonneau. 1993. Towards Coordinated Temporal Multimedia Presentation. Pp. 139-147 in M.T. Maybury, Ed., *Intelligent Multimedia Interfaces*. Menlo Park, Calif.: AAAI Press.

Grosz, B., and R. Davis. 1994. A Report to ARPA on Twenty-First Century Intelligent Systems. *AI Magazine*, 15(3):10-20.

Kushmerick, N., S. Hanks, and D. Weld. 1995. An Algorithm for Probabilistic Least-Commitment Planning. *Artificial Intelligence*, 76(1-2):239-286.

Lucas, P., S.F. Roth, and C.C. Gomberg. 1996. Visage: Dynamic Information Exploration. In *Proceedings of the Conference on Human Factors in Computing Systems*. New York: ACM Press.

McKeown, K.R. 1993. Tailoring Lexical Choice to the User's Vocabulary in Multimedia Explanation Generation. Pp. 226-233 in *Proceedings of the 31st Annual Meeting of the Association for Computational Linguistics*. Somerset, N.J.: ACL.

McKeown, K.R., S.K. Feiner, J. Robin, D. Seligmann, and M. Tanenblatt. 1992. Generating Cross-References for Multimedia Explanation. Pp. 9-16 in *Proceedings of the National Conference on Artificial Intelligence*, Menlo Park, Calif.: AAAI Press.

Moore, J.D. 1995. *Participating in Explanatory Dialogues: Interpreting and Responding to Questions in Context*. Cambridge, Mass.: MIT Press.

Moore, J.D., and V.O. Mittal. 1996. Dynamically Generated Follow-Up Questions. *IEEE Computer*, Vol. 75-86. (July).

Moore, J.D., B. Lemaire, and J.A. Rosenblum. 1996. Discourse Generation for Instructional Applications: Identifying and Exploiting Relevant Prior Explanations. *Journal of the Learning Sciences*, 5(1):49-94.

Pryor, L., and G. Collins. 1996. Planning for Contingencies: A Decision-Based Approach. *Journal of Artificial Intelligence Research*, 4:287-339.

Roth, S.F., and W.E. Hefley. 1993. Intelligent Multimedia Presentation Systems: Research and Principles. Pp. 13-58. in Mark T. Maybury, Ed., *Intelligent Multimedia Interfaces*. Menlo Park, Calif. AAAI Press.

Roth, S.F., J. Kolojejchick, J. Mattis, and J. Goldstein. 1994. Interactive Graphic Design Using Automatic Presentation Knowledge. Pp. 112-117 in *Proceedings of the Conference on Human Factors in Computing Systems*. New York: ACM Press.

Roth, S.F., J. Kolojejchick, J. Mattis, and M. Chuah. 1995. Sagetools: An Intelligent Environment for Sketching, Browsing, and Customizing Data Graphics. Pp. 409-410 in *Proceedings of the Conference on Human Factors in Computing Systems*. New York: ACM Press.

Wahlster, W., E. Andr, W. Finkler, J.J. Profitlich, and T. Rist. 1993. Plan-Based Integration of Natural Language and Graphics Generation. *Artificial Intelligence*, 63(1-2):387-428.

Zilberstein, S., and S.J. Russell. 1993. Anytime Sensing, Planning and Action: A Practical Model for Robot Control. Pp. 1402-1407 in *Proceedings of the 13th International Joint Conference on Artificial Intelligence*. Chambery, France.

RESOURCE DISCOVERY AND RESOURCE DELIVERY

Kent Wittenburg
Bellcore

The promise of a national information infrastructure (NII) includes the ability for every citizen to access certain fundamental information and services. I would assume that examples of fundamental information and services would include directory information (analogous to the present white and yellow pages); local, state, and federal government information, ranging from tax help to local library and social services to environmental regulations; and, lastly, a panoply of commercial services, such as audio/video broadcasting and n-way conferencing, virtual storefronts, and banking services that will emerge on some form of an infrastructure that combines elements from present telephony, broadcasting, and data networks.

Today's World Wide Web is the closest approximation we have to the NII of the future. One way to proceed in revealing the pertinent research issues is to ask where the current World Wide Web falls short in light of the goal of universal access. Besides the problem of physical access via networks and user premise hardware, I see two major problem areas: (1) the resource discovery problem, which I take to be a product of the chaotic, fundamentally democratic nature of the Web, and (2) the resource delivery problem, which has many dimensions, including complications brought about by differing bandwidth capacities, differing user interactive devices, and differing user cognitive (dis)abilities.

The goals that I see in these two areas can be stated simply:

- With respect to resource discovery, every literate citizen should have access to directory and finding services that are within that user's capacity to use. For example, every citizen should be easily able to locate the local library or school system's offerings on the NII and select an appropriate service.
- With respect to resource delivery, every literate citizen, including those with vision or hearing disabilities, should be able to access information and/or services at a certain minimum bandwidth using any device with certain minimum resources (audio, screen size, color, etc.). For example, a blind person who has use of an interactive device based entirely on audio should still be able to find and access the local library or school system's offerings.

RESOURCE DISCOVERY RESEARCH ISSUES

The resource discovery problem is one that is patently obvious to anyone trying to use the World Wide Web today. Currently, the strategies for finding resources are:

- ask a friend or colleague;
- subscribe to mailing lists or publications that give updates on resources of interest to subscribers;
- use general-purpose search services, such as AltaVista (http://www.altavista.com); and
- use subject-cataloging sites such as Yahoo (http://yahoo.com) or those provided by Internet access providers or mom-and-pop miniguides.

The first two strategies actually may be more promising as a basis for future research activities and tools than we may think at first blush. I would hazard a guess that most of today's knowledge workers whose responsibilities include keeping apace with developments in their areas of expertise have evolved a strategy of managing a personal view of the World Wide Web that is populated largely by resources found through serendipitous contacts with colleagues and friends as well as received as through netnews, mailing lists, and print or electronic publications. One of the research challenges I would pose is to create tools and methods for larger communities to leverage the millions of individual efforts that are already taking place for organizing information. Two exemplars of such community-based efforts at resource discovery are Bellcore's Group Asyncronous Browsing project (http://www.w3.orgpub/Conferences/WWW4/Papers/98/) and ATT's PHOAKS work (http://weblab. research. att.com/ phoaks/).

Search-based services are faced with the problems of how to manage and structure the astoundingly huge hit sets returned by their queries, how to include some form of quality control, and how to surmount, or shall we say circumvent, the inevitable precision/recall trade-offs. Further, there is the problem of combining and manipulating results from different search services and other relevant information broker sources. Efforts to achieve some standardized distributed object-like protocols so that different search services can be integrated is a step in the right direction (http://www-db.stanford.edu/~gravano/standards). Another needed direction is in how to integrate search with structural browsing and in fact with community-based sources of information as above. In general, there needs to be much more work on how to integrate filters and views over a domain, so that, for instance, a user does not have to deal with the results from a general query whose domain is the world when all he or she is looking for is the library down the street. For an every-citizen interface there is also the fundamental difficulty that effective use of today's general-purpose search engines requires a degree of sophistication beyond the reach of a substantial part of the population.

As for subject cataloging efforts, the major problems are the magnitude of manual labor required to keep up with the rapidly changing Web and the self-evident truth (which not everyone agrees with) that a single universal hierarchical classification of every piece of information on the Web, even if it existed, would not be very useful. The private customized subject catalogs one finds on the home screens of certain access providers or networks are fine as far as they go, but they will not scale. One of the major issues is how to build effective interfaces for browsing multiple hierarchies in an integrated fashion and, again, how to impose views over a massive collection of hierarchies that might be influenced by such factors as quality ratings, personal or group histories, popularity, and geographic locality.

PROPOSED PROJECTS: RESOURCE DISCOVERY

In the commercial marketplace we can expect that competing directory and search services will fight it out on the Web, but a danger is, of course, that a few companies may monopolize the area and make it difficult for the little guys to make themselves known. The business models for directory services seem at the moment to rely primarily on advertising (or pseudoadvertising) revenues. For instance, one has to pay a lot of money to get a link placed on Netscape's browser menu (http://www.netscape.com). What is difficult to see coming from the private sector are efforts that leverage the search services collectively and that integrate other helpful sources such as public sites (Library of Congress, for instance). Note that such services would violate the current economic models since the private provider no longer has control over the end-user's screen and cannot then leverage advertising revenue. In that light I would suggest that at least one major project coming out of a government funding effort concentrate on proposing standards and economic models for information brokering services so that integrated resource discovery tools become possible. We also need to experiment with building public registries so that nonprofit and governmental bodies can be easily found and their services utilized by the appropriate populations. One representative initiative in the earth science area is the USDAC project sponsored by the National Aeronautics and Space Administration (http://usdac2.rutgers.edu/).

Another major thrust I would see is in projects whose goal is to build interfaces that integrate information-brokering services enabled in part by the distributed substrate mentioned above. In the relatively short term, we can expect to see incremental improvements from the private sector in interfaces for search and, say, graphical browsing. An appropriate subject for longer-term combined unversity and private research lab efforts is to experiment with prototype interfaces for integrating distributed search services, structurally oriented graphical browsing, community-based sources, geographic location services, and so on.

Lastly, there needs to be more basic research to understand and model human resource discovery behavior, leading to evaluation metrics that might be used to judge competing techniques and systems. The Xerox PARC work on information foraging (http://www.acm.org/sigchi/chi95/Electronic/documnts/ papers/ppp_bdy.htm) is one exemplar of this line of research. The ultimate test will be success at allowing nonsophisticated users to find what they need, but it is not obvious at this point how to compare and evaluate competing systems and methods.

RESEARCH ISSUES: RESOURCE DELIVERY

As mentioned, the multidimensional resource delivery problem is characterized by constraints such as differing bandwidth capacities, differing user interactive devices, and differing user cognitive (dis)abilities. There are many ways in which to address these issues. My own perspective is approach it from the information provider's point of view. If I as an information provider need to get fundamentally the same content (and services) presented along so many dimensions, what is the technology that will aid me to do so?

The situation today is simply a horror show, although the advent of standard HTML, tools for format conversion, and cross-platform Java are major breakthroughs. The basic issue is how one moves beyond HTML to generate truly interactive interfaces for devices ranging from high-end workstations at T1 bandwidth to palm-sized wireless devices at less than 2K bits per second, for users with their full faculties and university training to economically disadvantaged and disabled users.

From a design perspective the problem is how to take the same content and design effective presentations and interactions for certain target points in this multidimensional space. This is a huge problem, and it is unreasonable to expect that each information provider must do this themselves from scratch for each piece of information they supply. The meager efforts to address this situation, as far as I can see, are coming from the private sector in the form of proprietary HTML-based tools that represent content in proprietary forms and then provide very limited help in designing for a very narrow range of alternatives.

The research communities have shown some interest in addressing multimodal and information-based graphical alternatives. I think that the most appropriate issue to address in the context of universal access is how to design effectively in the face of very strong constraints (such as audio-only interfaces) given a common content representation. One must understand not only how to create an appropriate design in general but also how to map to an instance of it from common content. Representing design knowledge (http://www.computer.org/conferen/vl95/talks/T1.html) is a crucial element in this enterprise. An example of a proposed mapping architecture can be found at http://community.bellcore.com/kentw/rg-for-ap5-abstract.html. Others can be found in Artificial Intelligence-oriented work on automatic presentation coming out of Columbia, Carnegie Mellon, ISI, and MITRE. However, it strikes me that all of this work is far from being able to deliver on the promise of automatic contruction of presentations and interactive interfaces to meet the needs of universal access. The major bottleneck, as far as I can see, is the lack of a common set of assumptions about the representation of content.

PROPOSED PROJECTS: RESOURCE DELIVERY

First, I would propose an effort at defining a common level of representation in the context of one or more particular information sets. For instance, the government might have an interest in seeing certain essential on-line services such as tax help currently available in HTML designed and delivered for a wider range of users and user devices. Rather than attempting to agree on a common representation in the abstract, which will be virtually impossible, I would suggest one or more concrete projects out of which a proposal for a common representation may emerge.

Second, I see a need for cataloging design knowledge relevant to particular points along this multidimensional delivery spectrum. These points need to be identified, of course, and then best-in-class example interfaces need to be built and abstracted. Again, this could be done in the context of a particular information domain of relevance to the government. Defining appropriate forms for design knowledge is, of course, a difficult problem in itself and would need to be addressed.

Lastly, I think basic research in architectures for systems that map from content to presentation instances needs to be fostered. These three proposals in the end require integration, but in the short run I think it is most appropriate to allow some independent efforts that can ultimately be brought together.

SEARCH AND PUBLISHING

Robert A. Virzi

GTE Laboratories Incorporated

SUMMARY

The national information infrastructure (NII) is already here. Bits and bytes buzz by us at an astounding rate just about wherever we go. The problem is not with the infrastructure—the databases, protocols, and physical transport media. The problem is that we do not have a national information superstructure—a set of access and publishing tools that are widely distributed, easy to use, cheap, powerful, and accessible through a variety of terminals that include computers, personal digital assistants, telephones, screen phones, cellular phones, pagers, and television sets. In my view the Web of tomorrow will be nothing like the Web of today in terms of who is using it and what they will expect from it. To get there from here, we need to make progress in three key technologies: (1) intelligent agent technologies, including searching and filtering tools, need to be made more comprehensive and transparent; (2) publishing tools need to evolve so that a greater variety of content producers can create information, in a greater variety of media; and (3) access needs to be possible independent of place (office, car, or home) and device (computer, phone, or TV set).

INTELLIGENT AGENT TECHNOLOGIES

The current generation of searching and filtering tools is inadequate in two key respects. First, the tools are not comprehensive, restricting searches to a subset of the available sources. For example, searching for a business's name on the Web may return me a pointer to the business's Web site, but it is unlikely to return a phone number that the business can be reached at. This is somewhat surprising considering that I can search for a business's phone number on the Web at any of several sites, yet these searches are not likely to tell me much about a business's Web presence. The net effect is that not only do I need to know the specifics of searching using any engine, I also need to know where to go to begin searching. The second user interface problem I have observed in searching and filtering mechanisms is that they tend to be rather opaque when it comes to in-forming the user of what was searched, what was rejected, why items may have been rejected, and how successes are prioritized. An ideal intelligent agent would make it easy for the user to express what he wanted done; confirm that the user's intentions matched the effected ac-tions; convey the breadth of the search, including gaps; and present re-sults in a clear way that matches the user's expectations.

PUBLISHING TOOLS

An interface to the NII for every citizen implies to me far more than the ability to find information. I have seen many reports in the press regarding the gap between information haves and have-nots. While I do not want to underestimate the importance of gaining access to informa-tion, I feel there has been far too little attention given to the gap between the content production capable and the incapable. If we succeed in pro-viding access to information for every citizen, I feel we will have fallen far short of the mark. What is needed are tools and technologies that will allow any citizen to produce and publish content. We need to break down the barriers to production so that the NII doesn't become the next form of television—a one-way pipe for the dissemination of carefully chosen messages by a select few. I believe that the goal of the NII should be not just many-to-many communication but any-to-any communica-tion. For this to happen, we need to find ways to make it much easier for people to produce content. We also need to understand and discuss new publishing models that include broadcasting but that also allow for "narrowcasting" of information.

I see the current barriers to widespread content production and pub-lishing as the high capital costs of computer ownership; the high level of technical savvy demanded by today's production, editing, and publish-ing tools; the literacy level required by what is predominantly a textual medium; and a lack of understanding on the part of the general popula-tion of the power of publishing content.

PLACE AND DEVICE INDEPENDENCE

As people come to rely on the NII more and more and as commercial endeavors begin to utilize it, the need to provide ubiquitous access will increase. Users will come to rely on the technology, and will demand access to it from their offices, homes, cars, hotels, airports, and other public places. In order to provide place independence, we must find a way to provide device independence. It should be possible to obtain or publish information on the NII without a computer. This is not to say that full functionality needs be provided from all types of terminals, but rather that the data appropriate to a given type of terminal should be presented. Once we have achieved device independence, place independence will follow automatically. And once we have place independence, people will come to rely on and use the NII heavily and automatically.

RESEARCH QUESTIONS

Based on the three key technological advances I see as necessary to providing an every-citizen interface to the NII, I will outline some research questions that I see as ripe for attack.

- *Search strategies.* How do people approach a search task? The design of search engines would benefit greatly from knowing what people expect to happen given a variety of scenarios. Free search engines such as AltaVista seem to demand different kinds of knowledge from the user than a visit to, say, Yahoo!, which relies on defined categories to a greater extent. Do either of these models map more naturally to users' cognitive styles? Are there task dependencies? Questions such as these seem eminently answerable today. Indeed, there is actually a large information sciences literature relevant to this area that has been strangely ignored.
- *Device-independent data structures.* Much of the information accessible today is highly tied to a particular class of display devices. Even multimedia objects (e.g., a movie) are not usually separable into independent streams if, for example, my device could play sound but not show moving images. This is unfortunate because in many instances degraded access to information is preferable to no access. This is a difficult problem, but it would be very useful to be able to separate the representation of the object as data from the device used to present it. The goal of this line of research would be to define a common representation for published objects, along with translation mechanisms to provide access to the objects from a variety of devices. Such a research project would have a fairly far horizon.
- *Publishing needs.* To create usable publishing tools, we need a better understanding of what it is that people will want to publish. This is more difficult than it might at first sound, because it is difficult to get consumers to think about how they will use something that is foreign to them. However, in order to build tools that support the publishing needs of every citizen, and to evolve the infrastructure in support of those needs, we need a better understanding of how people want to use the system.

I would emphasize that this could not be accomplished by looking at people's home pages today. We are in an age where the broadcasting model predominates. People and businesses put on the Web what they are willing to let anyone see. As Web-based security improves, we will move to a narrowcasting model where the publisher can be assured of limiting access to a select group. In some cases, this may lead to pay-for-services sites. In other cases people will use the security to "privately publish" information, so that they may, for example, access an appointment schedule via their car phone.

• *Market research.* Although it is likely far outside the bounds of what the National Research Council would consider as a project for study, there is a basic lack of understanding as to what consumers (i.e., citizens) actually want out of the NII. Without this basic understanding we run the considerable risk of building the wrong thing. In the late 1980s, telephone companies were scrambling to find a way to deliver switched video to the home. Luckily, before the huge capital costs were sunk, these same companies began to understand that maybe this was not what their customers actually wanted. In point of fact, something much simpler and cheaper could meet most consumer needs, and that is the direction we are traveling now. I am concerned that we may not have done our homework on the NII. Building it does not ensure that they will come.

SECURITY

Stephen Kent
BBN Corporation

EVOLUTION OF NATIONAL INFORMATION INFRASTRUCTURE ELEMENTS

As the national information infrastructure (NII) moves into the twenty-first century, it is evolving into a more sophisticated collection of information-processing and telecommunications systems. One of the most pressing challenges is to offer greater functionality, and incorporate greater security and privacy for these systems while providing a user interface that is comprehensible, comfortable, and easy to learn by average citizens.

Residential telephone services, which used to provide only simple point-to-point connection, now offer Call Waiting, Call Answering, Caller ID, Call Trace, Call Back, multiplexing of multiple numbers onto a single line (with distinct ring patterns), etc. Cellular telephones and pocket pagers began as expensive devices affordable only by professionals or those whose companies paid the bills. Now they are used by many "everyday" citizens, and they offer increasingly sophisticated capabilities (e.g., two-way nationwide paging). Airline passengers can initiate and receive phone calls on many flights.

Local television was once defined by a small number of channels, dominated by three major networks, and delivered via VHF and UHF signals. Today, cable and satellite (including direct-broadcast satellite) systems offer tens (soon hundreds) of channels, many with specialized program material. Some television delivery systems allow a user to select a channel via interaction with integrated, on-screen, time- and subject-oriented schedules.

Computers, which used to be large, isolated, centralized systems costing millions of dollars, have become inexpensive, portable, and networked. Computer communication, which was initially slow, expensive, and not very extensive, has become fast, cheap, and almost as ubiquitous as telephone service. Local-area networks provide high-speed access in buildings and on campuses, while wide-area nets connect systems around the world. Emerging wireless computer communications systems promise to make mobile computing connectivity as easy and common as cellular phone service.

Citizen interaction with organizations, both businesses and government agencies, used to require face-to-face meetings, filing of handwritten forms, or telephone calls. Automated touch-tone response systems, tied to databases and enabled with synthesized voice response technology, have greatly increased the range of information that citizens can access and have expanded the times at which such data can be accessed. Credit card balances, frequent flier account information, and tax refund status can all be checked through calls to toll-free numbers. Stock and mutual fund trades and bank fund transfers can be initiated via similar means, all without direct interaction with a human being and on a 24-hour basis.

Today, many of the systems that have provided automated telephone access capabilities are moving to Internet-enabled access. This provides a much more powerful and convenient interface, enabling a wider range of data access with faster response and interaction characteristics. Businesses and government agencies are moving rapidly to make information available over the Internet, via the World Wide Web. Massachusetts now supports payment of traffic tickets over the Web, as a first step toward making government more responsive and accessible to citizens. Businesses of every stripe, from financial institutions to mail-order catalog merchants, are providing client access via the Web, in addition to the telephone.

A VISION OF NEAR- AND INTERMEDIATE-TERM NII INTERACTIONS

Within the next 5 to 10 years significant improvements in many NII element interfaces will be implemented and widely deployed. The use of technologies such as cable modems, ADSL, and ISDN will significantly improve Internet access speeds for residential users. Continuing improvements in computer technology will increase local processing speed, enabling more sophisticated user interface software. The advent of very low-cost computers, designed specifically for Web browsing and using a television as a video interface, promises to expand the subscriber base into many more households. Using this model, one can imagine an NII in which citizen interaction with government agencies, businesses, and with one another make substantial use of this environment.

Requests for generic data from a vast array of government databases can be made and instantaneously satisfied via Web browsers interacting with servers coupled to massive databases. Interactions for a variety of personal transactions with government agencies also will be enabled (e.g., filing tax forms, making tax payments, or checking one's Social Security account status).

Many catalogs and periodicals now delivered in hard-copy form can be delivered via the Web, as some already are. After browsing on-line catalogs, clients will place orders for items to be shipped via the postal system or express delivery services, all via the Web. All forms of financial transactions (e.g., credit and debit card purchases, checks, cash exchanges, stock and mutual fund transactions) will be available via the Internet, and many will make use of these facilities instead of hard-copy instruments.

SECURITY, INTERFACES, AND THE NII

As elements of the NII evolve, as described above, they offer increased functionality and improved performance, usually at lower prices. However, security and privacy concerns often are overlooked in this rush to enhance the NII. Cellular phone calls are not only easy to intercept, but the account information used for billing is even easier to acquire via automated means. It has been estimated that the lack of attention to security, if only for this billing authorization information, has cost the cellular phone industry hundreds of millions of dollars in lost revenue. Digital paging systems are highly vulnerable to interception, raising privacy concerns. Theft of service for cable and satellite TV delivery systems is often decried as depriving those industries of significant amounts of revenue. The Caller ID feature for telephone systems is both a blessing and a curse, from a privacy perspective.

As companies have connected corporate computer and network systems to the Internet to facilitate user access, the overall security of these systems has often been degraded. Most of these Internet connections are secured by firewalls, a technology that usually constrains the Internet so as to reduce its capability (even for authorized users) and which ultimately fails to provide high-quality security for the computers being protected. The ease with which electronic mail can be intercepted or forged is appalling. As the first tentative steps are taken toward consumer-level Internet electronic commerce, the on-line literature is replete with examples of technical opportunities for fraud.

For many of these NII elements the technology for improving security and privacy has been available for some time, but often it has not been implemented. Sometimes the reasons are purely economic (e.g., the cost of adding security technology is perceived to make the resulting product noncompetitive). Sometimes time-to-market concerns prevent incorporation of security features (i.e., the delay imposed by adding security features would allow a competitor to offer a product or service sooner and thereby capture market share). However, in some cases the difficulty of providing a good user interface for security technology has been a major impediment.

As underlying communications and computing systems become more complex, there is a natural tendency for the user interface to become more complex, though that need not always be the case. For example, WIMP (windows, icons, menus, pointers)-based operating system interfaces can mask substantial underlying complexity, as illustrated by the contrast between the Apple Macintosh and DOS interfaces at corresponding points in time. However, within the context of a paradigm such as WIMP, increased functionality often results in increased complexity for users, as both Windows 95 and Mac users can attest.

Computer systems have become more complex, and network interactions have become commonplace in the desktop and laptop systems that users employ in home environments. Providing security for such systems has become increasingly difficult. In the 1970s and 1980s much research was devoted to the development of secure operating systems, primarily for use with multiuser systems (e.g., time-sharing systems and servers). However, all of this research into secure operating systems yielded very little that has been commercially successful or widely deployed. Today, operating systems for the desktop computers most commonly used in home environments (e.g., Windows 95 and Mac), have very few security features. Yet these may be the models for the systems that citizens will most commonly employ in their interactions with the NII.

An alternative model, suggested by the "network computer" paradigm promoted by companies such as Oracle and Sun, is a Java interpreter and a Web browser as the operating system replacement. Given the many security problems that have been discovered in Web browsers such as the Netscape Navigator and the rash of Java-based security problems that have been described in the literature, this is hardly an encouraging alternative paradigm.

In either case, networked computers of some sort will provide an every-citizen interface to many NII elements. There are fundamental and difficult problems associated with developing highly functional and secure networked computer systems; these problems are exacerbated when there is a requirement to make the systems easy to use by all citizens.

WHAT IS THE HARD PROBLEM?

The fundamentally hard problem, as alluded to above, is one of trying to make an increasingly complex system, operated by untrained users, secure in the face of attacks by sophisticated adversaries. Various aspects of this problem are examined below.

As noted above, firewalls are typically used in corporate environments to provide "secure" connectivity to the Internet. One of the major reasons for adopting this strategy is that those responsible for corporate computer security find themselves unable to effectively manage security for individual desktop computers. Instead, by inserting a firewall at the perimeter of the corporate network, the site security administrator can focus his or her attention on managing a single (or small number) of computers devoted to a well-defined and limited task (i.e., controlling the flow of Internet traffic across the security perimeter).

In contrast, security management of individual desktop systems is hard because these systems are often directly under the control of users, executing a wide range of software, and based on operating systems that are insecure out of the box.

The control afforded by firewalls is in direct opposition to the Internet goal of facilitating the flow of information between clients and servers. Security administrators are constantly fighting a battle to protect desktop systems and servers by controlling the flow of data (using fairly crude tools), while users clamor for unbridled access to Internet resources. The best a security administrator can hope for is to implement a packet-filtering policy that satisfies most user demands while minimizing attack opportunities. This tug of war has become worse with the advent of the Web and Java. The Java model calls for loading software from servers into users' computers for local execution, rather than transmitting data for display by a browser and so-called helper applications.

In a home environment, if the typical citizen makes use of the same operating system and many of the same applications and is assumed to be even less technically sophisticated that his or her office counterpart, there is even less likelihood that he or she will be able to manage the system in a secure fashion. Moreover, since the system may connect directly to a wide range of Internet servers without the benefit of an intervening firewall managed by a security administrator, the opportunities for successfully attacking such computers are almost boundless. The network computer (NC) model transforms the problem but does not solve it. Proponents of low-cost NCs describe simple systems without local disk storage and with a minimal operating system (e.g., similar to a Web browser). Applications are downloaded onto the NC over the net, for local execution, via high-speed connections.

Historically, one of the most difficult security problems to address is one in which potentially hostile software is imported into a target machine and executed. The "confinement problem" refers to this situation, where the imported software is supposed to be constrained in its access to user data, being granted only the access necessary to perform its advertised task. A Trojan horse is malicious imported software that performs some apparently useful function but also executes some sort of attack on the target system (e.g., destroying data or acquiring data for the attacker). In conventional systems the first challenge for an attacker using a Trojan horse was the problem of introducing his or her software into the target. If stealing data is the goal of the attack, the second problem faced by the attacker is one of exfiltration (i.e., sending the data back to the attacker). In an Internet environment, especially in the context of Web use, this second challenge essentially disappears. Confinement, if successfully implemented, addresses Trojan horse attacks by limiting the data and system resources available to the imported software.

In the past a security-savvy user would never import software into his or her system from other than well-known sources (e.g., major vendors). The introduction of "shareware" and "freeware" into a desktop computer, distributed over the Internet or downloaded from an on-line service such as AOL or CompuServe, flies in the face of this traditional security convention. Yet software distributed in this fashion has become quite popular and is widely used in corporate as well as home computer environments. Functionality has won out over prudent security practice, even though examples of Trojan horse attacks via these software sources are not unknown.

The Java model takes the imported software notion to its ultimate conclusion; it creates a legitimate path for infiltration of software (Java "applets") into user computers, typically via the Internet and the Web. To make this potentially dangerous situation less so, Java applets are supposed to be constrained in terms of the operations they can perform in the client computer. For example, applets are not supposed to have access to the local file system, to read or write user files. Unfortunately, vulnerabilities in the initial implementations of Java interpreters have not successfully confined applets, as promised. Even if these Java security problems are fixed, it is not clear that this simple model of highly constrained applet behavior will persist. Historically, useful applications have required access to user files, both for reading and writing. If applets are to become powerful tools performing increasingly sophisticated tasks for users, it seems unlikely that this stringent constraint will remain. Thus, one should assume that applets will, in the future, be granted access to user data, whether the data are locally resident on a full-fledged computer or stored on some network file server. Functionality almost always wins out over security.

An even more serious concern is that the user of a Java-enabled Web browser (or of a network computer in the future) may not even know when applets are being loaded into his or her computer. Today, many corporate security administrators urge users to disable Java support in their Web browsers to minimize the potential for this sort of security problem.

While use of Java is still rather minimal on the Internet, in time many Web pages may become Java applets, and disabling Java may prevent access to so many sites that users are forced to permit Java execution. So even if the user interface were to alert the user when an applet is downloaded, how would a user know whether that event posed a danger?

In principle, if Java environments evolve to a point where the known vulnerabilities are successfully addressed, the user could control which applets were loaded and what operations they were authorized to perform. But is this a realistic expectation? This represents the critical security user interface issue for the NII.

Previous research on computer security showed that it was quite difficult to establish a constrained execution environment for imported software (i.e., to address the confinement problem). Few operating systems were successfully developed to meet this challenge, and very few are deployed today. Java does help address this problem by providing an interpreted environment, and thus it should be possible to remove many means by which imported software might try to circumvent the constraints imposed by the user. However, so far the Java environment has proven to be vulnerable to circumvention by interpreted code, just as security controls in traditional operating systems have proven vulnerable to circumvention by compiled code.

In those operating systems that have attempted to solve the confinement problem, a user interface capable of administering the fine-grained access control required for confinement has been very complex. Compartmented mode workstations represent the most widely deployed systems that offer some form of operating-system-enforced confinement. These Unix-based systems are exceedingly difficult to administer, and the granularity of confinement offered is relatively crude compared to what a corporate or home user might require for controlled execution of applets. To date, there is no indication of how to structure a user interface to make confinement of imported software generally understandable even to fairly sophisticated computer users.

RELATED PROBLEMS AND RESEARCH DIRECTIONS

As noted above, confinement is a hard computer security problem that has been studied for almost 20 years. To protect users against malicious imported software (e.g., applets), it will be necessary to offer fine-grained access control to confine the execution of this software. This problem may be easier to solve in a more restricted environment such as that envisioned for network computers, but it is still a hard problem.

Thus, the first research problem is the development of an interface that is intelligible to users to empower them to manage confinement for imported software.

Many of the forms of interaction alluded to above require authentication in order to provide security. The user must be authenticated to the server, and the server must be authenticated to the user. The current proposals for how to accomplish this requirement center around the use of public key cryptography and certificates (e.g., for validating digital signatures and for exchanging keys). However, we have no experience with public certification systems of the scale required to support all of the citizens of the United States, and all of the commercial and government service providers.

In small-scale trials of certification systems for applications such as e-mail, one of the problems that quickly becomes apparent is the difficulty of presenting the right amount of authentication information to the user. If one displays full certification path data, the user will almost certainly be overwhelmed. If the only data displayed are from the final certificate in a path, suitable constraints must be imposed on the certification path validation algorithm to prevent "surprises." However, configuring and managing certification path validation parameters appears to be a fairly complex task in the general case. Noting that the average citizen cannot program a video cassette recorder successfully, it is hard to imagine how this individual could manage a more complex certification validation system. This problems shows up in many ways.

The Java architecture calls for applets to be digitally signed to verify their provenance (e.g., to detect modification of the applet after it was released by the developer or vendor). However, if it is hard to display the right level of detail to a user once the signature is validated, the signatures may not really address the fundamental problem of provenance. Authenticating the identity of a server to which the user has connected poses a similar problem. Small variations in the spelling of a server's name embedded in a public key certificate could easily lead a user to believe that he or she was connected to one (legitimate) server when another had actually been contacted.

This analysis suggests that a critical area requiring additional research is how to provide a user interface to manage certification graphs, so that users are truly aware of the identities of the people and organizations with whom they are dealing in cyberspace.

Many proposals for securing transactions generated by a user rely on the user employing a private digital signature key to sign the transaction. However, the user never directly sees the data being signed; he or she relies on software on his or her computer to indicate what is being signed. Thus, a user's signature may be applied to transactions or messages other than the ones he or she intends if malicious software manipulates the user interface.

Several proposals call for citizens to make use of kiosks for some transactions, both with government and commercial entities. This seems especially attractive as a means to empower low-income households that might not otherwise have access to services via a home computer. However, not long ago, criminals managed to place a fake ATM (automated teller machine) in a shopping mall as a means of acquiring user bank account numbers and PINs (personal identification numbers). A higher-tech version of this scam could be effected with kiosks and might be much harder to detect. The fake kiosks could provide access to legitimate servers on behalf of the user, completing valid transactions on his or her behalf. However, without the user's permission, kiosks could also effect unauthorized transactions at the same time (e.g., applying the user's signature to unauthorized transactions for money transfers).

A final research problem area is how to provide a user interface for personal cryptographic tokens so that users will be protected from malicious software that will attempt to misapply a user's digital signature capability.

RESEARCH TO SUPPORT WIDESPREAD ACCESS TO DIGITAL LIBRARIES AND GOVERNMENT INFORMATION AND SERVICES

Ben Shneiderman
University of Maryland

The rapid growth of the World Wide Web provides compelling testimony to the impact of improved user interfaces. Although FTP (file transfer protocol), Gopher, WAIS (wide area information service), and other services produced active usage, it was the appearance of easy-to-use embedded menu items and appealing graphics that produced the current intensity of use. Public interest continues to grow dramatically, and national policy is being effected in terms of providing access to government information and services.

Early adopters, who are typically technologically sophisticated, are highly motivated to overcome poor designs and push beyond the difficulties to achieve their objectives. However, the much larger number of middle and late adopters are less likely to tolerate chaotic screens; unnecessarily lengthy paths; slow response times; inconsistent terminology; awkward instructions; inadequate help facilities; and missing, wrong, or out-of-date information.

A proactive approach can ensure that the emerging technology will provide accessible, comprehensible, predictable interfaces that serve the needs of the majority. A prompt and moderate level of research effort can shape the evolution of user interfaces to match the skills, needs, and orientation of the broadest users. Topics might include the following:

- Cognitive design strategies for information-abundant Web sites, including metaphor choice (library, shopping mall, television channels, etc.), navigation design, and visual overviews;
- Recognition and support for the distinct needs of diverse user communities, such as elderly, young, handicapped, lower-income, minority, and rural users, plus those with poor reading skills;
- Control panels to allow user tailoring to individual abilities, limitations, and technology;
- Strategies to cope with efficient construction and maintenance of text and graphic versions, multiple browser support, varied user display devices, and voice output;

- Empirical studies of high- versus low-fanout strategies (shallow versus deep trees), compact vertical design to reduce scrolling, benefits of reduced/increased graphical treatments, and impact of slow response time;
- Web site construction languages and templates, software tools to verify visual and textual consistency, Web site management and terminology control, and thesaurus construction;
- Sequencing, clustering, and emphasis of information items according to designer goals;
- Web-oriented user interface design to support browsing directories, searching for key phrases in document databases, and performing database searches;
- Design strategies to support evolutionary learning of complex sites and services;
- Easy-to-use facilities to permit user construction of informational Web sites, community services, and entrepreneurial initiatives;
- Low-cost computing devices and low-cost network access the "Web-top computer";
- Refined feedback and evaluation methods to guide designers, including usability testing, expert reviews, field trials, interviewing users, focus groups, e-mail surveys, and e-mail suggestion boxes;
- Simple privacy protection and secure transmission of financial, medical, or other data;
- Image compression methods to reduce file sizes while best preserving image detail, texture, and color richness; and
- Logging and monitoring software, visualization of usage patterns for individuals and aggregates, and cost-benefit analyses.

Coordination with relevant groups can avoid redundant efforts and support common goals. Current activities include the following:

- Library of Congress National Digital Library Program, in cooperation with the University of Maryland (ben@cs.umd.edu);
- National Research Council project on ordinary-citizen interfaces (Alan Biermann, Chair, Duke University, awb@cs.duke.edu)[the project reported on in this volume].
- Stanford University effort to coordinate database services (contact: Hector Garcia-Molina, hector@cs.stanford.edu);
- U.S. government efforts such as GILS (Government Information Locator Service);
- USACM project: The Interface Between Policy and Technology in Providing Public Access to Government Data (contact: Randy Bush, randy@psg.com);

- Joint effort on digital libraries by the National Science Foundation, National Aeronautics and Space Administration, and Defense Advanced Research Projects Agency; and
- International efforts (e.g., Canada, Singapore, Italy).

ON APPLICATION AREAS

COMMUNITY COMPUTING PROJECTS

Aki Helen Namioka

Computer Professionals for Social Responsibility

INTRODUCTION

In the fall of 1993, Computer Professionals for Social Responsibility (CPSR) published a position paper titled "Serving the Community: A Public Interest Vision of the National Information Infrastructure." CPSR, a national nonprofit organization with a history of addressing issues of computing technology and its societal impacts, was in the unique position of being able to articulate concerns about the national information infrastructure (NII) from a public-interest perspective while drawing from the technological expertise of its members. Since the mid-1980s and into the 1990s, CPSR had taken positions on such topics as privacy, civil liberties, and free speech, with respect to electronic information. The 1993 position paper urged the adoption of several policy and design guidelines that CPSR believes would serve the public interest in the development of a new national information infrastructure. The policy guidelines are as follows:

- Consider the social impact of NII development.
- Guarantee equitable and universal access to network services.
- Promote widespread economic benefits.
- Promote diversity in content markets.
- Provide access to government services over the NII.
- Protect the public spaces necessary to foster community development.
- Encourage democratic participation in the design and development of the NII.
- Think globally rather than nationally.
- Guarantee functional integrity throughout the network.

The policy guidelines are accompanied by the following design recommendations:

- Emphasize ease of use.
- Provide full service to homes, workplaces, and community centers.
- Enable all users to act as both producers and consumers.
- Address privacy and security issues from the beginning.
- Develop open and interoperable standards.
- Encourage experimentation and evolution.
- Require high reliability.

In addition, CPSR also strongly endorses the principles set forth by the Telecommunications Policy Roundtable in Washington, D.C., of which CPSR is a member. The principles are as follows:

- *Universal access:* All people should have affordable access to the information infrastructure.
- *Freedom to communicate:* The information infrastructure should enable all people to effectively exercise their fundamental right to communicate.
- *Vital civic sector:* The information infrastructure must have a vital civic sector at its core.
- *Diverse and competitive marketplace:* The information infrastructure should ensure competition among ideas and information providers.
- *Equitable workplace:* New technologies should be used to enhance the quality of work and to promote equity in the workplace.
- *Privacy:* Privacy should be carefully protected and extended.
- *Democratic policy making:* The public should be fully involved in policy making for the information infrastructure.

CPSR added one more principle based on its members' experiences as designers and users of networking systems:

- *Functional integrity:* The functions provided by the NII must be powerful, versatile, well documented, stable, reliable, and extendable.

These guidelines provide a framework for discussion that is just as relevant today as in 1993. Since 1993, local, state, and national legislation and commercial development have eroded many of these principles— recent examples being the Telecommunications Reform Act of 1996, Washington State's Harmful to Minors Bill, and the city of Tacoma's tax on Internet service providers. We have also witnessed the explosive growth of the Internet. These developments, combined with CPSR's experiences and observations with community technology projects, such as the Seattle Community Network and Virtually Wired, have given us additional insights into what "public interest" really means.

EVERY-CITIZEN'S ACCESS—"INFOUTOPIA" VERSUS REALITY

Since Vice President Al Gore's introduction of the term *information highway* into our vocabulary during the 1992 campaign, private, public, and commercial organizations have been speculating about what the infoway might look like and how it will be used. Creative scenario builders, science fiction writers, and even successful entrepreneurs like Bill Gates have painted visions of a "wired" future. But all of these scenarios make one underlying assumption—that the technology will be available (i.e., affordable and accessible) for all who want to participate.

Gary Chapman, director of the 21st Century Project, in a 1996 article in *CIO* magazine, cautioned information executives that chief information officers in public services must ensure that information technologies will be the cutting edge and not the cutting wedge of social progress. Chapman noted that computer use, particularly Internet use, in poor households (annual incomes of less than $10,000) is almost nonexistent. At the same time, public-sector organizations are being pressured to develop on-line systems that are available to the public over the "Net."

The State of Washington has been struggling with this type of pressure. In response to public demand and expectations, state agencies were already putting information on the Web and trying to grapple with the impact of maintaining an "additional" mode of dissemination, not a replacement for an existing process. A governor's task force on electronic public information access was legislated to make policy recommendations to assist state agencies in transitioning to the information age. One of the major issues facing these agencies is the cost of making the information available electronically.

In his article Chapman suggests that a partial solution to the problem of creating a society of information haves and have-nots is to focus more attention on funding and supporting community computing projects that make technology more affordable and accessible. For the past few years, CPSR members, in various locations around the country, have been involved in projects that focus on making technology available to everyone.

COMMUNITY COMPUTING—PUBLIC ACCESS TO CYBERSPACE

Douglas Schuler (1996), former chair of CPSR, in his new book, *New Community Networks: Wired for Change*, discusses two forms of access to community computing resources: community networks and community computing centers. In 1992, CPSR/Seattle started a community network for the Seattle area. One of the purposes of the project was to implement an on-line service that was grounded in principles that the organization believed in—thus the formation of the Seattle Community Network (SCN). It is no coincidence that the policy and principles that govern SCN are similar to the CPSR guidelines introduced at the beginning of this paper. The SCN principles are as follows:

- Commitment to access,
- Commitment to service,
- Commitment to democracy,
- Commitment to the world community,
- Commitment to the future.

In addition, SCN developed a policy statement as the underlying governing framework. The high-level guidelines for network users are:

- Free speech: SCN is committed to maintaining free speech rights for all participants.
- Free access: SCN is committed to maintaining free access to information for all participants.
- Right to privacy: SCN is committed to maintaining the privacy of individuals.
- Due process: SCN is committed to maintaining the right to due process of individual users of the network.

SCN is just one of over 200 community network projects in the country, most providing free or very low-cost access to on-line services to communities. SCN provides e-mail, discussion forums, newsgroups, and

Web services to anybody who fills out a registration form. The SCN system is available through terminals in all branches of the Seattle and King County public library system.

However, availability of on-line services is only half of the equation of making technology accessible and affordable. Access to the hardware that is needed to connect to any on-line service is the other half. This is where community computing centers are filling a societal need. In several American cities people are making computing resources available to the public in community centers, schools, housing projects, and Internet cafes. Often these resources are available to the general public at little or no cost. Projects such as Virtually Wired in Boston, Plugged In in East Palo Alto, and Playing to Win centers across the country provide a communal space where people can learn computer skills and explore the resources of the Internet and World Wide Web.

INSIGHTS

Many lessons have been learned from observing and participating in making computing resources available to a large and diverse group of people. For example, gender balance is possible in the on-line community. When the SCN project started in 1992, the commercial on-line service subscribers were mostly males (at least 85 percent) and Caucasian. From the very beginning, SCN has managed to attract an almost 50-50 mix of male and female volunteers and participants. In 1993-1994, as SCN was doing its initial community outreach, entire families would attend meetings on how to become information providers. Early participants included the Older Women's League, the Seattle Folklore Society, and the Seattle Philharmonic.

Nontechnical people were enthusiastic about the SCN project. Unlike other on-line services, SCN was community focused; it provided a low-cost, low-threat way for people and organizations to be information providers and users. Educators, environmentalists, and librarians were SCN's earliest and strongest supporters, even in the days before the World Wide Web and Mosaic. Like other on-line services, SCN provides popular services like e-mail, forum newsgroups, and Web access—through Lynx. Because SCN tries to be sensitive to the lowest common denominator with respect to Web access, all information providers are strongly encouraged to design their pages for a graphics or a character-based browser. This is an important design consideration when creating Web pages for a wide range of people.

Coralee Whitcomb, director of Virtually Wired, in a recent discussion, shared her requirements for community computing. These include free e-mail for everyone; a stable interface (something that lasts more than 6 months); topic-focused search engines organized around specific areas (commercial, government, public sector, health care, nonprofits, medical research hospitals); public access centers (e.g., Washington Information Network kiosks located in public spaces throughout Washington State) containing on-line government information (including committee reports and campaign finances) that are as common as public pay phones and free on-line services to schools with the schools given controlled freedom to resell it, thereby providing some financial support for a community computing center.

Participating in these projects has also created indirect benefits that are not purely related to the services being offered. SCN has been the training ground for many unemployed volunteers who have later gone on to find jobs in the computing industry. Whitcomb also made the following points:

> 1. Never underestimate peoples' need for other people. We don't take to on-line help and waiting on hold, especially those who have put off learning about this stuff. 2. Public access [and] community networking are doing the marketing dirty work that industry doesn't want to do. We're the ones drawing in the reluctant, fearful, non-English speakers, disabled, poor, slow, you name it—they can't be bothered. Without us there will be no universality in this technology because industry will not do what it takes to truly distribute it. 3. People are extremely giving, especially computer geeks. Virtually Wired's most important role is providing socially disabled, homeless, recovering addicts, lonely hearts, real community with real people. None of our volunteers have any money and they have terrific talent, yet they give away their talent to have a place "where everybody knows their name." 4. Computing can be terrifically social. Sharing, tutoring, and just sitting next to each other is a good feeling. Some use basketball courts; others use public access. Midnight computing is a good idea (like midnight basketball). 5. Experience is worth a thousand words. No amount of hype will develop the context most of us need to invest in a computer and ISP [Internet service provider] without a solid reason. Public access places can provide the key experience to let people decide whether it is for them or not. 6. Public access can help develop an appreciation for the many noncommercial uses of the Net. We are going to have a big campaign democracy theme happening this fall, so people will become aware of the potential for citizenship.

CONCLUSION

Looking back on the CPSR principles that were articulated in 1993 and our experiences since then with the public at large, it appears that many of them have been validated. Providing available computing and a forum where everybody can be both a consumer and a producer of information is an essential component of a free society.

REFERENCES AND FURTHER READING

Chapman, Gary. 1996. "No Cover, No Minimum," *CIO*, July.

Computer Professionals for Social Responsibility (CPSR). 1993. Serving the Community: A Public Interest Vision of the National Information Infrastructure.

Miller, Steven. 1996. *Civilizing Cyberspace—Policy, Power, and the Information Superhighway*. ACM Press, New York.

Schuler, Douglas. *1996. New Community Networks: Wired for Change*. Addison-Wesley, Reading, Mass.

LIFELONG LEARNING

Gerhard Fischer
University of Colorado, Boulder

A UBIQUITOUS GOAL

Lifelong learning has emerged as one of the major challenges for the knowledge society of the future. This challenge is recognized by the international community as a variety of recent events indicate: (1) 1996 was the European Year of Lifelong Learning; (2) UNESCO (United Nations Educational, Scientific, and Cultural Organization) has included lifetime education as one of the key issues in its planning; and (3) the G7 group of countries has named lifelong learning as a main strategy in the fight against unemployment. Despite this great interest, there are few encompassing efforts to tackle the problem in a coherent way. Lifelong learning cannot be investigated in isolation by looking at one small part of it, for example, K-12 education, university education, or worker reeducation.

LEARNING AS A NEW FORM OF LABOR

The previous notions of a divided lifetime—education followed by work—are no longer tenable. Learning can no longer be dichotomized, spatially and temporally, into a place and time to *acquire* knowledge (school) and a place and time to *apply* knowledge (the workplace). Professional activity has become so knowledge-intensive and fluid in content that learning has become an integral and inseparable part of adult work activities. Professional work cannot simply proceed from a fixed educational background; rather, education must be smoothly incorporated as part of work activities. Similarly, children require educational tools and environments whose primary aim is to help cultivate the desire to learn and create, and not simply to communicate subject matter divorced from meaningful and personalized activity.

Lifelong learning is a continuous engagement in acquiring and applying knowledge and skills in the context of authentic, self-directed problems. It is applicable to the educational experience of both children and adults; it brings the child's experience closer to meaningful and personalized work, and it brings the adult's experience closer to one of continued growth and exploration. Lifelong learning is grounded in descriptive and prescriptive goals such as the following: (1) learning should take place in the context of authentic, complex problems (because learning is more effective when people understand its impact); (2) learning should be embedded in the pursuit of intrinsically rewarding activities; (3) learning on demand needs to be supported because change is inevitable, complete coverage of relevant information and knowledge is impossible, and obsolescence of acquired skills and knowledge is unavoidable; (4) organizational and collaborative learning must be supported because the individual human mind is limited; and (5) skills and processes that support learning as a lifetime habit must be developed.

DESIGN

Lifelong learning integrates and mutually enriches the cultures of work and education. Central to this vision in our own research is the notion of design activities, a model of work that is open-ended and long term in nature, incorporates personalized and collaborative aspects, and combines technical and aesthetic elements. Design (as practiced by engineers and architects designing infrastructure and buildings, lawyers designing briefs and cases, politicians designing policies and programs, educators designing curricula and courses, and software engineers designing computer programs) is an argumentative process, involving ongoing negotiations and trade-offs. It is also a collaborative process, making increasing use of new social structures brought about by the advent of computer networks and "virtual communities." The communality that binds design activities together is that they are centered around the production of a new, publicly accessible artifact. It is impossible for design processes to account for every aspect that might affect the artifact designed. Therefore, design must be treated as an evolutionary process in which designers continue to learn new things as the process unfolds, new requirements surface, and technologies change.

RETHINKING, REINVENTING, AND REENGINEERING EDUCATION

A deeper understanding and more effective support for lifelong learning will contribute to the transformation that must occur in the way our society works and learns. Investments in information technology have so far produced disappointing results because both industry and education tend to use these technologies simply as support mechanisms for existing practices rather than as vehicles to promote fundamentally new ways to create artifacts and construct knowledge. A major finding in current business reengineering efforts is that the use of information technology has had disappointing results compared to the investments made in it. Although a detailed causal analysis of these findings is difficult to obtain, it is generally agreed that a major reason is the fact that information technologies have been used to mechanize old ways of doing business rather than fundamentally rethinking the underlying work processes.

We claim that a similar argument can be made for current uses of technology in education: it is used as an add-on to existing practices rather than a catalyst for fundamentally rethinking what education should be about in the next century. As an example, the "innovation" of making transparencies available on the World Wide Web rather than distributing paper copies of them in class takes advantage of the Web as an electronic information medium, but contributes little in the way of introducing new epistemologies. Old frameworks of education do not get changed by using technology in a "gift-wrapping" approach where traditional instructionist, fixed-curriculum, decontextualized, rote learning is "wrapped" with new technologies such as computer-based training, intelligent tutoring systems, multimedia presentations, or the World Wide Web. We need computational environments to support "new" frameworks for education such as lifelong learning, the integration of working and learning, learning on demand, authentic problems, self-directed learning, information contextualized to the task at hand, (intrinsic) motivation, collaborative learning, and organizational learning.

MYTHS AND MISCONCEPTIONS

The current debate about the ability of computation and communication to change education fundamentally is (in our opinion) based on a number of basic myths and misconceptions. The most prevalent of these are the following:

• *Computers by themselves will change education.* There is no empirical evidence for this assumption based on the past 30 years of using computers to change education (e.g., computer-assisted instruction, computer-based training, intelligent tutoring systems). Technology is not a "deus ex machina" that can solve the existing problems of education. Traditional, instructionist approaches are not changed by the fact that information is disseminated by an intelligent tutoring system.

• *Information is a scarce resource.* "Dumping" even more decontextualized information on people does not seem to be a big step forward in a world where people already suffer from information overload. Instead, technology should provide ways to say the right thing at the right time in the right way.

• *The content, value, and quality of information and knowledge are im-*

proved simply because information is offered in multimedia or over the Web.
Media alone do not turn irrelevant or erroneous information into more
relevant information. We must create innovative technologies (e.g., design environments, simulations, visualizations, critiquing) to let people
experience knowledge in new ways.

- *Ease of use is the greatest challenge or the most desirable goal for new
technologies.* Usable technologies that do not serve the needs and concerns
of people are of no value. Rather than assuming that people should and
will be able to do everything without a substantial learning effort, we
should design computational environments that offer a low threshold for
beginners to get started and a high ceiling for skilled users to do the
things they want.

- *The myth of the Nobel Prize winner*—one of the earlier arguments in
support of the information superhighway was that every school child
would have access to a Nobel Prize winner. Although this argument is
true (or soon will be) at the level of technical connectivity, it is hard to
imagine that Nobel Prize winners will look forward to getting a few thousand e-mail messages a day.

- *The single or most important objective of computational media is reducing the cost of education.* Although we should not ignore any opportunity
to use technology to lower the cost of education, we should not lose sight
of an objective that is of equal if not greater importance: increasing the
quality of education.

- *Human learning is equal to machine learning.* Although we have
deepened our understanding of human learning through progress in
machine learning, there are fundamental dimensions, such as motivation
and competing requirements for a person's time, that make human learning a much more complex and interwoven activity than machine learning. There is substantial empirical evidence that the chief impediments to
learning are not cognitive. It is not that students cannot learn; it is that
they do not wish to.

CHALLENGES

Making learning a part of life creates many challenges, requiring creative new approaches and collaboration between many different stakeholders. For illustration, a few of them are mentioned here:

*1. The educated and informed citizen of the future: "super-couch potato"
consumers or enlightened designers?* The major innovation that many powerful interest groups push for with the information superhighway is to
have a future in which everyone can demonstrate creativity and engagement by selecting one of at least 500 television channels with a remote

control. The major technical challenge derived from this perspective becomes the design of a user-friendly remote control. Rather than serving as the "reproductive organ of a consumer society" (Ivan Illich), educational institutions must fight this trend by cultivating "designers," that is, by creating mind-sets and habits that help people become empowered and willing to contribute actively to the design of their lives and communities. This goal creates specific challenges for computational artifacts, such as the support of end-user programming and authoring.

2. *The "basic skills" debate.* If the hypothesis that most job-relevant knowledge must be learned on demand is true, we must ask ourselves the question: What is the role of "basic skills"? For example, if the use of software packages dominates the use of mathematics in the workplace, shouldn't a new function of mathematics education be to have students learn to use these mathematical artifacts intelligently? Another important challenge is that the old basic skills such as reading, writing, and arithmetic, once acquired, were relevant for the duration of a human life; modern basic skills (tied to rapidly changing technologies) will change over time.

3. *Can we affect motivation?* As mentioned above, there is substantial empirical evidence indicating that the chief impediments to learning are not cognitive but motivational. This raises the challenge of creating learning environments in which learners will work hard, not because they *have* to but because they *want* to. We need to alter the perception that serious learning must be unpleasant rather than personally meaningful, empowering, engaging, and fun. Our research has developed computational environments that address these motivational issues; for example, systems have explored making information relevant to the task at hand, providing challenges matched to current skills, creating communities (among peers, over the Internet), and providing collaborative access to *real practitioners and experts.*

4. *School-to-work transition.* If the world of working and living relies on (a) collaboration, creativity, definition, and framing of problems; (b) dealing with uncertainty, change, and distributed cognition; (c) coping with distributed knowledge; and (d) augmenting and empowering humans with powerful technological tools, then schools and universities should prepare students to function in this world. Industrial-age models of education and work (e.g., based on Skinner and Taylor) are inadequate to prepare students to compete in the knowledge-based workplace. A major objective of the lifelong learning approach is to reduce the gap between school and workplace learning. Current research addresses some of the major school-to-work transition problems and develops answers to the following questions:

- How can schools prepare learners and workers for a world that relies on an interdependent, distributed, nonhierarchical information flow and rapidly shifting authority based on complementary knowledge?
- What basic skills are required in a world in which occupational knowledge and skills become obsolete in years rather than decades?
- How can schools (which currently rely on closed-book exams, the solving of given problems, etc.) be changed so that learners are prepared to function in environments requiring collaboration, creativity, problem framing, and distributed cognition?
- To what extent will lifelong learning and new approaches to learning and teaching—such as learning on demand, learning while working, relations, and the involvement of professionals in schools—prepare learners for work?

LIFELONG LEARNING: AN IMPETUS FOR DESIGNING EVERY-CITIZEN INTERFACES

There is general agreement that as we approach the next century and next millennium, our society is changing to a knowledge and information society. There will be new opportunities and new challenges in all dimensions of our lives. But the future is not out there to be discovered: it has to be *invented and designed.* Making learning a part of life and the implications this has for how, under the influence of new media, human beings will think, create, work, learn, and collaborate in the future are major considerations for the design of every-citizen interfaces to the national information infrastructure (NII). Although the technologies surrounding the NII are important, we should not forget that they are means to ends and that we need to develop a deep understanding of these ends.

FURTHER INFORMATION

Background information about the ideas articulated in this position paper can be found on the World Wide Web:

1. About the Center for LifeLong Learning & Design (L^{3}D) at the University of Colorado, Boulder, and its research activities: http://www.cs.colorado.edu/~l3d/

2. A slide show of a presentation to the National Science Foundation about lifelong learning: http://www.cs.colorado.edu/~l3d/presentations/gf-nsf-9.95/

3. About Agentsheets, a computational substrate to support the development of design environments, simulations, and visualizations: http://www.cs.colorado.edu/~l3d/systems/agentsheets/

4. About the Agentsheets Remote Explorium, an environment to turn the Web from an information dissemination medium into a collaboration medium: http://www.cs.colorado.edu/~l3d/ systems/remote-explorium/

5. AboutWebquest, a system that exploits the Web with interactive learning games:

- About the system itself: http://www.cs.colorado.edu/~corrina/mud/

- A paper describing the system: http://www.cs.colorado.edu/~corrina/WebQuest/

6. About "SimCity in 10 Minutes" describing the philosophy of the Center for Lifelong Learning and Design on end-user programming: http://www.cs.colorado.edu/~corrina/simcity/

SUPPORTING LEARNING IN COMMUNITIES OF PRACTICE

Charles Cleary

Northwestern University

LIFELONG LEARNING: A KEY FUNCTION FOR THE NATIONAL INFORMATION INFRASTRUCTURE

The National Information Infrastructure Advisory Council (NIIAC, 1995) has identified education, particularly, lifelong learning, as one of five key areas requiring attention in the development of the NII. Although the NIIAC does not argue for its focus on lifelong learning, the case for the importance of lifelong learning is now familiar to most education researchers:

- The range of skills and knowledge that individuals now need for satisfying, productive lives is so broad and unpredictable that we can no longer hope to teach them all they need during the traditional school years.
- Many types of technical knowledge have but short half-lives, so individuals need to continually reeducate themselves if they are to keep current.
- Individuals change careers increasingly often, and, when they do, they frequently need to augment or rebuild their skills base.
- Learning is increasingly intertwined with "regular" work, as individuals and organizations see continual improvement as an integral part of doing work.
- Learning is *fun* and so people wish to continue learning even after the traditional school years end.

In short, the need to support lifelong learning is well established, but the mechanisms for doing so are less well defined. This position paper addresses the question: How can we apply the NII to foster lifelong learning?

COMMUNITIES OF PRACTICE AS COMMUNITIES OF LEARNING

To support learning we must begin by considering how people learn most effectively. For instance, consider these four themes from recent educational research:

- *Motivation is critical.* Learning is most effective when learners are able to pursue challenges they care about.
- *Transfer is hard.* It is easiest for people to apply what they learn when they learn it in a context like that in which they will need to apply it. Traditional "teach-em-and-test-em" methods of teaching often lead to inert knowledge.
- *Skills are more important than facts.* A good speechmaker must command both impressive writing skills and broad factual knowledge. But skills are harder to acquire than facts. So people are more often concerned with learning *how* (e.g., how to draft a speech) than learning *that* (e.g., that George Washington was the first president). To learn skills, people must practice them (learning by doing).
- *Support is essential.* People learn to do complex tasks best when they receive coaching. People are ready to learn when they have tried something out and have failed. But they need advice to help them understand why they failed and to determine how to improve their performance.

These themes point out that people learn most readily when they care about what they are learning, when they try to solve problems in realistic contexts, and when they have access to coaching when they get stuck. Although these constraints may not be satisfied very often within the walls of today's schools, they *are* satisfied in many situations outside school. In particular, they are satisfied when people who share an interest in a domain support each other in advancing their learning. Such groups, which have been labeled *communities of practice*, are quite common. From a group of engineers who are concerned with similar problems to an investment club to a swimming team, people often join together in communities of practice.

Communities of practice can provide fertile support to help individuals learn throughout their lifetimes. As an example, consider a group interested in fostering literacy. Such a group can help with *motivation.* A college student who thinks he may want to dedicate his career to increasing literacy levels can sit in on a few events that the literacy group sponsors to make sure that the field matches his expectations before he commits to it. The group can help with *skill building.* The literacy group can enable the college student to engage in real tasks (e.g., helping run reading groups) and work on real problems (e.g., selecting appropriate material for a particular reading student). Both the group and the college student benefit. Furthermore, communities of practice also often provide established routes for scaffolding learning, whereby new members begin with simple tasks and work their way up to expert-level tasks. Finally, the group can also help with *coaching.* If the college student runs into trouble when he tries to find appropriate reading materials, he can turn to the literacy group for advice from a senior member.

Communities of practice can also serve as engines for advancing group learning. An organization learns most effectively when it can harness the experiences and energy of all of its members. Often the learning cycle begins with the most junior members in a group. For instance, when a new member asks a question that the group cannot readily answer, then the group learns of a need for new learning. When the group works to develop an answer, the group advances its theory of its domain. When someone later tries out that answer and finds a wrinkle in it, the cycle begins again. Acting alone, the members of the community will run into only a few problems and be able to generate a few potential answers. When they join in a group, the members can leverage each other's specific experiences to build significantly more powerful understandings of their domain.

Given that communities of practice provide an effective and relatively widespread mechanism for supporting lifelong learning, it is not surprising that the NIIAC links them together in its report (NIIAC, 1995):

> By providing people of all ages with opportunities for lifelong learning and workplace skills development, the NII should enhance each individual's ability to create and share knowledge and to participate in electronic communities of learning.

Still, the question remains: *How* can we apply the NII to support communities of practice?

AN APPROACH TO SUPPORTING COMMUNITIES OF PRACTICE

Communities of practice can effectively support both individual and group learning. For a community to operate smoothly, it requires frequent and flexible communication between its members. Furthermore, if a group is to grow to significant size, it requires some way to leverage the experience of its thought leaders, so that they do not become overwhelmed with demands for coaching. Because of these constraints, few communities of practice function effectively today if they contain more than a few dozen members or members who are geographically separated.

The foundation provided by the NII can potentially enable members of a community to communicate across the boundaries of space or time. However, this potential is yet to be realized. To effectively support communities of practice, improved applications must be developed that will run on top of the NII.

What sorts of applications are these? As an example case, imagine that an independent business consultant would like to learn how to better diagnose a client's problem. He is a member of a geographically dispersed group of independent consultants. What sorts of applications can be provided that will help the consultant take advantage of the resources of the group (and that will help the group develop resources that are worth taking advantage of)?

Three separate classes of applications are needed. The most fundamental is that groups require *organizational memories* to keep track of what their goals are, what they know, and what they would like to learn. As a simple example, the business consultant might tap into a "memory" of business cases to search for one that is similar to his client's. However, organizational memories alone are not sufficient because too often the knowledge they contain lies inert. Accordingly, groups also require two classes of applications that actively deliver knowledge to the point of need. First, groups require *performance support tools* that help users perform tasks effectively. For instance, the consultant could make good use of a performance support tool that leads him through the process of making an effective diagnosis, feeding him appropriate advice or factual content from the group's organizational memory as it becomes relevant. Additionally, groups require *training systems* that enable individuals to learn how to perform tasks in a safe environment. For example, once the consultant makes his diagnosis, he could benefit from a training simulation that helps him learn how to position his recommendations to his client in his final presentation. Again, these training systems will rely on the knowledge contained in the organizational memory, both for raw case material and for coaching knowledge about how to respond to common failures or queries.

ORGANIZATIONAL MEMORIES

The most straightforward function of a group's memory is to help members of the group publish their expertise to each other and to "outsiders." If my brother-in-law happens to be an expert investor and I wish to know how to allocate my retirement funds, it would be reasonable for me to want some advice from him. However, the problem arises that 15 other people ask for the same advice in the same week, particularly if he is a member of a large investment club. People who develop a specialty do not want to have to answer the same questions time and again. Instead, they require some mechanism for publishing what they know. Unfortunately, current media are not particularly effective at publishing large bodies of complex interrelated knowledge. So we require improved group memories that provide more effective mechanisms for publishing knowledge.

Additionally, organizational memories should be *dynamic*, changing as the group modifies and expands on its ideas. Organizational memories should help groups keep track of what their goals are, what they know, and what they would like to learn. Current systems are not particularly effective at helping communities develop new knowledge (or capture the new knowledge they do develop). When a novice asks a question for which the community has not yet developed an answer, what should happen? The question should be posted and perhaps routed to those who have an interest in (or responsibility for) developing an answer. These people must develop their opinions, perhaps collaboratively. Differences in opinions must be ironed out or at least understood. The results of this discussion need to be captured in a form that makes it readily available, as needed, to those who later develop a need that it can address.

Today, applications such as e-mail and usenet news support some of the functions required to support knowledge building. However, the hard problem is integrating all of these functions, particularly those having to do with capturing the results of discussions, thereby helping groups to pull together a consensus point of view from a collection of disparate opinions. Complicating this task is the observation that the same piece of content may be relevant in quite different situations (e.g., a counterexample to someone making a claim, a piece of advice to someone facing a problem, an illustration to someone asking a question). To build dynamic memories, the *indexing problem*—determining how to label content so that it can be retrieved in the range of situations in which it will be relevant—must be tackled.

PERFORMANCE SUPPORT

Members of a community of practice rely on each other for support and advice as they perform their work. However, it is not always possible to access the right expert at the right time. Accordingly, we require performance support tools that help members tap into a community's organizational memory. This support can take a range of forms, including providing cases that are similar to the situation in which a user finds him- or herself, abstract templates for how to perform a task, and automated tools that actually perform the task for a user.

When a person tries to leverage each of these types of support, he or she is likely to have a range of sorts of questions. For example, someone who is trying to find a case in a performance support system might want to ask questions such as:

- "How should I go about choosing a case?"
- "What mistakes am I likely to make?"
- "Who can help me understand if I have chosen an appropriate case?"

If a performance support system only provides raw content (e.g., cases) and does not also answers such questions, it is likely to leave some users confused about how to apply the content that it does provide. Accordingly, performance support tools should not only provide raw content, they should also allow their users to ask a range of types of questions about that content.

SIMULATION-BASED TRAINING

People learn by doing. For instance, to become a good investor, one must do a lot of investing. But investing is a risky business. So it is best to practice in a safe, controlled environment, one that allows effective coaching to be delivered as it is required. Simulation-based training environments can allow people to learn by doing without the risk of catastrophic failure.

More generally, it is often easiest to explain what a domain is about to prospective members of a community by letting them try completing a task in the domain. Similarly, it is often easiest to help existing members learn new skills by allowing them to have a go at them. Since performing tasks in the real world is often expensive and does not permit adequate coaching, giving members simulated experiences is a sensible approach.

However, good simulations require good content. A simulation builder must identify which *tasks* are important to simulate, what *case material* may be used as grist for the simulation, what *errors* users are likely to make, and what *coaching* is appropriate to deliver when those errors occur. Importantly, this is the same type of content that an effective organizational material should provide.

THE NII'S ROLE

The NII can, in theory, help those with similar interests work together, even though they may be separated by barriers of space and time. This potential, if realized, promises to revamp how we as individuals learn throughout our lifetimes and how we as a society grow our capabilities. However, to realize this potential, we must move beyond general goals to a specification of the types of applications we desire the NII to support. Only then can we create the particular research agendas needed to develop these applications.

REFERENCE

NIIAC. 1995. *Common Ground: Fundamental Principles for the National Information Infrastructure.* First Report of the National Information Infrastructure Advisory Council. March.

ON SELECTED POPULATION GROUPS

EXTENDING KNOWLEDGE ACCESS TO UNDERSERVED CITIZENS

Wallace Feurzeig
BBN Systems and Technologies

ISSUES AND GOALS

If we are serious about making available the rich human and information resources of the national information infrastructure (NII) to all citizens, we have to address the great, and growing, knowledge gulf between the "haves" and "have-nots" in American society. This disparity poses a real threat to our political and social lives. It is at variance with our history and our democratic ideals. Many citizens who are economically underserved are also "informationally disadvantaged" (National Telecommunications and Information Administration, 1995). The knowledge empowerment made possible by the new information technologies must become available to all. We must work toward democratizing access to effective use of networking technology by all Americans who are capable of benefiting from its use. We need to provide the underserved not only with access to these potentially empowering information resources but also support in their use through education, training, and acculturation.

Researchers at BBN and elsewhere have done preliminary work along these lines to better understand the issues. Though neither systematic nor comprehensive, this work identifies some key research questions and suggests specific directions for more substantial action-oriented research efforts.

INTERNET USE BY LOW-INCOME FAMILIES

A recent study conducted from December 1994 to January 1996 probed the barriers, benefits, and perceived worth of the Internet to six low-income urban families in Florida, a group representative of the traditionally underserved and informationally disadvantaged population (Bier, 1996). The researchers asked what these families would actually do on-line given unrestricted Internet access in their homes. Each family was lent a home computer, high-speed modem, and printer; was provided with dial-up point-to-point Internet access; and was given training on the use of the mouse and keyboard. The computers were equipped with an interface security program, an integrated productivity package, several educational games, a typing tutorial, and a set of Internet utilities. Families were taught how to communicate with each other electronically and how to locate and acquire resources from the Internet. Additional training and technical support were available on demand for the duration of the project. Through interviews, visits, and telephone and e-mail interactions, researchers obtained data on the amount of time participants spent on-line, the sites they visited, the information they sought, and the obstacles they encountered. The participants made use of virtual hospitals, medical dictionaries, and physicians' desk references. They joined support groups, investigated scholarships, and made local transportation arrangements. They investigated appliances, employment listings, and local calendars of events. They e-mailed, chatted, and surfed the World Wide Web; made friends; felt personally empowered as learners; and gained a new sense of community. The results showed that Internet access enabled "powerful emotional and psychological transformations" on the part of the participants.

EDUCATIONAL SOFTWARE USE BY EDUCATIONALLY DISADVANTAGED STUDENTS

During the past two years, my colleagues at BBN have used the computer program RelLab (for Relativity Laboratory) to teach the concepts of relative motion to educationally disadvantaged inner-city high school students in Boston (Horwitz, 1995). The program enables users to construct and run relativity "thought experiments." The inner-city students worked on the same sequence of activities as the educationally advantaged suburban students with whom we worked earlier—and with almost identical results. They advanced steadily from simple Galilean (low-speed) relativity problems to complex ones involving the frame independence of the speed of light and its implications for simultaneity, time dilation, and length contraction. Along the way they exhibited the same frustrations and overcame the same obstacles as the suburban students, and they progressed at about the same rate. Moreover, they showed as much interest and had as many breakthroughs as their advantaged peers. The only real differences were that the inner-city students were considerably less verbally communicative than the suburban students and almost all were severely educationally deprived. This was particularly evident in the case of math. Their knowledge of the decimal system was spotty and unreliable, and they had great difficulty graphing data. Despite their competence on the computer, they were hopeless at pencil-and-paper tasks with the same material, particularly written tests. Based on posttest interviews of the students, it appeared that their poor performance was due not only to knowledge gaps but also to significant deficits in reading comprehension.

During the past year BBN researchers have also been using another educational computer program, GenScope, to teach the concepts of genetics to suburban and inner-city students in high school biology classes. GenScope enables users to explore and experiment with genetics models. It has proved engaging to both male and female students of widely differing ages, backgrounds, and ability levels. The most interesting results have come from the inner-city population, where students who had learned very little from a conventionally taught biology class learned a great deal about complex genetic processes working with GenScope and used their new knowledge effectively to accomplish a variety of analytical and constructive tasks. Moreover, they remembered what they had learned, and some were able to give accurate and detailed explanations weeks later in interviews conducted away from the computer. However, we found the same results as those noted above with RelLab—though the inner-city students often learned to do sophisticated genetics on the computer, their knowledge rarely transferred to paper-and-pencil tests. They were unable to express in writing the complex knowledge they exhibited on the computer. Given the software tools and support, educationally disadvantaged students acquired and applied complex reasoning, but their knowledge was *locked in*. They lacked the basic reading comprehension and communications skills that are fundamental for success in education and skilled occupations. The challenge is to help students like these acquire the verbal literacy that will enable them to participate more fully as citizens in the knowledge society.

RESEARCH ISSUES

The positive outcomes shown in the study of Internet use by low-income families are indeed impressive and encouraging. This work cries out for replication and suggests new questions for further research. What are the key requirements for making such Internet use productive? What skills and motivation must users possess to begin with? What kind of training and ongoing support are required? How much on-site help is required, and how practical and effective is on-line mentoring in augmenting initial training? Can the facilities, training, and support be provided not only or not primarily in the home but also in social settings like community organizations, churches, local schools (after-school programs), and particularly libraries—places with expert human information resources?

The results from the use of sophisticated learning technology by inner-city high school students—their success in acquiring and using complex knowledge contrasting strongly with their difficulty in communicating that knowledge—are more problematic and troubling and raise another set of research questions. Can high school students who fail to acquire competence in reading, writing, and communications skills overcome these deficits later? Are these difficulties remediable by tutoring? Or is there a literacy learning barrier for English (analogous to the putative foreign-language age block) that makes the acquisition of fluency in reading and writing English enormously difficult after a certain age or developmental level?

These questions provide a rich source of cognitive, educational, ethnographic, and technological research investigations, from intensive small-scale studies of individual development to long-term longitudinal programs involving large populations. Rather than providing brief summaries of possible research projects across this wide spectrum, I will focus on a single project that is motivated by both of the preliminary studies discussed above and that has important implications for advancing the goal of universal citizen participation and empowerment through educational networking.

The productive use of the Internet by low-income citizens would not have been possible if they did not bring to these activities a fairly high level of functional literacy. The stunted development of literacy skills among the inner-city high school students severely limited their social participation and learning opportunities, despite their inherent intellectual abilities. Effective utilization of the NII, no matter how rich its user interface and information resources, will require that its users bring a modicum of literacy. But our nation has an enormous number of citizens who do not meet that test. I describe a research project that seeks to address, through the use of new interface technology and associated in-structural activities, a most severe literacy problem—that of American adults who are functionally illiterate.

THE ADULT ILLITERACY PROBLEM

The development of a technologically literate work force is a national imperative for the United States in the face of increasing international competition. Major federal initiatives such as the School-to-Work Opportunities program and the Advanced Technology Education program have been created to address this critical need. However, these efforts will be severely hampered if the country's massive adult illiteracy problem is not solved. In confronting our formidable economic challenges we need to recognize that the most central and essential prerequisite for virtually all types of new jobs is functional literacy—the ability to read and comprehend text and to use various forms of word processing and other communications software.

Workplace literacy surveys indicate that over 90 percent of current occupations require reading. A recent study by the U.S. Department of Labor and the American Society of Training and Development found that, on average, workers spend more than 1.5 hours each day reading such materials as forms, charts, manuals, electronic display screens, and general literature. Further, these requirements are increasing: only 4 percent of new jobs can be filled by people with the lowest levels of literacy, as compared with 9 percent of existing jobs. According to the study, even the one-third of American workers who perform production and service delivery will need to read at an eighth-grade level. The remaining two-thirds will need to read at postsecondary and higher levels. Levels of literacy that were once acceptable will be marginal by the year 2000.

However, the stark reality is that the number of adults in the U.S. population with unacceptable levels of literacy is enormous. Already, more than one out of five adult Americans are functionally illiterate, and their ranks are swelling by about 2.3 million persons each year. Nearly 40 percent of minority youth and 30 percent of semiskilled and unskilled workers are illiterate. Illiteracy costs the United States over $225 billion annually in corporate retraining, lost competitiveness, and industrial accidents. The implication is clear: our goal of providing a modern competitive work force hinges very directly on our ability to achieve a massive improvement in adult functional literacy during the next decade. This cannot be accomplished through the use of human teaching alone. There simply are not enough reading instructors. Their teaching must be augmented by the creation and widespread application of an effective technology for automating literacy tutoring.

Although for a small fraction of illiterates the ability to read is impeded because of neurological problems, and for others there are learning difficulties that are not associated with sensory or motor problems, the primary cause of illiteracy among Americans is a failure to learn to read. Learning to read requires time and practice. Research indicates that once the basics of learning to read are in place, a grade-level gain in reading ability takes approximately 100 hours of engaged literacy training time. Further, at beginning levels of reading, individual feedback, motivation, and guidance are critical. For most adult illiterates a major obstacle to effective reading development lies in two simple facts—the human resources do not exist to provide the teaching support that is needed, and there is no way to adequately increase their number to provide such support during the next several years. A sufficient force of trained professionals and paraprofessionals at the level of expertise required cannot be developed, even with a massive injection of funding. The only option is the effective introduction of appropriate technology.

RESEARCH PROJECT ON ADULT ILLITERACY

My thesis is that one technology in particular—computer-based speech recognition—provides the central and essential capability required for launching a significant attack on a major segment of the adult illiteracy problem. The reason for this view is straightforward. Many adults who have serious reading difficulties can speak English intelligibly, even when their speech is in a dialect other than standard U.S. dialects. We at BBN plan to begin from their strength—their ability to *speak* English. They know how easy it is to talk and how hard it is for them to read. They do not know that their own speech can be transformed into text, that there is a direct, albeit complex, correspondence between the two forms of language. Even though they cannot initially read the text that is produced, they know that it is their own, that they created it from their own speech. So in a very real sense they know what the text "says." Further, they can repeat the utterance, either in its entirety or partially, a word or phrase at a time. In doing so, they begin to get a handle on the translation problem through a procedure they substantially control, in ways and at rates they find comfortable.

The starting point in this instructional strategy is to have the computer generate a speech utterance. The trainee is then asked to repeat the utterance, to "say the same thing." The speech recognition system prints the correct text corresponding to the utterance, but it remembers the trainee's articulations of the constituent words and phrases, including those not spoken in standard English. So the system develops a knowledge of the trainee's idiosyncratic pronunciations and the text of the words and phrases to which they correspond. This information will be used to generate the correct English text in activities where the trainee takes the initiative in generating the utterances.

This training strategy is distinctly different from traditional approaches based on giving trainees a reading task from the start. Instead, reading skills are developed in a more natural and gradual way from speaking and listening skills that, to begin with, are a great deal stronger. The transition from the scaffolding of speech-driven pattern matching to text-driven decoding and interpretation is not simple, but the confidence inspired in the trainee by being able to begin to make sense of text should substantially help in confronting and bridging this gap. In later phases of the training, students will be engaged more in practice activities to extend their vocabulary and to apply reading in contexts of use through task-oriented activities. The training sessions will involve the use of workplace literacy materials, including interactive simulations, games, and extended stories, gradually increasing in the level of challenge and complexity. The functional literacy tasks will be based on those defined by the National Adult Literacy Survey, particularly those in the first three levels (e.g., interpreting bus or airline schedules; following written and illustrated instructions from a manual or display for such tasks as repairing a paper jam in a copying machine). Interactive computer simulations of such tasks will involve the development of procedural reasoning and problem-solving skills in addition to reading comprehension skills.

This approach requires continuous, real-time, high-accuracy, dialect-sensitive speech recognition. With the introduction of such new and powerful facilities, the development of a literacy trainer incorporating two-way interactive speech technology has become feasible. Earlier speech recognition systems were not capable of recognizing with high accuracy, naturally spoken utterances involving large vocabularies and complex grammars. Moreover, they were not "speaker independent" in that their accuracy for any speaker was highly dependent on whether the system was tuned to the speech characteristics of that speaker, through a tedious, time-consuming "training" process. All this has changed with the introduction of systems such as the BBN HARK recognizer. Given the vocabulary and grammar associated with a student session, HARK can recognize utterances with a word accuracy of around 95 percent. Furthermore, the system can readily be configured to recognize speakers with Haitian, Cambodian, Hispanic, and other common dialects.

This experimental research and development project would be conducted jointly by industry and university researchers. I envisage a 10-year program to implement a comprehensive yet inexpensive training system, demonstrate its instructional capabilities, and evaluate its learning benefits with a representative group of trainees chosen to exemplify a wide range of literacy problems. A two-year small-scale pilot to develop a prototype system and demonstrate the instructional approach might constitute the first stage of the project. It would endeavor to show how speech-mediated literacy training technology can effectively be used to make major inroads on our national illiteracy problem. Speech scientists, instructional researchers, and software developers are keenly interested in participating in the proposed work. The project would have the long-term goal of substantially reducing the adult illiteracy problem in the United States and opening the way for fuller participation of all citizens in the knowledge society.

REFERENCES

Bier, Melinda. 1996. Personal Empowerment in the Study of Home Internet Use by Low-Income Families. World Wide Web article, http://www.educ.ksu.edu/projects/jrce/v1/Bier/article.html.

Horwitz, Paul. 1995. Electronic communication, Department of Education discussion group on a National Technology Plan, March 20, Kirk Winters, moderator. Archived in inet.ed.gov under NTPlan.

National Telecommunications and Information Administration. 1995. *Falling Through the Net: A Survey of the "Have-Nots" in Rural and Urban America*. Washington, D.C.: U.S. Department of Commerce.

ELECTRONIC ACCESS TO SERVICES FOR LOW-INCOME POPULATIONS

Adam Porter
University of Maryland

INTRODUCTION

Much of the Internet's popular appeal stems from its potential to provide a global virtual marketplace for goods and services. Already high-profile projects are under way to develop video on demand, virtual malls, and massive digital libraries. In addition to these glamorous products, more mundane government services will some day be delivered (in whole or in part) via the Internet. These services might include Medicare, welfare and unemployment, immigration, and job placement and training assistance. Since many of these services exist to serve low-income populations, it is important to determine whether low-income users differ from other Internet users and, if so, what implications this has on user interface design.

For the past several years I have been working with a nonprofit group called Raising Hispanic Academic Achievement (RHAA). RHAA is located in the Washington, D.C., metropolitan area and provides academic tutoring and mentoring to several hundred Latino children and their parents. Over 70 percent of these children come from families whose annual income is below $20,000 and many receive government services such as those described above.

SURVEYING THE USER COMMUNITY

I conducted an informal survey of this user community to help understand its characteristics and needs. This is not a scientific sample, and it is clearly incomplete. Nevertheless, it provides some insight into issues to consider when designing interfaces for these types of government services. The survey identified several characteristics that might not be found in other user communities:

- *Non-English speaking.* Many respondents are first- or second-generation Americans. Consequently, many do not speak English at all or have limited proficiency.

• *Limited educational background.* Many of the respondents have not completed high school. Moreover, they have had little exposure to computers and computer programming.

• *Limited literacy.* Since many of the respondents do not speak English and have limited education, functional illiteracy in English is high. Furthermore, 20 percent (estimated) of the parents I surveyed are also illiterate in Spanish.

• *Limited access to computers.* Few of the respondents have computers in their homes. Those who do tend to have lower-end machines with limited storage and printing capabilities. Almost all have phone or pager service. Some of those without home computers have access to the Internet through schools and/or public libraries.

CONSIDERATIONS FOR USER INTERFACE DESIGN

Based on this survey I have identified several issues and concerns that should be considered when developing user interfaces. Many of these, of course, will apply to other communities as well. I have grouped these issues into three categories: (1) computer literacy, (2) language literacy, and (3) limited computer resources.

Computer Literacy

• *Simple predictable interfaces.* Users often have to formulate queries to search large information spaces. Frequently, they must write these queries using SQL or logic programming languages. Since many of these users have no programming experience, this type of interface leads to errors and should be avoided when possible. Also, interfaces should be predictable, not changing from use to use, since this can lead to confusion.

• *Rapid, incremental, and reversible control.* Users should be encouraged to navigate large information spaces quickly and easily. Rather than programming queries, users should be able to visually define queries and then refine them rather than recomputing from scratch. Also, each operation should be reversible.

• *Training.* One research area that should be explored is the development of novice versus expert interfaces. To support novice users better, error recovery and prevention schemes will be important, as will further study into architectures for "help" systems.

Language Literacy

• *Direct manipulation.* Since even experts make frustrating typing mistakes when using textual interfaces, the illiterate will find these interfaces unusable. Although direct manipulation interfaces alleviate some of these problems, there is still a strong need for more effective visual presentation approaches.

- *Audio support.* For people who cannot read or whose language is unwritten (e.g., certain Creole languages), audio support may be necessary. In these cases, text-to-speech systems may provide low-cost conversion of written content.
- *Culturally appropriate presentation.* Different languages are presented and organized differently. They have different accent marks, character sets, and orientations in which words are read and written. (This problem also appears in commercial software development where products must be internationalized.) Rather than expending scarce resources to translate content, reformat output, and redevelop character-processing code, some research should be devoted to low-cost translation systems, flexible software architectures, reconfigurable browsers, and so forth.

Limited Computer Resources

- *Presentation on low-bandwidth devices.* Many people do not have computers in their homes and have limited access elsewhere. As interface developers we cannot assume that everyone is using Netscape. We need to explore methods for low-cost conversion of content for different devices (e.g., phones, beepers). For example, Lucent Technologies has developed a language that allows HTML documents to be presented in one way for a phone and in another way for a standard browser.
- *Users without fixed Internet addresses.* Low-income people may have computer access only through public channels, such as libraries and schools, rather than at home. Notification services that assume a fixed or a forwarding address will be inadequate. Some research issues to consider are secure identification mechanisms and flexible locator services.
- *Long-running services.* Providing services may require many steps, with human intervention at several points. Therefore, users may need to suspend long-running services and resume them later (possibly from a different physical location, with different computer resources, user names, etc.). Consequently, architectures need to be developed for incremental interaction and interfaces that summarize interaction histories.

SUMMARY

This paper explores the design of user interfaces for systems that provide electronic access to government services. Since these systems exist to serve low-income populations, I conducted an informal survey of one low-income population to understand their needs. The survey indicated that low-income populations will have many novice computer users, require support for languages other than English, and have limited access to computer resources. Since redeveloping content for every user community would be prohibitively expensive, this situation presents a wide variety of research challenges. Three of the most interesting topics are (1) visual presentation and searching of large information spaces, (2) low-cost translation and conversion of content, and (3) flexible software architectures and interaction patterns.

ACCESS FOR PEOPLE WITH DISABILITIES

Larry Goldberg
WGBH Educational Foundation

INTRODUCTION

The barriers that prevent persons with limited sight, hearing, or mobility from gaining access to the fruits of the emerging national information infrastructure (NII) are not all that different from the barriers that face all the other millions of Americans who have, voluntarily or not, opted out of participation. Limited bandwidth, limited technological resources, limited technological facility, limited income, limited time, and limited interest are the restraints bifurcating our society. This division is self-perpetuating in that without interventions like the promotion of every-citizen interfaces the gap will widen and feed on itself.

For people with disabilities, input/output issues are the core concerns. Disabled people share with their able-bodied colleagues concerns about the complexity of systems, training needs, flexible and intelligent interfaces, and so forth. But without the ability to input commands and data and receive appropriate output, the rest of the issues are irrelevant.

TODAY'S MEDIA

For the more basic, one-way components of the NII (i.e., television in its broadcast, cable, satellite, video-on-demand formats), provision of access to the content flowing over these pipelines continues to be an after-the-fact retrofit. That is, upon finalization of programming, closed captions or video descriptions are added. In the case of the former, caption data are encoded into the vertical blanking interval (VBI) of the television signal and delivered and displayed to the end user via a set-top box or built-in decoder chip. In the case of the latter, an additional audio track is added to the master video and delivered to the end-user via an auxiliary audio channel (the Second Audio Program) on stereo televisions and video cassette recorders.

Though widely utilized for decades (closed captioning) and years (descriptions), these technologies are by no means 100 percent reliable, owing to both system errors and human errors. Research into fail-safe mechanisms for delivery of these data would provide the benefit of consumer confidence and programmer satisfaction.

In addition, the distribution plants of the major broadcasters and cable system operators often either cannot traffic the extra audio channel for video description or will strip those descriptions prior to delivery to the home. Preliminary research into digitization of the auxiliary audio channel and encoding into the VBI (like in the captioning process) has been conducted with promising but inconclusive results. The added question requiring an extra user appliance for decoding VBI-encoded audio needs to be examined. Research may determine means of adding such capability into today's or next-generation television systems.

Production of access services also is time and labor intensive. Though trivial in terms of the overall cost of mass media production, budgets for access services are carefully scrutinized. This has become an even greater concern as the sources of information and entertainment continue to grow. As we approach the ability for every citizen to become a programmer/distributor, the need to facilitate and lower the cost of producing and adding access adjuncts or alternate means of output (text and audio) becomes more dire.

Potential research in this area needs to focus on the utilization of speech-to-text and text-to-speech technologies. Neither has yet been developed to the point of aiding in the production or distribution process of either captions or descriptions, but both show tremendous promise. Today, most of the burden for providing captioning on live programming falls on a extremely small group of highly skilled "stenocaptioners" who can outgun any speech recognition engine available today.

Captioning has clearly proven itself to be a service that serves populations far beyond the originally intended audience. Early optimistic explorations into the use of captioned television for early and remedial readers has been followed by exploitation of captioning for students of English as a second language.

Computer manufacturers are now building caption displays into their "personal computer/televisions" with the added capability of downloading caption data for archiving and indexing purposes. And researchers in the field of digital video storage have long been excited about the use of captions as indices for large-scale video databases for research, archiving, and production uses.

Perhaps more trivial but ever more evident, captioned television has become widely used in environments that require an alternative to audio output, such as health clubs, bars, libraries, and for late-night television watching.

Video description uses for additional populations have just begun to be explored and would certainly benefit from significant research projects.

Preliminary work has begun to determine the potential of description to assist students and adults with learning disabilities, especially attention deficit disorder. Additional similar benefits may be discovered through research into video description's impact on information retrieval where masses of data and information clutter could be reduced through "descriptive guides."

Embedded description has also been suggested as a potentially useful way of indexing large visual databases if coupled with intelligent speech recognition. Little or no research has yet been conducted in this area, but that may point the way to another repurposing of an access technology.

NEW MEDIA

In the worlds of nonlinear and digital multimedia, interactive media, and advanced television, many problems remain to be solved. Standards are either evolving or have not yet been considered for incorporation of captioning and description in all of these venues. Early efforts at creating such standards ignored the ancillary uses of these technologies and threatened to lock in bad designs.

For example, the ability to display text in the emerging DVD (Digital Video Disk or Digital Versatile Disk) format has been designed with language translation as the primary purpose for text display. Since the DVD format has mostly been designed in Japan, the text is being created through bit-mapped graphics files, not ASCII text as in broadcast closed captioning. This has resulted in many unforeseen design flaws: the inability of a DVD player to address the closed-captioning circuitry in television sets, the inability to flexibly change fonts or type sizes, and the inability to use the text as a search engine.

These decisions are made as new media products rush to market, with little attention paid to the best-possible design for the built-in access services and how they can be configured for universal applicability. Similar concerns are being directed toward the designs of the alternate audio features of advanced television and DVD.

As great a concern has been expressed about the "appliances" people will be using to access the Internet or other digital information and entertainment systems. With personal computers the ability to add software or hardware to assist those with special needs is relatively straightforward (though not without significant programming and development efforts). But if every citizen will be accessing the new services via "thin clients," smart phones, set-top boxes, or low-end, low-cost browsing boxes attached to television sets, the ability to add such services as speech synthesis or output to refreshable Braille or large-print displays is problematic.

When digital sound files are sent over the Internet and received via these boxes, how will the boxes turn the sound into text for deaf people?

Research into the ability to incorporate these alternate output modes into inexpensive information appliances can result in more accessible low-end browsers for every citizen, including blind and deaf people. Incorporation of new access standards into digital media formats (such as QuickTime, Active Video, and RealAudio) will facilitate the ability of low-end browsers to display incorporated access technologies. All of these research challenges can be addressed in the short term (one to five years), except perhaps for the need for a fully capable speech recognition technology, which, after 20 or more years of effort, still requires many years to approach the speed, accuracy, and other capabilities needed for use by deaf people.

It has been the experience of those in the world of media access that these design and research challenges are not complex (certainly not as complex as the creation of the new media themselves). When focused attention and resources are applied to the problems, solutions are readily discovered, especially when approached by consortia of public and private practitioners and researchers. Early awareness and design-from-the-blueprint-stage thinking obviate the need for expensive and inefficient retrofits that are resisted by producers and consumers alike.

SUGGESTED UNIFORM RESOURCE LOCATORS

http://www.wgbh.org/caption
http://www.wgbh.org/dvs
http://www.wgbh.org/ncam
http://trace.wisc.edu

ON KEY PROCESSES

CROSS-DISCIPLINARY, SOCIAL-CONTEXT RESEARCH

John Leslie King
University of California, Irvine

A key challenge in developing an every-citizen interface to the national information infrastructure is in recognizing the ongoing evolution in our concepts of what the "interface" encompasses. The development of concern over interface issues in the past 30 years reflects the complexities of these issues and provides some direction for improving these interfaces.

BACKGROUND

The term *interface* in the computing field has been appropriated by a relatively narrow community of interest, namely those interested in human-machine interactions at the ergonomic and perceptual level. Most of this study, which goes under the name of human-computer interaction (HCI or CHI) is strictly limited to studies of individual human actors interacting with specific packages of hardware and software. This focus of work has been very successful, producing among other things the innovations of "pointing" aids such as the mouse, trackball, touchscreen, and digital pad, as well as the graphical screen interface ubiquitous in all modern operating systems. These advancements have their intellectual

411

roots in fairly circumscribed zones of disciplinary concern, namely cognitive psychology and human factors engineering. In essence the focus of this line of work is on the human working with a computer-based system.

In the past several years the HCI focus has broadened somewhat to include small groups of individuals each working with a computer-based system but for the purpose of working collaboratively with other members of the group. This is a significantly different conceptual focus, with individuals working through the computer to interact with other individuals. Prominent developments in this domain have been technologies for computer-mediated communication, "groupware," and computer-supported cooperative work. The intellectual roots of this work go beyond cognitive psychology into other realms of the social sciences, especially social psychology, but also into anthropology, organizational psychology and sociology, and economics. The applications of these technologies have caught the attention of scholars interested in fundamental questions of human discourse, social network construction and maintenance, identity and personality formation and expression, and the social construction of meaning and reality. These rapidly growing areas of interest have been stimulated by the stunning speed with which major components of the national information infrastructure such as the Internet and the World Wide Web have invaded social life in all dimensions.

These developments illustrate the evolving capacity of computer-based systems to affect basic human activities and reflect the fact that the concept of "interface" between humans and information technology is an elastic concept that expands to deal with the new opportunities and problems presented by technological change. Three observations can be made from this evolving concern with interface.

1. The parochial concerns of any particular group that engages interface issues at any given moment tend to appropriate and dominate the evolving meaning of interface-related research. The routine disciplinary politics of research institutions affect researchers in the interface field. Interface research was for many years (and to a considerable degree still is) politically marginalized within the field of academic computer science. Even within the interface field, some researchers whose work is fundamentally grounded in psychology feel themselves to be marginalized by those whose work is based on traditions of engineering in which psychology plays little part. The lesson here is that the dominant definitions of what constitutes the "real" issues in interface research and what constitutes the "right" approaches to doing such research are very misleading. It is necessary to look beyond these politically constructed definitions of what ought to be done and focus on the broader challenges of what emerging applications will require.

2. The trend in conceptual evolution of interface concerns is generally "upward" in the layers of social focus, from the individual to small group, to organizational, sectoral, institutional, and cultural. To the extent that being human involves essential attributes of group identity, organization of production and consumption, formation and sustainment of social order and culture, and so on, these too require attention in interface research. This notion is captured well in recent use of the term *usability* to describe research aimed at developing information technologies that actually accomplish what those who use them desire. This focus has clearly emerged in the computer-supported cooperative work (CSCW) research community and has appeared as well in discussions of organizational usability and even institutional usability of information technologies. It is certain that a concern about every-citizen interfaces to the national information infrastructure must embody such perspectives. While it is true that at some level all interface issues can be traced to rudimentary human-computer interface concerns as represented by the parochial HCI community, these broader issues of usability involve concerns that have nothing at all to do with the narrow HCI focus and must be addressed by research methods that traditional HCI researchers would never consider.

3. Although the concern with interface issues is usually tied to the evolving HCI, CSCW, and other perspectives, important aspects of research into group, organizational, and institutional usability have been under way for many years. Although largely ignored by the computer science research community, the vast range of economically vital computing applications in organizational information processing have drawn much attention from researchers in management information systems, library and information science, medical informatics, and other fields. Transaction-processing systems, which remain among the largest and most complex computerized information systems, were made possible only by careful study and learning-by-doing design to meet interface needs at the individual, work group, organizational, and institutional levels. To pick just one case in point, designers of the airline reservations system, which literally revolutionized air travel, had to overcome numerous complicated problems at all social levels, including being modified to comply with court-ordered remedies against unfair competitive practices. Similar stories can be told regarding credit data-reporting systems, financial accounting and reporting systems, personnel management systems, computer-integrated manufacturing systems, and so on. The lesson here is that a great deal of useful information on the development of effective interfaces at the higher social levels is available in the applications-oriented research communities.

RESEARCH NEEDS

The point of the discussion above is not to argue against further investment in the well-established traditions of research in computer science, HCI, and so on. Such investments have yielded great payoffs and will continue to do so in the future. Instead, the point is to place in the foreground the need for focused research on the "higher-level" issues of interface development at the group organization, sectoral, institutional, social, and cultural levels. Moreover, these are not merely desirable venues for research investment, but rather are as essential to the goal of an every-citizen interface as well-established domains of federally supported research. Unfortunately, such research has been comparatively underfunded. There are numerous advocates of more traditional research needs to articulate requirements for such research. I will focus on the needs of the higher-level challenges.

The primary goal of research into the higher-level challenges of interface design is to reduce the cost and increase the speed of effective design. A great many extraordinary information technologies have been developed that demonstrate the virtues of good interfaces and that are highly usable in routine production. But the cost of developing them has been quite high because most of the systems have been built on the ruins of expensive failed efforts. It has been estimated that as many as half of large information systems projects fail to meet their objectives, and a significant fraction of those fail altogether. Many examples can be drawn from public-sector projects such as the disastrous World Wide Military Command and Control System (more than $5 billion), the Federal Aviation Administration's advanced technology program to replace the aging air traffic control system (more than $2 billion), and California's write-off of its ambitious overhaul of motor vehicle information systems (a mere $55 million). Similar failures abound in the private sector, but they are more easily hidden from view. The American Airlines effort to replicate its marvelous success in airline reservations systems in the French national railways and in its Encompass freight management system come to mind as just two examples. Research into higher-level challenges is aimed at learning what works and what does not and putting that knowledge to work.

The following constitute important areas of needed research investment at the higher level:

- *Synthetic studies that pull together the extensive social learning already accumulated through important development projects.* Most large-scale system development efforts occur in operational settings, not research laboratories. Research on such systems must be done in vivo, in the living systems.

There are significant problems with doing such research that need to be acknowledged. Among others, such research usually presents researchers with difficulties in gaining access to the right study sites, reluctance of organizations to reveal their failures due to fear of embarrassment, reluctance to reveal details of successes for competitive reasons, and the high cost of travel and time on site. But these are really no more troublesome than the challenges faced by numerous other research communities that must go to the field for their data collection. The synthetic research suggested here must be theoretically driven, but ultimately it is empirical in nature and akin to research traditions in engineering and management. The questions are: What works? What doesn't work? And why?

• *Analytical studies of the likely evolutionary pathways of complex sociotechnical systems over time.* It is increasingly recognized that information technologies do not merely allow efficiency and effectiveness improvements in well-established activities. Much more importantly, they enable fundamental changes in the nature of the activities themselves. The whole "reengineering" movement, which was articulated by people from organizational information systems backgrounds, is predicated on the argument that fundamental changes in what is to be done are required, displacing the traditional focus on how things are to be done. Much of the learning about what will "really" happen is inevitably going to be empirical—we will watch and see. But advances in conceptual tools such as game theory have made possible much more sophisticated modeling of possible interactions among actors under different assumptions, including enablement from new information technologies. Such studies seldom provide real predictive power in the sense that they can tell designers or decision makers exactly what to do. But they have been applied with great success in narrowing the search space around the likely outcomes under different assumptions—a contribution that can greatly improve the efficiency in design of complex systems that must be built through learning by doing processes such as prototyping. Significant increases in investment in such research are needed.

• *Collaborative research and development projects that allow different development strategies to be tested in real settings.* There are numerous recommended strategies for improving the design of complex sociotechnical systems. Many of these have evolved from the traditions of system design and software engineering and range from structured analysis and design techniques to participatory design. Unfortunately, our understanding of the efficacy of these approaches amounts to little more than folklore. There have been few systematic studies to demonstrate the utility of these approaches in real development situations and the contingencies under which the different approaches offer advantages. Moreover, this lack of systematic study makes it difficult to identify holes in existing knowledge and theory that require further research attention.

These kinds of studies require multidisciplinary research approaches, involving specialists from information and computer sciences, management, and the social sciences. In many cases, particularly where applications are in expert domains (e.g., medicine), subject matter specialists will be needed as well.

AUDIO ACCESS TO THE NATIONAL INFORMATION INFRASTRUCTURE

John C. Thomas
NYNEX Science and Technology

GOALS

There are trade-offs among the goals given below and the costs. While each is a desirable direction, any of these goals, if pushed to an extreme, could render other goals impossible.

- *Universality.* Every citizen should have some way of gaining access to information that has been made public. In some cases this may require special devices, language help, training, or economic assistance.
- *Privacy.* Individuals should have the ability to create, store, and modify information and restrict the access others have to that information. Information created about individuals by others should also be restricted in ways that the individual has some power over. At a minimum, individuals should know who has what information about them and should know when new information is being collected.
- *Security.* Information should be safe from unauthorized destruction, alteration, or copying.
- *Usability.* Information should be presented in a form that is maximally useful. This depends on the person, the task, the context, and their access to the system.
- *Empowerment.* The individual should be free to determine how, when, and where he or she access information. For example, some people may prefer, for certain tasks, a very "active" system in which agents make frequent suggestions. Others may prefer a more passive system.
- *Responsibility.* Economic or other incentives should be in place so that limited resources (bandwidth, storage capacity, computer power, creative human power that produces new information) are not simply "taken" for free by whoever gets there first. There should also be some incentive for those who create information to keep on creating.
- *Translatability.* Information entered in one medium should be capable of being translated into another medium. Not only should documents be easily translatable into another machine's format, but faxes

should be translatable into ASCII, spoken words into ASCII, and, ultimately, even pictures and video should be somewhat describable as text.

• *Ubiquity.* People should have access from anywhere to information (perhaps at a premium). They should not have to physically move very far to gain this access.

RESEARCH APPROACH

In 13 years at IBM I saw many excellent results (in human-computer interaction and effective software development process) of research in our labs; other labs and universities have a minuscule impact on what was actually done at IBM. In starting the artificial intelligence laboratory at NYNEX, I led each group to have a long-term vision of where to push the technology but to choose a portfolio of short- and medium-term projects that pushed toward that vision but also provided a real benefit for NYNEX. This was not motivated primarily by a desire to stay funded—though that was a consideration too—but because I believe it is far too easy to "partial out" the really difficult issues of artificial intelligence (AI) if one works on "toy systems." I do not believe there are "frictionless planes" when it comes to human psychology or building complex systems. Only through applied work is real progress made.

The ultimate goal of speech synthesis, for example, might be to read text as a good human actor might. However, a little reflection will show this (and all other similar problems!) to be coextensive with the "general AI" problem. While this is a worthy vision, a mundane step we took in this direction was to work on a better synthesizer for names and addresses, focusing on improving the prosody. Here the approach of the main investigators (Kim Silverman and Ashok Kalymanswamy) was not to "prove" that a particular approach to prosody was the "right" one but to use everything that worked and to do their own original research when they hit unsolved problems.

None of this philosophy should be taken as meaning that there is no place for theory or no place for university research. We have had a number of good collaborations with universities, including MIT and the University of Colorado, where we work on real problems for a while and then spend time theorizing. But the theorizing is based on experiences with real problems, and the theory is then applied to the next real problem.

I also believe that working on complex, real-world problems requires the cooperation, and perhaps the friendly competition, of numerous research groups. The speech community has shown remarkable progress working together through the Defense Advanced Research Projects Agency in collecting and sharing data, trying various approaches, and publishing results. The dawning commercial success of this technology is a further driver toward progress. I believe, therefore, that the way to develop the research agenda for issues about providing an every-citizen interface to the national information infrastructure is to start doing it. As we run into problems, we should use those problems to define the research agenda.

RESEARCH ISSUES

I propose that we develop an audio access to the Internet. Such a system would allow anyone access to the Internet over an ordinary POTS telephone line by using spoken commands. Quite obviously, this would not provide the identical experience that sitting in front of a keyboard (for an experienced typist) and a huge full-color monitor might. Nonetheless, such a system will have several major practical benefits and would serve as a focal point for pushing some important technologies.

First, the penetration of personal computers into the lowest socioeconomic status quartile is low and staying low. This would allow people without the financial resources immediate access to the Internet. It would also allow people who are reluctant to buy a computer because they don't see the value of Internet access (or other computer applications) to "try out" Internet access without a significant up-front investment. Individuals could use such access to listen to speeches of political candidates on particular issues, find out about their benefits and bills, find out about community events and safety messages, find transportation schedules, get sports results, and so on. Some of this information currently does exist in various audio forms, but typically it is not updated very frequently, and users must dial a different number for each type of information.

Second, there are families and work groups where most of the group has Internet access but a few do not. An audio access to the Internet would allow such a group or family to communicate much more effectively.

Third, even people who do have computer access to the Internet find themselves in situations (e.g., in their cars, at payphones, at hotels without modems) where they do not have computer access but could use a phone to find important financial and trip information, listen to their e-mail, etc.

Fourth, audio input/output is already becoming an important enhancing medium for the Internet. Welsh lessons that include audio are available from Brown University. One can listen to music, people's voices, and sounds. Ideally, one might well navigate more easily through voice commands. In addition, speaker verification could add another level of security to Internet transactions.

Fifth, there are people with special needs (blind or paralyzed users) for whom audio access to the Internet would be crucial. In addition to these special needs, there is a huge population of people in the United

States who can speak and listen to English but cannot read or write it. In a stroke, such an interface would help enfranchise and educate them.

In addition to providing practical benefits, a workable audio access to the Internet will force us to improve several important technologies.

- *Speech recognition.* While some access to the Internet could begin immediately, access could be improved via larger, speaker-independent vocabulary. Another improvement could be made if the system "adapted" on-line to the dialect and vocal tract configuration of individual speakers. Performance in some conditions will also be enhanced by better noise cancellation techniques.
- *Speech synthesis.* While current levels of intelligibility would be useful, certainly further enhancements can and should be made in the areas of aesthetic appeal, proper name and special symbol pronunciation, and prosody. In some cases, the Internet may provide additional clues for the synthesizer. For instance, in e-mail, the name and subject fields give potential clues about how the contents should be pronounced. Hypertext markup language (HTML) tags in Web sites may give additional structural information about pauses and emphasis.
- *Picture and video understanding.* To provide some (not complete) audio information about pictures, graphics, and videos available on the Internet, an automatic scene describer would provide a cheaper solution than having human beings try to keep up with the exploding information by describing each scene. By having HTML tags and verbal materials to provide some structure and context, the task for machine scene understanding could be made more tractable, but there are still unsolved research issues here. The solutions would have other applications as well, including digital movie making and editing and security.
- *Natural language processing.* Much of the information on the Internet is in the form of text. Being able to do a better job of indexing, summarizing, and locating text would drive better natural language processing. Again, the HTML tags of Web sites provide a potential additional source for natural language understanding systems.
- *User interface design.* How should a dialogue over the phone be structured? Under what conditions should it be all speech and when should DTMF also be used? When is explicit confirmation needed? How can speech/audio be used as an adjunct to screen-based systems?
- *System integration.* Perhaps a mobile phone user would like to browse for certain kinds of information and bookmark Web pages for later perusal on a screen. How can the various networks be internetworked?
- *Speaker verification.* Perhaps the user could be presented with a phrase to repeat in his or her own voice. This could be used to help

authenticate transactions. Clearly, better verification techniques would help make the system more secure and user friendly.

• *Media translation.* Speech recognition and synthesis are special cases, but it would also be nice to be able to translate a fax document into an e-mail document that could then be read over the phone. In general, information should be capable of being input in any medium and output in any other medium. While the (typed) fax to e-mail issue is nearly solved, handwriting still provides a challenge. We still do not see systems adapting to handwriting as well as humans do.

• *Adaptive recognition.* The human being seems to be very good at "speaker-independent" speech recognition. Yet a selection made by "pasting together" words from a random speaker seems very difficult for a human to understand compared to one from any single speaker. Today's speech recognition systems don't seem to care. Apparently, humans are doing something in the way of rapid speaker adaptation that we do not understand well enough to incorporate into a machine. Similarly, we are quite good at "adapting" to a particular individual's handwriting. Again, we don't know how to program a computer to do this very well. Similarly, if we view a graph, photo, or movie on a particular device in a particular lighting context, we make a fairly quick adaptation to the style and other aspects of context. And, again, we don't know how to do this very well in a machine. I believe a key to significant improvement in a number of the technologies listed here is a better understanding of how humans do adaptive recognition. Rather than studying it in a toy domain, however, I believe we should observe and test how people do this in a real context doing a real task.

• *Intelligent searching.* Today's search engines on the Internet are not very precise. They typically return very many false-positives. Audio input/output with natural language processing gives the possibility of more selective searches and also provides strong motivation since audio scanning is more onerous than visual scanning. One potential source of information is to use the user's current task and past history to help focus a search. Such an approach forces us to examine privacy and security issues.

All of these technologies could be explored in their own right, but I think that exploring them in the context of trying to provide a real-world system will produce the best research results as well as a practical benefit.

APPENDIXES

A

WORKSHOP AGENDA AND PARTICIPANTS

AGENDA

Wednesday, August 21, 1996

6:00-7:30 p.m. **Welcoming Reception**

Thursday, August 22

7:30-8:30 a.m. **Continental Breakfast**

8:30-8:45 **Workshop Introduction and Objectives**
Alan Biermann, Steering Committee Chair

8:45-10:15 **People and Functions: Uses of Information Infrastructure and Implications for Interfaces**
Moderator: Tora Bikson
Panel: Larry Goldberg, Sara Kiesler, John King, Robert Kraut, Bruce Tognazzini

10:15-10:30 **Break**

10:30-Noon **Communication and Collaboration**
Moderator: Barbara Grosz
Panel: Austin Henderson, Gary Olson, Candace Sidner, Lee Sproull, Loren Terveen

Noon-1:15 p.m. **Lunch**

1:15-2:45   **Information Dimensions**
                 Moderator: Bruce Tognazzini
                 Panel: Susan Hockey, Mark Weiser, Moshe Zloof

2:45-3:00   **Break**

3:00-5:00   **Input-Output Methods and Paradigms**
                 Moderator: Gregg Vanderheiden
                 Panel: Ron Cole, Thomas DeFanti, John Makhoul, Alan
                 Newell, Daniel Siewiorek, Andries van Dam, Stephen
                 Weinstein

5:00-5:15 p.m.   **Day 1 Wrap-up: Comments from Invited Observers
                 and Instructions for Day 2**
                 Alan Biermann

5:15-6:15   **Reception and Demonstrations**

6:15-7:30   **Dinner**

                 Friday, August 23

7:30-8:30 a.m.   **Continental Breakfast**

8:30-10:15   **Parallel Sessions**
                 Parallel Session A1: Agents and System Intelligence
                 Moderator: Alan Biermann
                 Panel: Steven Feiner, Craig Knoblock, Mark Maybury,
                 Johanna Moore, Katia Sycara, Kent Wittenburg
                 Parallel Session A2: Design and Evaluation
                 Moderator: Thomas Landauer
                 Panel: Sara Czaja, Dennis Egan, Alan Newell, John
                 Thomas, Robert Virzi

10:15-10:30   **Break**

10:30-Noon   **Parallel Sessions: Application Dimensions**
                 Parallel Session B1: Lifelong Learning
                 Moderator: Gerhard Fischer
                 Panel: Charles Cleary, Wallace Feurzeig, John Richards,
                 Elliot Soloway, John Thomas
                 Parallel Session B2: Work and Home Life
                 Moderators: John Makhoul and Stephen Weinstein
                 Panel: Louis Hecht, Stephen Kent, Sara Kiesler, Robert
                 Kraut, Mark Laubach, Adam Porter

Parallel Session B3: Public Interest and Health Care
Moderators: Tora Bikson and Bruce Tognazzini
Panel: Patricia Brennan, David Crocker, Sara Czaja, John
King, Aki Namioka, Lee Sproull, Michael Traynor

Noon-1:15 p.m. **Lunch**

1:15-2:15   **Parallel Sessions Concluded**
                 Complete reports for presentation in plenary session

2:15-2:30   **Break**

2:30-3:00   **Parallel Session Presentations**

3:00-5:00   **Synthesis—Setting the Research Agenda**
                 Moderator: Alan Biermann
                 Panel: Steering Committee

5:00   **Adjourn**

PARTICIPANTS

Alan Biermann, *Chair*, Duke University
Tora Bikson, RAND Corporation
Patricia Brennan, Case Western Reserve University
Charles Cleary, Learning Sciences Corporation
Ron Cole, Oregon Graduate Institute
David H. Crocker, Brandenburg Consulting
Sara Czaja, University of Miami
Thomas DeFanti, University of Illinois at Chicago
Dennis Egan, Bellcore
Steven K. Feiner, Columbia University
Wallace Feurzeig, BBN Corporation
Gerhard Fischer, University of Colorado
Larry Goldberg, National Center for Accessible Media
    WGBH Educational Foundation, Corporation for Public Broadcasting
Barbara Grosz, Harvard University
Louis Hecht, Open GIS Consortium Inc.
Austin Henderson, Apple Computer
Susan Hockey, University of Alberta (affiliation at time of workshop:
    Center for Electronic Texts in the Humanities, Rutgers University and
    Princeton University)
Stephen T. Kent, BBN Corporation
Sara Kiesler, Carnegie Mellon University
John L. King, University of California, Irvine
Craig Knoblock, University of Southern California
Robert E. Kraut, Carnegie Mellon University

Thomas Landauer, University of Colorado
Mark Laubach, Com21 Inc.
John Makhoul, BBN Corporation
Mark T. Maybury, Mitre Corporation
Johanna Moore, University of Pittsburgh
Aki Namioka, Computer Professionals for Social Responsibility
Alan Newell, University of Dundee
Gary Olson, University of Michigan
Adam Porter, University of Maryland
John Richards, Turner Educational Services Inc.
Candace Sidner, Lotus Development Corporation
Daniel Siewiorek, Carnegie Mellon University
Elliot Soloway, University of Michigan
Lee S. Sproull, Boston University
Katia Sycara, Carnegie Mellon University
Loren Terveen, AT&T Research Laboratories
John Thomas, NYNEX Science and Technology
Bruce Tognazzini, Healtheon Corporation
Michael Traynor, Cooley Godward LLP
Andries van Dam, Brown University
Gregg Vanderheiden, University of Wisconsin
Robert Virzi, GTE Laboratories
Stephen Weinstein, NEC America Inc.
Mark Weiser, Xerox Palo Alto Research Center
Kent Wittenburg, Bellcore
Moshe Zloof, Hewlett Packard Laboratories

INVITED OBSERVERS

Susan A. Brummel, General Services Administration
Y.T. Chien, National Science Foundation
Dinah F.B. Cohen, Department of Defense, Computer/Electronic
    Accommodations Program
Eileen Collins, National Science Foundation
Helen Gigley, Office of Naval Research
Thomas Kalil, National Economic Council
Michael R. Nelson, Office of Science and Technology Policy
Gary W. Strong, National Science Foundation

B

STEERING COMMITTEE MEMBERS' BIOGRAPHIES

Alan W. Biermann is a professor of computer science at Duke University. His research is in the areas of automatic programming and natural language processing. In recent years, he has developed, with the help of colleagues and students, a series of voice-interactive dialogue systems for office applications, equipment repair, and tutoring.

He has co-edited two books on automatic programming and is author of *Great Ideas in Computer Science: A Gentle Introduction*, The MIT Press, 1990 (second edition, 1997). He is on the editorial boards of the *Journal of Symbolic Computation* and the *International Journal of Speech Technology*. Biermann received the BEE and MS degrees from The Ohio State University in 1961 and a Ph. D. from the University of California, Berkeley in 1968, all in electrical engineering and computer science. He is a member of the Institute for Electrical and Electronic Engineers, the Association for Computing Machinery, the American Association for Artificial Intelligence (AAAI), and the Association for Computational Linguistics (ACL). He is a fellow of the AAAI and past president of the ACL.

Tora Bikson is a senior scientist in RAND Corporation's Behavioral Sciences Department. She received B.A., M.A., and Ph.D. (1969) degrees in philosophy from the University of Missouri at Columbia and M.A. and Ph.D. (1974) degrees in psychology from the University of California at Los Angeles. Since 1980, Dr. Bikson's research has investigated properties of advanced information technologies in varied user contexts, addressing such issues as what factors affect the successful incorporation of innovative tools into ongoing activities; how these new work media influence group structures and interaction processes; what impact they have on task and social outcomes as well as user satisfaction; and what individuals and organizations need to know to use them effectively. She has pursued these questions as principal investigator for projects funded by NSF, the Office of Technology Assessment, and the John and Mary R. Markle Foundation. Her work emphasizes field research design, intensive case studies, and large-scale cross-sectional studies addressed to the use of computer-based tools in organizational settings. Dr. Bikson is a member of Data for Development (a United Nations' Secretariat providing scientific guidance on the use of information systems in developing countries) and a technical consultant to the U.N. Advisory Commission on the Coordination of Information Systems. She is a frequent reviewer for professional papers and has authored a number of journal articles, book chapters, and research reports on the implementation of new interactive media. She is a member of the AAAS, ACM, APA (fellow), Computer Professionals for Social Responsibility, and the Society for the Psychological Study of Social Issues. Dr. Bikson recently served on the NRC's CSTB Committee to Study the Impact of Information Technology on the Performance of Service Activities.

Thomas A. DeFanti, Ph.D., is director of the Electronic Visualization Laboratory (EVL), a professor in the department of Electrical Engineering and Computer Science, and director of the Software Technologies Research Center at the University of Illinois at Chicago (UIC). He is also the associate director for virtual environments at the National Center for Supercomputing Applications (NCSA) at the University of Illinois at Urbana-Champaign.

DeFanti is an internationally recognized expert in computer graphics. In the 24 years he has been at UIC, DeFanti has amassed a number of credits, including: use of his graphics language and equipment for the computer animation produced for the first Star Wars movie; early involvement in video game technology long before video games became popular; contributor and co-editor of the 1987 NSF-sponsored report *Visualization in Scientific Computing*; recipient of the 1988 ACM Outstanding Contribution Award; an appointment in 1989 to the Illinois Governor's Science Advisory Board; and, his appointment as a University Scholar for 1989-1992. DeFanti is also a Fellow of the Association of Computing Machinery. He serves on the Technical

Advisory Board of the Internet II and is a co-principal investigator of the National Computational Science Alliance.

Gerhard Fischer is director for the Center for Life-Long Learning and Design (L^3D) at the University of Colorado at Boulder. He is also a professor in the Computer Science Department and a member of the Institute of Cognitive Science at the University of Colorado. Dr. Fischer's research interests are human computer communication, artificial intelligence, and education and computers, design, cognitive science, and software engineering. He is a member of the Association for Computing Machinery, American Association for Artificial Intelligence, Cognitive Science, Gesellschaft für Informatik, Institute of Electrical and Electronics Engineers, and Computer Professionals for Social Responsibility. Dr. Fischer has written extensively in his field. He received his M.A. in mathematics from the University of Heidelberg, Germany, his Ph.D. in computer science from the University of Hamburg, Germany, and a degree in habilitation in computer science at the University of Stuttgart, Germany.

Barbara J. Grosz is Gordon McKay Professor of Computer Science in the Division of Engineering and Applied Sciences at Harvard University. She has written several seminal papers in discourse processing, and developed the discourse component of a number of natural language processing systems. She is widely regarded as having established the research field of computational modeling of discourse. A fellow of the American Association for the Advancement of Science and the American Association for Artificial Intelligence (AAAI), she is past president of the AAAI, was chair of IJCAI-91, and is a member and former chair of the Board of Trustees of the International Joint Conferences on Artificial Intelligence, Incorporated. Her current research encompasses four problem areas: computational theories of discourse and discourse processing, computational models of collaborative planning, investigations of the interactions between intonation and discourse, and techniques for combining natural language and graphics. Before joining the faculty at Harvard, she was director of the Natural Language program at SRI International, and co-founder of the Center for the Study of Language and Information. Professor Grosz received an A.B. in mathematics from Cornell University and a Ph.D. in computer science from the University of California, Berkeley.

Thomas Landauer is a professor of psychology and fellow of the Institute of Cognitive Science at the University of Colorado. He received his

B.A. in anthropology in 1954 from the University of Colorado, his M.A. in anthroplogy and psychology in 1958, and his Ph.D. in social psychology in 1960. His work includes basic and applied research, prototype building and testing, exploratory development, and design-methodology studies on a variety of topics, including (1) electronic text delivery systems (hypertext, digital libraries, multimedia), (2) simplified e-mail for residential use, (2) advanced information retrieval methods, e.g., Latent Semantic Indexing (LSI), fisheye views, and unlimited aliasing, (3) methods for evaluating and improving user interfaces, e.g., heuristic evaluation, (4) empirical and theoretical studies of interface design issues, e.g., command names and menu organization, and (5) a wide variety of other topics, including cryptographic time stamping for digital documents, neural nets for speech recognition, and computer-enhanced communication sytems (MUDs). He was awarded a fellowship with the AAAS and the American Psychological Association (APA) (experimental psychology and engineering psychology) and is a charter member of the American Psychological Society (APS). Dr. Landauer has two patents, one pending, on software design for text and multimedia information retrieval using Latent Semantic Indexing.

John Makhoul received his B.S. degree in electrical engineering from the American University of Beirut in 1964, his M.S. degree in electrical engineering from the Ohio State University in 1965, and his Ph.D. degree in electrical engineering from MIT in 1970. Dr. Makhoul is chief scientist for Speech and Signal Processing at BBN Corporation, Cambridge, Massachusetts, and a research affiliate with the Speech Communication Laboratory at MIT. Dr. Makhoul conducts research in speech analysis, synthesis, and compression, speech enhancement, automatic speech recognition, neural networks, and digital signal processing, including linear prediction, spectral modeling, lattice structures, and adaptive filtering. Dr. Makhoul is a fellow of the IEEE and of the Acoustical Society of America.

Bruce Tognazzini, a leading authority on software design, has been designing human-machine interfaces for more than 35 years. At Apple, he headed up both the Apple II and Macintosh human interface efforts. At SunSoft, as distinguished engineer in the Office of Strategic Technology, he led the Starfire project, outlining the future of computing. He is currently chief designer at Healtheon, a new start-up devoted to moving the medical industry onto the Internet. "Tog" has written dozens of papers, articles, and columns, is a contributing author of three books on human interface design, and is the sole author of two books, *Tog on Interface* and *Tog on Software Design*, both from Addison-Wesley.

Gregg Vanderheiden is a professor in the Human Factors Division of the Department of Industrial Engineering at the University of Wisconsin, Madison. He is also director of Trace Research and Development Center at the Waisman Center at the University of Wisconsin. He received his B.S. in electrical engineering (1972), M.S. in biomedical engineering (1974), and Ph.D. in technology in communication, rehabilitation, and child development, all from the University of Wisconsin, Madison. He is the principal investigator on more than 140 grants and projects in the area of rehabilitation engineering, access to national and next-generation information systems, computer access systems, and augmentative communication and writing for children and adults with disabilities. His activities include research, development, commercial facilitation, information summary, and training (pre-service and in-service). Dr. Vanderheiden has worked with industries on topics in a wide range of areas relating to more flexible interface design, disability access, and nomadicity. Interface extensions from Dr. Vanderheiden's work are included in most all of the major operating systems today, including MacOS, Windows 95, Windows NT, OS/2, and Unix/X-Windows.

Stephen Weinstein is employed at NEC America, Incorporated. Prior to that, he was a member of the Multimedia Communications Research Division at Bell Communications Research. His research concentrations are network communication of data, modems, and information transfer and retrieval. He is a fellow of IEEE and received the Centennial Medal from IEEE in 1984. Dr. Weinstein received his S.B. in 1960 from MIT, his M.S. in 1962 from the University of Michigan, and a Ph.D. in 1966 in electrical engineering from the University of California.